How to BEAT HOUSE- WORK

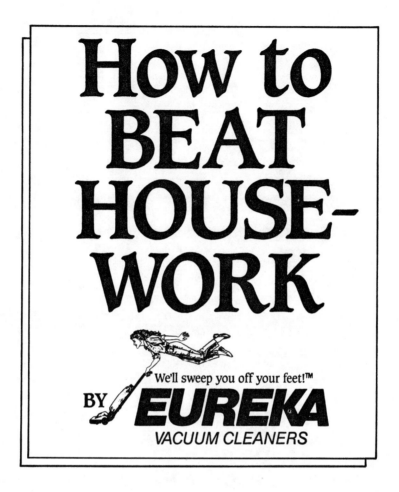

We'll sweep you off your feet!™

BY **EUREKA**

VACUUM CLEANERS

PUBLICATIONS INTERNATIONAL, LTD.
Lincolnwood, Illinois

ISBN 0-88176-435-3

CONTENTS

Nobody lives the way they used to.

Lifestyles have changed. Goals and needs have changed. You're under terrific time pressures every day. Even if you wanted to, you couldn't spend a lot of time cleaning. You have too many other things to do. Nobody understands this better than Eureka.

Not many years ago, many women spent their time keeping their homes spotless. It was expected. Not any more. The way we live has changed; an immaculate home is no longer a goal for most of us. But a certain amount of housework has to be done. When you tackle it, and how much you do, is up to you.

The profile of the American household has changed; the people responsible for cleaning in these households has also changed. More than 50 percent of American women are in the work force. This means are there more working wives and working mothers. More husbands and fathers are doing housework. More people live alone; singles, of both sexes, face housework hassles.

Eureka has designed this book to help *everyone* beat housework. All you need is the right tools and to know how to use them efficiently. Eureka is a cleaning expert. We're putting everything we know to work for you.

EUREKA'S GOT A SYSTEM

Your Eureka vacuum cleaner is one of five different basic types developed by Eureka to handle the full spectrum of cleaning needs. There are many different models within each category, of course, but five categories make up the Eureka Cleaning System:

- Upright
- Self-Propelled
- Canister
- Power Team
- Cordless

First, let's consider the upright, self-propelled, canister, and power team models. (Cordless models have their own special time-and-work-saving features and a special place further on in this book.) The Eureka Cleaning System has an answer for your cleaning problems no matter what kind of home you have or how much time you have to clean it. Each of these four kinds of cleaners has its own special cleaning expertise. In the following pages, we'll look at them one at a time.

What kind of vacuum cleaner do you need?

The Eureka vacuum cleaner you have may handle all your cleaning needs, all by itself. It will certainly do an excellent job wherever you use it. But we're not just talking about vacuuming carpets. We're talking speed, convenience, and getting as much cleaning as possible done and doing it as quickly as possible.

If you have a two-story house, consider a heavy-duty vacuum cleaner for downstairs, where the tracked-in dirt accumulates, and a lighter vacuum cleaner for upstairs, where lint and light dust gather. With two vacuum cleaners, you'll never have to lug a vacuum cleaner up and down the stairs.

Stairs can be a drag to clean, but if you have a smaller Eureka cleaner, sized for stairs and other steep or narrow places, it can cut the work—and the time—in half.

Above-floor cleaning can take more time than vacuuming carpeting from wall to wall. You'll speed up the job if you let your vacuum cleaner handle it.

Consider this: A 9-by-12-foot carpet can hold as much dirt as one and a half times its own weight and still look clean; that is about 85 pounds of embedded dirt. This is the most difficult kind of dirt to clean because it is likely to be ground into carpet fibers.

Both seen and unseen dirt can damage carpeting. When you walk across a dirty carpet, dirt scrapes against the carpet fibers and cuts into them, eventually causing the carpet to break down and to lose its beauty and resilience. Some people think that vacuuming wears out carpeting, but the opposite is true: Vacuuming is the only way to remove the embedded dirt that wears out carpeting.

Dirt in carpets and throughout your home also has an impact on health. Many people have allergic reactions to household dust, dirt, and mold. Asthma, emphysema, and other respiratory conditions are aggravated by dirt, animal dander, and other particles that regular vacuuming safely removes from the environment of your home.

Let's see what the Eureka Cleaning System can do for you!

Eureka Standard Uprights

Eureka Standard Upright.

Eureka Standard Uprights are especially good for . . .
- Wall-to-wall carpets and large rugs.
- Carpeted areas with heavy traffic.
- Deep-pile carpeting.

Eureka upright vacuum cleaners are used mainly for rugs and carpeting, rather than for above-floor cleaning. They handle carpeting effectively because their motors are positioned directly above the dirty surface for the maximum cleaning power. Uprights also use a motor-driven brush roll to loosen dirt so it can be drawn into the vacuum cleaner by the suction.

Features of Eureka Standard Upright Models and what they mean to you.

Note: See your Owner's Manual for the features that apply to your specific Eureka vacuum cleaner.

- **Carpet-Height Controls:**
  Dial-A-Nap® is a rotating dial that adjusts cleaner efficiency to any carpet height.
  Rugulator® is a sliding-scale carpet height adjustment that is more precise than preset dial positions.
- **Edge Kleener**® carpet nozzle cleans right up to baseboards on both sides.
- **Top-Fill Dust Bag** holds more dirt because the dirt falls into a separate compartment at the bottom. Old dirt doesn't clog incoming airflow (that's for efficiency), and bags last longer between changes (that's for economy).
- **Triple Filter System** is the best yet for home use. Nonwoven filter, 100-percent knit fabric bag, and disposable paper dust bag clean incoming air *three times.*
- **Extra-Long Cords** (up to 30 feet) add to your cleaning range so you don't have to stop to change outlets.
- **Headlight** brightens dark places where dirt hides.
- **3-Position Handle** adjusts vertically in storage or for use with above-floor tools, horizontally for cleaning all the way under furniture, and in-between for regular vacuuming.
- **Tool Kits** adapt uprights for convenient above-floor and hard-surface-floor cleaning.
- **Low-Profile Design** glides easily under furniture.

Eureka Ultra offers these *additional* features:
- **ESP**® **(Extra Suction Power) Motors,** up to 6.5 amps, are heavy-duty, high-power motors that deliver up to 50 percent more cleaning power than standard uprights from Eureka.

- **Brushed Edge and Corner Kleener™** gets dirt from corners and along baseboards.
- **Automatic Carpet Height Adjustment** saves time and the bother of manually adjusting for different carpets.
- **Vibra-Groomer II**® uses seven rotating beater bars on its brush roll to create 20,000 pulsations a minute! Vibrating action loosens deeply imbedded dirt and suction whisks it away. It has chrome-plated steel construction with lifetime-lubricated bearings.
- **Large Rear Wheels** let Ultra maneuver smoothly over carpet from room to room.

Eureka Self-Propelled Uprights

Eureka Self-Propelled Upright.

Eureka Self-Propelled Uprights are especially good for . . .
- Large rugs and carpets.
- Homes of senior citizens and people with physical limitations.
- Carpeting of anyone who wants effortless, fast vacuuming.

Using Eureka self-propelled vacuum cleaners is the fastest, easiest way to clean extensive carpeted areas and large area rugs. They are also effective on smaller carpets. The smooth, self-propelled action makes cleaning effortless. Eureka self-propelled vacuum cleaners never jerk or surge unexpectedly. All you do is guide the vacuum cleaner; it does all the work. Self-propelled is a dream come true for those who don't have the time, the inclination, or the physical ability to vacuum the standard way.

Features of Eureka Self-Propelled Models and what they mean to you.

Note: See your Owner's Manual for features that apply to your Eureka vacuum cleaner.

- **Fingertip Control** makes cleaning almost effortless. Just a light touch for forward or reverse. Let go and the drive motion stops. You're always in control.
- **Transmission System** responds smoothly, predictably—no jumps, no surprises.
- **ESP® (Extra Suction Power) Motors,** up to 7.5 amps, are heavy-duty, high-power motors that deliver up to 50 percent more cleaning power than standard uprights from Eureka.
- **Manual Control** lets a Eureka self-propelled cleaner operate like a standard upright.
- **Vibra-Groomer II®** uses seven rotating beater bars to create 20,000 pulsations a minute! Vibrating action loosens deeply imbedded dirt to be whisked away by the vacuum cleaner. Chromed steel construction with lifetime-lubricated bearings insures dependable service.
- **Rugulator®** is a sliding-scale carpet height adjustment that's more precise than preset dial positions.
- **Top-Fill Dust Bag** holds more because the dirt falls into a separate compartment at the bottom. Old dirt doesn't clog incoming airflow (that's for efficiency); bags last longer between changes (that's for economy).
- **Triple Filter System** is the best yet for home use. Nonwoven filter, 100-percent knit fabric bag, and disposable paper dust bag clean incoming air *three times.*
- **Extra-Long Cords** (up to 30 feet) allow cleaning of large areas without stopping to change outlets.
- **Headlight** brightens dark places where dirt hides.

Precision® Self-Propelled offers these *additional* features:

- **Electronic Speed Control** on Model 5175 adjusts the cleaning power precisely to the cleaning job.
- **Control Panel** on/off switch and Cordaway® release button puts both controls up high where they're easy to reach.
- **Cordaway®** retracts the cord at the touch of a button and stores it out of sight.
- **On-Board Bag Storage** keeps new bags right at hand and tells at a glance when to buy more.
- **Wraparound Furniture Guard** provides extra protection for walls and furniture.
- **Exclusive Built-In Lift-and-Carry Handle** is designed for balanced and easy movement up and down stairs or when closet storage is required.

Eureka Standard Canisters

Eureka Standard Canister.

Eureka Standard Canisters are especially good for . . .
- Hard-surface floors and above-floor surfaces.
- Apartments, dorm rooms, and small homes.
- Homes with a variety of floor surfaces.
- Stairways and second stories
- Upholstery and furniture.
- A second all-purpose vacuum cleaner.

Eureka canisters are used primarily for cleaning hard-surface floors and above-floor surfaces. Because of their portability and their design, canisters are superior to uprights for cleaning walls, woodwork, shelves, and furniture. Compact, lightweight canisters, such as the Mighty Mite® (see the next section for more information), also have powerful motors that enable them to clean quickly.

Features of Eureka Standard Canister Models and what they mean to you.

Note: See your Owner's Manual for the features that apply to your specific Eureka vacuum cleaner.

- **Powerful Motors** (1.0 to 4.3 peak horsepower) are lifetime-lubricated and quiet-running for longer service.
- **All-Steel Construction** makes for durability and long service life. Bright, baked-on finishes provide an attractive decorator look.
- **On/Off Toe Switch** starts and stops cleaner at a touch of the toe.
- **Triple Filter System** is the best yet for home use. It filters incoming air *three times*. Dusty air doesn't get into the motor or back into the room. This helps keep your home clean.
- **Hinged Top** flips wide open for easy bag and filter changing.
- **Crush-Resistant Hose** is long and flexible and lets you clean floors, corners, ceilings, or walls.
- **Long Cords** extend cleaning range without stopping to change outlets.
- **Soft Furniture Guard** protects woodwork and furniture from nicks and scratches.
- **Attachment Sets** include special tools for cleaning carpets, draperies, upholstered furniture, and more.
- **Tool-Pak®** built into the cleaner holds attachments securely in place, right on the cleaner.
- **Edge & Corner Kleener™ Carpet Nozzle** cleans right up to baseboards and into corners.
- **Large Carrying Handle** provides a balanced, easily accessible lifting point.
- **Easy Maneuverability** comes from one swivel wheel in front and two fixed wheels in back. Cleaner rolls smoothly over floors, rugs, even thresholds.

Eureka Mighty Mite® Canisters

Eureka Mighty Mite®.

Eureka Mighty Mite® canisters are especially good for . . .
- Smaller houses and apartments with several kinds of flooring.
- Above-floor cleaning.
- Stairs.
- Spilled dry food or dirt.
- Furniture and woodwork.

The Mighty Mite® is the perfect vacuum cleaner for small apartments and for fast cleanups in larger homes.

Features of Eureka Mighty Mite® and what they mean to you.

Note: See your Owner's Manual for features that apply to your Eureka vacuum cleaner.

- **Powerful Motors** (1.0 to 3.0 peak horsepower) are lifetime-lubricated and quiet-running.
- **Sturdy ABS Construction** combines high-impact durability with attractive decorator colors.
- **On/Off Power Switch** is located conveniently on the handle for easy use.
- **Triple Filter System** is the best yet for home use. Cleans incoming air *three times*. Dusty air doesn't get into the motor or back into the room.
- **Direct Hose Connection** fits firmly into the cleaner and locks in place.
- **Attachment Sets** include special tools for cleaning carpets, draperies, upholstered furniture, and more.
- **Edge & Corner Kleener™ Carpet Nozzle** cleans right up to baseboards and into corners.
- **Tool-Pak®** stores attachments conveniently right on the cleaner.
- **Extra-Long Hose** provides a 7-foot "reach" for hard-to-get-at places. It's crush-resistant.
- **Convenient Snap-Latch** lets the hinged front panel swing wide open and makes dust bag changing quick and easy.
- **20-Foot Power Cord** permits wide-sweep cleaning. It wraps neatly around the cleaning base, secured by a quick-release clip.
- **Light, Compact** Mighty Mite® is easy to lift, carry on stairs, and store in small spaces. An added convenience for above-floor cleaning is the optional shoulder strap, available at extra cost.
- **Blower Port** reverses airflow through the hose to blow dirt out of hard-to-reach places.

Eureka Power Teams

Eureka Power Teams are especially good for . . .
- Hard-surface floors as well as carpeted floors.
- Above-floor cleaning.
- Stairs.
- Cleaning under furniture and beds.
- One vacuum cleaner households where they are needed to clean above-floor surfaces and hard-surface floors as well as to remove embedded dirt from carpets.

Eureka power teams are canister vacuum cleaners with motorized cleaning heads. In addition to doing everything a canister does, a power team also cleans rugs and carpets as effectively as an upright. The canister motor provides suction while a second motor, located in the powerhead, drives an agitator with a revolving brush roll.

Features of Eureka Power Team Models and what they mean to you.

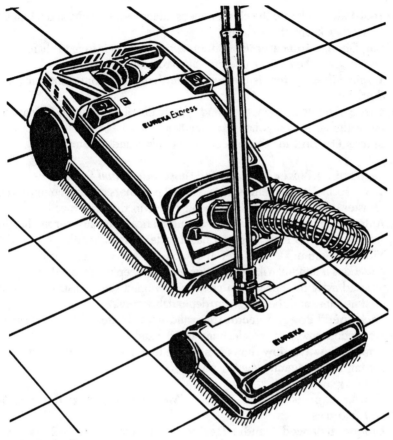

Eureka Power Team.

Note: See your Owner's Manual for the features that apply to your specific Eureka vacuum cleaner.

- **Powerful Motor** (up to 4.3 peak horsepower) is lifetime-lubricated and quiet-running—the most powerful Eureka canister motor.
- **Vibra-Groomer III®** is a power-driven steel brush roll that vibrates imbedded dirt from carpet fibers with double brush action so it can be vacuumed away.
- **Roto-Matic® Powerhead** with second motor is a compact, low-profile design with automatic carpet-height adjustment. It switches from carpet to hard-surface-floor cleaning with one touch of a control.
- **Cordaway®** retracts the cord at the touch of a button and stores it out of sight.
- **Edge & Corner Kleener™ Carpet Nozzle** cleans right up to baseboards and into corners.

- **Tool-Pak®** built into the cleaner keeps attachments handy, and a hinged dust cover keeps them clean.
- **Bag Change Indicator** lights automatically when it's time to change the dust bag, so the cleaner operates at maximum efficiency.
- **Triple Filter System** is the best yet for home use. Filters incoming air *three times*.
- **Large Wheels** ride smoothly and quietly on all surfaces, so it's easy to move the cleaner anywhere in your home.
- **Stands On End** for convenient use on stairs and for storage.

Vactronic™ Power Teams offer these *additional* features:
- **Two-Motor Power Teams** use up to 4.0 peak horsepower motors at the canister, plus a compact, high-speed motor in the powerhead.
- **Roto-matic® Powerhead** adjusts automatically to any carpet height from low nap to high shag and has a wide cleaning swath.
- **Vibra-Groomer II®** uses seven rotating beater bars to create 20,000 pulsations a minute! Vibrating action loosens deeply imbedded dirt to be whisked away by the vacuum cleaner. Chromed steel construction with lifetime-lubricated bearings, for dependable service.
- **Vactronic™ Power Selector** uses solid-state electronics to adjust canister suction power to the cleaning job at hand.
- **Power View Window** shows at a glance that beater bar/brush roll is revolving for maximum cleaning power.

Eureka Express® Power Touch™ (Model 8295) offers these *additional* features:
- **Unique Balanced Handle Design** and its light weight—25 percent lighter than conventional Power Teams—make Eureka Express® easy to carry upstairs, downstairs, all around the house.
- **Comfort-Grip Power Touch™ Handle** puts controls at your fingertips: Turn brush roll in powerhead "on" or "off" and adjust motor speed to the cleaning job at hand.
- **LED "Power Available" Light** on the handle indicates that cleaning power is "on."
- **Digital Power Indicator** (Model 8295) on the canister reads out cleaning power in use and cleaning power in reserve and helps adjust power use to need.

Cleaning or In-Betweening™

Now for the *rest* of Eureka's Cleaning System. Here's a cleaning concept that fits right into the life you live today. We call it In-Betweening™—between-cleaning cleanups™ that can help you put off heavy-duty cleaning for a very long time.

A lot of the cleaning you do removes surface dirt—dumps, spills, litter, lint, and unidentified bits of stuff that accumulate every day. This mess gets tracked all over your home. But you don't need to spend time *deep cleaning* to handle daily dirt if you have the proper tools to clean it up before it gets tracked around or ground in where it fell.

In-Betweening™ is the answer. Clean up the little dirt while it's still little. Your Eureka cordless vacuum cleaner will help you In-Between instead of clean. Eureka cordless vacs are light, compact, rechargeable quick-fixers that swoop up the small stuff, before it has a chance to grow. Until you need them, they wait quietly in their charging stands. (You never need to buy new batteries.)

No matter which kind of deep-cleaning Eureka vacuum cleaner you have, you may want to talk cordless with your Eureka dealer. Eureka cordless and In-Betweening™ keep you on top of cleaning. By keeping things looking good, you can put off full-scale cleaning until you have the time.

Eureka Cordless Quick Up®

An In-Betweening™ Stick Vacuum Cleaner

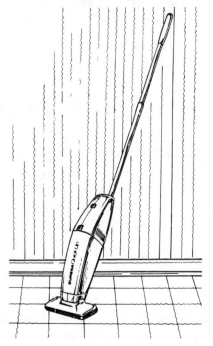

Eureka Quick Up®.

Eureka Cordless Quick Up® is especially good for . . .
- Quick cleanups of crumbs, cold ashes, sand, and any other dry spill any-where in the house.
- Dorm rooms.
- Hobby areas.
- Hard-surface floors or carpets.
- Hard-to-get-in places and cleaning under furniture.

Quick Up® is ideal for In-Betweening™ all over your house. Its versatil-ity makes Quick Up® the perfect working partner for your full-size vacuum cleaner.

Features of Eureka Cordless Quick Up® and what they mean to you.

Note: See your Owner's Manual for features that apply to your Eureka cordless cleaner.

- **Cordless Convenience**—no twists, no kinks, no limits on where you can clean with a Quick Up®.
- **Rechargeable Battery** runs 15 minutes on one charging—plenty of time for quick pickups.
- **Lightweight**—an easy-to-use 3 pounds and 8 ounces.
- **Versatile** for hard-surface floors *and* short nap carpet.
- **Large Dust Cup** removes easily and cleanly for quick emptying; reus-able filter requires no bags.
- **Low Profile** gets under furniture easily.
- **Self-Storing** on its wall-mounted charging stand.

Eureka Cordless Mini Mite®

An In-Betweening™ Hand Vacuum Cleaner

Eureka Cordless Mini Mite® is especially good for . . .
- Quick cleanups of dry spills and litter anywhere.
- Cars, boats.
- Pets.
- Workbenches and hobby areas.
- Children's activity areas.
- Fast cleanup of dust bunnies.

Mini Mite® is ideal for In-Betweening™ in your house, your car, your workshop, and anywhere else spills and litter happen. Its versatility makes Mini Mite® the perfect working partner for your full-size vacuum cleaner.

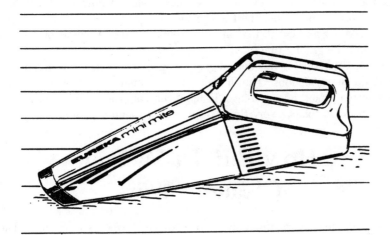

Eureka Mini Mite®.

Features of Eureka Cordless Mini Mite® and what they mean to you.

Note: See your Owner's Manual for features that apply to your Eureka cordless cleaner.

- **Cordless Convenience**—goes anywhere anytime.
- **Rechargeable Battery** runs 5 to 8 minutes on one charging—plenty of time for quick pickups.
- **Snap Latch** releases the front for easy emptying.
- **Dust Cup** empties easily; no bag to handle.
- **Trigger Switch** is spring loaded for instant on/off.
- **Charge Indicator** light shows the power is on.
- **Self-Storing** charging unit attaches to the wall or sits on the counter.

The Choice Is Yours

Eureka's Cleaning System helps you beat housework with In-Betweening™ and deep-cleaning when you need it. You can count on Eureka for as much or as little cleaning power as you need. The point is that Eureka is here to help you clean anytime.

As mentioned earlier, the models used to explain the Eureka Cleaning System are representative of categories. Your specific Eureka vacuum cleaner may have different features. But no matter which Eureka vacuum cleaner you own, you can be sure that it is an expert cleaner you can count on. Your Owner's Manual will tell you exactly which features you have and how to use them to their best advantage.

Mini Mite® and Quick Up® are each one-of-a-kind. A couple of the best ideas in a long, long time!

While you're giving this book a general once-over, take a few minutes to read the next sections. They'll help you understand how your vacuum cleaner works and help you keep in mind the important safety precautions you'll need to follow every time you use your vacuum cleaner.

How Eureka Vacuum Cleaners Work

Airflow cleans carpeting and above-floor areas when you vacuum. The "on" switch of a Eureka vacuum cleaner activates the motor, which creates the suction inside the body of the vacuum cleaner that pulls in dirt particles and air. Once inside the machine, the dirt is carried with the air through filters that trap the particles but allow the air to flow through the machine and out the exhaust opening. Eureka uprights and power teams include a beater bar or brush roll to agitate the dirt out of the carpet; this enhances their cleaning action.

Since airflow cleans carpeting, the amount of airflow determines how well a carpet is cleaned. The amount of airflow is affected by the size of the vacuum cleaner's motor (power rating), the motor's placement, the construction of the fan chamber, and the design of the paper bag.

Since the *size of the vacuum cleaner's motor* is not the only factor that determines airflow, you cannot compare the cleaning capacity of vacuum cleaners simply by comparing their power ratings. Although a standard unit of measure for airflow exists (CFM, or cubic feet of air per minute), vacuum-cleaner manufacturers do not use this rating system consistently.

The *placement of the motor* affects airflow differently in canister and upright vacuum cleaners. Canisters have an indirect air system; the air is drawn indirectly through the fan chamber because it is drawn through the bag first. Canister motors need to be more powerful than upright motors because air must be pulled from greater distances (up to ten feet) through the hose and pipes.

Uprights have a direct air system; air is pulled through the fan chamber first and then blown into the bag. Since air travels a much shorter distance (five to seven inches) than it does through canister vacuums, less motor power is required for an upright to maintain the same amount of CFM as a canister.

The *construction of the fan chamber* (the number of fins on the fan) affects the amount of airflow. Eureka motors have ten fins for maximum CFM.

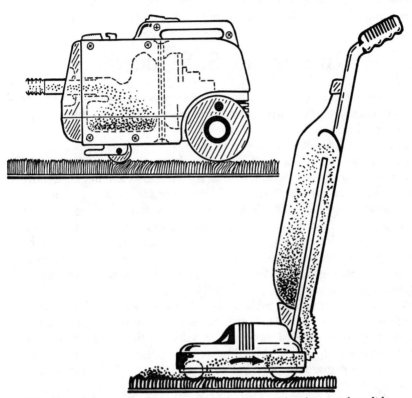

Airflow through your vacuum cleaner brings dirt into the cleaner where it is trapped in the dust bag.

The *design of the disposable dust bag* and the quality of the paper also determine the amount of airflow. The purpose of the paper bag is to trap dirt, but at the same time, the bag must be porous enough to allow air to pass through. A bag made of poor-quality paper with closed pores or a bag that is full of dirt blocks the passage of air, reducing the cleaning power of the machine. A genuine Eureka replaceable bag, made of high-quality filter paper, will make your Eureka clean better. Changing the bag often will allow your vacuum cleaner to clean at its most efficient best. Very fine particles can restrict airflow and decrease performance even before the bag appears to be full. For this reason, when you vacuum carpet fresheners or cleaners, powder, plaster dust, or similar fine substances, the bag may need to be changed more often than usual.

Eureka bags are designed by Eureka engineers to fit Eureka vacuum cleaners. Eureka large-capacity bags fill from the top, dropping dirt to the bottom of the bag and out of the way. Suction power stays stronger longer. Eureka bags hold more dirt, so you change bags less often, saving time and money. A generic bag, which claims to fit all vacuum cleaners, can leak or break, spreading hair, dust, and dirt and making an enormous mess.

Important Safeguards

Accidents due to misuse can only be prevented by the person who is using the machine. To guard against injury, basic safety precautions should be observed.

Read and follow all safety instructions.

Electric shock could occur if a vacuum cleaner is used outdoors or on wet surfaces unless the vacuum cleaner is a cordless vacuum or a wet/dry vac that has been specifically designed for use under these circumstances.

A vacuum cleaner is safe when it is used to perform cleaning functions as they are specified in the owner's guide. Should damage occur to electrical or mechanical parts, the vacuum cleaner and/or accessory should be repaired by the manufacturer or an Authorized Service Center before you use the machine again, in order to avoid further damage to the machine or physical injury to yourself.

A damaged power cord could cause electrical shock or fire. To minimize this possibility, observe the following precautions: Do not run the vacuum cleaner over its power cord. Avoid closing a door on the power cord or pulling it around sharp edges. When disconnecting the power cord from an electrical outlet, grasp the plug. Pulling it out by the cord itself can damage cord insulation and internal connections to the plug.

Your vacuum cleaner creates suction and may contain a revolving brush. To avoid bodily injury from suction or moving parts, the vacuum cleaner brush, hose, wands, and attachments should not be placed against or in close proximity to loose clothing, jewelry, hair, or body surfaces while the vacuum cleaner is connected to an electrical outlet.

Whenever possible, plug your vacuum cleaner into a standard wall outlet. The use of extension cords or light sockets with inadequate current could result in electric shock or fire.

To avoid electric shock, always plug your vacuum cleaner into a 3-prong grounding receptacle if your vacuum cleaner is provided with a grounded electrical system and has a 3-prong grounding plug.

Attachments such as insecticide and paint sprayers can cause toxic, flammable, explosive, or suffocating vapors in indoor areas. Use only those attachments that are recommended by the manufacturer of your vacuum cleaner.

Disconnect your vacuum cleaner from the electrical outlet before changing bags, filters, brushes, or belts. You could receive bodily injury from moving parts should the power switch accidentally be turned on.

When you use your vacuum cleaner to vacuum another electrical appliance, such as removing lint from a clothes dryer, be sure to disconnect the appliance being vacuumed from the electrical outlet in order to minimize chances of electric shock.

Guide the power cord firmly when retracting it on vacuum cleaners with Cordaway® to prevent the plug from becoming a flying object.

Do not use your vacuum cleaner in areas where flammable and/or explosive vapors or dust is present to avoid the possibility of fire or explosion. Some cleaning fluids can produce flammable vapors. Areas on which dry-cleaning fluids have been used should be completely dry and thoroughly aired before being vacuumed.

To avoid fire hazard, do not pick up matches, hot fireplace ashes, or smoking material with a vacuum cleaner.

Keep your work area well lighted to avoid picking up harmful materials, such as liquids, sharp objects, or burning substances, and to prevent tripping accidents. Proper storage of the vacuum in a closet or other out-of-the-way area immediately after use will also prevent accidents caused by tripping over the vacuum cleaner.

Use care when operating your vacuum cleaner on uneven surfaces, such as stairs. A falling vacuum cleaner could cause bodily injury and/or damage the machine.

Store your vacuum cleaner indoors in a cool, dry area. Preventing exposure to the weather will help avoid electric shock and/or damage to the vacuum cleaner.

Exercise strict supervision to prevent injury when using your vacuum cleaner near children or when a child is operating the vacuum cleaner. Do not allow children to play with vacuum cleaners, and never leave a vacuum cleaner plugged in and unattended.

Before plugging in your vacuum cleaner, be sure your electrical outlet voltage is within 10 percent of the voltage listed on the rating plate located on the underside of the vacuum cleaner.

Hold On To Your Eureka Owner's Manual

Save your Owner's Manual, cherish it, and never let it go! Your Owner's Manual is the source for information on how to keep your specific Eureka vacuum cleaner running like new for years. Your manual will also tell you what to do if your vacuum cleaner fails to run right.

The manual explains how to change dust bags, belts, and filters. It also tells you how to clean and care for your Eureka vacuum cleaner. You need the information in the manual and won't find it anywhere else. Store your manual where you'll be able to find it when you need it. If you don't, you can almost be sure that the first time you need your manual you won't be able to find it.

One very good way to keep your manual from getting lost is to keep it where you store your vacuum cleaner. Then you'll see it every time you get out your vacuum cleaner. Tape it on the wall, pin it up with pushpins, or put it in a manila envelope labeled "Eureka Owner's Manual." Another good way to take care of your Owner's Manual is to put it in a loose-leaf notebook where you store the owner's manuals for your other appliances.

ALL ABOUT FLOORS

Dirt from the street collects on feet and gets walked into your house a dozen times a day. The little dumps and spills of daily living accumulate with startling speed. Eureka's Cleaning System can help you handle every floor in your home the fast, easy, no-hassle way.

Carpets and Rugs

For In-Betweening™ spilled popcorn, dumped ashtrays, and crunched potato chips, a Mini Mite® or Quick Up® will swoosh away the mess in seconds. But eventually you'll have to clean the entire floor. You can rely on your Eureka vacuum cleaner to clean carpets and rugs quickly and thoroughly.

VACUUMING YOUR CARPET
Later in this section, we'll talk about dealing with spots and stains, about specific cleaning techniques, and even about repairing carpets. But first, some general tips for carpet cleaning.

The easiest way to tackle a large job, like vacuuming a wall-to-wall-carpeted room, is to break it down into sections. When you mow the lawn, you make sure you go over all of it. When you vacuum wall-to-wall carpeting, you can be sure to cover every inch if you divide the floor into quarters. Vacuum an entire quarter before moving on to the next.

When you vacuum a carpet, especially a thick, plush carpet in which dirt is sure to be deeply embedded, take your time. One pass with even a high-powered Eureka upright is not enough. Go over each section of carpeting several times. Work slowly to allow the suction to remove all the ground-in dust and dirt.

The experts at Eureka have found that you really do need to vacuum your rugs and carpets about once a week, more often in areas of heavy traffic. Frequent vacuuming prolongs the life of your carpet because it prevents a buildup of gritty particles that can cut carpet fibers. Every few weeks take a little extra time and use your crevice tool for in-depth cleaning around baseboards and radiators and in other hard-to-reach places.

When we say that you need to vacuum areas of heavy traffic frequently, we're not just talking about hallways and the route to the kitchen. People move their feet around when they sit and grind dirt from their shoes into the carpeting, so you'll need to pay special attention to the carpet in front

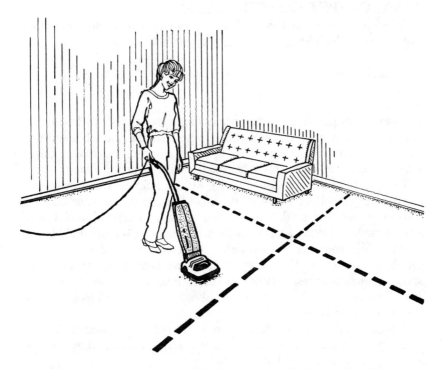

To make sure that you cover the entire surface of your wall-to-wall carpeting when you vacuum, divide it into quarters and thoroughly clean each one before going on to the next.

of chairs and couches, and under desks. Vacuum areas of heavy traffic with a crisscross pattern of overlapping strokes.

A surefire way to cut your cleaning time in half is to put thick mats or throw rugs at all the entrances to your home, both inside and outside the doors. Eureka has found that these mats intercept and trap loose dirt, keeping it from being tracked through your house. Compared with cleaning a whole room, throwing a washable rug into the washing machine or vacuuming a doormat takes practically no time at all.

After thoroughly vacuuming your rugs or carpet, you may find yourself faced with carpeting that is still not quite clean. Regular use of your Eureka vacuum cleaner will keep dirt from building up too fast, but eventually you'll need to deep-clean your carpet or have to deal quickly and effectively with spots and stains. Each kind of stain requires special treatment, and the cleaning pros at Eureka have discovered the best and quickest ways to clean up most kinds of spills. When it is time to deep-clean your carpet, turn to the section of this chapter that deals with shampooing carpet, and you'll find time-tested advice on the best, easiest, and fastest ways to clean.

BASIC CARPET CONSTRUCTION

Before you start to think about cleaning your carpet, let's consider the four major features that distinguish one carpet from another:

- Fiber
- Pile and Density
- Padding
- Texture

Fiber: Many people think that wool is the best carpet fiber when money is no object. But many synthetic fibers reproduce the natural qualities of wool, and some may resist stains better than wool does. Wool carpet releases soil easily, and it is resilient and does not support flame.

The quality of wool carpeting varies widely. Inferior wool carpets will shed, stain, and pill. A good synthetic carpet is better than inferior wool.

Most carpet sold in the United States is not made of wool but of synthetics. Nylon is the best synthetic carpet fiber. It is more durable and carefree than other man-made fibers. A well-constructed nylon carpet is an excellent investment. Carpet made from synthetic fibers treated with special chemicals to resist stains may cost as much as good wool carpeting, but it may be worth the additional initial cost because it will look good for a long period of time.

Polyester and acrylic are less expensive carpet fibers. Because both of these kinds of fibers show soil and mat relatively quickly, they are best reserved for areas of low traffic.

Polypropylene (olefin) carpets are primarily used for basements and outdoor areas because the fiber resists moisture and fading.

Pile and Density: A carpet's performance is affected by its pile (carpet height) and density (number of tufts per square inch) as well as by its fiber content. High-pile carpeting may look especially soft and luxurious initially, but its height makes cleaning it difficult. The pile may "lay over," causing people to walk on the sides of the yarn instead of on its surface. For most homes, high-density, low-pile carpeting will wear best. Eureka recommends a maximum pile height of .375 inches and a density of 64 tufts per square inch.

Before you buy carpeting, give it a "palm test." This is a relatively accurate test of a carpet's wearability. Run the palm of your hand over the carpet's surface. If the fibers are flexible and bend easily, the carpet will wear out quickly. If the fibers resist the pressure from your hand, the carpet should wear well.

Padding: Carpet padding does a lot more than put spring in your step when you walk across a carpeted room. Padding increases the life of a carpet by protecting the carpet backing that holds carpet fibers in place. Padding also absorbs noise and insulates a room from drafts.

Carpet padding is rated by weight. In most cases, thicker and heavier pads offer better protection than thinner and lighter pads. Eureka recommends a minimum padding thickness of one-half inch.

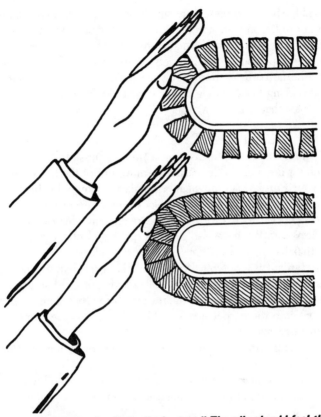

Before buying carpeting, give it the "palm test." The pile should feel thick, tight, and springy when you brush your palm over it. Fold a corner of the carpet to see if the backing shows through the pile.

Texture: The texture of a carpet distinguishes one kind of carpeting from another. When carpeting is manufactured, loops of spun fiber are stitched through a backing. The loops can be cut and twisted to create various textures, or they can be left uncut. Varying the length of the loops or combining loops with cut pile creates a sculptured look.

Selecting the texture, fiber, and color of carpeting is a highly personal choice, but living with your choice and maintaining it may not be all that you had hoped if you do not choose wisely. Eureka's carpet experts suggest that a good-quality, thick-pile carpet in a combination of muted, dark tones is the best carpet choice for most homes.

Industrial-grade, tightly woven carpets not only wear like iron, but they feel like iron when you walk on them or kids play on them. Low-pile carpet, such as indoor/outdoor carpet, is difficult to maintain because it shows dirt. A thick, plush carpet will hide dirt, but a short-pile, solid-color carpet reveals every speck of dirt and every tiny bit of litter, not to mention crumbs.

Light-gold, white, and pastels are simply gorgeous carpet colors, but unless you plan not to live in your home, these elegant, light-colored carpets will be a disaster in a few months. No matter how faithfully you keep mats at the entrances and wipe your feet, all carpets eventually get soiled. There is no way to keep airborne particles from industrial pollution, street oils, heating gas, and home cooking from settling on the carpet. So do yourself a big favor and choose a color that won't show soil.

CARPET TREATMENTS

We all want to put off for as long a time as possible the day when we have to either deep-clean the carpet or move out of the house. In addition to using your Eureka vacuum cleaner regularly to keep dirt from becoming embedded in carpet fibers, the Eureka cleaning experts have found that carpets treated to resist dirt and static really stay clean longer than untreated carpeting. We have also found a quick and effective treatment for a carpet that has picked up household or pet odors.

A soil-retardant is a chemical treatment that coats carpet fibers to make them less able to absorb water- and oil-based spots and spills. Tea, milk, coffee, and winter slush are the main causes of carpet stains because they quickly soak into the carpet fibers and backing unless the carpet has been treated to resist soil.

Soil-retardants can be applied to new carpets or to newly cleaned carpets. These chemicals may appear to be easy to apply, but Eureka's experience bears out the manufacturers' advice that you apply soil retardants only with professional equipment, using the recommended application techniques.

Carpets can also be treated with antistatic agents. This treatment will not only eliminate the irritation of mild electric shocks every time you change the channel on your television or touch a light switch, but it will also keep your home and carpet cleaner because static electricity has a magnetic effect on dust particles in the air.

There are many antistatic sprays on the market, but Eureka's cleaning pros have found that ordinary fabric softener works as well as many commercial antistatic products. Just as fabric softener takes static cling out of your laundry, it can remove static shock from your carpet. Spray your carpet lightly with a mixture of 5 parts water and 1 part liquid fabric softener. Let the carpet dry thoroughly before you walk on it. The result will be a shockless carpet.

Carpet odor can be eliminated without resorting to deep-cleaning. The cleaning team at Eureka sprinkles baking soda on the carpet before vacuuming. If you prefer, you can use 1 cup borax mixed with 2 cups cornmeal, but you must let this mixture stand on the carpet for at least an hour before vacuuming. Remember that these fine particles may stop the airflow through your Eureka disposable dust bag sooner than larger dust particles, and a bag that appears to be only partially filled may need to be changed. Don't forget to check the filter on your canister as well.

CLEANING SPILLS

You know that there is no way to prevent spills on carpeting, short of living in the kitchen. But the kitchen floor also has to be cleaned. Over the years at Eureka, we've found that in many ways it's as easy, if not easier, to maintain a carpet as it is a hard-surface floor. If you treat spills quickly and correctly, most of them are not disastrous to your carpet. Prepare for the worst, stock up on the cleaning and stain-removing supplies you'll need, and go ahead paint your toenails in the bedroom, drink red wine in the living room, and let the kids make Christmas cards around the dining room table—your carpet really can take it.

Eureka has learned the secret of spot and stain removal through experience and by consulting with homemakers and carpet manufacturers: Clean spots and spills immediately. It's that simple. If you catch the spill when it's fresh, before it has become a stain, you've got three chances out of four of removing it totally. So when something spills, immediately move into action and follow this procedure:

- Carefully blot or scrape the entire stained area before applying any cleaning solution. Remove as much of the spill as possible. If you just start right in cleaning, you'll make an even bigger mess because the cleaning solution you pour on will only spread the stain over more of the carpet.

Before applying cleaning solution, blot the stained area to remove as much of the spill as possible.

- Before using any cleaning solution, test your carpet in an inconspicuous area to make sure the cleaner won't damage or discolor it. Since you want to move fast once a spill occurs, Eureka suggests that you test the cleaning agents that you keep on hand before you have to use them to make sure that they will not harm your carpeting. (For example, you would not want to use any kind of acetone-based cleaner on acetate carpeting because it would dissolve the carpet fibers.) For detailed information, consult the section of this book that deals with cleaning solutions.
- Do not rub the spill because rubbing might spread the problem to a larger area of the rug. When you apply spot cleaner, work from the outside of the stain toward the inside to avoid spreading the stain. You'll probably want to start cleaning the worst part of the stain first, but most substances stain as they dry. Cleaning the stain from the outside edges in toward the center gathers up the spill in order to get rid of it completely.
- After an application of a cleaning solution, blot up all the moisture. Eureka has found that a clean, white bath towel is unsurpassed for drying carpet and brushing the nap back up to a standing position.
- After blotting the carpet, if you feel there is still too much moisture, place a ¾-inch-thick stack of white cloth towels over the spot and weight them with a heavy object.

CARPET STAIN–REMOVAL GUIDE

Later in this book, you'll find a very thorough guide to spot and stain removal. Eureka has researched and completely tested the best and quickest methods for removing just about every kind of stain from just about every kind of surface. But we've found, as we're sure you know, that certain kinds of stains are more likely to happen to carpets than others. So this is a quick-reference guide (in alphabetical order) to Eureka's best cures for the most common carpet spots and stains.

Acid Stains

Acid spills, such as toilet-bowl cleaner, drain cleaner, and vinegar, demand especially quick action. Dilute them immediately with baking soda and water or with club soda. You can tell by feel and smell when the acid spill has been cleaned up. Then apply a solution of ammonia (1 part) and water (10 parts). Rinse with cold water, let dry, and vacuum.

Alcoholic Beverages

If someone spills an alcoholic drink on your carpet, quickly dilute the spot with cold water so that the alcohol does not have time to attack the dyes. Absorb the excess liquid. Then mix 1 teaspoon mild detergent, 1 teaspoon white vinegar, and 1 quart warm water. Apply the solution to the spot. Let the carpet dry. If the spot remains, reapply the solution. Let the carpet dry completely. Vacuum gently.

Blood
Absorb as much of the blood as you can. Then mix 1 teaspoon mild detergent, 1 teaspoon white vinegar, and 1 quart warm water. Apply the solution to the spot. Let the carpet dry. Apply dry-cleaning fluid, and let the carpet dry completely. Vacuum gently.

Butter
The first step in cleaning up a butter spill is to scrape up as much solid butter as you can or to absorb all the melted butter that you can. Apply dry-cleaning fluid. Let the carpet dry. If the spot remains, reapply the fluid, and let the carpet dry thoroughly. Then vacuum.

Candle Wax
Eureka's cleaning experts have discovered that the easiest way to remove candle wax from your carpet is to press an ice cube against the drip. The wax will harden and can then be pulled off. Treat any remaining traces of wax with dry-cleaning fluid. Let the carpet dry, and vacuum.

Another way to remove candle wax on carpeting is to place a blotter over the spilled wax, and press with a warm iron until the blotter absorbs the melted wax. Move the blotter frequently so that it doesn't get oversaturated. Remove traces of the wax with spot remover. Let dry, and then vacuum.

Candy
Candy that contains no chocolate is usually easily removed from carpet. Scrape up as much of the candy as you can. Mix 1 teaspoon mild detergent, 1 teaspoon white vinegar, and 1 quart warm water. Apply the solution to the spot. Let the carpet dry. If the spot remains, reapply the solution. Let the carpet dry. Vacuum gently.

Chewing Gum
Chewing gum can be a sticky mess, so harden it by pressing an ice cube against the blob of gum. The gum will harden and can then be pulled off. Treat any remaining traces of the chewing gum with dry-cleaning fluid. Let the carpet dry, and then vacuum.

Chocolate
The longer chocolate is allowed to stay on your carpet, the more difficult it is to remove. Scrape the chocolate from the carpet. Mix 1 teaspoon mild detergent, 1 teaspoon white vinegar, and 1 quart warm water. Apply the solution to the spot. Rinse well with clear water, making sure you don't drench the carpet. Let the carpet dry. Vacuum gently.

Coffee
Blot spilled coffee immediately. Then mix 1 teaspoon mild detergent, 1

teaspoon white vinegar, and 1 quart warm water. Apply the solution to the spot. Let the carpet dry. Apply dry-cleaning fluid, and let the carpet dry again. Vacuum gently.

Crayon

Dropped crayons have a knack for getting stepped on and ground into carpeting. Scrape away excess crayon and remove the rest by placing a blotter over the crayon stain and pressing it with a warm iron until the blotter absorbs the melted crayon. Move the blotter frequently so that it doesn't get oversaturated. Apply dry-cleaning fluid, and let the carpet dry. Reapply if necessary, and then vacuum.

Egg

Like all protein stains, spilled eggs need to be cleaned up immediately. Scrape up as much cooked egg as possible or mop up raw egg. Mix 1 teaspoon mild detergent, 1 teaspoon white vinegar, and 1 quart warm water. Apply the solution to the spot. Let the carpet dry. If the spot remains, reapply the solution. Let the carpet dry. Vacuum gently.

Fruit

Eureka knows that fruit stains can be very hard to remove if they are allowed to set, but if you act quickly this method usually prevents a permanent stain. Scrape up spilled fruit, and absorb fruit juice. Mix 1 teaspoon mild detergent, 1 teaspoon white vinegar, and 1 quart warm water. Apply the solution to the spot. Let the carpet dry. If the spot remains, reapply the solution. Let the carpet dry. Vacuum gently.

Gravy

If you accidentally rock the gravy boat, wipe up as much of the spilled gravy as you can. Mix 1 teaspoon mild detergent, 1 teaspoon white vinegar, and 1 quart warm water. Apply the solution to the spot. Let the carpet dry. Apply dry-cleaning fluid. Let the carpet dry. Vacuum gently.

Hand Cream

When you inadvertently squirt hand lotion on your carpet, wipe up the spill immediately. Apply dry-cleaning fluid. Let the carpet dry. If the spot remains, reapply the dry-cleaning fluid. Let the carpet dry, and then vacuum.

Ink

Fast action is essential when you spill ink on carpet. Immediately apply dry-cleaning fluid. Let the carpet dry. If the spot remains, reapply the dry-cleaning fluid. Let the carpet dry thoroughly, and vacuum.

Lipstick

Open tubes of lipstick have a way of falling into the hands of curious toddlers or just falling, period. When your carpet acquires a telltale trace of lipstick, scrape away as much of the lipstick as you can. Apply dry-cleaning fluid, and let it dry; then mix 1 teaspoon mild detergent, 1 teaspoon white vinegar, and 1 quart warm water. Apply the solution to the spot. Let the carpet dry. If the spot remains, reapply the solution. Let the carpet dry. Vacuum gently.

Mildew

The first step in removing mildew stains is to kill the fungus. To do this, mix 1 teaspoon disinfectant cleaner and 1 cup water. Apply the solution to the mildewed carpet, and blot. Then to remove the stain, apply a solution of ammonia (1 part) and water (10 parts). Blot, rinse, and let dry. Vacuum. Keeping the area totally dry is the only way to prevent the reoccurrence of mildew, which can eventually break down carpet fibers.

Milk

Blot up the spilled milk. Mix 1 teaspoon mild detergent, 1 teaspoon white vinegar, and 1 quart warm water. Apply the solution to the spot. Let the carpet dry. Vacuum gently.

Mud

When muddy boots and shoes get past the mats at the entrances to your home, allow the mud tracked onto your carpeting to dry completely, and then brush or scrape off as much as possible. Mix 1 teaspoon mild detergent, 1 teaspoon white vinegar, and 1 quart warm water. Apply the solution to the spot. Let the carpet dry. If the stain remains, apply dry-cleaning fluid, and blot dry. When the spot is completely dry, vacuum gently.

Nail Polish

Apply dry-cleaning fluid or amyl acetate, acetone, or nail-polish remover to the spilled polish. Test the solvent you plan to use on an inconspicuous part of the carpet. Never apply acetate, acetone, or nail-polish remover to acetate carpet fibers. If the stain remains, mix 1 teaspoon mild detergent, 1 teaspoon white vinegar, and 1 quart warm water. Apply the solution to the spot. Let the carpet dry. Vacuum gently.

Salad Dressing

A misplaced slosh of salad dressing can be removed easily from most carpeting. Absorb as much salad dressing as you can. Mix 1 teaspoon mild detergent, 1 teaspoon white vinegar, and 1 quart warm water. Apply the solution to the spot. Let the carpet dry. If the spot remains, reapply the solution. Let the carpet dry. Vacuum gently.

Soft Drinks

The carbonation in soft drinks will help you clean spilled drinks quickly, but act fast because some of the dyes in the drinks can permanently stain your carpet. Blot up the spilled drink. Mix 1 teaspoon mild detergent, 1 teaspoon white vinegar, and 1 quart warm water. Apply the solution to the spot. Let the carpet dry. If the spot remains, reapply the solution. Let the carpet dry. Vacuum gently.

Tea

The tannic acid in black tea is a potent dye, so move quickly when tea is spilled on your rug. Blot up the tea spill. Mix 1 teaspoon mild detergent, 1 teaspoon white vinegar, and 1 quart warm water. Apply the solution to the spot. Let the carpet dry. Apply dry-cleaning fluid. Let the carpet dry. Vacuum gently.

Urine

Mix 1 teaspoon mild detergent, 1 teaspoon white vinegar, and 1 quart warm water. Apply the solution to the spot. Let the carpet dry. If the spot remains, reapply the solution. Let the carpet dry. Vacuum gently.

Vomit

Treat vomit quickly. Blot up as much as possible, then dilute immediately with baking soda and water or with club soda. Then apply a solution of ammonia (1 part) and water (10 parts). Rinse with cold water, let dry, and then vacuum.

Wine

When red wine is spilled on your carpet, dilute it with white wine, then clean the spot with cold water, and cover with table salt. Wait ten minutes, then vacuum up the salt.

SPECIAL PROBLEMS

When you look across a flawless expanse of new carpet, you hate to think of all the potential disasters that lie ahead for your beautiful floor. Eureka understands this better than anyone. After so many years of cleaning carpeting and listening to people who live with and clean carpeting, Eureka has become well acquainted with many special carpet problems, and we've learned how to deal with them. When your carpet is burned, stained, or discolored, you can simply move a big chair over the spot and forget about it, or you can use one of the simple methods developed and tested by Eureka to restore your carpet to its original good looks.

- If the spot remover you use alters the color of your carpet, try touching up small places with artists' acrylic paint. If that doesn't work, try a felt-tip marker or a permanent-ink marker of the appropriate color. Go slowly and blend the color into the fibers.
- To raise depressions left in carpet by heavy furniture, try steaming. Hold a steam iron close enough for steam to reach the carpet, but don't let the

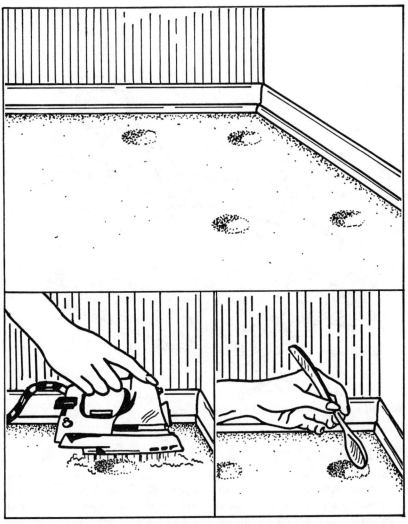

Raise depressions in carpet by steaming the area and then lifting the fibers by scraping them with the edge of a spoon.

iron touch the fibers, especially if they are synthetic, because they could melt. Lift the fibers by scraping them with the edge of a coin or spoon.

- If a carpet thread is loose, snip it level with the pile. If you try to pull out the thread, you risk unraveling part of the carpet.
- To repair a small area burned down to the carpet backing, snip off the charred fibers, and put white glue in the opening. Then snip fibers from a scrap of carpet or an inconspicuous part of the carpet (perhaps in a closet). When the glue gets tacky, poke the fibers into place. If the burn isn't all the way down to the backing, just snip off the charred tips of the

Snip off a loose carpet thread even with the pile.

fibers with scissors. The slightly shorter length of a few carpet fibers will never be noticed.
- To repair a large burned area in a carpet, cut out the damaged area and substitute a patch of identical size and shape. Secure the new piece of carpeting with double-faced carpet tape or a latex adhesive.

DEEP–CLEANING CARPETS

There comes a time in the life of every carpet when vacuuming can no longer restore its clean appearance. Since you don't want to rush into a major cleaning job, Eureka has developed the following checklist for dirty carpets. If any of these descriptions fit your carpet, then it is time to deep-clean it.
- The carpet is matted and feels sticky to bare feet.
- The carpet is no longer the same color as the remnant you saved when the carpet was new.
- The carpet has grimy circles around the chairs where people sit to read or watch TV.

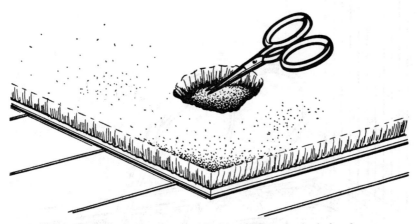

To repair burned carpet, clip away the blackened fibers. In the hole, glue new fibers cut from a carpet scrap.

To repair severe damage, cut out a square of carpet and replace it with a scrap piece held in place with double-faced carpet tape.

- The carpet releases a dust storm when you run across the room to answer the phone.

Eureka recommends having your carpet professionally cleaned unless you have the time and patience to do a thorough cleaning job. One of the reasons that many people believe that carpets soil faster after they have been shampooed is that some people clean only the surface of their carpeting when they think they are deep-cleaning it. The only method that

A steam carpet cleaner injects streams of hot cleaning solution deep into carpet pile and, almost simultaneously, it extracts the moisture and soil.

Eureka has found to clean carpeting down to the backing is to agitate it with a shampooer and rinse it with an extractor.

Should you decide to rent carpet-cleaning equipment and shampoo your carpets yourself, we at Eureka suggest that you allow plenty of uninterrupted time for the task. This is a very big job, and rushing it will mean disappointing results. To speed drying, you should also plan to shampoo carpets during dry periods of the year or when the heating system is operating.

Before cleaning your carpeting, Eureka recommends that you test for colorfastness. Moisten a white towel with the cleaning solution that you are going to be using and apply it to an inconspicuous area. If the towel does not pick up any color from the carpet, it is probably safe to use the solution on the entire carpet.

Remove as much furniture from the room as possible, and place foil or plastic film under the legs and bases of the remaining furniture to prevent stains. (The foil or plastic should be left in place until the carpet is completely dry.) Vacuum the carpet thoroughly, then spot-clean and pretreat stains before shampooing the carpet.

The cleaning experts at Eureka want to remind you to follow the instructions printed on the carpet cleaner you rent, but here are a few additional hints that we hope will make shampooing your carpet easier.

- Use single strokes over the carpet surface.
- Do not apply heavy pressure with the machine.
- Wipe cleaner solutions and foam from woodwork and furniture immediately to prevent damage to the wood or upholstery.
- Fluff damp fibers against the nap after shampooing to aid drying and prevent matting.
- Make sure the room is well ventilated after cleaning to speed drying.
- Try not to walk on carpets until they are dry.

SURFACE–CLEANING CARPETS

It may be possible for you to put off shampooing your carpets almost indefinitely if you are willing to spend extra time each month to keep them clean. Eureka has adapted a carpet-cleaning method sometimes used by professional cleaners to clean the surface dirt from carpets. This is not a deep-cleaning operation. It is a carpet-maintenance technique intended to prevent carpets from needing a major shampooing too often.

If you vacuum your carpets frequently, most dirt accumulates on top of the carpet fibers and is not transferred to the backing. Moisten a two-inch-thick pad, made from a Turkish towel or other heavy-duty cloth, with carpet-cleaning solution, and wring out the excess moisture in a roller mop bucket. Mount the pad on a household floor polisher and run it over the carpet. The pad picks up and absorbs surface grime and soil. When the cloth becomes dirty, turn it over and repeat the process. When both sides are dirty, rinse the pad in the mop bucket, wring, and repeat.

RUG CARE

With the following exceptions, Eureka suggests that you clean and maintain rugs in exactly the same way you take care of carpets. Remember to vacuum both the top and bottom surface of a rug to keep dirt particles from wearing out rug fibers. Eureka has collected the following hints to help you care for rugs with special needs:

Natural Fibers: After vacuuming the surface and underneath fiber, sisal, and grass rugs, remove dirt and restore moisture to the rugs with a damp cloth.

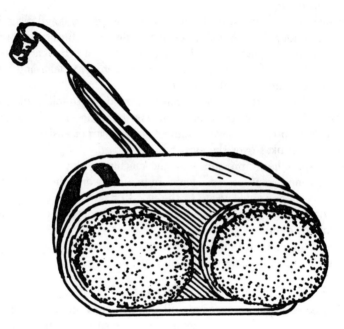

Mount a two-inch thick pad that has been moistened with carpet cleaner on your floor polisher to surface-clean your carpeting.

Fur: Clean fur rugs by working multiple applications of cornmeal through the pile until the cornmeal shakes out clean. Then lightly vacuum the remaining granules. A fur rug can also be spot-cleaned with a damp cloth, but don't get the pelt wet.

Washable Fibers: Air dry round or oval throw rugs to retain their shape, but don't hang them over a clothesline; dry them flat.

Hard-Surface Floors

VACUUMING HARD–SURFACE FLOORS

The Eureka Company has been making vacuum cleaners since before your grandmother started keeping house, and in all those years, we've learned a great deal about cleaning floors—not just rugs and carpets, but all kinds of floors. Unlike other methods of attacking the dirt that piles up on floors, using your Eureka vacuum cleaner doesn't just push dirt around. Whether it's a Mini Mite®, Quick Up®, or Eureka canister, your vacuum cleaner gets dirt off your hard-surface floors and puts it neatly in a bag so it's ready to be taken out of your home for good.

Vacuuming hard-surface floors before you wash them saves you time because when you wash or polish the floor there is no dirt to grind into the floor covering or turn to mud. To not only speed up cleaning but get your home really clean, always vacuum the floor before you clean it with water or wax.

The experts at Eureka recommend that you vacuum your wood and other hard-surface floors about once a week, more often in areas of heavy traffic or if the floor is dark or very shiny. Lint and dust show up faster on polished surfaces than they do on carpeting, so use a Mini Mite® or Quick Up® between regular cleanings to keep your floor sparkling with a minimum of effort. Frequent vacuuming prolongs the life of the floor because it prevents a buildup of grit that can scratch hard-surface flooring.

The techniques you use to vacuum a carpeted room should also be used when you vacuum an uncarpeted room. Eureka reminds you never to use an upright or power team powerhead on a hard-surface floor; both the vacuum and the floor are likely to be damaged permanently. A Eureka canister, power team, or upright vacuum with a floor-nozzle attachment or a Quick Up® is best for removing dust and debris from all hard-surface floors. Vacuum the floor thoroughly, going back and forth across each section. Eureka has found that two slow strokes are usually sufficient to pick up the loose dirt. (Use a small-brush attachment to clean around baseboards and radiators and in other hard-to-reach places.)

CLEANING HARD-SURFACE FLOORS

There are probably many different kinds of hard-surface floors in your home. Your Eureka vacuum cleaner can help you maintain all the floors in your home, from the concrete in your basement to the parquet under the oriental rug in the living room. Unfortunately, weekly vacuuming with your Eureka is not all it takes to keep a hard-surface floor looking its best. So Eureka has developed quick and easy cleaning methods to help you speed through the heel marks and the sticky stuff that accumulate on your hard-surface floors.

The first step toward efficient floor cleaning is to know what your floor is made of. The cleaning method that works for one surface may ruin another. We suggest that you glance through this part of the book and look for the types of surfaces you will be cleaning. In each section, we've told you everything you need to know to care for a particular kind of floor, so you don't need to read the whole thing. All you have to do is to follow the advice for your particular floor covering.

Whenever you go to the grocery or hardware store, you will find an array of specialized cleaning products. Many commercial products are very good at cleaning what they are designed to clean. Which products you use to clean your floors is entirely up to you. We have included some tried-and-true recipes for cleaners that can be made from products you're likely to have in your cupboards. These solutions and methods don't necessarily work better than commercial products, but they all work as well. We know;

A Eureka Quick Up® quickly cleans hard-surface floors.

we've tested them. So if you have time to clean your bathroom floor, but you've run out of the cleaner you usually use, try the homemade remedy—it will save you money, and it will save you time, since you won't have to run out to the store before you start to clean.

Asphalt Tile

An asphalt-tile floor won't retain leg imprints when you replace your old favorite TV chair in the family room with a snazzy new one. But even though asphalt tile recovers well from indentations, we suggest that you use plastic, not rubber, casters and cups on furniture legs to minimize scratches and indentations. Although asphalt is resilient, you should know that grease, oil, and solvents—such as kerosene, gasoline, naphtha, and turpentine—or harsh cleaning preparations and strong soaps as well as scouring can leave the surface of your floor looking like the moon.

If you take the time to damp mop your asphalt floor every week, you will not have to wash and polish it as often as if you allow dirt to build up. But make sure that the cleaner/polish you use can withstand damp mopping. If it can't, you will have to reapply it. We've found that adding a cup of fabric softener to a half pail of water will prevent damp mopping from dulling the shine on your floor.

When you decide to wash the floor, don't flood the floor with water; excess water can seep into the seams and loosen adhesives that hold down the flooring.

Remove heel marks by dipping fine-grade (000) steel wool in liquid floor wax and rubbing the spot gently. Wipe with a damp cloth.

The *fastest* way to clean an asphalt floor is with a one-step cleaner/polish. If you use a commercial water-based polish, don't shake it before use.

The *best* way we've found to clean an asphalt floor takes longer than using a one-step, but it gives an asphalt-tile floor a more durable finish than other cleaning methods. Mix ¼ cup low-sudsing, all-purpose cleaner; 1 cup ammonia; and ½ gallon cool or cold water. **Caution:** Wear rubber gloves, and work in a well-ventilated area when using this powerful solution. Apply the cleaner to the floor with a sponge mop, using pressure for heavily soiled areas. Rinse with cool, clear water for spotless results. Apply two thin coats of a water-based, self-polishing floor finish, allowing the floor to dry between coats. Apply the polish with a long-handled wax applicator that has a washable chenille pad.

Brick

Your brick floor may appear to be very durable because of its hard, fired surface. But in reality brick is porous and stains easily. For this reason, the best way to care for your brick floor is to keep it sealed and waxed. You'll need to use a commercial sealer for brick.

Damp mopping with a sponge mop or string mop after vacuuming will prevent dirt from building up on your brick floor, so you can put off washing and/or stripping the floor. Try adding a cup of vinegar to the mop water; the floor will glisten without being polished—a real time-saver.

If you use a water-based, self-polishing liquid wax, you'll occasionally have to strip the wax buildup before you rewax. Use a solvent-based wax

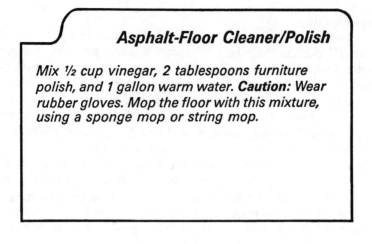

Asphalt-Floor Cleaner/Polish

Mix ½ cup vinegar, 2 tablespoons furniture polish, and 1 gallon warm water. **Caution:** *Wear rubber gloves. Mop the floor with this mixture, using a sponge mop or string mop.*

so that you don't have to strip your floor. A solvent-based polish can be applied over a water-based polish, but a water-based polish cannot be applied over a solvent-based polish. The solvents in the wax dissolve the layer of wax that is on the floor every time solvent-based wax is applied, so there is no wax buildup.

If your floor has a wax buildup, you can remove it by applying a wax-stripping product with a scrub brush or floor-scrubbing machine that has a brush attachment. Rinse the floor thoroughly with clear water after applying the stripper according to the manufacturer's directions. Do not clean your brick floor with acids, strong soaps, or abrasives.

Caring for a porous brick floor is a lot of work no matter what you do. If you use a solvent-based wax on the floor, you have to seal it. If you use a water-based polish, you'll occasionally have to strip the wax buildup.

While the following method of caring for a brick floor is not as effective as a treatment with stripper, sealer, and paste wax, it is a quick and inexpensive way to take care of your brick floor. Since this homemade solution contains ammonia, you strip the floor every time you wash it, eliminating wax buildup. Most acrylic liquid waxes are self-sealing, allowing you to skip the application of a sealer. Clean and strip the floor with a solution of ¼ cup low-sudsing, all-purpose cleaner; 1 cup clear ammonia; and ½ gallon cool or cold water. **Caution:** Wear rubber gloves, and work in a well-ventilated area when using this powerful solution. Apply the solution to the floor with a sponge mop, using pressure for heavily soiled areas; rinse with cool, clear water for spotless results. Then apply two thin coats of an acrylic floor wax.

Ceramic Tile, Glazed

Before there was vinyl, there was glazed ceramic tile for people like us who quickly say no, thank you, when it comes to complicated and time-consuming cleaning projects. Highly glazed ceramic tile is an almost carefree

> ## Cleaner for Glazed Ceramic Tile
>
> *Mix ¼ cup low-sudsing, all-purpose cleaner; 1 cup ammonia; and ½ gallon cool or cold water. **Caution:** Wear rubber gloves and work in a well-ventilated area when using this powerful solution. Apply the solution to the floor with a sponge mop, using pressure for heavily soiled areas; rinse with cool, clear water for spotless results. Dry with a soft cloth.*

floor covering. It requires little more than regular vacuuming and damp mopping.

We suggest that you damp mop with an all-purpose cleaner, using a synthetic scouring pad and nonabrasive cleaner for stubborn spots. Then dry the floor with a soft cloth to avoid streaks. If the freshly mopped floor dries with a luster-dulling film, mop it again with water containing a cup of white vinegar, and the floor will glisten.

Ceramic Tile, Unglazed

Unlike shiny, easy-to-care-for glazed tile, unglazed ceramic tile is porous and must be sealed to resist stains. Your new unglazed ceramic-tile floor needs to be sealed with a commercial sealer and a water-based wax.

Damp mopping with a sponge mop or string mop after you vacuum will allow you to put off washing and rewaxing the floor until it is really dirty. We've discovered that if you put a cup of vinegar in the mop water, your unglazed ceramic tile floor will glisten.

About once a year, you will need to strip the wax buildup on your tile floor and rewax. A floor-scrubbing machine that has a brush attachment really saves time on this job, but if you don't have or can't rent a machine, a scrub brush can be used to apply the wax-stripping product. Rinse the floor thoroughly with clear water after applying the stripper. Do not clean your unglazed ceramic-tile floor with acids, strong soaps, or abrasives.

When you rewax the floor, you can use either a water-based, self-polishing wax or a paste wax. We recommend that you use the following home-made solution in conjunction with a water-based, acrylic self-polishing wax. This method is not as effective as a treatment with stripper, sealer, and paste wax, but we have found that it works nearly as well, and it's quick and inexpensive.

Clean and strip the floor with a solution of ¼ cup low-sudsing, all-purpose cleaner; 1 cup clear ammonia; and ½ gallon cool or cold water. **Cau-**

tion: Wear rubber gloves and work in a well-ventilated area when using this powerful solution. Apply the solution to the floor with a sponge mop, using pressure for heavily soiled areas; rinse with cool, clear water for spotless results. Then apply two thin coats of an acrylic floor wax.

Concrete

If you're like most people, you probably put off dealing with the concrete floors in your unfinished basement and garage for as long as possible. The result is that they get really dirty because concrete is very porous and soaks up stains quickly. While few of us are so fastidious as to seal or paint our garage floors, the time you take to seal a basement floor, especially if it is new, will save time in the long run, since the sealed floor will require little more cleaning than vacuuming. When your basement floor does have to be washed, go ahead and get it really clean by washing it with a strong, all-purpose cleaning solution.

After you have gotten rid of the loose surface dirt, we suggest you use the following homemade cleaning solution. It works as well as a commercial heavy-duty cleaner, and it's much less expensive.

Cleaner for Concrete

Mix ¼ cup low-sudsing, all-purpose cleaner; 1 cup clear ammonia; and ½ gallon cool or cold water. **Caution:** Wear rubber gloves, and work in a well-ventilated area when using this powerful solution. Apply to the concrete floor with a sponge mop, using pressure for heavily soiled areas; rinse with cool, clear water for spotless results. Let the floor dry.

Garage floors are not a pretty scene. They soak up oil and grease stains, gather piles of litter, and collect road dirt. But not many people spend much time in the garage, so you don't need to attack the mess very often.

We suggest that you spread kitty litter to absorb oil and grease and that you keep the garage door closed so that leaves and other windblown debris don't collect in your garage.

When it comes time to clean the garage floor, sweep out the dirt, dust, and kitty litter with a stiff broom. You should work from the back of the garage to the front. Then get out the garden hose, and flush the floor with clear water. You can scour tough globs of dirt with your stiff broom or blast them with a jet of water.

Cork

A cork floor recovers quickly from the pressure of chair legs and the wear and tear of heavy foot traffic, but water will do it in every time; even the small amount of H_2O in water-based cleaners is too much wet for a cork floor. You must use only solvent-based cleaners and polishes to maintain cork-tile flooring.

A new cork floor should be sealed with varnish, shellac, or lacquer. Paint or lacquer thinner, alcohol, and other chemicals will damage these sealers, so try not to use them near the floor.

You can remove heel marks from your cork floor by applying a solvent-based wax, polish, or cleaner to a rag and rubbing the mark.

The fastest way to clean a cork floor is with a one-step product specifically formulated to clean and polish cork floors. Unfortunately, the fastest way is not the best way to care for cork. Eureka suggests that if your floor is new or a focal point of your home, you should take the time twice a year to clean the floor with a liquid wood-floor cleaning product and to rewax. Use a liquid cleaner/wax that soaks into the floor. Wipe up the excess liquid, and allow the floor to dry, then buff it with a floor polisher.

The second step of this process is to apply a liquid or paste solvent-based wax. No stripping will ever be necessary because the solvents in the new wax will strip off the old wax. Shake solvent-based liquid polishes vigorously before use. All you have to do to renew the shine between cleanings is to buff the floor when it appears dull.

Flagstone and Slate

These natural-stone flooring materials are similar in that they have rough, porous surfaces and are set into grout. This type of flooring wears

Cleaner for Flagstone and Slate

Mix ¼ cup low-sudsing, all-purpose cleaner; 1 cup clear ammonia; and ½ gallon cool or cold water. **Caution:** Wear rubber gloves, and work in a well-ventilated area when using this powerful solution. Apply to the floor with a sponge mop, using pressure for heavily soiled areas. Rinse the floor thoroughly with clean water. Apply sealer, then buff.

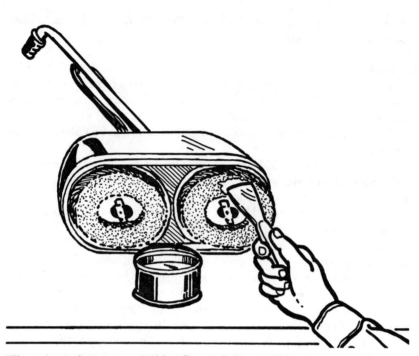

When you apply paste wax with a floor-polishing machine, use a spatula to spread a small amount of wax directly on the brushes.

like rock, but it will look like it should have been left outside if it is not cared for properly. Flagstone and slate floors must be sealed with a commercial sealer, not lacquer or varnish.

The best way to seal a flagstone or slate floor is with a sealer for terrazzo and slate. After the sealer dries, apply two thin coats of an acrylic floor finish with a long-handled wax applicator fitted with a lamb's wool pad, or apply paste wax with a floor-polishing machine. To do this, use a spatula to spread a small amount of paste wax directly on the brushes of the polisher. Slowly operate the polisher back and forth to apply an even, thin coat of wax. When dry, buff the floor.

A self-polishing liquid will build up on your floor, and you'll occasionally have to strip the wax buildup and rewax. Applying a wax-stripping product with a floor-scrubbing machine that has a brush attachment will keep you off your knees, but if you don't have a machine, a scrub brush will work. After applying the stripper according to the manufacturer's directions, rinse the floor thoroughly with clear water. Then apply wax to the floor.

To keep ahead of dirt, damp mop flagstone or slate floors with a sponge mop or string mop, using clear water, an all-purpose cleaning solution in warm water, or water to which fabric softener has been added. Wring the mop until it doesn't drip, and apply it to the floor in slow, even strokes with

Linoleum Cleaner/Polish

Mix ½ cup vinegar, 2 tablespoons furniture polish, and 1 gallon warm water. **Caution:** *Wear rubber gloves. Mop the floor with this mixture, using a sponge or string mop.*

just enough pressure to loosen and pick up dirt. If the freshly mopped floor dries with a luster-dulling film, you can mop it again with water containing a cup of white vinegar; the floor will glisten.

Linoleum

Sad but true, linoleum must be waxed to shine and stand up to foot traffic effectively. But once it is waxed, the only regular maintenance a linoleum floor needs is vacuuming and an occasional swipe with a damp mop. A cup of vinegar in the mop water will bring up the shine on the floor, so you can delay rewaxing until it's really necessary.

Remove heel marks from linoleum by dipping fine-grade (000) steel wool in liquid floor wax. Rub the spot gently, and wipe with a damp cloth.

A water-based cleaner/polish or an all-purpose cleaning solution is best for the routine care of a linoleum floor. Solvent-based products can soften and damage linoleum. Scouring the floor, flooding it with water, or using very hot water or strong soaps are other no-nos for linoleum floors.

We have discovered that the fastest way to clean a linoleum floor is with a one-step cleaner/polish, but the best way to clean the floor is to mop it with an all-purpose cleaner. Dissolve the cleaner in very warm water, rinse, and apply two thin coats (let dry between coats) of a water-based, self-polishing liquid. Use a long-handled wax applicator fitted with a washable chenille pad.

Occasionally, you'll have to remove wax buildup with an all-purpose cleaner or stripper. We recommend that you always test a corner of the floor before stripping the whole thing to make sure the product you're using won't permanently damage the flooring.

Marble

Marble flooring is becoming more and more popular for almost every room in the house; it's available in a variety of colors, with a polished or nonpolished finish, and in an array of new thicknesses and shapes. Non-polished marble is very porous, stains easily, and must be sealed with a commercial sealer. Don't use varnish or lacquer to seal marble; it quickly peels off. Polished marble is less porous but can still be stained; we recommend a commercial marble sealer for this finish also.

Marble floors look great after being damp mopped with a sponge mop or string mop, using clear water, an all-purpose cleaning solution in warm water, or a mixture of 1 cup fabric softener and ½ gallon water. Wring the mop until it doesn't drip, and apply the mixture to the floor in slow, even strokes with just enough pressure to loosen and pick up dirt. If the mopped floor dries with a luster-dulling film, mop it again with water containing a cup of white vinegar. The floor will glisten—it sure beats rewaxing.

Water-based, self-polishing liquid wax is a fast, shiny finish for marble. There's only one problem with using it (and it's a big one): Occasionally, you'll have to strip the wax buildup and rewax. Applying a wax-stripping product with a floor-scrubbing machine with a brush attachment makes the job slightly more pleasant than crawling around on your knees with a scrub brush. After applying the stripper according to the manufacturer's directions, rinse the floor thoroughly with clear water. Then apply wax to the floor.

You can use either a water-based self-polishing wax or a paste wax. If you use a water-based polish, don't shake it before use. A solvent-based polish can be applied over a water-based polish, but a water-based polish cannot be applied over a solvent-based polish. If you use a paste wax, test it in a corner to see if it will discolor the flooring. If a solvent-based paste wax is used, rewax to strip the old wax and to renew the shine.

Quarry Tile

Like brick, quarry tile looks durable, but this unglazed clay tile is really very porous and readily soaks up stains. Quarry-tile floors have to be well sealed with as many as three coats of sealer and further protected by a high-quality wax. Our years of experience in cleaning floors have failed to turn up a truly easy way to seal a quarry-tile floor. But if you do it right, you won't have to do it very often.

The best way we have found to seal a quarry-tile floor is with a commercial sealer for terrazzo and slate. After the sealer dries, apply two thin coats of an acrylic floor finish, using a long-handled wax applicator fitted with a lamb's wool pad, or apply paste wax with a floor-polishing machine. To do this, use a spatula to spread a small amount of paste wax directly on the brushes of the polisher. Slowly operate the polisher back and forth to apply an even, thin coat of wax. When the wax is dry, buff the floor.

To keep your sealed-and-waxed quarry-tile floor looking really terrific, all you have to do is damp mop it occasionally after you vacuum. If the mopped floor dries with a luster-dulling film, you can restore the shine by mopping it again with water containing a cup of white vinegar.

When it comes time to strip the wax buildup and rewax, apply a commercial wax-stripping product with a floor-scrubbing machine that has a brush attachment. After applying the stripper according to the manufacturer's directions, rinse the floor thoroughly with clear water. Use a non-abrasive powder and a synthetic scouring pad for stubborn spots.

If you plan to use a paste wax, such as those used on wood floors, test the wax in a corner to see if it will discolor the tile. You will never have to strip the wax. Rewaxing will strip the old wax and renew the shine.

Rubber Tile

Rubber tile is slightly delicate; it can be damaged by exposure to direct sunlight, and it is easily wrecked by strong cleaners. Care for rubber tile in much the same way that you maintain asphalt tile, but you'll have to be a little more careful.

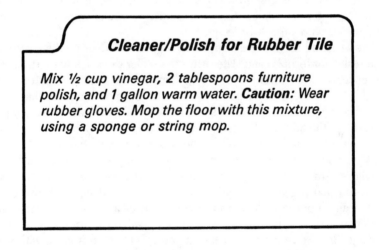

Cleaner/Polish for Rubber Tile

Mix ½ cup vinegar, 2 tablespoons furniture polish, and 1 gallon warm water. **Caution:** Wear rubber gloves. Mop the floor with this mixture, using a sponge or string mop.

None us has time to wash floors on a weekly basis, but most of us can find time to pass a damp mop over the floor after we've vacuumed it. This will delay for a long time the day when you finally have to mop. A trick we've found to make a rubber-tile floor look freshly waxed is to add a cup of fabric softener to a half pail of water. This prevents damp mopping from dulling the shine on your floor. Also, be sure that you use a cleaner/polish that can withstand damp mopping; if it can't, you'll end up reapplying the cleaner/polish every time you mop.

The quickest way we have found to clean a rubber-tile floor is to use a water-based cleaner/polish or an all-purpose cleaning solution. Eureka recommends that you read the product label for precautionary measures and test any cleaner in a corner before using it on the entire floor.

Occasionally, remove wax buildup with a cleaner or wax stripper. Follow stripping with two thin coats of self-polishing wax; allow to dry between coats. Two thin coats make a much more durable, long-lasting finish than one coat, which may dry slowly and leave a gummy, dust-collecting mess on your floor.

Remove heel marks from rubber tile by dipping fine-grade (000) steel wool in liquid floor wax. Rub the spot gently, and wipe with a damp cloth.

Solvent-based products can soften and damage a rubber-tile floor. Also, keep scouring pads, strong soaps, and hot water away from rubber tile. Flooding the floor with water will also cause big problems; excess water can seep into the seams and loosen the adhesives that hold down the flooring.

Terrazzo

Terrazzo is a very durable floor that was once used only in schools and other public buildings, but is now showing up in bathrooms and entrance halls in homes. This flooring is made of marble chips set in cement. After it cures, terrazzo is ground and polished. As durable as it seems, we have found that terrazzo stains easily and must be sealed with a commercial sealer, not with varnish or lacquer.

We've found that the best way to seal a terrazzo floor is with a commercial sealer for terrazzo and slate. After the sealer dries, apply two thin coats of an acrylic floor finish, using a long-handled wax applicator fitted with a lamb's wool pad, or apply paste wax with a floor-polishing machine. To do this, use a spatula to spread a small amount of paste wax directly on the brushes of the polisher. Slowly operate the polisher back and forth to apply an even, thin coat of wax. When the wax is dry, buff the floor.

After you have gone to the trouble to properly seal your terrazzo floor, it will reward you by being very easy to care for. All a terrazzo floor needs to keep it looking good is a quick going over with a damp mop, using clear water, an all-purpose cleaner in warm water, or a mixture of 1 cup fabric softener and ½ gallon water. If your mopped floor dries with a luster-dulling film, we've discovered that if you quickly mop it again with water containing a cup of white vinegar, the floor will glisten.

Occasionally, you'll have to strip the wax buildup on your floor and rewax if you use a water-based, self-polishing liquid. Apply a commercial wax-stripping product with a floor-scrubbing machine that has a brush attachment. After applying the stripper according to the manufacturer's directions, rinse the floor thoroughly with clear water. A nonabrasive powder and a synthetic scouring pad will remove stubborn spots without scratching the floor.

Vinyl

Vinyl floor coverings are ideal for to everyone who hates to clean. They are truly easy-care, and there are many excellent products on the market that are designed to maintain a sparkling vinyl floor in one quick step.

If you don't want to use one of these products, the best way to clean a vinyl-tile floor is with an all-purpose cleaner dissolved in water. After you

Cleaner/Polish for Vinyl

Mix ½ cup vinegar, 2 tablespoons furniture polish, and 1 gallon warm water. **Caution:** Wear rubber gloves. Mop the floor with this mixture, using a sponge or string mop.

have cleaned the floor, rinse the tile with clear water to make sure no film remains to dull the finish. When the floor is dry, apply two thin coats of water-based, self-polishing floor finish, allowing the floor to dry between coats. Apply the wax with a long-handled wax applicator fitted with a washable chenille pad.

It will be a long time before you need to do anything more for your floor than to wipe up spills and vacuum. But if you want to damp mop after vacuuming, add a cup of fabric softener to a half pail of water to prevent damp mopping from dulling the shine on your vinyl floor.

Remove heel marks from vinyl floors by dipping a synthetic scouring pad in liquid floor wax. Rub the spot gently and wipe with a damp cloth.

Vinyl, "No-Wax"
A "no-wax" vinyl floor is a breeze to maintain. All you have to do is keep it clean, and damp mopping after vacuuming goes a long way toward doing that. Obviously, you don't have time to mop the kitchen floor after dinner every day, so go ahead and wipe up spills with a sponge dipped in dishwashing liquid, scrub off heel marks with a synthetic scouring pad, and put off washing the floor until it gets really sticky, if you want to.

When it's finally time to wash the floor, use an all-purpose cleaning solution. Always be sure to read the product label for precautionary measures and instructions. We have also found that it pays to test any cleaner in a corner before using it on the entire floor.

Sometimes a "no-wax" floor dries with a luster-dulling film; don't panic, just mop it again with water containing a cup of white vinegar, and the floor will glisten like new.

If your "no-wax" floor loses its shine in high-traffic areas, use a gloss-renewing product available from the manufacturer of your floor or another commercial product designed for this purpose. Never throw just anything you have around the house on the dull floor: Solvent-based products or cleaners that contain pine oil can soften and permanently damage a vinyl-tile floor. Also, do not scour "no-wax" vinyl, use strong soaps and hot water, or flood the floor with water. Excess water can seep into the seams and loosen the adhesives that hold down the flooring.

Wood

There is almost nothing as elegant as a glimmering wood floor. The sight of such a floor speaks to us of glamor, good living, and a lot of very hard work on somebody's part (preferably not yours). It's true that you have to take care of a wood floor, but you don't have to break your back to do it if you care for it our way.

The product used to seal a wood floor determines how it can be cared for. Varnish, shellac, polyurethane, and lacquer are used to finish floors, but only polyurethane requires no further treatment, including waxing. The integrity and beauty of wood floors not finished with polyurethane can be maintained only by using solvent-based cleaners and polishes. Water should never be used on wood floors, except those treated with polyurethane; these can be damp mopped. If you have the choice and don't want to spend your time maintaining your wood floor, we recommend that you have your wood floors finished with polyurethane.

For those of you who have lacquered, varnished, or shellacked floors, the fastest way to clean a wood floor is with a one-step cleaner/polish. After vacuuming the floor, pour the solvent-based liquid on a small area and rub lightly with a clean, dry wax applicator. Working on a small section at a time, stroke the floor in the direction of the grain. Blot up any excess liquid with a clean cloth.

As it sometimes happens, the best way to clean a wood floor is not the fastest; so if you want a long-lasting shine on your wood floor, you will have to spend more time and follow this tested method. After vacuuming the floor, apply a liquid wood-floor cleaner with a dry wax applicator or a cloth on a small area at a time. Let it soak for 3 minutes, and wipe up the excess. When the floor is dry, buff with a floor polisher. **Caution:** This is a combustible mixture; use in a well-ventilated area.

Unless you always take off your shoes at the door, you'll probably have to apply a liquid or paste solvent-based wax to your wood floor about twice a year. No stripping is necessary because the solvents in the new wax will strip off the old wax. Make sure the room is well ventilated when using solvent-based waxes and polishes.

YOUR CLEANING CLOSET

A well-stocked cleaning center is the hurried housecleaner's best friend. You will be more likely to start your cleaning chores and to finish the task if you have everything you need on hand and in one place. A cleaning closet will save you time and steps; it is the efficient beginning to all the quick and easy cleaning methods in this book.

Your Eureka vacuum cleaner with a set of cleaning tools and your Mini Mite® or Quick Up® are the most essential tools in your cleaning closet. But you will also need an assortment of other cleaning tools and products. You may not need everything that's listed here, but as you read this section, think about the cleaning tasks you perform regularly and stock your cleaning closet with the tools that will help you accomplish them most efficiently and quickly.

Before you supply your cleaning closet, make sure the closet has a place to store all the cleaning tools and products you buy. If you can't fit them all into one orderly place, you'll waste time digging around under the sink for the cleanser and going out to the garage for your mop. Put up pegboard or hooks to hang brushes and mops. They'll not only be easier to lay your hands on, but they'll last longer if they are hung. Install plenty of shelves to hold bottles and cartons. This will get dangerous cleaning products out of the reach of children and give you space to store a full battery of cleaning supplies, so that when you find time to clean, everything you need will be handy.

Tools of the Trade

Baskets are used for carrying supplies from one room to another and for collecting the dirty ashtrays you want to take to the kitchen to wash, the collectibles you want to polish, and/or the toys the kids left in the family room.

Brushes are available in an assortment of sizes: a hard-bristled scrub brush, toilet brushes (one for each bathroom), a radiator brush, and other soft- and medium-bristled brushes for scrubbing and dusting.

Buckets with double compartments hold both your cleaning solution and rinse water.

Chamois are expensive, but they will last almost indefinitely when properly handled. Nothing absorbs water better than soft leather, so your chamois is perfect for drying washed cars and windows. After you use it, wash your chamois in a detergent solution, rinse thoroughly, squeeze out

Storing all your cleaning equipment and supplies in one place—your cleaning closet—will save you time and effort every time you clean.

the water, stretch it to full size, and place it on a flat surface to dry. Don't wash a chamois with soap.

Cleaning cloths are made from worn-out clothes, sheets, and towels. Cotton or linen, white or light-colored fabrics are best.

Mops should have detachable heads for easy cleaning.

Rubber gloves only protect your hands if you wear them. Don't forget to put yours on whenever you work with cleaning solutions.

Scouring pads are made of both synthetics and steel wool. Keep a variety in your cleaning closet.

Sponges should be tossed out as soon as they start to shred. Have plenty on hand.

Stepladders, at least three feet tall, are a safe substitute for the unsteady chair or stack of boxes you may have been standing on to clean hard-to-reach places.

Window squeegees speed window washing, but if you don't have one, an old windshield wiper is a good stand-in for a commercial squeegee.

Cleaning Agents

In addition to your vacuum cleaners and other cleaning tools, you need to have on hand several basic cleaning supplies and the special cleaning agents for your Stain-Removal Kit. (You'll find out more about this emergency first aid kit for spots in "How to Beat Spots and Stains" in this book.)

All-purpose cleaners remove grease and grimy dirt.

Ammonia is available in clear or sudsy form. It is an excellent cleaner or cleaning booster for many household surfaces. It is a grease cutter, wax stripper, window cleaner, and general soil remover. If you object to the strong odor of ammonia, buy a scented product, but neither scented ammonia nor sudsy ammonia is suitable for stain removal.

Baking soda is one of the most versatile cleaning products available. Used by itself in dry form, it acts as a very mild scouring powder that will not scratch even the most delicate surfaces. Add water to make a paste, and use baking soda to scour dirty surfaces. Combined with other ingredients, it makes a very good cleaning solution that also deodorizes.

Bleach helps remove stains and whiten laundry, and it's also good for cleaning toilets.

Flour is useful for some cleaning tasks. Always use flour in its dry form because it creates a gluey paste when mixed with water.

Lemon juice, either bottled or squeezed from a cut lemon, provides the mild acid reaction needed for many cleaning solutions.

Liquid dishwashing detergents are used for many cleaning tasks in addition to doing dishes.

Vinegar is also an acid; it can usually be substituted for lemon juice. White vinegar should be used to clean fabrics, but cider vinegar is adequate for other applications.

Waxes, polishes, and oils shine and protect wood, leather, brass, chrome, silver, glass, and other surfaces.

CLEANING STRATEGIES

No one has time to clean anymore. There is too much else to do. But most of us would prefer not to come home to a total disaster area, so cleaning has to be dealt with sooner or later.

The time it takes you to tidy up is time taken away from work and play, and it has got to be time well spent. With the right cleaning strategy, you can keep the drudgery to a minimum and give yourself the maximum of valuable living time.

Cleaning is hard work, but with your Eureka vacuum cleaners, the right tools and cleaning products, a game plan, and the helpful cleaning tips in this book, your cleaning load will be lighter than ever before. You'll enjoy a neat living environment and time to devote to yourself, your family, and your friends.

Hurried does not have to mean helter-skelter. Your cleaning schedule for both regular and seasonal care should be organized in a way that makes you comfortable: You may choose to clean for an hour every morning, two hours after work, or all Saturday morning. As long as you have a schedule that leaves room for spontaneity, you'll stay ahead of housework.

Concentrate on one room at a time; don't run all over your house or apartment pushing dirt around here and there. Stick with one room until it is sparkling clean. You'll have the reward and encouragement of its good looks when you're ready to proceed to the next task.

Basic day-to-day chores, such as beds, dishes, baths, laundry, and floor care, require a firm routine. Big tasks, such as closets, ovens, and silver, are often best tackled on impulse and require an elastic plan. If a big chore is hanging over your head and you keep putting it off, wait. It will be there when you are up to it, and you'll probably do a better job if you are ready to tackle it. Remember that when you are in the mood to clean, your cleaning tasks will get done much faster if there are no interruptions. So turn on the answering machine and send the kids who are too little to help to visit a friend, and concentrate on the task at hand.

Most big cleaning jobs will go much faster if you have help. Divide the labor among all the members of the household, including the children, or invite a friend to help out. You can reciprocate when his garage needs cleaning.

Cleaning Plan

Here is a general plan for cleaning a home. We hope you'll use it as a starting point for making your own cleaning strategy.

EVERY DAY

- Remove litter from carpets and hard-surface floors with your Quick Up® or Eureka canister vacuum cleaner.
- Wash dishes, and wipe countertops and cooking appliances.
- Empty kitchen garbage containers.
- Wipe basins and bathtubs.
- Make beds and straighten rooms.

AS NEEDED

- Vacuum carpets and hard-surface floors thoroughly with your Eureka vacuum cleaner.
- Vacuum upholstery and drapes with the upholstery tool and use the crevice tool in the seams of furniture coverings.
- Dust and/or polish furniture.
- Clean the range and wipe out the refrigerator.
- Wash kitchen and bathroom floors.
- Clean toilets, fixtures, and bathroom mirrors.
- Change bed linens.
- Empty wastepaper baskets.

SEASONAL

- Surface-clean rugs and carpets, using a carpet-cleaning solution or an absorbent powder.
- Remove old wax, apply new wax, and buff hard-surface floors.
- Wash throw rugs.
- Shampoo upholstered furniture.
- Wash lamp shades, walls, and woodwork.
- Dust books, pictures, and lamps.
- Clean mirrors, TVs, picture frames, and art objects.
- Clean ovens, microwave, refrigerator, freezer, and other appliances.
- Wash bathroom carpeting and shower curtain.
- Organize closets.
- Turn mattresses, wash pads and pillow covers, and air or wash pillows.
- Clean screens and wash windows.

YEARLY

- Vacuum rug pads and the backs of rugs.
- Shampoo carpets, clean rugs, and turn rugs to equalize wear.
- Wash curtains, blinds, and shades, and clean draperies.
- Clean closets and cabinets.
- Wash or dry-clean bedspreads, blankets, and slipcovers.
- Clean out the garage, basement, and workshop.

EMERGENCIES

- Remove spots and stains while they are fresh.

Dust or Vacuum, Which to Do First?

If you have mats at all the entrances to your home, both inside and outside, you'll cut your cleaning time almost in half. Mats also make dusting the first logical step in cleaning, since your floors and carpets will not release clouds of dust as you go about your cleaning tasks.

Anyone who tells you not to dust until you have vacuumed your floors needs a new vacuum cleaner. A Eureka vacuum cleaner, with a Eureka filter bag and clamps that don't leak, will not spew dust over cleaned surfaces. If your vacuum cleaner releases dust or has a dusty or burning smell when you turn it on, you either need a new vacuum filter or need to replace the bag. You should change the disposable dust bag frequently so that your vacuum will clean with maximum efficiency.

Dusting is more than picking up minute particles of lint or airborne residue on a picture frame. Dusting is scraping dirt and grime off windowsills; vacuuming eraser rubbings and food crumbs; getting all the ashes, orange seeds, and gum wrappers off the living room furniture; and on and on. If you vacuum the floor first, all the litter you dust off other surfaces can end up on your freshly vacuumed floor.

The best plan is to dust with your vacuum cleaner. Instead of releasing dust and debris into the air and onto other surfaces in the room, start at the ceiling and dust everything from moldings to baseboards with your Eureka vacuum cleaner. Your vacuum cleaner will remove dust from hard-to-reach areas, such as the tops of doors and the inside areas of radiators, and do a much more thorough cleaning job than a dust cloth.

When Company Comes on 10-Minute Notice

The phone rings; it's a friend from school in town for a meeting or one of your mother's cousins who happens to be in the neighborhood. The surprise visitor will be at your door in 10 minutes, and your home must be ready to go on show. The following whirlwind routine will help you present a neat facade.

- Gather everything that is sitting where it doesn't belong in the entry and living areas, and dump it all into an empty laundry basket. Hide the filled basket in a closet.
- Wipe out the ashtrays, stack newspapers and magazines on the coffee table or floor, and plump the furniture pillows.
- Give the bathroom sink and toilet a once-over, and straighten the rug

and towels. Shine the mirror with tissue, and shove scattered items back into the medicine cabinet.
- Rinse the dishes, and stack them neatly in the kitchen sink or put them in the dishwasher. Wipe the countertops.
- Close the doors to rooms you don't want to display.
- Try to relax.

Clean a Room Quickly

Before you start to clean a room, face the fact of dirt. Cleaning is dirty work and your clothes will get soiled, so dress the part. Pull on a pair of old jeans, roll up the sleeves on a tattered shirt, and attack the grime with your full attention.

Gather together all the cleaning supplies you will need. Carrying them in a tote basket will save extra steps between your cleaning closet and your work site. Then, take everything out of the room that does not belong in it. Put small decorative items into a basket and out of harm's way, and put the dirty items that you want to clean separately, such as ashtrays and metal objects that need polishing, in a box or basket and take them to the kitchen. Don't redistribute anything until you have finished cleaning the room.

Pull all the furniture out from the walls. Turn back rugs at the edges, and take up small scatter rugs to make vacuuming the floor easier. Choose a starting point, and work your way around the room. The law of gravity applies: Dust settles downward, so to avoid dirtying what you have just cleaned, always work from the top down. Clean floors last.

With the appropriate attachment on your Eureka vacuum cleaner, dust moldings, door frames, draperies, lamp shades, blinds, shutters, pictures, wall hangings, mantels, shelves, vents, radiators, and baseboards. Vacuum upholstered furniture, as well as wood, plastic, and chrome furniture. Wipe smudges off doorknobs, light switches, and walls with an all-purpose cleaner.

Hard-surface floors are next. Using the floor-brush attachment on your Eureka vacuum cleaner, thoroughly vacuum all hard-surface flooring, such as tile, linoleum, vinyl, and wood. Now straighten the rugs that were folded back for cleaning, and vacuum them slowly. Fluff up the carpet pile.

That's it. Simply replace the furniture, dust your bric-a-brac and replace it, and your room is clean. You don't have to polish the wood furniture, wash the windows, or scrub the floors; save these special tasks for another time. It is more efficient.

Here are some quick tips to make this easy method for cleaning a room even easier:
- Carry two buckets or a bucket with two compartments when you are washing items that also need rinsing.

- Vacuum before cleaning with a liquid cleaning solution to avoid making mud.
- Go easy on cleaners. Soap or wax used sparingly clean and beautify surfaces. Use too much, and you will have to spend time removing the buildup and streaks.
- When you are cleaning something up high, don't stand on tiptoe: Grab a stepladder. If you are cleaning down low, sit on the floor. Straining up or down is tiring, inefficient, and bad for your back.

CLEANING YOUR BATHROOM

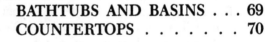

If there's a growing collection of dust balls under your bed, a drawerful of tarnished flatware in the sideboard, or a month's worth of newspapers on your coffee table, you can live with that. But a grimy bathroom is another story. If there is one cleaning job that really must be done each week no matter what, it's cleaning the bathroom. There is no way to get around it. But you can make this unpleasant task a whole lot easier if you and everyone else who uses the bathroom quick-cleans it every day.

Bathrooms tend to become both dirty and messy. The obvious solution to bathroom clutter is to create storage for the things most bathrooms are not designed to store, such as hair dryers, makeup, electric shavers, and magazines. Clear countertops not only look cleaner, but they are quicker to clean, because there's no clutter to clean around and under. But even the best-designed bathroom is prone to soap scum and streaky surfaces. The most efficient way to clean your bathroom is to clean it often.

Most bathrooms are made of materials that are easy to keep clean. Tile and porcelain surfaces are stain-resistant if dirt and scum are not allowed to build up on them. Make it a firm rule in your home to rinse out the tub or shower stall immediately after you use it. Rinse it while you are still wet and in the tub or stall. Simply spray water from the shower head on all interior surfaces, then lather soap onto a damp sponge, swish it around the tub or stall, and rinse. The basin can be given a similar treatment each evening by the last person who uses it.

Keeping tile and porcelain surfaces clean so that they never need to be scoured not only saves time, but it also protects these surfaces from unnecessary wear and keeps them looking their best. Most scouring powders and nonabrasive cleaners will safely rid tile and porcelain surfaces of dirt, but if stains have to be removed with harsh abrasives, the porcelain or ceramic tile will be scratched. These tiny scratches invite more dirt build-up, and your cleaning problems increase.

The toilet and floor can wait for a weekly cleaning. When it's time to clean your bathroom thoroughly, reach for your Eureka vacuum cleaner before you do any wet cleaning. Vacuum the floor and countertops while they are completely dry. This will speed your cleaning: There won't be any loose hairs to wrap themselves around your sponge, and you won't make mud on the floor when water splashes out of the basin while you're cleaning it. Wash the floor after you have completed all the other bathroom-cleaning chores.

Bathtubs and Basins

Most bathtubs and basins are made of porcelain. If the fixtures are older, chances are the material is porcelain on cast iron. These fixtures may not be as acid- and alkaline-resistant as newer porcelain-on-steel tubs and basins. Cultured marble is also used for one-piece basin/countertops. Fiberglass tubs, which are lighter and easier to install than steel tubs, are used in new-home construction and remodeling, but they are not as durable as porcelain-coated steel. If you have a fiberglass tub, you will have to be especially careful when you clean it to avoid scratching the surface.

Since it is better to keep a bathtub clean than to scour it periodically, we suggest that you add bubble bath or a capful of detergent to your bathwater to prevent bathtub rings. If you prefer a clear-water bath, you can remove rings while the water drains from the tub by rubbing a nylon-net ball or pad around the tub. Keep your ring-eliminator in the soap dish.

Porcelain basins and tubs should be cleaned with powdered cleanser or nonabrasive liquid cleanser. Sprinkle a mild abrasive powder on a damp sponge and apply it to the porcelain surface of the tub or basin. Use a synthetic scouring pad on stubborn soil. Rinse with clear water. When you clean the bathtub and basin, also remove hair from the traps in the drains to prevent clogging.

Cultured-marble or fiberglass tubs and basins should be cleaned with a commercial fiberglass-cleaning product or nonabrasive liquid cleanser. Apply either product with a damp sponge and rinse with clear water.

If you have an older bathroom, rust stains are often a problem. We've found that commercial rust removers are very effective. **Caution:** Wear rubber gloves when you work with these products because they contain acid. You can also clean discolored porcelain fixtures with a paste made of

Cleaner for Bathtubs and Basins

*This solution cleans porcelain as well as cultured-marble and fiberglass fixtures. Mix ½ cup vinegar, 1 cup clear ammonia, and ¼ cup baking soda in 1 gallon hot water. **Caution:** Wear rubber gloves, and work in a well-ventilated area when using this powerful solution. Apply the solution to the fixtures with a sponge, scrubbing if necessary, and rinse with clear water.*

cream of tartar moistened with hydrogen peroxide or a paste made of borax moistened with lemon juice. Scrub the paste into lightly stained areas with a brush, and rinse well.

If your old porcelain bathtub has yellowed, try rubbing the tub with a solution of salt and turpentine. **Caution:** Wear rubber gloves when you work with this solution. Rinse well.

When you're down on your knees scrubbing the bathtub and get a closeup view of a grimy rubber or vinyl bathtub mat, don't waste time scouring the mat. Just toss it into your clothes washer with several bath towels. The terry cloth scrubs the mat, and everything will come out clean.

Countertops

Bathroom countertops are sloshed, splotched, and splattered with everything from hair spray to shoe polish. In most homes, countertops are made of materials that can stand up to the assault: ceramic tile, cultured marble, and plastic laminate. Because these materials are durable, they are easy to clean.

CERAMIC TILE

Glazed ceramic tile is virtually stainproof, but this isn't true of the grout between the tiles, which is porous and soft. To compound the problem, grout is often white to contrast with dark tiles or to match gleaming, white tiles. Either way, stained or mildewed grout is very noticeable and makes your whole bathroom look grubby.

A toothbrush or nailbrush is the best tool for cleaning grout. To remove mildew, dip the brush in chlorine bleach and gently scrub the affected grout. You can also clean grimy grout with a typewriter eraser. If spots persist, hide them. We've found you can camouflage stained grout with a white

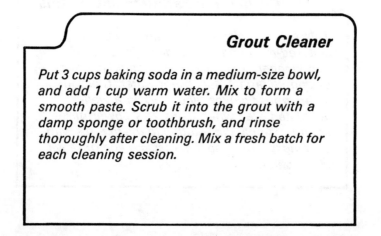

Grout Cleaner

Put 3 cups baking soda in a medium-size bowl, and add 1 cup warm water. Mix to form a smooth paste. Scrub it into the grout with a damp sponge or toothbrush, and rinse thoroughly after cleaning. Mix a fresh batch for each cleaning session.

Ceramic-Tile Cleaner

Mix ½ cup vinegar, 1 cup clear ammonia, ¼ cup baking soda, and 1 gallon warm water. **Caution:** Wear rubber gloves, and work in a well-ventilated area when using this powerful solution. Apply it to the countertop with a sponge, and rinse with clear water. Wipe dry to prevent water spots. Mix a fresh batch of this cleaner for each cleaning session.

If you can't remove stains from the grout between your bathroom tiles, conceal the spots with white shoe polish.

fingernail pencil or white liquid shoe polish. (If you get shoe polish on the tiles, let it dry, and then wipe it off with a damp rag.)

Even though ceramic tile resists dirt and rarely needs cleaning, you may sometimes have to clean it; so here are a few suggestions:

- Never use harsh abrasive cleaners that might scratch the glaze.
- Sparkle your bathroom walls and countertops by rubbing the ceramic tile with car wax, and buff after 10 minutes.
- If you use an aerosol-foam or spray tile-and-grout cleaner, follow the manufacturer's instructions, and rinse with clear water to finish the job.

Cultured-Marble Cleaner

*Mix ½ cup vinegar, 1 cup ammonia, and ¼ cup baking soda in 1 gallon hot water. **Caution:** Wear rubber gloves, and work in a well-ventilated area when using this powerful solution. Apply it to the cultured marble with a sponge, rinse with clear water, and buff dry. Dirt and soap film are quickly and inexpensively removed with this mixture.*

CULTURED MARBLE

Cultured marble resembles real marble, but it is a lot more versatile and much easier to care for. Unlike plastic laminate, cultured marble is not a thin veneer; if you scratch or burn it, you can often repair the damage.

We recommend that you avoid using abrasive cleaners and steel-wool pads to clean cultured marble; they will scratch the surface, making it difficult to keep clean. Mildly abrasive liquid and powdered cleansers should be applied directly to the wet surface of the countertop to dissolve dirt and soap film. Rinse well, and buff dry with a soft cloth.

PLASTIC LAMINATE

Plastic laminate is very durable if you don't scratch it, chip it, knock off its edges, burn it, scrub it, let water seep under it, stain it, or otherwise mistreat it. Plastic laminate is made of thin layers of plastic superimposed on craft paper and overlaid on particle board or plywood. The color of most plastic laminate is only in the top layer. The glossy, mat, or textured surface is also laid on. This is the reason plastic laminate cannot be restored if it is damaged; all its beauty is on the surface.

We regularly apply an appliance wax or light furniture wax to protect and brighten plastic-laminate surfaces.

During your weekly bathroom-cleaning session, wipe your plastic-laminate countertop with a damp cloth or sponge. We've found that a two-sided scrubbing pad with fiber on one side and a sponge on the other works especially well. Moistened slightly with water, the fiber side is just abrasive enough to loosen greasy smears and other soil. Turning the scrubber over, use the sponge side to wipe the surface damp-dry. When a spot or stain persists, first sprinkle baking soda on the spot and scrub gently. If this doesn't take care of the problem, apply a polishing cleanser with a wet sponge.

Drains

In most homes, the bathroom sink is a dressing table as well as a wash-basin, and everyone in the family shampoos in the shower. Hair and soap are washed into bathroom drains day and night, and the cruddy mess can quickly jam up the works. All that is needed to clean some clogged drains is to clear the trap of hair and soap curds. Regular clearing of the traps saves your plumbing, and it also cuts down on cleaning time, since when water flows out of the basin and tub quickly, it doesn't allow dirt to settle on these surfaces.

When clearing the trap doesn't clear the drain, you'll have to take stronger measures. First, use a plumber's helper and plunge the drain. (We suggest that you keep one handy in the bathroom.) Before you use the

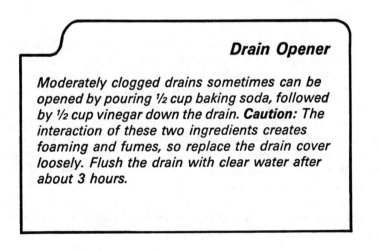

Drain Opener

*Moderately clogged drains sometimes can be opened by pouring ½ cup baking soda, followed by ½ cup vinegar down the drain. **Caution:** The interaction of these two ingredients creates foaming and fumes, so replace the drain cover loosely. Flush the drain with clear water after about 3 hours.*

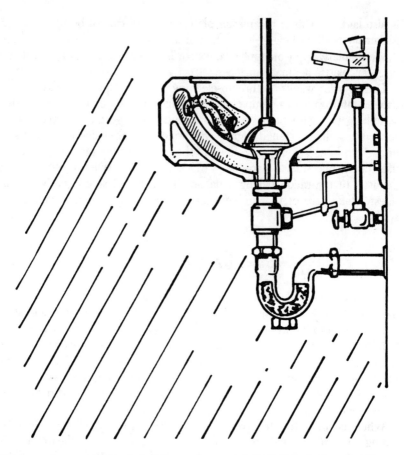

Before you use a plumber's helper to plunge your bathroom basin, plug the overflow opening with a washcloth.

plunger in the bathroom basin, plug the overflow opening. This allows the plunger to exercise its maximum suction effect on the clogged drain.

If plunging does not open the drain, use a chemical drain opener. These products must be handled with special care because they are caustic and harmful to skin and eyes. Use them in a well-ventilated area, and follow the manufacturer's instructions. Commercial drain openers are sold in granular, liquid, and pressurized forms. Granular products utilize lye to do their work, liquid drain openers use lye and other chemicals, and pressurized products work by chlorofluorocarbon propellants and pressure. If you use a granular drain opener, you must first remove standing water from the sink; this is not necessary for liquid and pressurized products. Chemical drain openers will damage porcelain enamel and should not be allowed to remain on the surface of your fixtures for any length of time.

If the first type of chemical drain opener you use does not work, do not use a different chemical drain cleaner unless the initial cleaner has been flushed away totally. Never use a plunger or a pressurized drain opener after using a chemical cleaner; it may cause dangerous chemicals to splash back onto you. Also, be sure to tell your plumber what you have put into the drain before he or she starts to work. The combination of ammonia and other household cleaners with chemical drain openers produces hazardous gases.

Hardware

If you get into the habit of wiping the sink and tub hardware after each use, you'll prevent water spots and keep your bathroom looking sparkling longer. You don't need to do anything special to care for most bathroom hardware—just clean it along with the tub and basin, using the same cleaning products and methods. Rinse well, and buff with a dry cloth.

Clogged shower heads are a common problem if you have hard water. You don't have to replace them, but you'll have to take them apart for cleaning. Remove the head from its fitting, dismantle it, and soak it in vinegar. Use a toothbrush to brush away mineral deposits. Clean the holes by poking them with a wire, pin, toothpick, or ice pick.

We've found that the fastest way to clean chromium and stainless steel is with baking soda applied to the surface with a dry cloth. It will remove fingerprints, smudges, and sticky residue with no further rinsing or wiping.

Treat wooden towel racks with an occasional application of furniture polish to bring up the shine and give a protective coating. Apply the polish with a soft cloth, and buff.

Bathroom Mirrors

The better your family's dental hygiene, the sooner you'll see spots before your eyes when you look in the bathroom mirror. As is true of other bathroom surfaces, daily wiping both delays and facilitates heavy-duty cleaning. You can quickly remove spots and spatters from a mirror with a damp facial tissue, and then polish it with a dry one.

If your mirror is clouded by hair spray, rubbing alcohol will wipe away the haze.

During the morning rush hour, if you're trying to shave while the shower is producing billows of steam in the same small bathroom, you can defog the bathroom mirror quickly by blowing hot air on it with a hair dryer. Running an inch of cold water in the bathtub before adding hot water eliminates fogging altogether.

Defog your steamy bathroom mirror with a blast of warm air from your hair dryer.

Mirror Cleaners

- *Mix ⅓ cup clear ammonia in 1 gallon warm water. Apply it with a sponge/squeegee, or pour the solution into a spray container and spray it directly onto the mirror. Buff with a lint-free cloth, chamois, or paper toweling. Vinegar may be substituted for ammonia.*
- *Pour vinegar into a shallow bowl or pan, then crumple a sheet of newspaper, dip it in the vinegar, and apply to the mirror. Wipe the glass several times with the same newspaper until the mirror is almost dry, then shine it with a clean, soft cloth or dry newspaper.*

Mirror Cleaner

Mix 2 cups isopropyl rubbing alcohol (70-percent solution), 2 tablespoons liquid dishwashing detergent, and two cups water. Stir until thoroughly mixed and then pour into a spray bottle. Spray directly onto the mirror. Buff with a lint-free cloth, chamois, or paper toweling.

Shower Curtains

Shower curtains need to be cleaned on a regular basis to remove built-up soap scum and water deposits. All shower curtains are washable; fabric curtains and some plastic ones can be washed in the machine. Use your regular laundry detergent when you wash fabric shower curtains, and follow the manufacturer's instructions for water temperature and wash/rinse cycles. When you machine wash plastic shower curtains, use the gentle cycle and cool water. Wash plastic curtains in ½ cup detergent and ½ cup baking soda, along with two large bath towels. To prevent a machine-washed shower curtain from wrinkling, add a cup of vinegar to the rinse cycle.

Washing a plastic shower curtain in the bathtub causes fewer wrinkles than machine washing. We've found a good method for doing this. Mix ½ cup vinegar, 1 cup clear ammonia, ¼ cup baking soda, and 1 gallon hot water, and apply the solution to the shower curtain with a sponge while it is lying flat in the bathtub. **Caution:** Wear rubber gloves, and work in a well-ventilated area when using this powerful solution. Let stand a few minutes to loosen the scum, and then scrub the curtain with a sponge or brush, adding more cleaner if necessary. Rinse well in warm water to which a few drops of mineral oil have been added; this will keep the curtain soft and flexible. Shake off excess water and hang to drip-dry.

Back fabric curtains with a plastic liner to preserve their good looks and to make them more effective. You can also back a new plastic shower curtain with your old plastic shower curtain. Hang the new curtain on the same hooks, but in front of the old curtain. The old curtain will take the beating from water and soap scum while the new one stays clean.

Mildew often develops on shower curtains. To discourage its growth, spray clean curtains with disinfectant. Make it your habit to shake excess water off the shower curtain after each use.

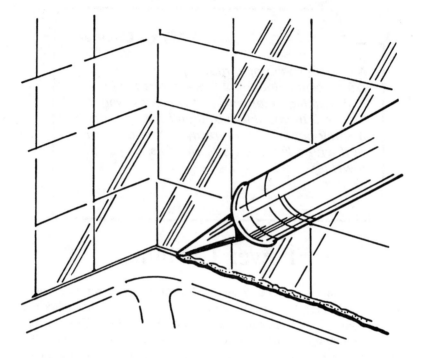

Maintain an unbroken bead of caulk where the tub or shower stall joins the bathroom wall to prevent water from seeping into the wall.

Shower Enclosures

Shower stalls would be self-cleaning, if soap scum, mildew, and mineral deposits didn't build up on the shower enclosure. We've collected the following helpful hints to make dealing with these cleaning chores easier.

- If your shower area is subject to mildew, spray it periodically with a mildew inhibitor and disinfectant.
- Leave the shower door open slightly to allow air to circulate; this will discourage the growth of mildew.
- Remove hard-water deposits on shower enclosures with a solution of white vinegar and water.
- Glass shower doors will sparkle when you clean them with a sponge dipped in white vinegar.
- Remove water spots on the metal frames around shower doors and enclosures with lemon oil.
- If the grout or caulking in your shower breaks away where the walls join the tub or shower floor, recaulk immediately to prevent water damage.

Shower-Stall Cleaner

Mix ½ cup vinegar, 1 cup ammonia, ¼ cup baking soda, and 1 gallon hot water. **Caution:** *Wear rubber gloves, and work in a well-ventilated area when using this powerful solution. Apply it to the walls of the shower with a sponge, scrubbing with a brush if necessary to remove all the scum. Rinse well with clear water, and wipe dry.*

Toilets

Cleaning the toilet is one of those grin-and-bear-it chores that you want to get through as quickly as possible. Many toilet-bowl cleaners and deodorizers claim that they'll help you do this. Some products are truly helpful, some are not. Most cleaners that are placed in the tank and are dispensed each time the toilet is flushed do little more than color the water. Some clean the bowl better than plain water, but in-tank cleaners are not a substitute for a regular scrubbing, when you also clean the seat and the rim of the toilet bowl.

Toilet bowls and tanks usually are made of vitreous china, which is nonporous and easy to clean. Before you clean your toilet, read the label on your cleaning product to learn its exact chemical makeup and how it should be used. Be especially careful never to mix products that contain chlorine

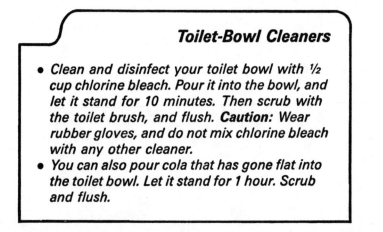

Toilet-Bowl Cleaners

- *Clean and disinfect your toilet bowl with ½ cup chlorine bleach. Pour it into the bowl, and let it stand for 10 minutes. Then scrub with the toilet brush, and flush.* **Caution:** *Wear rubber gloves, and do not mix chlorine bleach with any other cleaner.*
- *You can also pour cola that has gone flat into the toilet bowl. Let it stand for 1 hour. Scrub and flush.*

bleach with ammonia-based products. Always wear rubber gloves when you work with toilet cleaners. They contain strong chemicals and should be flushed immediately after the bowl has been cleaned. You should be careful not to allow cleaners to remain in the toilet or to touch other bathroom surfaces.

We suggest that you keep a long-handled brush for cleaning only toilet bowls.

The exterior of a toilet should be cleaned with the same products you use for tubs and basins. Wipe the toilet seat, the tank, around the rim, and around the base when you clean.

CLEANING
YOUR
KITCHEN

(continued)

CLEANING YOUR KITCHEN
(continued)

M any of our ancestors hid their kitchens in their basements or backyards or off in some far, dark corner of the house. That was one way to keep the family from knowing you hadn't gotten around to cleaning the oven for a few years. Today, most of us have a different attitude about kitchens. We want our kitchens to be light, sparkling (or cozy) multiuse family centers, complete with computers and couches, VCRs and miniature vegetable patches. Gathering the family around the hearth or the induction cooktop is a terrific idea. But don't forget that in the middle of all the activity and nice furniture, there's still a kitchen, where you're going to be spilling milk and burning toast.

Cooking is a messy task: You can't make an omelet without breaking eggs, dripping egg white down the outside of the bowl onto the counter, dropping a shell on the floor and stepping on it. The only way to deal with the mess in the kitchen is to control it with quick, daily cleanups.

In most households, there are cooks and there are eaters. Use this division of labor to everyone's advantage for regular kitchen maintenance. Cooks are responsible for blotting spills when they happen and getting dirty cooking utensils into the sink or dishwasher. But after dinner, the cleanup crew (previously known as the eaters) takes over from the cooks. They'll vacuum crumbs with a Eureka Mini Mite® or Quick Up®, do the dishes, wipe the countertops and appliances, clean the sink, and take out the garbage.

Keeping the kitchen fairly clean beats having to spend regular long stretches of time cleaning it. But there are still plenty of unavoidable kitchen chores that will eventually have to be done. We don't need to tell you how often to clean your kitchen; it will tell you. When your feet stick to the floor in front of the refrigerator, or worse, when you skid by the range on an oil slick, you know it's time to mop the kitchen floor. When the mustard jar can't be pulled out of the spreads bin on the fridge door because it's embedded in dried catsup, you'll have to clean the refrigerator. Some of us don't wait until our kitchens get this bad before we clean them, but all of us want to get kitchen cleaning out of the way so we can get on to better things. At Eureka we understand this and want to help you. We've developed vacuum cleaners like the Quick Up® and Mini Mite® that are ideal for quickly getting cracker crumbs off the kitchen floor and spilled dry cereal out of the cutlery drawer. We've also collected hints on the fastest and best ways to clean everything in your kitchen. So when it's time to attack your messy kitchen, turn to Eureka, and we'll help you beat kitchen cleaning.

Countertops

Kitchen countertops have to be ready for anything—a smack from a floury handful of bread dough, a slice from a paring knife that goes off course, or a slosh of grape juice intent on staining the surface. Acrylic, ceramic tile, cultured marble, marble, plastic laminate, and wood countertops can take this kind of abuse if we make it up to them with regular, gentle cleaning and care. These surfaces are all easy to clean; if they can't take it, they should get out of the kitchen.

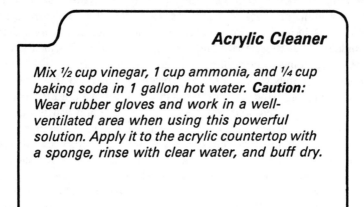

Acrylic Cleaner

Mix ½ cup vinegar, 1 cup ammonia, and ¼ cup baking soda in 1 gallon hot water. **Caution:** Wear rubber gloves and work in a well-ventilated area when using this powerful solution. Apply it to the acrylic countertop with a sponge, rinse with clear water, and buff dry.

ACRYLIC

You have to go out of your way to harm an acrylic countertop. A very hot pan or lighted cigarette will leave a permanent burn mark on the surface, but scouring powder or steel wool will remove most stains and scratches. For routine cleaning, use mildly abrasive liquid or powdered cleansers, applied directly onto the wet surface to dissolve dirt. Rinse well and buff dry with a soft cloth.

CERAMIC TILE

Both glazed and unglazed ceramic tile are used for kitchen countertops. Unlike many other surfaces, ceramic-tile countertops can take the heat; you don't have to fumble around searching for a trivet whenever you need to find a safe place to set a hot pot. Ceramic tile itself is extremely durable, but the grout between the tiles is soft, porous, and prone to cracks.

Use a toothbrush or nailbrush to scrub grout clean. To remove mildew and other stains, dip the brush in laundry bleach. When you clean grout, don't use harsh abrasive cleaners, which might scratch the glaze on ceramic tile. Many aerosol-foam and spray tile-and-grout cleaners are available.

Grout Cleaner

*Put 3 cups baking soda in a medium-size bowl and add 1 cup warm water. **Caution:** Wear rubber gloves. Mix to form a smooth paste; scrub it into the grout with a toothbrush and rinse thoroughly after cleaning. Mix a fresh batch of cleaner for each cleaning session.*

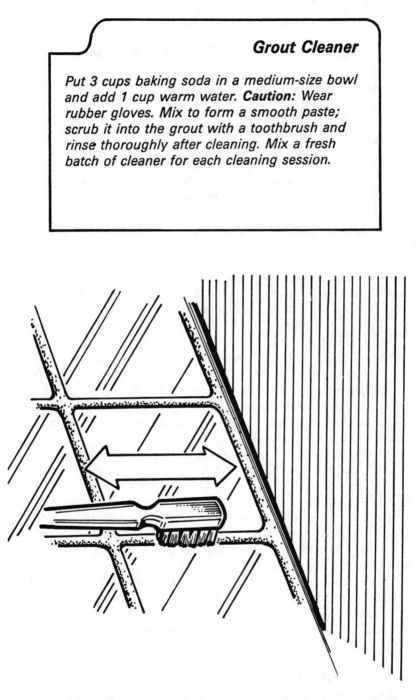

Use a toothbrush to scrub the grout between the tiles in your ceramic-tile countertop.

Ceramic-Tile Cleaner

*Mix ½ cup vinegar, 1 cup clear ammonia, ¼ cup baking soda, and 1 gallon warm water. **Caution:** Wear rubber gloves and work in a well-ventilated area when using this powerful solution. Apply the solution to the countertop with a sponge and rinse with clear water. Wipe dry to prevent water spots. Mix a fresh batch of cleaner for each cleaning session.*

Follow the manufacturer's instructions, and rinse with clear water to finish the job. **Caution:** Wear rubber gloves to avoid skin contact with these powerful cleaners, and take care not to breathe the mist from spray cleaners.

CULTURED MARBLE

Cultured marble is an acrylic material that resembles real marble, but it's easier to care for because it is less porous and does not have to be sealed.

Avoid abrasive cleaners and steel-wool soap pads; they will scratch the surface. Mildly abrasive liquid or powdered cleansers should be applied directly to the wet surface to dissolve dirt and soap film. Rinse well and buff dry with a soft cloth.

Hot pots and lighted cigarettes will leave permanent burn marks on cultured marble.

MARBLE

Marble countertops are porous and susceptible to stains, but they are not affected by heat. Seal marble with a special stone sealer to reduce its porousness, and wipe up wine, fruit juice, and other acid food spills immediately to prevent permanent surface etching.

Abrasive and caustic cleaners will mar the surface of marble, and oil polishes and soft waxes may discolor it. Many appropriate commercial cleaners are available, but borax rubbed into the surface with a moistened cloth will also clean marble. Rinse with warm water and buff dry with a soft cloth.

PLASTIC LAMINATE

Most kitchens have plastic-laminate countertops. They're practically seamless, giving cooks a smooth, waterproof work surface that is easy to clean. Unfortunately, wetness is not the only difficulty we must expect our

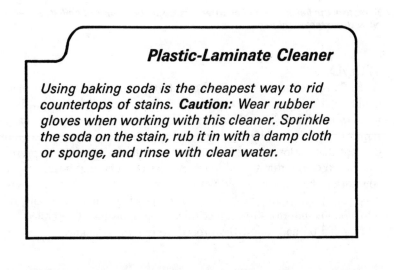

Cultured-Marble Cleaner

*Mix ½ cup vinegar, 1 cup ammonia, and ¼ cup baking soda in 1 gallon hot water. **Caution:** Wear rubber gloves and work in a well-ventilated area when using this powerful solution. Apply it to the cultured marble with a sponge, rinse with clear water, and buff dry.*

kitchen countertops to overcome: There are also hot cooking pots, sharp knives, and red-wine vinegar, to name a few. Plastic laminate burns, scratches, and stains fairly easily, so you'll have to be considerate of your countertops to keep them looking good. Regular applications of appliance wax or light furniture wax will help plastic-laminate surfaces to resist stains and scratching. Never use abrasive cleansers or steel wool on laminate countertops, and always use a cutting board.

For general cleaning, a two-sided scrubbing pad with fiber on one side and a sponge on the other works particularly well. Moistened slightly with water, the fiber side is just abrasive enough to loosen greasy smears and other soil. Turning the scrubber over, use the sponge side to wipe the surface damp-dry. When a spot or stain persists, apply a polishing cleanser with a wet sponge. Then rinse and damp-dry the countertop.

Plastic-Laminate Cleaner

*Using baking soda is the cheapest way to rid countertops of stains. **Caution:** Wear rubber gloves when working with this cleaner. Sprinkle the soda on the stain, rub it in with a damp cloth or sponge, and rinse with clear water.*

To restore the finish of wood countertops, apply two coats of boiled linseed oil with a steel-wool pad.

WOOD

Butcher-block and other wood countertops require more care than you might expect, if you don't want them to look like they belong in the back room of a butcher shop. You can restore a wood countertop that has been scratched and stained by sanding it and applying a wood-preservative product, but that's a lot of work. You'll save time in the long run by preserving your wood countertop's good looks. Always use a cutting board on a wood countertop, just as you would with any other surface. Wipe up stains and keep your wood countertops as dry as you possibly can. Periodically, rub oil into wood countertops to protect them from moisture. Use boiled linseed oil or salad oil and follow the procedure described below.

Remove stains with a solution of ¼ cup chlorine bleach in 1 quart warm water. Rinse, dry, and coat with oil.

To get rid of odors, rub the surface with a slice of lemon.

Wood-Countertop Cleaner

*Baking soda cleans and deodorizes wood surfaces. Mix ½ cup baking soda in 1 quart warm water. **Caution:** Wear rubber gloves. Rub the paste into the wood countertop, using a synthetic scouring pad. Rinse well with clear water and pat dry to remove excess moisture. When completely dry, restore the finish by using boiled linseed oil or salad oil, rubbed in with a fine-grade steel-wool pad. Treat the countertop with two coats of oil, applied 24 hours apart, and blot up the excess oil after each application.*

Drains

We all know that cooking grease combined with bits of food jams kitchen-sink drains, and we know that prevention is the best cure for the problem. But most of us will have blocked kitchen drains anyway.

As soon as a drain begins to run slowly, treat it; don't wait until no water drains out. If you suspect that the problem is a grease deposit, dissolve it by pouring boiling water or boiling water and baking soda down the drain.

If this treatment does not open the drain and if either a dishwasher or a garbage disposal is connected to it, call a plumber immediately. If no appliances utilize the drain, you can attempt to open it with a plumber's helper.

If plunging fails to unclog the drain, use a chemical drain cleaner. These products must be handled with special care because they are caustic and harmful to skin and eyes. Use them in a well-ventilated area and follow the manufacturer's instructions carefully. Commercial drain openers are sold in granular, liquid, and pressurized forms. Granular products utilize lye to do their work, liquid drain openers use lye and other chemicals, and pressurized products work by chlorofluorocarbon propellants and pressure. Before you use a granular drain opener, you must remove standing water from the sink; this is not necessary for liquids.

Try using a plumber's helper to plunge your clogged kitchen drain before you use a chemical drain cleaner.

If the first type of chemical drain opener you use does not work, do not use a different drain opener unless the initial cleaner has been flushed away totally. Never use a plunger or a pressurized drain opener after using a chemical cleaner; either one may cause dangerous chemicals to splash back onto you. Also, be sure to tell your plumber what you have put into the drain before he or she starts to work. The combination of ammonia and other household cleaners with drain cleaners produces hazardous gases.

Floors

The first step in cleaning any kind of kitchen floor is to reach for your Eureka vacuum cleaner. Whether it's a Mighty Mite®, Quick Up®, or Eureka canister, your vacuum cleaner doesn't just push dirt around the floor, it gets rid of it. When you vacuum a floor before you mop it, there's no loose dirt left on the floor to become mud when it's mixed with your floor-cleaning solution, and no loose dirt to scratch the floor as it is being mopped. To accelerate kitchen-floor cleaning, use your Eureka vacuum cleaner to clean dirt from the floor, then use your mop to wash the floor.

A vacuum-cleaner crevice tool or a small-brush attachment cleans around baseboards and radiators in the kitchen, just as it does in the rest of the house. But a crevice tool is especially effective in the kitchen, where you can use it to clean places you might not otherwise be able to reach. Use it to remove crumbs from the floor under the range, to get at dust that settles behind the refrigerator, and to clean other dirty, hard-to-reach places.

Kitchen floors come in a variety of materials. Knowing the specific material that your floor is made of is an important factor in its care, because floors can be damaged by using the wrong cleaning method or product. Beyond this consideration, the choice of which products you use to clean your kitchen floor is totally up to you. If you happen to run out of the floor-cleaning product you usually use and don't have time to run out and buy more, try one of the homemade cleaning solutions in this book. They are made from products you're likely to have in your cupboards. These solutions and methods don't necessarily work better than commercial products, but they all work very well. The following solution is recommended for asphalt, linoleum, rubber-tile, vinyl, and "no-wax" vinyl floors.

One-Step Floor Cleaner/Polish

*Mix ½ cup vinegar, 2 tablespoons furniture polish, and 1 gallon of warm water. **Caution:** Wear rubber gloves. Mop the floor with this mixture, using a sponge mop or string mop.*

ASPHALT TILE

Eureka suggests that you damp mop asphalt kitchen floors frequently to prevent dirt from building up. Use a cleaner/polish that can withstand this treatment. A cup of fabric softener added to a half pail of water may prevent damp mopping from dulling the shine on your floor.

When you wash the floor, don't flood it with water; excess water can seep into the seams and loosen adhesives that hold down the flooring. The fastest way to clean an asphalt floor is with a one-step cleaner/polish. If the mopped floor dries with a luster-dulling film, mop it again with water containing a cup of white vinegar, and the floor will glisten.

The best way to clean an asphalt floor is with an all-purpose cleaner dissolved in water and applied with a sponge mop. After you wash the floor, rinse the tile with clear water to make sure no film remains to dull the finish. When the floor is dry, apply two thin coats of a water-based, self-polishing floor finish, allowing the floor to dry between coats. Apply the polish with a long-handled wax applicator that has a washable chenille pad.

Remove heel marks by dipping fine-grade (000) steel wool in liquid floor wax and rubbing the spot gently. Wipe with a damp cloth.

LINOLEUM

Linoleum must be waxed in order to look shiny and to stand up to foot traffic effectively. After vacuuming the floor, use a damp mop to clean your linoleum kitchen floor. If the mopped floor dries with a luster-dulling film, we've found that mopping it again with water containing a cup of white vinegar will make the floor sparkle.

Use a water-based cleaner/polish or an all-purpose cleaning solution for routine care. Read the product label for precautionary measures. If you use a water-based polish, don't shake it before use.

Occasionally, remove wax buildup with an all-purpose cleaner or stripper. Always test a corner before stripping to make sure the product won't permanently damage your linoleum flooring. This is particularly true of older linoleum.

Do not use solvent-based products. They can soften and damage linoleum. Also, don't scour the floor, flood it with water, or use very hot water or strong soaps.

If you have time and the inclination, the best way to clean a linoleum floor is first to mop it with an all-purpose cleaner dissolved in very warm water. Then rinse, and apply two thin coats (let dry between coats) of a water-based, self-polishing liquid polish. We recommend you use a long-handled wax applicator with a washable chenille pad.

Remove heel marks by dipping fine-grade (000) steel wool in liquid floor wax. Rub the spot gently and wipe with a damp cloth.

RUBBER TILE

Rubber tile is similar to asphalt tile, but it can be ruined by strong sunlight and is more susceptible to damage by strong cleaners, abrasive cleansers, and very hot water.

Damp mop your rubber-tile floor after vacuuming. A cup of fabric softener added to a half pail of water may prevent damp mopping from dulling the shine on your floor. If you use a cleaner/polish that cannot withstand damp mopping, you must reapply the cleaner/polish instead of just damp mopping.

Use a water-based cleaner/polish or an all-purpose cleaning solution for routine care. Read the product label for precautionary measures and test any cleaner or stripper in a corner before using it on the entire floor.

Do not use solvent-based products on a rubber-tile floor. They can soften and damage the tile. Also, do not scour the tile, use strong soaps and hot water, or flood the floor with water. Excess water can seep into the seams and loosen the adhesives that hold down the flooring.

Occasionally, remove wax buildup with a cleaner or wax stripper. If you use an all-purpose cleaning solution, follow it with two thin coats of self-polishing wax; allow to dry between coats. Do not shake a water-based liquid polish before use.

Remove heel marks by dipping fine-grade (000) steel wool in liquid floor wax. Rub the spot gently and wipe with a damp cloth.

VINYL

Damp mop vinyl floors after you vacuum them. A cup of fabric softener added to a half pail of water may prevent damp mopping from dulling the shine on your floor. If you use a cleaner/polish that cannot withstand damp mopping, you must reapply the cleaner/polish.

For fast, routine care of a vinyl kitchen floor, we recommend a water-based cleaner/polish. Read the product label for precautionary measures and test any cleaner or stripper in a corner before using it on the entire floor. Occasionally, remove wax buildup with a cleaning solution that contains ammonia or with a wax stripper.

Do not use solvent-based products or cleaners that contain pine oil on a vinyl floor. They can soften and damage the flooring. Also, do not scour the floor, use strong soaps or hot water, or flood the floor with water. Excess water can seep into the seams and loosen the adhesives that hold down the flooring.

The best way to clean a vinyl-tile floor (if you have the time) is with a powdered cleaner dissolved in warm water and applied with a sponge mop. If you use an all-purpose cleaner, rinse the tile with clear water to make sure no film remains to dull the finish. Adding a cup of white vinegar to the rinse water will make your floor glisten. When the floor is dry, apply two thin coats of a water-based, self-polishing floor finish, allowing the floor to dry between coats. Apply the wax with a long-handled wax applicator that has a washable chenille pad.

Remove heel marks from vinyl floors by dipping a synthetic scouring pad in liquid floor wax. Rub the spot gently and wipe with a damp cloth.

VINYL, "NO-WAX"

A "no-wax" vinyl floor requires less care than other kitchen floors. Just vacuum regularly and damp mop.

Use an all-purpose cleaning solution to wash the floor. Read the product label for precautionary measures and test any cleaner in a corner before using it on the entire floor. If the mopped floor dries with a luster-dulling film, mop it again with water containing a cup of white vinegar, and the floor will shine.

If your "no-wax" floor loses its shine in high-traffic areas, use a gloss-renewing product available from the manufacturer of your floor or another commercial product formulated for this purpose.

Do not use solvent-based products or cleaners that contain pine oil on a vinyl floor. They can soften and damage the flooring. Also, do not scour the floor, use strong soaps and hot water, or flood the floor with water. Excess water can seep into the seams and loosen the adhesives that hold down the flooring.

Remove heel marks by dipping a synthetic scouring pad in cleaner. Rub the spot gently and wipe with a damp cloth.

WOOD

If you have wood floors in your kitchen, you should either seal the floor with polyurethane or oil the wood. Varnish, shellac, and lacquer, which are used to seal wood floors in other parts of the house, are not suitable for the kitchen. They don't like to get wet.

A wood floor that has been sealed with polyurethane can be damp mopped and cleaned with water-based cleaning solutions. Be sure to read the product label. You may want to wax the floor to protect it from wear and tear, but the floor will shine, resist water, and repel stains without having been waxed.

A wood kitchen floor sealed with an oil-based floor finish is not as impervious to wet spills as a floor sealed with polyurethane, but it may wear better. Oil penetrates wood, while varnishes, including polyurethane, sit on top of the wood and are scratched and worn away with normal use over time. Kitchen floors take more abuse than most other floors in your house, so an oiled floor, which has a finish that you restore every time you clean, may look better longer than a kitchen floor that is varnished.

We recommend that you wash your kitchen's wood floor with flax soap, following the package directions. Flax soap both cleans and seals the floor with a light coating of oil.

The *fastest* way to clean wood floors that are sealed with varnish, lacquer, or shellac is with a one-step cleaner/polish. After vacuuming the floor, pour the solvent-based liquid on a small area and rub lightly with a dry wax applicator. Working on a small section at a time, stroke the floor in the direction of the grain. Blot up excess liquid with a clean cloth.

The *best* way to clean a wood floor takes longer but gives a kitchen floor much-needed extra protection from moisture. Use a liquid-wax cleaner. After vacuuming the floor, apply the cleaner with a dry wax applicator or a cloth. Work on one small area at a time. Let the cleaner soak for three minutes and wipe up the excess. When the floor is dry, buff it with a floor polisher. **Caution:** This is a combustible mixture; use in a well-ventilated area.

Remove heel marks by applying a solvent-based wax, polish, or cleaner with a rag. Rub the mark away.

Hardware

Get in the habit of wiping faucets and taps when you swab the counters after meals. This will prevent water spots and give your kitchen a sparkling look with very little effort on your part. Clean hardware when you clean the sink, using the same cleaning product and method. Rinse well and buff with a dry cloth. Wash greasy drain baskets in the dishwasher.

If you live in an area that has hard water, you'll need to remove mineral deposits from faucet heads. Remove the head from its fitting, take it apart, and soak it in vinegar. Then brush the mineral deposits loose with a toothbrush. If the holes remain clogged, poke them clear them with a wire, pin, toothpick, or ice pick.

Large Appliances

Large appliances are basically big, enamel-coated metal boxes that clean up with the swipe of a wet cloth. With the exception of rangetops that have at least four depressions to trap and hold spilled food, the outsides of appliances present no cleaning problems. You give them a once-over when you do your countertops, and that's that. Inside large appliances, there's another story. Glaciers form in your freezer. The gunk under the crisper drawer in your refrigerator looks like a high school science project. There's enough lint in your dryer to stuff a pillow. Any day now, you wouldn't be surprised to find that someone had started mining the mineral deposits in your dishwasher. What goes on in the oven and under the cooktop on your range should not be mentioned in polite company.

If you keep up appearances by regularly wiping sticky fingerprints off the refrigerator door and gummy drips off the front of the dishwasher, you can put off cleaning the messes that lurk within your large appliances until you have time to deal with them thoroughly. When you do find the time to tackle the interiors, we're here to help with time-tested hints to speed you through your work.

CLOTHES WASHERS AND DRYERS

Clothes washers and dryers are kept out of sight in most homes, and many of us tend to let them get pretty dirty. But cleaning the outside surfaces of your clothes washer and dryer is not just something to do while you wait for a repair person. Wet clothes are dirt magnets, and keeping these appliances clean will save you having to rewash clothes that drop on a dirty dryer.

The top of each unit is made of powdered paint, which is a very durable material. The sides are finished with baked enamel, which is very much like that you would find on your automobile. Other parts are made from metal, durable plastics, and metal-coated plastics.

Read the manufacturer's instruction booklet for the best methods for caring for your particular machines, including cleaning the dryer filter and washing-machine filter (if they are not self-cleaning).

For top drying performance, lint trays and the areas around them should be free of lint. When lint builds up, clean the inside of your dryer with your vacuum cleaner. After unplugging the dryer from the electrical outlet, attach the hose to the blower end of your vacuum cleaner and move the nozzle over the interior of the dryer's spinner basket, starting at the top and working down the sides. This will blow the lint into the air-intake opening. After removing as much lint as possible in this way, reverse the vacuum-cleaner hose, placing it at the suction end, and remove any lint still left inside the dryer.

Wipe the exterior of the machines with a damp cloth, using a synthetic scouring pad for stubborn soil. Baking soda will clean and shine enamel surfaces. Dip a damp sponge in soda and rub it over the soiled area. Because baking soda is not abrasive, it does not scratch the enamel, but it works as well as scouring cleansers. Rinse well with clear water and buff dry with a soft, absorbent cloth.

Commercial kitchen-appliance waxes will leave a protective wax coating on your washing machine and dryer, but be careful not to get wax on the plastic parts.

To clean the interior and hoses of your clothes washer, pour 1 gallon white-wine vinegar in the tub and run the washing machine through a normal cycle at the highest water level.

DISHWASHERS

Baking soda cleans your dishwasher inside and out. Dip a damp cloth in soda and use it to clean smudges and fingerprints from the exterior; the same method will also remove stains from the liner. Use a synthetic scouring pad to clean stubborn soil.

Use a spray glass cleaner to polish chromium trim. Commercial kitchen-appliance waxes will leave a protective wax coating on your dishwasher, but be careful not to get wax on the plastic parts.

If your dishwasher has a butcher-block top, clean it by saturating a cloth or fine-grade (000) steel-wool pad with vegetable oil, rub it into the wood, and allow the oil to soak overnight. Wipe up any excess oil the next day.

If the interior of your dishwasher retains odors, sprinkle 3 tablespoons baking soda in the bottom of the machine and allow it to sit overnight. The odors will be washed away with the baking soda during the next wash cycle. To prevent the liner from retaining odors, occasionally leave the dishwasher door open to air.

Here's a quick way to remove mineral deposits from your dishwasher. Use this method only for dishwashers with porcelain interiors. It cannot be used on dishwashers with plastic interiors. Place a glass bowl containing ¾ cup bleach on the lower rack. Load the dishwasher with glasses and dinnerware only and run it through the wash and rinse cycles. Then put 1 cup vinegar in the bowl and run the dishwasher through another complete cycle.

FREEZERS

Freezers require little care other than wiping off smudges and fingerprints and defrosting (if you have a manual defrost model).

Defrost the freezer when the frost gets to be ½-inch thick. Turn off the freezer controls and remove all the food. Put the food in an ice chest, wrap it in layers of newspaper, or store it tightly packed in your refrigerator. Open the door of the freezer and allow the ice to melt partially. When it is the consistency of slush, scrape the ice away with a wooden or plastic scraper. You can speed the melting process by setting shallow pans of hot water on the freezer shelves. Do not put food back into the freezer until you have wiped off any condensation that develops and the freezer has been running for at least half an hour. Whenever you defrost your freezer, clean dust from behind the grill at the bottom of the freezer with your Eureka vacuum cleaner.

Place a box of baking soda in the freezer every other month to control freezer odors.

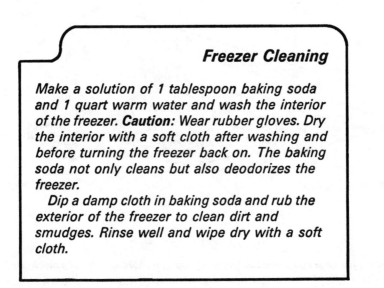

Freezer Cleaning

Make a solution of 1 tablespoon baking soda and 1 quart warm water and wash the interior of the freezer. **Caution:** Wear rubber gloves. Dry the interior with a soft cloth after washing and before turning the freezer back on. The baking soda not only cleans but also deodorizes the freezer.

Dip a damp cloth in baking soda and rub the exterior of the freezer to clean dirt and smudges. Rinse well and wipe dry with a soft cloth.

MICROWAVE OVENS

If you keep a microwave oven clean, you'll never have to "clean" it. Just wipe the exterior when you do the kitchen countertops, and wipe the interior after each use. A synthetic scouring pad will remove stubborn soil. Use a mild dishwashing detergent, baking soda, or glass cleaner. Wash the glass tray in the sink or the dishwasher when it is soiled. Never use a commercial oven cleaner in a microwave oven.

RANGE HOODS

Some range hoods are vented to the outside and remove grease, steam, and cooking odors from the kitchen. But other hoods do not have outside vents and rely on replaceable charcoal filters to clean smoke and odors from the air. Both vented and nonvented hoods have fans to draw air and smoke from the cooking area, and both need to be cleaned to keep them free from grease buildup and working effectively.

Wipe the exterior and interior of the range hood. Use a solution of hot water, dishwashing detergent, and ammonia to cut the grease; wear rubber gloves. Remove the filter cover and wash it in soapy, hot water. Allow it to dry completely before replacing. Wipe the blades of the fan with an ammonia solution. Clean metal mesh filters when they are dirty, and replace the filters on nonvented range hoods every six to nine months or as often as the manufacturer recommends. Washing charcoal filters will reduce their effectiveness.

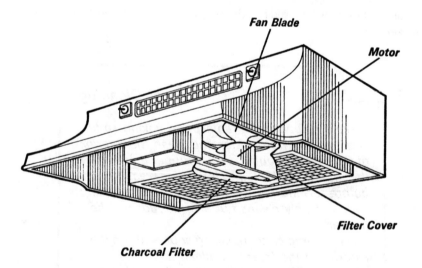

Wash the filter cover and fan blades but not the charcoal filter of a nonvented range hood.

RANGES

The best way to care for all the parts of a range is to clean them continually, never allowing spilled food or grease spatters to become baked on. If you wipe up spills as soon as the stove is cool, they will not bake onto the surface and cleaning will stay simple.

Ceramic Cooktops

The ceramic cooktop is a glass cooktop with electric heating elements under the glass. While smoothtops may appear to be easy to clean, special care must be taken to avoid damaging or discoloring the ceramic surface.

Wait until the top cools to wipe up spills; never use a wet sponge or cloth on a hot panel. Don't set soiled pots or pans on the surface; they can mar it permanently. Abrasive cleaning products will scratch the surface, discoloring it and making it difficult to keep clean.

The best way to clean a ceramic cooktop is to sprinkle a nonabrasive cleanser or baking soda over the surface and rub with a synthetic scouring pad or sponge. Rinse well with clear water and buff dry with a soft cloth for a clean finish.

Gas and Electric Stovetops and Range Exteriors

The exteriors of most gas and electric ranges are baked-on porcelain enamel, the trim is usually chromed steel or brushed aluminum, and the control knobs are plastic.

Wipe the surface around the heating elements after each use. Use a synthetic scouring pad for stubborn soil. Harsh abrasives or steel wool will damage the stove's enamel finish.

Wash reflector bowls, or drip pans, and grids in warm soapsuds whenever food or grease is spilled on them. Clean reflector bowls will help your stove to cook more efficiently; blackened and dull reflector bowls absorb heat rather than reflecting it back up to the cooking pot. Whenever you remove the bowls from the stovetop to wash them, use your vacuum-cleaner hose to draw out crumbs and other particles that collect beneath them. Many stovetops can be raised for access to this area.

Gas burners should be washed occasionally. Clear the holes with a fine wire or a pipe cleaner. Don't use a toothpick; it could break off and clog a hole. To prevent rust, quickly dry the gas burners in a warm oven after they have been washed.

Electric heating elements are self-cleaning and should never be submerged in water. If you need to clean an element, first turn off the power to your electric range at the service panel.

Remove all the control knobs when you clean the exterior of the range to make the job easier. Soak the knobs in sudsy, warm water and dry them with a soft towel before putting them back in place.

Commercial appliance-cleaning products will not only clean and shine the surface of your range but also will leave a protective wax coating.

Oven Cleaner

Pour 1 cup ammonia in a glass or ceramic bowl, place it in a cold oven, and allow it to sit in the closed oven overnight. The next morning, pour the ammonia into a pail of warm water and use this solution and a sponge to wipe away the loosened soil. **Caution:** *Wear rubber gloves whenever you work with an ammonia solution. The fumes are strong at first, but they soon dissipate.*

Ovens

There are many strong cleaning products designed to clean traditional ovens. **Caution:** Most oven cleaners are dangerous when they come in contact with your skin or eyes. Wear rubber gloves and protect your eyes while cleaning. Don't breathe the spray mist or the fumes. Avoid dripping oven cleaner onto any surfaces other than those it is intended to clean. Always carefully read and follow the manufacturer's instructions when you use a commercial oven cleaner.

When you clean a traditional oven, use strips of aluminum foil to protect the heating elements, oven wiring, and thermostat from commercial oven cleaners.

Many ranges are equipped with self-cleaning or continuous-cleaning ovens. A self-cleaning oven uses a pyrolytic, or high heat, system to incinerate oven grime, creating a powdery ash. A continuous-cleaning, or catalytic, system eliminates small spatters through the porous porcelain-enamel finish on the oven liner, which absorbs and spreads soil to promote cleaning at normal temperature settings. Large spills must be wiped up; they will burn and may permanently stain the oven surface. Dust continuous-cleaning ovens frequently and self-cleaning ovens after the cleaning cycle, using the small-brush attachment of your Eureka vacuum cleaner to remove dried food particles and/or ash.

Follow the manufacturer's instructions when using the cleaning cycle of a self-cleaning oven, and follow the manufacturer's recommendations for caring for a continuous-cleaning oven. Neither kind of oven should be cleaned with commercial oven cleaners. A continuous-cleaning oven should never be scrubbed with abrasives or powdered cleansers; these products will damage the surface.

REFRIGERATORS

A frost-free refrigerator should be cleaned when it's dirty. Clean a manual-defrost refrigerator when you defrost the freezer compartment.

Remove ashes from self-cleaning ovens with your Eureka vacuum cleaner.

Wash the drip pan whenever you defrost and/or clean your refrigerator.

Defrost the freezer section of your refrigerator when the frost gets to be ½-inch thick. Turn off the freezer controls and remove all the food. Put the food in an ice chest or wrap it in layers of newspaper. Remove all shelves, bins, racks, and trays and wash them in a mild soapsuds solution. Dry thoroughly.

To speed defrosting, prop open the door of the freezer compartment. If your refrigerator is a manual-defrost model, placing shallow pans of hot water on the shelves will melt frost buildup quickly. When the ice is the consistency of slush, scrape it away with a wooden or plastic scraper. Never use sharp tools to scrape frost and ice from the freezer.

Do not put food back into the freezer until you have wiped off any condensation that develops and the freezer has been running for at least a half hour. Wipe the interior of the refrigerator to prevent puddles from remaining in the bottom when you replace the bins.

Vacuum dust from the area behind the bottom grill of your refrigerator at least twice a year. Clean the condenser coils with your Eureka vaccum cleaner's crevice tool about once a month.

Control refrigerator odors with a box of baking soda placed at the back of a shelf. Replace the box several times a year. Also, place a box of soda in the freezer if odors are a problem there.

Do not wash ice trays in a detergent solution; this can remove the special nonstick coating that some of them have.

Commercial kitchen appliance wax will remove smudges and dirt and leave a protective wax coating on the exterior of the refrigerator, but baking soda will also clean and shine your refrigerator. Rub the exterior with a damp cloth dipped in baking soda, rinse well, and wipe dry.

TRASH COMPACTORS

Follow the manufacturer's cleaning instructions for the interior of your trash compactor. Clean it when necessary, watching out for small glass particles that may be left from the trash.

Generally, the bags made especially for a particular trash compactor will give you the best results. Remember that no compactor is designed to handle wet garbage. Empty your trash compactor frequently and use a deodorant spray to discourage bad odors.

Routinely wipe the exterior of your trash compactor to remove smudges and fingerprints. Use a commercial kitchen-appliance wax or baking soda to polish it.

Small Appliances

The little machines that line up along our kitchen countertops or park themselves in our appliance garages save us time and effort when we cook. But they sometimes seem to use up the time they've saved us in the amount of time they take to clean. Food sloshes out of blenders and spins out of food processors. Blades and cutters hide food in their intricate designs and can cut our fingers when we try to clean them. Even though most small appliances are designed to be easy to clean, they still have to be cleaned. We'll show you quick and easy ways to do this without endangering your fingers.

BLENDERS AND FOOD PROCESSORS

Always read and follow the manufacturer's cleaning instructions. Most plastic work bowls and blender jars can be washed in your dishwasher, some cannot. Some blades are dulled by repeated exposure to dishwasher detergents, some are not.

If you wipe the bases of food-preparation appliances after each use, you will rarely have to scrub them. The blender jar is almost fun to clean; fill it with a warm detergent solution and run the blender for about 15 seconds at high speed. Rinse well and dry. To retain the sharpness of the blades, do not wash the blender's assembly in the dishwasher.

Wash the food-processor work bowl, cover, pusher, blade, and discs in warm, soapy water or in the dishwasher. Because the blade is razor sharp, to be safe, carefully wash it by hand. If you leave the blade in the rack of the dishwasher, you might cut your hand when you are loading or unloading other items.

A glass cleaner is excellent for cleaning stainless-steel blender bases and trim. Simply spray it on and buff dry immediately with a soft cloth. An all-purpose cleaner or a solution of baking soda and water cleans plastic blender and food-processor bases.

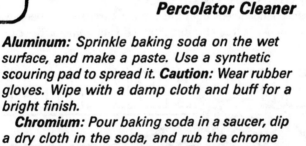

Percolator Cleaner

Aluminum: Sprinkle baking soda on the wet surface, and make a paste. Use a synthetic scouring pad to spread it. Caution: Wear rubber gloves. Wipe with a damp cloth and buff for a bright finish.

Chromium: Pour baking soda in a saucer, dip a dry cloth in the soda, and rub the chrome surface. This will remove fingerprints, smudges, and even sticky residue with no further rinsing or wiping. Kitchen flour rubbed on the surface with a dry cloth will also remove greasy film and smudges.

Stainless Steel: Sprinkle baking soda on the wet surface and scrub with a synthetic scouring pad. Caution: Wear rubber gloves. Wipe with a damp cloth and buff with a soft, dry cloth.

COFFEE MAKERS

Drip coffee makers are easy to clean; they require a new filter; washing the pot, lid, and basket in a detergent solution; and a quick wipe of the base with a damp cloth.

Percolators need thorough, occasional cleanings to get rid of oil build-up on the stem, basket, and interior walls that can affect the taste of the coffee.

Allow a heated percolator to cool before cleaning. We recommend that you use a synthetic scouring pad, never harsh abrasives or steel wool, to remove stubborn soil from percolator parts. If the surface becomes scratched, oil and other coffee residues will accumulate in the scratches.

Wash all percolator parts in a warm detergent solution after each use. If your percolator is not immersible, wipe the exterior with a damp cloth and buff dry. Clean the spout and tubes of a percolator with a percolator brush and a warm dishwashing-detergent solution.

Commercial products formulated to clean percolators are very effective, but we've found that the following method for cleaning percolators works equally well: With the stem and basket in place, fill the percolator completely full with cold water and add 6 tablespoons baking soda. Plug in the machine and allow the percolator to run through its complete cycle. Wait for 15 minutes, unplug the machine, and empty the solution. Wash in a mild detergent, rinse, and dry. (Adding ¼ cup white vinegar to a potful of water and running it through the brewing cycle will also clean the percolator.)

ELECTRIC CAN OPENERS

Your can opener needs light but regular care. Remember always to unplug a can opener before cleaning it, and do not immerse the case in water.

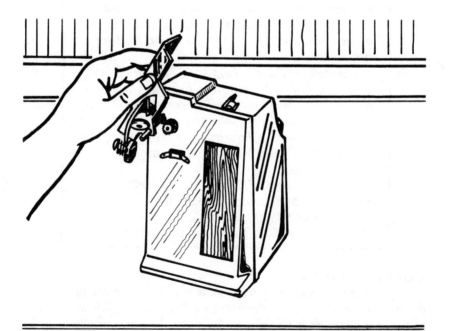

Remove the cutting wheel and lid holder from your electric can opener to clean them in hot, sudsy water.

Wipe the can opener after each use to remove food spills or drips. Use a sponge dampened in a warm soapsuds solution made from liquid dishwashing detergent. Buff dry.

Periodically, remove the cutting wheel and lid holder and soak them in hot, sudsy water. Scrub caked-on food with a toothbrush; rinse, dry, and replace the parts.

ELECTRIC IRONS

The obvious problem with a clogged steam iron is that it doesn't deliver enough steam. An even worse problem is the tendency of clogged irons to become suddenly unclogged and spew white mineral globs all over your best dark suit or favorite silk blouse. A clean iron speeds your pressing and protects your clothes.

Water-Reservoir Cleaner

Remove mineral deposits from the water reservoir when the steam action begins to decrease. Pour a solution of ⅓ cup white vinegar and ⅓ cup water into the water reservoir. Heat the iron and let it steam for about 3 minutes. Unplug the iron and position it, soleplate down, on a small glass dish that has been placed in a larger shallow pan. Allow the water to drain from the vents for about an hour. Drain away remaining solution and flush the reservoir with clear water before using the iron.

Soleplates

Follow the manufacturer's instructions to keep the steam vents from becoming clogged with mineral deposits. Some irons use tap water; others require distilled water. When you clean the soleplate of your iron, be sure to remove cleaning-product residue from the vents. We use a cotton swab or pipe cleaner. A sharp knife or other metal tool is likely to scratch the soleplate.

Commercial products are available to clean hot irons. But if you don't have one of these products, you can use a damp cloth dipped in baking soda to clean the soleplate of a slightly warm iron. Scrub starch buildup or other soil. Rinse well with another damp cloth, taking particular care to clear the vents.

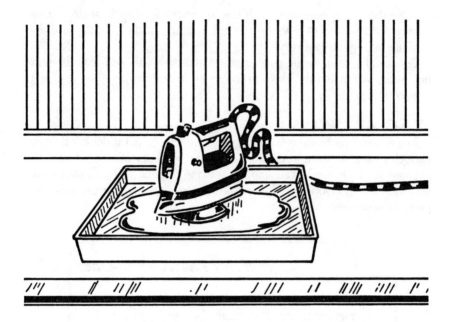

After you clean the water reservoir of your iron with a vinegar solution, allow the solution to drain out the steam vents by placing the iron soleplate down on a small dish.

Water Reservoirs

Even if your steam iron is designed to be used with tap water, you should use distilled water if you live in a part of the country that has hard water. Melted frost from the freezer is a good substitute for distilled water.

GARBAGE DISPOSERS

Garbage disposers are self-cleaning, but they can get smelly, especially if you let food sit in them for any length of time. To keep your disposer odorless and running smoothly, operate it with a full stream of running cold water. Flush the disposer for a few seconds after turning it off to ensure that all debris is washed away.

We know that you've heard this before, but we all need to be reminded to keep the following materials out of the disposer: metal, wood, glass, paper, or plastic objects; fibrous organic waste, such as artichoke leaves and corn husks; and caustic drain cleaners.

If an unpleasant odor begins to come from your disposer, eliminate it by tearing up the peels of citrus fruit and putting them into the disposer. Grind them with a stream of cold running water and enjoy the fresh smell. Another excellent method for clearing odors from your disposer is to sprinkle baking soda over several ice cubes and grind them in the disposer.

HOT TRAYS

A quick wipe with a damp sponge usually is sufficient to clean a hot tray, but if spilled food is baked on, stronger measures are needed. Remember never to immerse a hot tray in water.

To remove baked-on food from a hot tray, we recommend a commercial oven cleaner. Heat the tray to a warm temperature and carefully spray it with the cleaner. Cover the outer perimeter of the tray and all plastic and wood parts with aluminum foil to prevent oven cleaner from touching these surfaces. Do not let oven cleaner seep into the crevice between the frame and the surface of the tray.

You'll need to allow the oven cleaner to stand on the tray for 10 minutes and then remove it with a clean, wet sponge. **Caution:** Follow the manufacturer's warnings for proper use of oven cleaners. Wear rubber gloves, protect your eyes, and do not breathe the spray or fumes.

TOASTER OVENS/BROILERS

When the puddle of cheese from last night's nachos meets the buttery crumbs from this morning's toast in the bottom of your toaster oven, you have a major mess, not to mention a fire hazard. Cleaning your toaster oven/broiler right after you use it prevents a squalid buildup of food spatters and crumbs, which is likely to become a permanent condition because baked-on messes are very difficult to remove from toaster ovens. Wipe the exterior of the oven and the crumb tray regularly, and wipe the interior of the oven with a warm dishwashing solution after cooking greasy foods. A synthetic scouring pad will remove stubborn soil from the tray and racks. The plastic parts are best cleaned with a warm detergent solution; buff the surfaces dry.

Clean a toaster oven only when it is cool and has been disconnected. Never immerse the oven in water, and don't use harsh abrasives, steel wool, or commercial oven cleaner to clean a toaster oven.

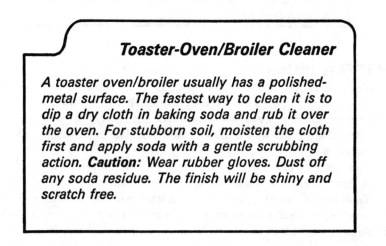

Toaster-Oven/Broiler Cleaner

*A toaster oven/broiler usually has a polished-metal surface. The fastest way to clean it is to dip a dry cloth in baking soda and rub it over the oven. For stubborn soil, moisten the cloth first and apply soda with a gentle scrubbing action. **Caution:** Wear rubber gloves. Dust off any soda residue. The finish will be shiny and scratch free.*

TOASTERS

Toasters are crumb catchers and smudge collectors; they need regular attention to keep them clean, shiny, and crumb free.

Remember to unplug the toaster and let it cool before cleaning it.

Wipe the exterior of the toaster regularly. Remove the crumb tray at the base of the toaster and shake out accumulated crumbs; wash the tray in warm soapsuds. If your toaster does not have a crumb tray, turn the toaster upside down and shake it over the sink or a large garbage can. Use a thin, soft-bristled brush to remove crumbs from the interior.

Never wash the inside of the toaster with water or immerse the whole unit. Metal utensils should not be used to clean the inside of the toaster. You can polish the exterior of your toaster with baking soda or flour, using the same method we use for toaster ovens/broilers.

Waffle-Iron Cleaners

Baked Enamel: Wipe the exterior surfaces of the waffle iron with a sponge dipped in a warm soapsuds solution made with a liquid dishwashing detergent. **Caution:** Wear rubber gloves. For stubborn soil, use a synthetic scouring pad. Rinse and buff dry with a soft cloth.

Metal: Rub baking soda or flour onto the surface with a dry cloth to remove light soil and smudges. If a spot persists, moisten the cloth and apply baking soda with a gentle scouring action. Dust off any remaining soda for a bright, scratch-free finish.

WAFFLE IRONS

Waffle irons need little care. The grids are made from seasoned cast iron or have a nonstick surface and generally do not require washing.

Wipe the exterior of your waffle iron and clean up batter spills after each use. Wipe the grids with a paper towel that has been dampened with vegetable oil.

If waffles stick to the grids and burn, you'll have to remove the grids and wash them in warm soapsuds, using a plastic brush to remove the burned waffle debris. Season the surface with a light brushing of vegetable oil.

Never clean a waffle iron until it is cool and has been unplugged. Do not immerse a waffle iron in water.

Kitchenware

COOKWARE

When was the last time you saw your face reflected in the bottom of a skillet or reveled in the warm glow of a copper pot you had just shined? If you can't remember, you probably have much too much to do to worry about keeping your pots, pans, and cooking utensils looking like new. Unless they're on display, a reasonably clean cooking pot functions just about as well as a sparkling clean one does. The amount of shine on your cookware is totally up to you. In this section, we'll tell you how to put a shine on stainless steel when you want to, but we'll also show you how to care for your cast iron easily and quickly.

Basic care for all cookware starts with reading the manufacturer's care instructions. Wash all pots and pans thoroughly inside and out soon after use. An exception to this is your omelet pan. Clean seasoned omelet pans with a paper towel. If baked-on food necessitates washing the pan in soapsuds, dry it thoroughly over a warm burner and rub vegetable oil into the warm pan with a pad of folded paper toweling.

Prevent heat stains on the outsides of pans by keeping gas flames low so that they cannot lick up the sides. Do not subject cookware to sudden temperature changes. Allow it to cool before washing or soaking.

We recommend that you clean scorched pans by bringing 1 teaspoon baking soda and 1 cup water to boil in the pan. Allow the pan to cool and wash it in soapy water. Substitute vinegar for baking soda to clean scorched aluminum pans.

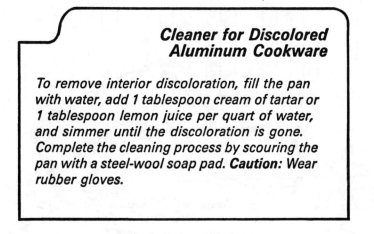

Cleaner for Discolored Aluminum Cookware

To remove interior discoloration, fill the pan with water, add 1 tablespoon cream of tartar or 1 tablespoon lemon juice per quart of water, and simmer until the discoloration is gone. Complete the cleaning process by scouring the pan with a steel-wool soap pad. **Caution:** Wear rubber gloves.

Aluminum

The only way to protect aluminum cookware from discoloration is never to wash it in an automatic dishwasher or let it soak in soapy water for long periods of time. We recommend that you don't allow food to stand in aluminum cookware and don't use it to store food; food that is acid-based can discolor or pit the metal.

Use a steel-wool soap pad to remove burned-on food from cast-aluminum cookware. Liquid nonabrasive bathroom cleanser or a paste of baking soda and water used with a synthetic scouring pad will polish both cast and sheet aluminum.

Cast Iron

Cast-iron cookware has a tendency to rust if it is not kept properly seasoned. Some new cast-iron cooking utensils come from the factory already sealed, but most will have to be seasoned before their first use.

We recommend that you season cast-iron cookware in the traditional way: Scour your pot with a steel-wool soap pad, then wipe the inside with vegetable oil, place it in a warm oven for two hours, and wipe off the excess oil. To maintain your cookware's seasoning, repeat this procedure periodically and whenever rust spots appear.

Wash cast-iron cookware in hot, sudsy water, then dry it thoroughly and store it in a dry cupboard without its lid in place. Never wash cast-iron cookware in the dishwasher; it will remove the seasoning and cause rust.

Clay

We recommend that you soak new clay cookware in water for about a half hour before using it for the first time. Be sure to soak both the top and

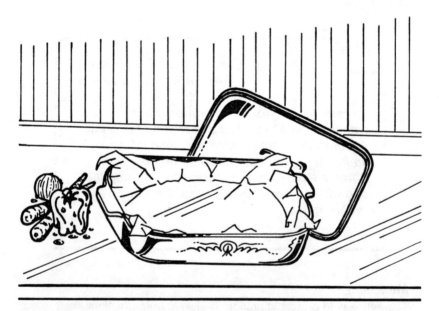

Line a clay pot with parchment paper to prevent stains from cooked food.

the bottom, then scrub them well with a stiff-bristled brush to remove clay dust.

Line the cooker with parchment paper to prevent the porous surface from absorbing food stains and strong flavors. If your clay pot becomes stained or takes on pungent odors, fill the cooker with water, add 1 to 4 tablespoons baking soda, and let it stand overnight.

Never put a hot clay cooker on a cold surface; the cooker might crack.

Wash clay cookware immediately after it cools to prevent food from drying and crusting, but never wash clay cookware in the dishwasher or scrub it with a steel-wool soap pad. Carefully dry the cooker before storing it to prevent mold. Storing clay cookware with its lid off will also discourage mold.

If mold spots appear on a clay cooker, brush the surface with a paste made of equal parts baking soda and water. Let stand 30 minutes, preferably in strong sunlight; brush the paste away, rinse well in clear water, and dry thoroughly in a well-ventilated location.

Copper

Copper darkens with use and exposure to air. If you prefer shiny copper, you can clean and polish it easily. Copper cookware is lined with other metals to prevent harmful chemical reactions with food. The lining is usually tin or stainless steel. If your copper pot has a tin lining, you must be careful not to scrape away the tin by stirring with sharp metal cooking utensils. You can have a copper pan retinned when the lining begins to wear thin, but this is an expensive procedure. We recommend that you use wood, nylon, or nonstick-coated spoons for stirring to prevent scratching the lining of copper cookware.

Some copper cookware comes with a protective lacquer coating that must be removed before the utensil is heated. Follow the manufacturer's

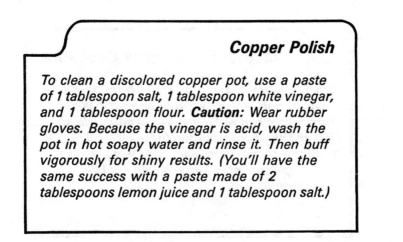

Copper Polish

*To clean a discolored copper pot, use a paste of 1 tablespoon salt, 1 tablespoon white vinegar, and 1 tablespoon flour. **Caution:** Wear rubber gloves. Because the vinegar is acid, wash the pot in hot soapy water and rinse it. Then buff vigorously for shiny results. (You'll have the same success with a paste made of 2 tablespoons lemon juice and 1 tablespoon salt.)*

instructions, or place the utensil in a solution of 1 cup baking soda and 2 gallons boiling water, let it stand until the water is cool, peel off the lacquer, wash, rinse, and dry.

Protect copper pans from scorching by making sure there is always liquid or fat in the pan before it is placed on the heat. When melting butter, swirl it around in the bottom of the pan and up the sides. Lower the heat as soon as the contents of the pot reach the boiling point.

Commercial copper-cleaning products do a good job of cleaning and shining copper cookware if you follow the manufacturer's instructions.

Enamelware

We suggest that you let enamel cookware cool before washing. Rapid changes in temperature can crack the enamel coating. If necessary, soak a dirty pot to loosen cooked-on foods. Use a synthetic scouring pad, never abrasive cleansers or steel wool, to scrub stubborn soil. Enamelware can be washed safely in the dishwasher.

Dishwashing detergent will clean enamel cookware quickly. Encrusted food or stains can be removed with a liquid nonabrasive bathroom cleanser.

Glass and Ceramic-Glass

Most heat-resistant glass and ceramic-glass cookware is designed for oven use only, but some can be used on stovetops. Read the manufacturer's instructions carefully to make sure that you use your cookware appropriately. All glass and ceramic-glass cookware is dishwasher safe.

Glass cookware that is allowed to boil dry is likely to shatter. If a pot boils dry, the safest way for you to handle this potentially explosive situation is to turn off the heat and leave the pot where it is until it has cooled.

You can remove mineral deposits from a glass coffeepot or teapot by boiling full-strength cider vinegar in the container for 15 minutes.

Cleaner for Nonstick Cookware

When you want to remove stains from nonstick-coated cookware, mix 2 tablespoons baking soda with 1 cup water and ½ cup liquid bleach. Boil the solution in the pan for several minutes until the stains disappear. After washing the pan, wipe the inner surface with cooking oil to season it.

Nonstick-Coated

Nonstick finishes or coatings are relatively thin and damage easily. We recommend that you use wood, nylon, or specially coated spoons and spatulas to prevent surface damage. Most nonstick-coated cookware can be safely washed in the dishwasher.

Wash new pans before using them and lightly coat the inside with vegetable oil. Apply vegetable oil again after each washing in the dishwasher and after treating stains, following the procedure described above. Do not soak pans in soapy water; the coating can retain a soap flavor.

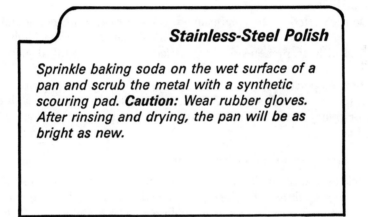

Stainless-Steel Polish

*Sprinkle baking soda on the wet surface of a pan and scrub the metal with a synthetic scouring pad. **Caution:** Wear rubber gloves. After rinsing and drying, the pan will be as bright as new.*

Stainless Steel

Stainless steel requires practically no special care. It is dishwasher safe, but if you wash it by hand, dry it promptly to prevent water spots.

Letting a pot boil over high heat for a long period of time or allowing a gas flame to lick up the sides of a pan will discolor stainless steel. Storing the cookware stacked with other pots may cause surface scratches.

Many commercial products will shine stainless steel. We recommend that you follow the manufacturer's instructions for the best results.

DINNERWARE

Almost every meal you eat at home results in dirty dishes. That could be more than a thousand sinkfuls of dishes annually. Washing dishes is one of the few housecleaning tasks that is truly unavoidable; the trick is to get it done and out of the way as quickly as possible. Here are a few hints to help you do dishes without doing yourself in.

Of course, the best hint for making dishwashing easier is to use a dishwasher. If you have a dishwasher, carefully read the manufacturer's instructions for loading, correct water temperatures, and preferred dishwasher detergents.

We recommend that you remove food residues from dinnerware as quickly as possible. Scrape dishes with a rubber scraper or plastic brush to prevent scratches. Never scrape plates with knives or other sharp objects. Rinse out coffeecups and teacups before residues have a chance to stain the cups. Use cool water to soak or wash dishes that have been used to serve eggs or cheese. Acid foods, such as tomatoes, vinegar, and wine, allowed to remain on glazed dinnerware can pit the surface.

To protect glass or china from chipping or breaking while you are hand washing it, use a plastic dishpan or rubber sink mat. You can also pad the bottom of the sink with a towel. Avoid abrupt changes of temperature when you wash china.

Do not wash delicate, hand-painted, gold- or silver-trimmed, or antique dinnerware in the dishwasher. Metal-trimmed dinnerware should also not be soaked in soapy water for long periods of time; this will damage the trim.

High temperatures may also damage dishes. Do not warm plates in the oven unless they are heatproof. Do not rinse glazed dinnerware with very hot or boiling water; this may cause the glaze to craze, or develop minute cracks.

FLATWARE AND CUTLERY

Most of us wash the knives, forks, and spoons we use at mealtimes along with our other dishes. If we're organized and wash dishes by hand, the flatware is washed after the glasses and before the plates. But washing flatware doesn't complete the cleaning process; unless you eat with stainless steel, your flatware will need to be polished occasionally.

Cutlery (knives and other cutting instruments) can be cleaned in the same way as flatware, but observe the manufacturer's instructions to be sure that the cutlery is dishwasher safe. Here are some of the best methods we've found for cleaning and polishing flatware and cutlery.

Always wash pewter and gold-plated flatware by hand and buff dry to bring up the shine and prevent water spots. Sterling silver and silver plate may be washed in the dishwasher, but they will need to be polished less often if they are washed by hand. Rinse salt and acid food off flatware as soon as possible to avoid stains.

Do not soak flatware or cutlery that has bone, ivory, or wood handles, and do not wash them in the dishwasher.

Use silver often; it tarnishes less and grows more beautiful with use. Store silver and gold flatware in rolls, bags, or cases made with tarnish-resistant cloth.

Do not allow stainless-steel flatware to touch anything made of silver in the dishwasher. It will set up an electrolytic action that pits the stainless steel and leaves black spots on the silver.

Wash flatware and cutlery with liquid dishwashing detergent. Fill the sink with hot water, add the detergent, and wash the flatware using a soft cloth or sponge to wipe away the soil. Never use an abrasive cleanser, steel-wool pad, or synthetic scouring pad. Avoid overcrowding the sink to prevent scratching your flatware. After it is clean, rinse with hot water, and buff with a soft towel to bring up the shine.

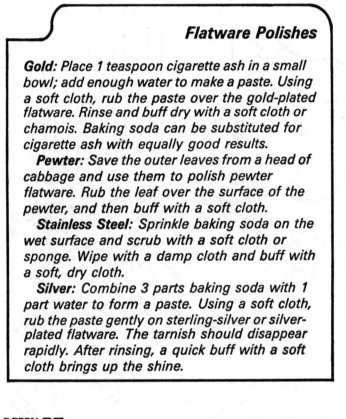

Flatware Polishes

Gold: *Place 1 teaspoon cigarette ash in a small bowl; add enough water to make a paste. Using a soft cloth, rub the paste over the gold-plated flatware. Rinse and buff dry with a soft cloth or chamois. Baking soda can be substituted for cigarette ash with equally good results.*

Pewter: *Save the outer leaves from a head of cabbage and use them to polish pewter flatware. Rub the leaf over the surface of the pewter, and then buff with a soft cloth.*

Stainless Steel: *Sprinkle baking soda on the wet surface and scrub with a soft cloth or sponge. Wipe with a damp cloth and buff with a soft, dry cloth.*

Silver: *Combine 3 parts baking soda with 1 part water to form a paste. Using a soft cloth, rub the paste gently on sterling-silver or silver-plated flatware. The tarnish should disappear rapidly. After rinsing, a quick buff with a soft cloth brings up the shine.*

GLASSWARE

Most glassware can be safely washed in the dishwasher, but gilt- and silver-trimmed glass, delicate crystal, milk glass, and ornamental glass must be washed by hand. If you have soft water in your area, we recommend that you wash all glassware by hand because the combination of soft water and dishwasher detergent will etch and permanently dull glassware.

Before you wash glassware, cushion the bottom of the sink with a towel or rubber mat. Add vinegar to the wash water or rinse water for more sparkle; ammonia in the wash water will cut grease on glassware. Wash glasses first, before cutlery or dinnerware. Slowly slide stemware into the wash water, holding the glass by the base; if you push a glass into the water bottom first, it could crack. Remove dirt from crevices with a soft-bristled brush; remove stains by rubbing with a cut lemon or washing in a vinegar

Slide a glass slowly into dish water, rim first. If you plunge the bottom of the glass in the water, it is likely to break.

solution. Let glassware drip dry upside down, or polish with a soft, lint-free cloth.

Clean stained decanters by filling them with water and adding 1 cup ammonia or vinegar. Soak overnight. If this solution does not clean the decanter, use two packs of powdered denture cleaner dissolved in water.

FOOD–PREPARATION, STORAGE, AND SERVING UTENSILS

Most food-preparation, storage, and serving utensils are made of plastic, rubber, metal, or wood. Because we use these tools every day, they should be easy to maintain. Metal is the easiest to clean, since it can be washed, does not retain food odors, and does not deteriorate in water the way wood does. The other materials, while relatively simple to care for, do need special treatment.

Metal

Metal cooking utensils, such as pancake turners, potato mashers, and cooking forks, are usually made of aluminum or stainless steel. They can be cleaned in hot, soapy water or put through the dishwasher. Never soak metal utensils with glued-on handles; the adhesive will weaken.

Plastic and Rubber

Plastic utensils and containers, such as orange-juice pitchers, covered storage bowls, and spatulas, and rubber food-preparation tools, such as scrapers, drain boards, and sink mats, are cared for in much the same way. We recommend that you don't expose plastic and rubber to high heat. Some plastics will melt and warp, and heat and sunlight can cause rubber products to crack.

Check the manufacturer's instructions to see if an item is dishwasher safe. Do not use solvents, harsh abrasives, or scouring pads to remove stains from plastic or rubber.

A thick paste made with equal parts baking soda and water is very effective for removing stubborn soil and stains from plastic and rubber utensils. It deodorizes as it cleans. Apply the paste to plastic with a sponge or soft cloth; a synthetic scouring pad can be used on rubber. **Caution:** Wear rubber gloves.

Another way to remove odor from a plastic container is to crumple a piece of newspaper into the container, secure the lid tightly, and leave it overnight. The paper will absorb the odor.

Wood

Wood food-preparation equipment, such as bowls, trays, rolling pins, spoons, salad utensils, and cutting boards, needs special care to prevent warping and cracking. Because wood is porous, it absorbs moisture. When it dries out, the wood may be rough because the water has raised the grain. We recommend that you periodically clean and oil cutting boards to restore their smooth surfaces and to protect them from moisture. Some salad bowls are finished with a waterproof varnish, but many people prefer to keep their bowls untreated to absorb seasonings and enhance the flavor of the salad.

Wipe woodenware immediately after using it with a sponge or paper towel moistened in cold water. If the item needs to be washed, don't let it soak in water and never put it in the dishwasher. Wash woodenware quickly; then rinse immediately, wipe dry, and air-dry thoroughly before storing.

Remove stains from woodenware with a solution of ¼ cup chlorine bleach and 1 quart warm water. Rinse and dry, then coat with vegetable oil. Get rid of odors by rubbing the surface with a slice of lemon.

Woodenware Cleaner

*Baking soda cleans and deodorizes wood. Mix ½ cup baking soda with 1 quart warm water and rub it on the wood surface. **Caution:** Wear rubber gloves. Use a synthetic scouring pad to clean a cutting board. Scour the gummy residue on the edges of the board. Rinse with clear water, blot the moisture with a towel, and air-dry completely. Bring back the natural wood finish by giving woodenware a coat of boiled linseed oil, salad-bowl finishing oil, or vegetable oil, rubbed in with a synthetic scouring pad. Apply two thin coats 24 hours apart, wiping off the excess a half hour after each application.*

CLEANING INSIDE YOUR HOME

(continued)

CLEANING INSIDE YOUR HOME

(continued)

B athroom and kitchen messes are unique, and we clean these rooms in special ways. But the other rooms of our homes are pretty much the same—rectangular cubes that collect dirt, clutter, grease stains, and dirty socks. When it comes to cleaning, a wall is a wall; it's not a family-room wall or a living-room wall. Which is not to say that all walls are cleaned in the same way. There are painted walls, papered walls, vinyl-covered walls, as well as all the other kinds of walls you have in your home. So in this chapter we're going to look into the best and quickest ways to clean the various surfaces in your home. (In the next chapter, we'll get to the furniture.)

The best way to clean all the above-floor areas in your home is to use your Eureka vacuum with its brush and crevice attachments. Regular vacuuming to pick up loose dirt on ceilings, walls, and woodwork saves you time and effort. Because dirt is not allowed to build up, you won't have to get out the buckets and brushes very often. Vacuuming before you clean with water or other cleaning solutions makes the job faster and easier; you're washing away only the sticky, gooey messes that need to be washed, instead of using a damp sponge to smear around loose dirt.

Ceilings

Most of us ignore our ceilings until cobwebs hang down so far they block our view of the television or until we're flat on our backs with flu. When we finally look up, we're likely to see a grayish, brownish haze, combining the smoke of burned toast with cooking grease and all kinds of airborne particles. If your ceiling has lost its original color, you'll have to brush away the cobwebs and wipe away the smog. It's not something you need to do very often, but we're here to help you when the time comes.

A few basic tips for ceiling cleaning:

- Lift cobwebs off ceilings with your Eureka vacuum cleaner and its brush attachment. Be careful not to crush cobwebs onto the ceiling; they will leave black smudge marks.
- Wash or clean ceilings before walls if you are cleaning the whole room. But watch out for drips; if you allow drips to run down walls, they may leave permanent marks.
- Protect furniture and floors with plastic drop cloths or newspaper while you clean the ceiling.
- Use a sponge mop to clean ceilings so you won't need a ladder.

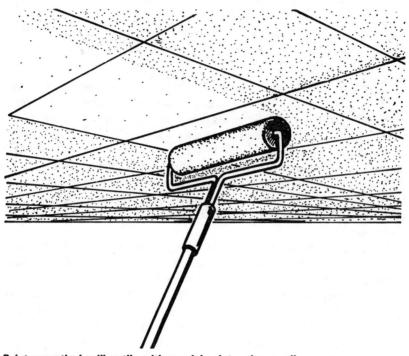

Paint acoustical ceiling tile with special paint, using a roller.

ACOUSTICAL TILE AND SUSPENDED PANEL

Acoustical ceiling treatments are made of porous materials to absorb noise. You can wash vinyl-coated acoustical ceilings. Use an all-purpose cleaning solution applied with a sponge mop. Noncoated tiles generally are not washable, but you can spot-clean them, using special products available at hardware stores. When an overall cleaning is needed, we recommend an application of acoustical-tile paint.

TILE

Vinyl-coated ceiling tile can be cleaned with an all-purpose cleaning solution. Nonwashable tiles can be spot-cleaned with products available at most hardware and paint stores. When an overall cleaning is needed, paint the tiles with either latex or oil-based paint.

PAINTED

The most frequently used ceiling paint is *latex*, which is easy to wash after it has "cured," or set for a period of time. The other kind of paint used on ceiling is *alkyd*, or oil-based; it is durable and washable and comes

Painted-Ceiling Cleaner

*Mix ½ cup vinegar, 1 cup clear ammonia, ¼ cup baking soda, and 1 gallon warm water. **Caution:** Wear rubber gloves, and work in a well-ventilated area when using this solution. Apply it to the ceiling with a sponge and rinse with clear water.*

in three finishes: flat, semigloss, and gloss. Flat and semigloss are most often used on ceilings, but some bathroom and kitchen ceilings are gloss.

We recommend that you clean painted ceilings with commercial liquid or powdered all-purpose cleaners, following the manufacturer's instructions, rinse with clear water, and allow to dry.

PAPERED

Paper-covered ceilings are not washable. When you need to clean them, we recommend that you use a commercial wallpaper cleaning product and follow the manufacturer's instructions for the best results.

We've found that you can remove smudges from papered ceilings by very gently rubbing the spots with an art gum eraser. General soil comes off when a piece of rye bread is wadded up and used like an eraser. To clean a grease spot, blot it with paper toweling and gently press cornstarch on the stain. After the cornstarch absorbs the grease, rub it off gently.

Vinyl-Covered Ceiling Cleaner

*Mix ½ cup vinegar and 1 quart water. Gently apply the solution to the ceiling with a sponge. **Caution:** Wear rubber gloves when you work with this cleaner. Don't let the ceiling get too wet; moisture could seep under the seams and loosen the backing of the vinyl.*

Vinyl-Covered Ceiling Cleaner

You can make a "dry detergent" to clean vinyl ceiling coverings. Mix ¼ cup dishwashing liquid with 1 cup warm water in a mixing bowl and beat the solution with an eggbeater to a stiff foam. Working in a small area, dip a sponge into the foam and apply it to the ceiling to loosen dirt. Rinse the detergent with a sponge dipped in clear water and squeezed dry.

Many ceilings are "papered" with washable vinyl. Some manufacturers of vinyl wall-coverings caution against using ammonia-based cleaners. Be sure to check the instructions for cleaning your particular ceiling, or test your ceiling covering in an inconspicuous area before you attempt to clean the entire surface.

PLASTER

Decorative plaster ceilings, as opposed to flat, painted plaster ceilings, can't be cleaned because of their unpainted surface and deep texture. When a plaster ceiling becomes dirty, the best treatment is first to vacuum it, using a brush attachment on your Eureka vacuum cleaner, and then respray it with plaster.

SPRAY–ON ACOUSTICAL FINISH

This rough, sound-absorbing finish is often used in new construction and remodeling. Spray-on acoustical finishes are relatively inexpensive and quick to apply. They cover cracks and other ceiling imperfections. But this kind of ceiling can't be cleaned. When the ceiling becomes dirty, the best thing to do is to vacuum it, using a brush attachment on your Eureka vacuum cleaner. Then respray it with a thin coat of the original finish. You can rent spray equipment at most paint stores.

Fireplaces

Whether your fireplace is so small that it fits neatly into a corner of your den or so massive that it spans the entire length of a wall, a fireplace is not a purely decorative piece. You can't just dust it off every once in a while and let it go at that. A fireplace needs regular care and cleaning to assure its safety and efficiency. Creosote, a flammable, tarlike substance that ac-

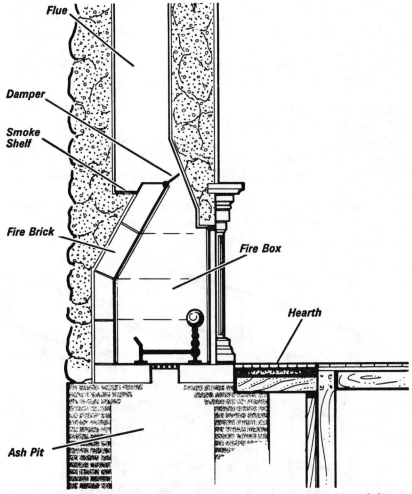

As a fireplace is used, soot builds up in the firebox and on the sides of the flue. To prevent problems, clean the chimney and ash pit regularly.

cumulates in the chimney and flue, must be removed to eliminate a potential fire hazard.

We suggest that you give your fireplace and its accessories routine cleanings throughout the wood-burning season; then you won't end up in the spring with an accumulation of soot, ashes, and creosote.

Use your Eureka vacuum cleaner frequently to prevent dust and soot from building up on the hearth. But do not vacuum until all the embers have been extinguished for at least 12 hours.

Burn only seasoned, well-dried wood to minimize dangerous creosote buildup.

Inspect the firebox, flue, and chimney yearly for creosote accumulation.

Do not use water to drown a fire; it will make a paste of the ashes that is difficult to remove. We recommend that you keep a fire extinguisher near the fireplace at all times.

Never use an abrasive cleanser inside the fireplace. Many leave a flammable residue, and they can wear away firebrick.

ANDIRONS AND BRASS OR BRASS–PLATED TOOLS

There are many commercially available products that can restore brass fireplace tools to their original beauty with a little time and effort. If you choose to use one, be sure to follow the manufacturer's instructions for the best results.

You can also clean andirons by dipping fine-grade (000) steel wool in cooking oil and rubbing gently. **Caution:** Wear rubber gloves to protect your hands. Apply polish to bring up the shine.

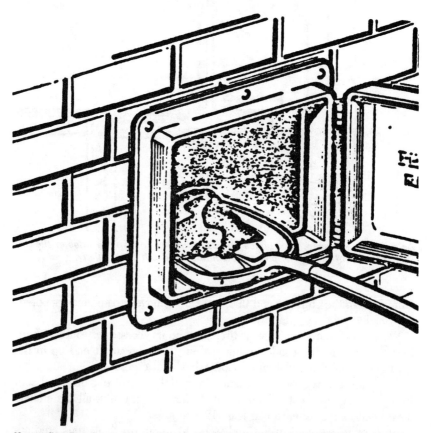

If your fireplace has a door to its ash pit on the outside of your house, open it to remove ashes.

CHIMNEY AND FLUE

Your fireplace chimney and flue must be cleaned properly at least every two years to assure a safe fire. But for the most efficient use of your fireplace, we suggest that you have it professionally cleaned once a year.

FIREBOX

The firebox is the part of the fireplace that contains the fire; it is commonly constructed of either metal sheeting or firebrick. Since the heat of the fire keeps the firebox clean (in much the same way a self-cleaning oven works), very little upkeep is required.

Gently scrub the walls of the firebox opening with a stiff-bristled brush (not a wire brush) to the height of the lintel (the steel brace that supports the masonry above the fireplace opening). Be gentle with firebrick because it crumbles easily. Be careful not to bend any edges on a metal firebox where it joins the flue. Bent edges leave openings to the wall studs where fire could spread.

If your fireplace does not have an ash pit, shovel the bulk of the ashes into a trash bag. Then use your Eureka vacuum cleaner to remove the remaining lightweight ashes.

FIRE SCREEN

Most fire screens are made of black-painted metal, but if your screen is brass plated, clean it as you would other brass objects.

If your brass-plated fireplace screen is coated with lacquer to protect its shine and this coating is cracked or peeling, you can clean it quickly with a solution of baking soda and boiling water (1 cup soda to 2 gallons water). Let the screen stand in the solution until it cools, then peel off the lacquer. You can either have the screen relacquered or clean and polish it.

You can also clean brass-plated fire screens by dipping fine-grade (000) steel wool in cooking oil and rubbing gently. **Caution:** Wear rubber gloves.

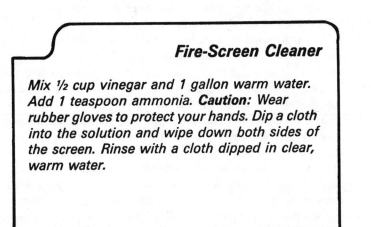

Fire-Screen Cleaner

*Mix ½ cup vinegar and 1 gallon warm water. Add 1 teaspoon ammonia. **Caution:** Wear rubber gloves to protect your hands. Dip a cloth into the solution and wipe down both sides of the screen. Rinse with a cloth dipped in clear, warm water.*

Cleaner for Glass Fireplace Enclosures

Remove smoke stains with a solution of ½ cup vinegar in 1 gallon warm water. Add 1 tablespoon clear ammonia. Either spray this mixture on the glass or wipe it on with a cloth. **Caution:** *Wear rubber gloves. Rinse with clear, warm water and dry with a clean cloth.*

GLASS ENCLOSURE

Glass enclosures for fireplaces defeat their purpose if you can't see through them. The best way to care for heat-resistant, tempered glass is to keep it clean. After every second fire, remove the residue of soot from the glass.

If soot has baked on your glass fireplace enclosure, scrape the glass very carefully with a glass scraper. Avoid scratching the surface by taking your time and using a sharp blade.

GRATE AND CAST-IRON TOOLS

If you burn green wood, your fireplace grate can accumulate a buildup of creosote or sap. If you always burn seasoned wood, you will probably never have to clean the grate.

We recommend that you remove creosote or sap that is not baked on the grate before you use the fireplace again. Take the grate outside and hose it down. If it is too cold to work outside, don't put off cleaning the grate; find a place to do this messy job inside. Sprinkle an abrasive cleanser on the grate; scrub with a stiff-bristled brush or use a steel-wool soap pad. No precautions need to be taken, but we recommend that you wear rubber gloves to protect your hands from abrasion.

If sap and creosote have baked onto your fireplace grate, the only way to remove the baked-on residues is with commercial oven cleaner. Work outdoors, wear rubber gloves, and observe all the manufacturer's suggested safety precautions. Allow the cleaner to sit overnight.

Unpainted iron surfaces, such as fireplace tools, that are not continuously exposed to the heat of the fire can rust. We suggest that you protect iron fireplace tools with liquid wax and buff them to bring up highlights.

MANTEL AND HEARTH

Warming the room is only a seasonal and secondary occupation for most fireplaces; their primary function is to look good. A mantel gives you a place to put Aunt Sarah's heirloom clock, something to arrange the living room furniture around, and somewhere to lean when you need to have a formal picture taken. A blackened mantel and a dusty hearth won't fill the bill; your fireplace is a showpiece and should look like one. But keeping up appearances does not require daily drudgery if you follow our hints.

The trim surrounding a fireplace is usually made from masonry tile or wood. Brick, marble, and ceramic tile are also used.

Brick

You can quickly remove smoke stains from above a fireplace opening by using an abrasive cleanser. Scrub the powder into the moistened brick surface and then rinse well with clear water to make sure no white residue remains.

If brick is especially dirty, use a commercial brick cleaner and a stiff-bristled brush. Rinse with clear hot water and wipe dry. **Caution:** Wear rubber gloves when using this strong solution, and keep it and other dangerous chemicals out of the reach of children.

Ceramic-Tile Cleaner

*Mix ½ cup vinegar, 1 cup clear ammonia, ¼ cup baking soda, and 1 gallon warm water. **Caution:** Wear rubber gloves, and work in a well-ventilated area when using this powerful solution. Apply the solution to the mantel and hearth with a sponge and rinse with clear water. Wipe dry to prevent water spots.*

Ceramic Tile

Both glazed and unglazed ceramic tile are used for mantels and hearths. Unglazed tile should be treated periodically with a sealer to keep its slightly porous surface from becoming stained. Glazed ceramic tile is virtually stainproof, but that isn't true of the grout that holds the tiles in place.

We recommend that you use a toothbrush or nailbrush to clean grout. Do not use harsh abrasive cleaners on stained grout; they might scratch the glaze on the ceramic tile.

Many aerosol-foam and spray tile-and-grout cleaners are available. Always follow the manufacturer's instructions, then rinse with clear water and buff dry to finish the job. **Caution:** Wear rubber gloves to avoid skin contact with these powerful cleaners, and take care not to breathe the mist from spray cleaners.

Marble

Remove dust from your marble mantel with your Eureka vacuum cleaner. Then wipe with a damp sponge to remove light soil.

Abrasive or caustic cleaners will scratch marble. Oil polishes and soft waxes may discolor it. Many commercial cleaners are available, but borax rubbed into the surface with a moistened cloth will also clean marble. Rinse with warm water and buff dry with a soft cloth. This technique also brightens light-colored marble.

Masonry Tile

Masonry tile is very easy to care for. We recommend that you sprinkle dry baking soda onto the tile. Rub it with a soft-bristled brush to absorb stains and clean the tile. Use your Eureka vacuum cleaner to remove the dry powder.

Oil Finish

This make-it-yourself polish is one of the best products for restoring the beauty of mantels that have an oil finish. Pour equal parts turpentine and boiled linseed oil into a jar, tighten the lid, and shake the solution to blend it thoroughly. **Caution:** *Wear rubber gloves. Pour a small amount of the mixture onto a soft cloth and rub the wood, following the grain. The wood will appear oily, but within an hour the polish will be completely absorbed, leaving a lovely soft sheen.*

Wood, Oiled or Waxed Natural Finish

Many commercial oil and wax finishes for wood are available. For the best results, follow the manufacturer's instructions. Never apply wax or furniture polish over an oil finish.

Wood, Painted

Mantels are usually painted with oil-based paints that are very easy to clean. First, use your Eureka vacuum cleaner to remove loose dirt. If your mantel has carved decorative elements, you may want to blow dirt from the carving by putting the hose in the blower end of your vacuum cleaner.

After you have removed dust from the mantel, mix 2 tablespoons dishwashing detergent in 1 gallon warm water. Wipe it on with a cloth or sponge. Don't let any excess run off; it can stain surrounding surfaces. We recommend that you clean from the bottom up to avoid streaking.

Radiators, Heat Vents, and Returns

Don't believe your eyes: The heating element in your room doesn't create dirt, it just collects it. Radiators, baseboard heating units, portable heaters, registers, and heat-distributing devices in the fireplace acquire dust from the air currents created by their heat. Unless you clean your heating outlets, they'll recirculate all that dirt onto your walls, draperies, and home furnishings. But when you clean them, you remove the dirt they have collected, quickly cutting down on dirt buildup in your home.

The best way to clean all kinds of heating units is to vacuum them with your Eureka vacuum cleaner. We suggest that you make it a habit to vac-

To clean dust from between the fins of your radiator, cover it with damp newspaper and blow the dirt into the paper with the blower of your Eureka vacuum cleaner.

Radiator Cleaner

After thoroughly vacuuming the radiator to remove dust, clean the unit with a solution made from ½ cup vinegar, 1 cup ammonia, and ¼ cup baking soda in a gallon of hot water. **Caution:** *Wear rubber gloves, and work in a well-ventilated area when you use this powerful solution. Place newspapers and/or drop cloths under the radiator to protect the floor from moisture, and apply the solution with a sponge or cloth. Use a long-handled brush to clean the fins of radiators; a ruler draped with cloth will also work. Rinse with clear water.*

uum heating units whenever you vacuum the floor. Use a crevice tool to get into hard-to-reach places. For tight spots, such as between the fins of radiators, use the blower end of the vacuum and blow the dust out onto wet newspaper.

If you have forced-air heat, remove the grids covering the vents and returns, and vacuum their backs. Also, clean inside the duct as far as the hose of your Eureka vacuum cleaner will reach.

Wash the surfaces of baseboard units and radiators with an all-purpose cleaner when they begin to look grimy.

Walls

Walls get dirty in the same passive way that ceilings do: Grime and dust float through the air, land on them, and stick. But walls also get dirty in more active ways—when toddlers try out their crayons, chocolate-bar eaters switch on lights, and exuberant chefs toss spaghetti. Unless you deal with the passive dirt buildup on walls, attempts to wipe up after your active family will result in a smeary mess or leave a streak of clean-wall color in sharp contrast to the rest of your wall.

Use your Eureka vacuum cleaner with a floor/wall brush to vacuum your walls whenever you clean the room. Go behind pictures and mirrors with the small-brush attachment.

Remove cobwebs carefully. Don't press them against the wall; they'll leave a smudge.

Use an all-purpose cleaner for cleaning washable walls. We recommend that you test the product by first washing an inconspicuous place to make

A bracelet made from a sponge or washcloth and held around your wrist with a rubber band will keep water from running down your arm when you wash walls.

sure it does not harm your wall. Wash walls from the bottom to the top, overlapping the cleaned areas to prevent streaks. We've found that you can keep water from running down your arm when you wash walls by making a bracelet from a sponge or washcloth held in place with a thick rubber band.

To remove transparent tape from a wall without marring the paint or wallpaper, use a warm iron. Through a protective cloth, press the tape with the iron to soften and loosen its adhesive backing.

Remove finger smudges while they are fresh. But do not scrub with excessive pressure, or use synthetic scouring pads or abrasive cleaners.

BRICK

A wall made of brick requires little attention if you use your Eureka vacuum cleaner to remove loose dirt regularly. A solution of hot water and an all-purpose cleaner will clean accumulated dirt and stains from the surface. If the mortar between the bricks is especially dirty, add chlorine bleach to the cleaning solution. Wet the areas below a smoke stain before you wash it; this will prevent runoffs from staining the lower tiers of bricks.

Slight smoke stains above a fireplace opening are quickly removed with abrasive cleanser. Scrub the powder into the moistened brick and then

When you wash a brick wall, wet the area below where you are cleaning, so that runoff dirty water does not stain it.

rinse with clear water, making sure no white residue remains. If spot-cleaning changes the color of the brick, you can even out the color by rubbing another brick of the same color over the discolored surface.

If the brick wall is especially dirty, use a commercial brick cleaner and a stiff-bristled brush. Rinse with clear, hot water, and wipe dry. **Caution:** Wear rubber gloves when using a strong solution, and keep it and other dangerous chemicals out of the reach of children.

CERAMIC TILE

We recommend that you clean both glazed and unglazed ceramic tile regularly with an all-purpose cleaning solution or a spray tile-and-grout cleaner. **Caution:** Use rubber gloves to avoid skin contact, and don't breathe the mist when spraying the tile. Scrub dirt from the grout with a toothbrush or nailbrush, taking care not to scratch the tile. After cleaning, a clear-water rinse is recommended. Then buff with a soft, dry cloth to bring out the shine on glazed tile.

You can clean darkened grout with a solution of ¼ cup liquid chlorine bleach and 1 quart water. Scrub this cleaner into the grout with a toothbrush and rinse with clear water.

Grout can also be cleaned with a paste made from 3 parts baking soda and 1 part water. Apply this to the grout with a damp cloth, scrub with a toothbrush, and rinse with clear water.

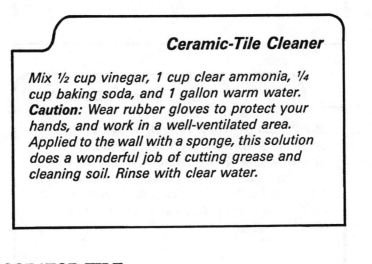

Ceramic-Tile Cleaner

*Mix ½ cup vinegar, 1 cup clear ammonia, ¼ cup baking soda, and 1 gallon warm water. **Caution:** Wear rubber gloves to protect your hands, and work in a well-ventilated area. Applied to the wall with a sponge, this solution does a wonderful job of cutting grease and cleaning soil. Rinse with clear water.*

DECORATOR TILE

Self-sticking decorator tiles, which are often vinyl-coated, are grease- and stain-resistant. A quick wipe with a sponge dipped in an all-purpose cleaning solution is usually all that is needed to keep them fresh and bright. You should try to avoid excessive moisture; it might seep between the seams and loosen the backing.

METAL TILE

We recommend that you wipe metal tile with a cloth dampened with an all-purpose cleaner and then buff with a soft, dry cloth to avoid streaking.

MIRROR TILE

You clean all mirror tiles in the same way, whether they are clear, smoked, or have a design painted or etched on them.

We recommend that you use one of the following homemade cleaners; they are as effective as commercial products and cost a lot less. Never use soap on mirror tile; it will streak and leave a film.

Cleaner for Mirror Tile

Mix ⅓ cup clear ammonia in 1 gallon warm water. Apply with a sponge/squeegee or pour the solution into a spray container and spray it directly onto the mirror tiles. **Caution:** Wear rubber gloves. Buff with a lint-free cloth, chamois, or paper toweling. Vinegar may be substituted for ammonia.

Cleaner for Mirror Tile

Mix 2 cups isopropyl rubbing alcohol (70 percent), 2 tablespoons liquid dishwashing detergent, and 2 cups water. Stir the solution until thoroughly mixed, then pour it into a pump bottle, and spray it directly onto the mirror tiles. Buff with a lint-free cloth, chamois, or paper toweling.

Cleaner for Mirror Tile

Pour vinegar into a shallow bowl or pan, crumple a sheet of newspaper, dip it in the vinegar, and apply to the tile. Wipe the mirror tile several times with the same newspaper until it is almost dry, then shine the tile with a clean, soft cloth or dry newspaper.

PAINTED

Most walls are painted with *latex*, which is easy to wash after it has "cured," or set for a period of time. The other kind of wall paint, *alkyd*, or oil-based, is more durable than latex, but it is more difficult to apply. Both types of paint come in three finishes: flat, semigloss, and gloss.

We recommend that you clean painted walls with a commercial all-purpose cleaner or use the following recipe for a homemade cleaner.

We have found that you can lift crayon marks off a painted wall by rubbing them carefully with a cloth or sponge dampened with mineral spirits or lighter fluid. Remove any shine by sponging it lightly with hot water.

Painted-Wall Cleaner

Mix ½ cup vinegar, 1 cup clear ammonia, ¼ cup baking soda, and 1 gallon warm water. ***Caution:*** *Wear rubber gloves, and work in a well-ventilated area when using this powerful solution. Apply the solution to the wall with a sponge and rinse with clear water. If your walls have a rough texture, use old nylon stockings or socks rather than a sponge because they won't tear and leave difficult-to-remove bits on the surface.*

PAPERED

Wallpaper is not washable. We recommend that you clean it only with commercial products, following the manufacturer's instructions for the best results. But we've found some simple, quick ways to clean up smears, spots, and writing on the wall between major cleaning.

- Smudges, fingerprints, and pencil marks can be removed from wallpaper by very gently rubbing the spots with an art gum eraser.
- General soil comes off when a piece of rye bread is wadded up and used like an eraser.
- To clean a grease spot, blot it with paper toweling and sprinkle cornstarch on the stain. After the cornstarch absorbs the grease, rub it off gently and vacuum.
- You can also place a white blotter over a grease spot and press it with a moderately hot iron. The blotter will soak up the grease. Repeat as required.
- To remove crayon marks from wallpaper, rub carefully with a dry soap-filled, fine-grade steel-wool pad. Or use a wad of white paper toweling

moistened with dry-cleaning solvent to delicately sponge the surface. Carefully blot and lift in small areas to prevent the solvent from spreading and discoloring the wallpaper.

Cleaner for Vinyl Wall Coverings

Mix ½ cup vinegar and 1 quart water and gently apply the solution to the wall with a sponge. **Caution:** *Wear rubber gloves. Don't use too much moisture; it could seep under the seams and loosen the backing.*

VINYL

If your wall coverings are made of vinyl, rather than paper, they're washable. Some manufacturers caution against using ammonia-based cleaners, so be sure to check the instructions for cleaning your vinyl wall covering or test the cleaning product you plan to use on your wall in an inconspicuous area.

You can also use a "dry detergent" to clean a vinyl wall covering. Mix ¼ cup dishwashing liquid with 1 cup warm water in a mixing bowl and beat the mixture to a stiff foam with an eggbeater. Working in a small area, dip a sponge into the foam and apply it to the wall to loosen dirt. Rinse the detergent with a sponge that has been dipped in clear water and squeezed dry.

WOOD PANELING

All wood paneling is not finished in the same way, so it is not cleaned in the same way. If your paneling was left natural or stained with a water-based stain and not sealed, the only way you should clean it is with your Eureka vacuum cleaner. If your paneling has an oil finish, you can clean it with a commercial oil-based product or our homemade cleaner, but avoid any cleaning product that contains wax. If your paneling has a waxed finish, use only wax-based cleaners.

Using your Eureka vacuum cleaner with the wall-brush attachment is the best way to clean loose dirt from all kinds of wood paneling. Never use water to clean wood. If you use a spray or aerosol cleaner/polish, follow the manufacturer's instructions carefully.

> ## Oil Finish
>
> *This make-it-yourself polish restores the beauty of wood paneling that has an oil finish. Pour equal parts turpentine and boiled linseed oil into a jar, tighten the lid, and shake the liquid to blend it thoroughly. **Caution:** Wear rubber gloves. Pour a small amount of the mixture onto a soft cloth and rub up and down the paneling, following the grain of the wood. The wood will appear oily, but within an hour the polish will be completely absorbed, leaving a soft sheen on your paneling.*

We've found that if you need to remove white water marks from wood paneling, you can rub mayonnaise into them. Wipe off the mayonnaise 12 hours later. The marks will have vanished.

Windows

You can avoid washing your windows by keeping the drapes drawn, the shades down, or the blinds closed. But life without windows is a little gloomy, so we suggest that you plan to wash your windows twice a year, usually in the spring and in the fall. If you get everyone in the household involved in window washing, you can probably finish the task on a Saturday morning.

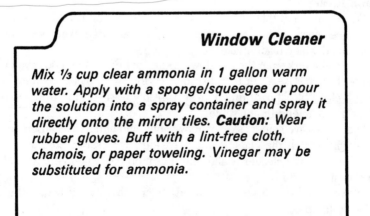

> ## Window Cleaner
>
> *Mix ⅓ cup clear ammonia in 1 gallon warm water. Apply with a sponge/squeegee or pour the solution into a spray container and spray it directly onto the mirror tiles. **Caution:** Wear rubber gloves. Buff with a lint-free cloth, chamois, or paper toweling. Vinegar may be substituted for ammonia.*

Wash windows on the outside with horizontal strokes and on the inside with vertical strokes. This makes it easy to track down streaks.

Put some of your crew to work inside and others outside. Tell those who are at work in the house to use vertical strokes; those working on the outside should use horizontal strokes. With this method, you can quickly track down streaks.

We recommend that you use a squeegee on a long handle or a sponge/squeegee combination to prevent streaks on large windows. An old windshield-wiper blade makes a good squeegee.

Wash windows from the top down to prevent drips on sections you've already cleaned. Use a soft toothbrush or cotton swab to clean corners. Rubbing a clean blackboard eraser over a freshly washed (and dried) window gives it a diamond-bright shine.

Soap will leave smudges on windowpanes, and abrasive cleansers or steel wool will scratch the glass. Window cleaners themselves pose a threat to woodwork. If the cleaner is allowed to drip on the windowsill, it can harm the paint or varnish.

We've found that if you wash windows on a hot or sunny day, the glass is likely to streak.

Window Cleaner

Pour vinegar into a shallow bowl or pan, crumple a sheet of newspaper, dip it in the vinegar, and apply to the window. Wipe the glass several times with the same newspaper until the window is almost dry, then shine the glass with a clean, soft cloth or dry newspaper.

Window Cleaner

Mix 2 cups isopropyl rubbing alcohol (70 percent), 2 tablespoons liquid dishwashing detergent, and 2 cups water. Stir the solution until thoroughly mixed and then pour it into a spray bottle. The alcohol keeps the cleaner from freezing on windowpanes in cold weather.

Window Cleaner

To remove built-up cooking grease or soot from windows, use a solution of 2 cups kerosene and 1 gallon warm water. Rub the mixture on the glass with a soft cloth and wipe the panes dry with clean paper toweling. **Caution:** Wear rubber gloves, and do not use this solution near an open flame because kerosene is flammable. This cleaner protects windows; water will bead on them in the same way it does on a waxed car.

Woodwork

Woodwork is constantly assaulted with the same kind of dirt and grime that hits walls. Most woodwork is painted, stained, or left natural with an oil or varnish finish. All woodwork should be vacuumed regularly with your Eureka vacuum cleaner. Don't forget the tops of doorjambs, window frames, cornices, and ledges as well as baseboards.

We recommend that you keep a small container of matching paint or stain handy to touch up nicks and scratches on woodwork.

When you wash door and window frames, work from the bottom up, using an all-purpose cleaner on painted surfaces to remove smudges and fingerprints. Clean stained and natural woodwork with a wood cleaner/polish. Do not use water or water-based cleaners on stained or natural woodwork except for light touch-ups that you buff dry quickly. Spray the cleaner onto a cloth instead of directly onto the woodwork to prevent staining adjoining surfaces.

Many commercial oil and wax finishes are available. For best results follow the manufacturer's instructions.

CLEANING YOUR HOME FURNISHINGS

(continued)

CLEANING YOUR HOME FURNISHINGS

(continued)

Copper
Gold
Ivory
Jade
Marble
Pewter
Porcelain
Silver

Metal
Plastic
Upholstery

Fabric • Leather • Vinyl

Wood

Oiled • Painted • Polished
• Specialty

Blinds
Curtains
Draperies
Shades
Shutters

I f your home is like most, much of your furniture probably does all kinds of things it wasn't intended to do. The upholstered chair by the front door is a catchall for schoolbooks and jackets. The dining table doubles as a sewing table, desk, or computer center. And many of us practically live in bed, snacking, reading, watching TV, or just recovering from the day at work. Grime builds up on the chair, lint sticks to the dining table, and cracker crumbs work their way into the mattress. Eventually, you've got to do something about cleaning your furniture or call a junk dealer to come and take it away.

We've found that you can maintain (or restore) the good looks of most furniture with the proper care. You can use (or misuse) your furniture the way you want, and still seat your great aunt in that upholstered chair, serve company dinner on the dining table, and roll over in your sleep without crunching crumbs. All the care most of your furniture requires is the regular removal of loose dirt with your Eureka vacuum cleaner and an occasional cleaning.

In this chapter, you'll find time-tested techniques for cleaning, polishing, and protecting the many different kinds of furniture and the treasured objects you have in your home. When your furniture requires more cleaning than a thorough going-over with your Eureka vacuum, you'll find information here to help you quickly restore its good looks and get it ready for company.

Bedding

When sheets and pillowcases are soiled, you can just toss them in the washing machine along with the rest of the wash. But other kinds of bedding require special care. The key to successful cleaning is to do it before the soil is heavy and to know the fabrics involved in order to use the right cleaning procedures. We suggest that you keep a file of manufacturers' care labels and refer to them when cleaning is necessary.

BEDSPREADS

Many bedspreads are washable. Before you wash your bedspread, we suggest that you dip a corner of it in the detergent solution you plan to use to check for colorfastness. If the color bleeds, have your bedspread dry-cleaned.

If it is safe to wash your bedspread, we advise you to wash it before it becomes heavily soiled. Treat spots and stains with a spray prewash product or liquid detergent. Use a large commercial washing machine for over-sized bedspreads. An overcrowded washer won't clean very well. Dry bedspreads across several clotheslines or in a large commercial dryer.

BLANKETS

Blankets are made of many different fibers and blends, but most of them are washable by hand or machine. Some wool blankets can be machine washed, some cannot. We recommend that you check the care label and follow the manufacturer's instructions.

Use your Eureka vacuum cleaner to remove dust and lint from blankets. We suggest that you also air blankets on a clothesline periodically to refresh them.

Before you wash a blanket, mend or replace bindings and treat spots and stains. Use a large commercial washer to wash large blankets. Fill the washer with water and put in the detergent so it can completely dissolve before you add the blanket. Use a gentle (delicate) wash cycle; long periods of agitation will mat blanket fibers. Also avoid overcrowding the machine. A fabric softener will increase a blanket's fluffiness and reduce static electricity.

Electric blankets should always be hand or machine washed, never dry-cleaned. Both cleaning solvents and mothproofing can damage the wiring in an electric blanket.

COMFORTERS AND QUILTS

Down-Filled

The down filling in comforters and quilts is held in place by tufts of yarn or by stitched-through patterns. Most down-filled comforters and quilts are washable, but some older ones are too fragile to be cleaned at home.

Follow the manufacturer's care instructions if they are available. Test older comforters and quilts for colorfastness by wetting an inconspicuous spot with the detergent solution you plan to use and blotting the area with a white blotter.

If comforters or quilts are in good condition, machine wash and dry them. Use cold wash water and rinse water and all-purpose detergent. Fragile down comforters and quilts should be hand washed in the bathtub or a deep laundry tub.

Drape the wet comforter or quilt over several clotheslines to allow excess moisture to drip out; reposition it periodically. If the comforter or quilt is strong enough to be dried in a clothes dryer, preheat the dryer to a low temperature and include a pair of clean, dry sneakers to help fluff the down. The dryer can also be set on air dry (no heat) to dry the quilt.

Wool-, Cotton-, and Synthetic-Filled

Padded bed coverings may be filled with wool, cotton batting, or polyester fiber. The filling is held in place by tufts of yarn or by stitched-through patterns. Most cotton- or polyester-filled comforters and quilts are washable, but older quilts may be too delicate to withstand washing. Some newer wool-filled or wool-covered comforters and quilts can be washed at home; others should be dry-cleaned.

Follow the manufacturer's care instructions if they are available. Test old quilts and comforters for colorfastness before attempting to wash them by wetting a small area with the detergent solution and blotting it with a white blotter. Clean patchwork quilts with the method that is appropriate for the most delicate fabric in the quilt. Never attempt to wash silk- or velvet-covered quilts and comforters.

For small- to medium-size quilts and comforters, use your home washing machine. For large quilts, use a commercial washer. Let quilts and comforters soak in the machine for about 10 minutes before starting them through a short, gentle (delicate) washing cycle.

Hand wash and line-dry old or fragile quilts and all quilts with cotton batting. Machine washing is too harsh and can cause cotton batting to bunch up. Use a bathtub or deep laundry tub, and allow the soap or detergent to dissolve in the wash water before adding the quilt.

MATTRESSES AND BOX SPRINGS

Mattresses are usually made with foam or springs and casings; some older mattresses were filled with hair, and futon mattresses are stuffed with cotton. All benefit from routine care: Vacuum mattresses and box springs, and turn the mattress over and around end-to-end to insure even wear. Use an upholstery attachment on your Eureka vacuum cleaner, and work carefully around any buttons on your mattress. Remove dust and blanket fluff from the edges of the box spring with your vacuum brush attachment.

We recommend covering mattresses with quilted or rubberized pads that can be quickly washed when they become soiled. Remove spots and stains promptly, but do not allow the mattress to become excessively wet when you spot clean it. Do not make the bed until the mattress is completely dry.

PILLOWS

Know the pillow's filling—down, feathers, foam, polyester, or kapok—so that you can use the appropriate cleaning method. For polyester-filled pillows, read the care-instruction tags; some polyester-filled pillows are washable, but some are not. Kapok is the silky covering of seeds from the ceiba tree; pillows with this stuffing need frequent airing but cannot be washed.

We recommend that you protect your pillows with a zip-on cotton or polyester cover, which you can wash regularly. Refresh pillows by airing them near an open window or hanging them on a clothesline outside.

Down and Feather

Fluff down and feather pillows when you make your bed to get rid of accumulated dust and to redistribute the filling. Before you wash a feather or down pillow, make sure it has no holes or ripped seams. Machine or hand wash feather and down pillows in cool water with cold-water, light-duty detergent. Wash two pillows at a time or add a couple of bath towels to balance the load. If the fabric is worn or the pillow is heavily stuffed, wash the feathers and ticking separately. Secure the feathers in a large muslin bag and stitch the opening closed.

Dry down and feather pillows in the dryer on the low-heat setting. Including a pair of clean, dry tennis shoes in the dryer will help distribute the down as it dries.

Foam
Hand wash and line-dry foam pillows. Change the hanging position hourly to dry the filling evenly. Never put a foam pillow in the dryer.

Polyester-Filled
Machine or hand wash polyester-filled pillows in warm water with an all-purpose detergent. A front-loading tumble washer rather than a top-loading machine works best for polyester pillows. Dry the pillows in the dryer on a moderate heat setting.

SLEEPING BAGS
Most sleeping bags are filled with polyester or down. Follow the manufacturer's washing instructions. We recommend that you wash your sleeping bag after each outdoor use. Treat spots and stains on the bag's cover with liquid detergent.

Wash down-filled sleeping bags in cool water with cold-water, light-duty detergent. Wash polyester-filled sleeping bags in warm water with all-purpose detergent.

If your sleeping bag can be machine dried, tumble it with a clean, dry tennis shoe to prevent matting and a clean, dry bath towel to absorb excess moisture. If you line-dry the sleeping bag, unzip it before drying.

Books and Records

Many of us have large and constantly expanding collections not only of books and records but also of audio- and videocassettes and compact discs. We've found that these newer media benefit from the same storing and cleaning methods that we recommend you use for books and records.

If you arrange books at the front of shelves, air will be able to circulate around them to prevent mustiness. You should also protect books from direct sunlight, which will fade the bindings and cause them to deteriorate.

The best way to clean books and slipcases for records, audio- and videocassettes, and compact discs is to vacuum them with the small-brush attachment on your Eureka vacuum cleaner. Tilt each book (or slipcase) back

Hold a book tightly shut when you remove soil from the edges of the pages with an art gum eraser.

and then forward, one at a time, on the shelf so you can remove the dust from the book's binding and edges.

To keep vinyl and imitation-leather book bindings looking as good as new, wipe the covers with a mild detergent solution, and then treat them with a light coating of petroleum jelly or vinyl dressing. Leather-bound books should be treated periodically with lightweight oil so that the leather won't dry out and crack.

To remove grease stains from books, rub the affected areas with soft white-bread crumbs. Badly soiled paper edges of books can be cleaned with an art gum eraser. Hold the book firmly by the covers so that you won't accidentally damage the pages if the book falls open.

If a book is damp, sprinkle the pages with cornstarch until the moisture has been absorbed, then vacuum the powder.

Vacuum your record, compact disc, and audiocassette collections and your stereo equipment regularly. If dust accumulates around the stylus, or needle, of your turntable, clean it with an artist's brush dipped in isopropyl alcohol. Clean lightly soiled records on the turntable. Gently hold a clean dust cloth on a record and allow the disc to turn at least three revolutions under the cloth. Since you are cleaning with the grooves, not across them, there is less chance of damaging the record.

Candlesticks

Candlesticks come in a vast array of styles, from simple, utilitarian models to ornate, elaborate designs. They can be made of a number of materials, including crystal, porcelain, silver, gold, brass, copper, pewter, or wood. The care of a particular candlestick depends on the material with which it is made. Routine cleaning consists of regular dusting and an occasional wipe with a damp sponge.

One problem common to all candlesticks is dripping wax. Remove a hardened wax drip by gently pushing it off the candlestick with the ball of your finger or your fingernail covered with a thin cloth to prevent scratching the surface. If the wax resists these methods, dip the candlestick in

A quick way to clean the crystals on your chandelier is to dip them in a solution of alcohol and water.

warm water to soften the wax for removal, or if the candlestick is not immersible, soften the wax with warm air from a hair dryer.

Silver candlesticks that have wax dripped on them can be cleaned unharmed if you put them in the freezer first. After the wax freezes, it will peel off easily.

Chandeliers

A chandelier can be cleaned without taking it down. Use your Eureka vacuum cleaner to dust your chandelier regularly and before cleaning it. In a drinking glass, mix a solution of ¼ cup denatured alcohol and ¾ cup water. Cover the floor or table under the chandelier with newspaper or a plastic drop cloth. Set up a ladder so that you can safely reach the pendants. Submerge the crystals in the glass for a few seconds, swishing them back and forth, and then let them air-dry.

Decorative Objects

Your prize possession may be a collection of pewter salt-and-pepper shakers depicting national monuments or the box of bone-handled knives your brother gave you on your birthday. You may treasure an alabaster figurine or an elephant-foot umbrella stand. The decorative objects you've collected and cherish add visual interest to your home and sometimes become treasured family heirlooms. They'll also need to be cleaned from time to time. Most of your things can be safely cared for at home, especially if frequent dusting has kept dirt from building up on their surfaces.

ALABASTER

Alabaster looks like marble and is made into vases, statues, lamp bases, and other ornamental objects. Although it comes in several colors and sometimes has a dark streak or band of color, the best-quality alabaster is pure white and translucent. It is fine-grained but soft enough to be scratched with a fingernail. Alabaster is easily broken, soiled, and weathered, and must be handled with care.

Dust alabaster frequently with a soft, untreated cloth or the small-brush attachment of your Eureka vacuum cleaner. We recommend that you gently blow dust away from intricate carving with the vacuum's blower.

An oil polish or soft wax will probably discolor alabaster, and abrasive or caustic cleaners will scratch it. Alabaster can be cleaned with commercial products that clean marble. **Caution:** Work in a well-ventilated area to avoid breathing fumes from these products; do not smoke while using them or work near an open flame because some marble-cleaning products are flammable.

Alabaster Cleaner

Clean alabaster with borax; it is mild enough not to scratch the surface. Dip a moistened cloth into a small amount of dry borax and rub it on the alabaster. Rinse with warm water and buff dry with a soft cloth.

BONE

Bone is an animal product, like ivory, and must be treated with special care. Dust bone frequently with a soft, untreated cloth or the small-brush attachment of your Eureka vacuum cleaner. You can also gently blow dust away from intricate carving with the vacuum's blower.

Occasionally, wash bone objects in mild soapsuds, rinse, and buff dry. Do not allow bone pieces that are cemented together to soak in water; the adhesive will loosen. Never wash bone-handled knives in the dishwasher.

BRASS

There are many brass polishes on the market. If you run out of the polish you usually use, we suggest you try one of the following solutions:

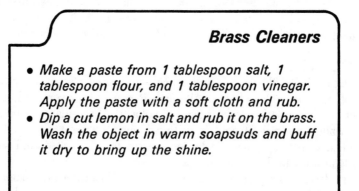

Brass Cleaners

- *Make a paste from 1 tablespoon salt, 1 tablespoon flour, and 1 tablespoon vinegar. Apply the paste with a soft cloth and rub.*
- *Dip a cut lemon in salt and rub it on the brass. Wash the object in warm soapsuds and buff it dry to bring up the shine.*

You can strip cracked and peeling lacquer from coated brass and brass-plated objects with a solution of baking soda and boiling water (1 cup soda to 2 gallons water). Let the article stand in the solution until it cools, then peel off the lacquer. You can either have the piece relacquered or clean and polish it yourself.

COPPER

You can clean and polish copper with one of the many commercial copper-cleaning products that are on the market. But if you don't have the cleaner you usually use on hand, try one of these methods:

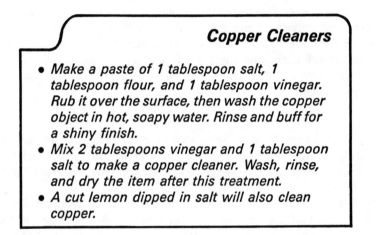

Copper Cleaners

- *Make a paste of 1 tablespoon salt, 1 tablespoon flour, and 1 tablespoon vinegar. Rub it over the surface, then wash the copper object in hot, soapy water. Rinse and buff for a shiny finish.*
- *Mix 2 tablespoons vinegar and 1 tablespoon salt to make a copper cleaner. Wash, rinse, and dry the item after this treatment.*
- *A cut lemon dipped in salt will also clean copper.*

GOLD

Gold has a brilliant luster that resists corrosion and tarnish. Gold is very soft and is usually combined with other metals to add hardness. The number of carats describes the purity of the gold: 24 carats is pure gold; 18, 14, and 10 carats have lesser amounts of gold.

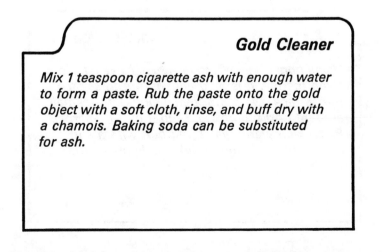

Gold Cleaner

Mix 1 teaspoon cigarette ash with enough water to form a paste. Rub the paste onto the gold object with a soft cloth, rinse, and buff dry with a chamois. Baking soda can be substituted for ash.

IVORY

Ivory, an animal dentin taken from elephants, hippopotamuses, walruses, and other sea creatures, is used for ornamental objects and piano keys. Dust ivory regularly with a soft cloth or the small-brush attachment of your Eureka vacuum cleaner. We recommend that you gently blow dust away from intricate carving with the vacuum's blower.

Occasionally wash ivory objects in mild soapsuds, rinse, and buff to dry. Do not allow ivory pieces that are cemented together to soak in water; the adhesive will loosen. Never wash ivory-handled knives in the dishwasher.

Keep ivory objects where light will reach them; continual darkness causes ivory to yellow. If you have a piece of ivory that is beginning to yellow, treat it with lemon and salt: Cut a lemon in half, dip it in salt, and rub it over the ivory. Let it dry, wipe the object with a damp cloth, and buff it dry for a bright finish.

JADE

Jade is used to make lamp bases, vases, carved ornaments, and jewelry. It is hard, heavy, and fine-grained. The color of jade ranges from white to dark green, with occasional tints of brown, mauve, blue, yellow, red, gray, or black.

Because jade is hard and not porous, very little care is required. Dust it regularly, and buff it with a soft cloth or chamois when it begins to look dull. If a jade piece becomes soiled or sticky, wipe it with a damp cloth and buff it with a dry cloth.

MARBLE

Marble is used to make tabletops, floors, countertops, walls, steps, fireplace facings, window and door sills, other building materials, and statuary. It comes in a variety of colors and has either a shiny or a mat finish.

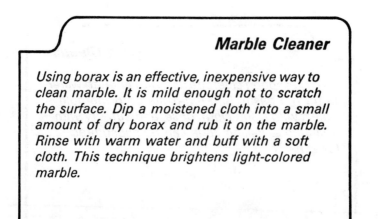

Marble Cleaner

Using borax is an effective, inexpensive way to clean marble. It is mild enough not to scratch the surface. Dip a moistened cloth into a small amount of dry borax and rub it on the marble. Rinse with warm water and buff with a soft cloth. This technique brightens light-colored marble.

Vacuum marble surfaces regularly using the small-brush attachment of your Eureka vacuum cleaner. Then wipe them with a damp sponge to remove light soil and buff to dry. Do not use abrasive or caustic cleaner on marble; it will mar the surface. We suggest that you not use oil polish or soft wax, it may discolor the marble.

Commercial polishes, some of which are flammable, are available for cleaning marble. Read and follow the manufacturer's directions.

PEWTER

Pewter can be cleaned with the outer leaves from a head of cabbage. Rub a leaf over the surface and then buff it with a soft cloth.

PORCELAIN

Porcelain and other types of clay are used to make vases, lamp bases, candlesticks, and figurines that depict everything from Elvis to Plymouth Rock.

Dust porcelain regularly with the small-brush attachment of your Eureka vacuum cleaner or a soft cloth. When a porcelain object becomes dirty, wash it in mild soapsuds, using warm water. Hot water can cause the glaze to craze. Pad the bottom of the sink with a towel and wrap another towel around the faucet to prevent breaking a delicate object in the sink. Never use abrasives or steel-wool pads on porcelain and do not wash it in the dishwasher.

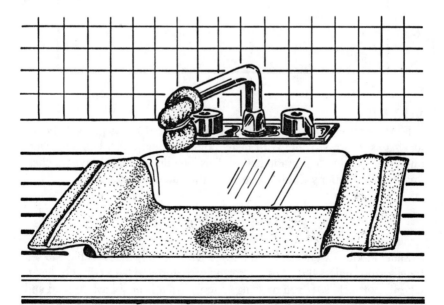

Padding the bottom of your sink with a towel and wrapping the faucet will protect delicate porcelain objects when you wash them.

> ### Silver Polish
>
> *Place tarnished silver in a glass dish, add a piece of aluminum foil, and cover with 1 quart hot water mixed with 1 tablespoon baking soda. A reaction between the foil and the silver will remove any tarnish. Don't use this process on silver objects with raised designs; you will lose the dark accents of the pattern.*

> ### Silver Polish
>
> *Make a paste of 3 parts baking soda to 1 part water. Using a soft cloth, rub the paste gently on the silver. Tarnish will disappear rapidly. After rinsing, buff the silver with a soft cloth to bring up the shine.*

SILVER

Silver is meant to be used. When properly cared for, it just gets better looking as it grows older. With many polishings and much handling, sterling silver will develop a satin patina. This blending of many tiny scratches, known as a "butler's finish," gives the silver an overall luster.

Fabric Flowers

Many fabric flowers copy real ones so authentically that it is hard to tell them apart—unless the fakes are coated with dust and have cobwebs hanging off their petals. If you're going to fool anyone, you'll have to read and follow the manufacturer's instructions for the care of your fabric flowers.

Remove dust with your Eureka vacuum cleaner set at low suction. Remove stubborn dust by gently wiping each petal with a soft toothbrush.

Wipe silk flowers with a damp sponge; don't wash them. Dip washable flowers in a mild solution of dishwashing detergent only when other cleaning methods have failed. Hang the flowers by the stems to dry, or use a hair dryer.

Perk up slightly wilted flowers with steam from a teakettle or a steam iron. You can freshen some sturdy fabric flowers by shaking them in a paper bag with dry cut oats, cornmeal, or salt.

Furniture

The furniture in your home can be made of just about anything, from stone to straw and plaster to plastic. All furniture lasts longer and looks better if you clean it regularly. Use your Eureka vacuum cleaner to remove dust and dirt, and when necessary, clean and polish your furniture using the techniques we suggest.

You'll need to know what your furniture is made of in order to select the proper cleaning and polishing methods. Before you clean a piece of furniture for the first time, read the product label carefully to learn safety pre-

Use your full-size Eureka vacuum cleaner or Mini Mite® to remove dust and debris from all your furniture.

cautions and whether the cleaner you plan to use suits the surface. If you do not know what your furniture is made of, test your cleaning product in an inconspicuous place before cleaning the entire piece.

Remove dust regularly with your Eureka vacuum cleaner, using the small-brush attachment, upholstery nozzle, and crevice tool. Remove the cushions from upholstered pieces, and vacuum in the crevices and along the trim. Don't vacuum a down-filled cushion unless you are sure it is protected with a tightly woven cover that will not allow any of the down to escape.

Treat spots and spills immediately, before they become stains, taking care to choose the appropriate spot remover for the kind of padding in upholstered pieces. Don't use solvent-based spot removers on cushions filled with foam rubber; solvents can deteriorate foam rubber.

Acid stains on upholstery should be treated especially quickly. Dilute them immediately with baking soda and water or with club soda. The same solution will also keep vomit stains from setting.

For more detailed information on cleaning spots and stains on furniture, see "How to Beat Spots and Stains" and the complete Stain-Removal Guide in this book.

METAL

Metal furniture requires no special care. Vacuum it regularly and wipe it with a sponge dampened with an all-purpose cleaning solution.

PLASTIC

Vacuum plastic furniture regularly with your Eureka vacuum cleaner's small-brush attachment. Wipe it occasionally with a sponge dipped in an all-purpose cleaning solution, and buff it dry to prevent streaks. We recommend that you remove stubborn spots with liquid detergent applied directly to the spot; then rub, rinse well, and buff dry. An abrasive cleanser

Plastic-Furniture Cleaner

Using baking soda is the cheapest way to rid plastic furniture of stains. Just sprinkle the soda on the stain, rub it with a damp cloth or sponge, and rinse with clear water.

or steel-wool pad will mar plastic and plastic laminate. Ammonia and alcohol-based products can cloud the surface.

Apply appliance wax or light furniture wax to brighten dull plastic surfaces. This treatment will also protect plastic from scratches.

UPHOLSTERY
Fabric
Shampoo or deep-clean upholstered furniture when vacuuming and spot cleaning fail to make it look fresh.

Most furniture upholstered in fabric can be shampooed safely at home; the exception to this is fabric marked "dry-clean only." But you can spot clean this kind of fabric with a solvent-based cleaner.

Many commercial fabric shampoos are available. If you use one, be sure to read the manufacturer's instructions.

You can shampoo upholstery with the stiff suds made by whipping dishwashing detergent and water. Use a soft-bristled brush to apply the foam.

Upholstery Shampoo

Mix ¼ cup dishwashing liquid with 1 cup warm water and whip the solution with an eggbeater. Apply the foam to the upholstery, a small section at a time, with a soft-bristled brush. Shake off any excess water. Rinse the upholstery by gently rubbing the fabric with a moist, clean cloth; rinse the cloth as necessary.

Leather

Leather must be cleaned with pure soap products (no detergents) and benefits from occasional applications of conditioner to restore moisture and bring up the sheen.

Leather-Upholstery Cleaner

A sudsy solution of soap flakes and warm water is a good way to clean leather upholstery. Apply the suds only, scrubbing gently with a soft-bristled brush; wipe clean with a damp sponge.

Vinyl

Vinyl upholstery is sometimes difficult to distinguish from real leather. It can be cleaned in the same way as leather or with a commercial cleaner developed especially for cleaning vinyl. Never use oil; it will harden the upholstery.

Vinyl upholstery is very durable, but it can easily be cut or punctured. This kind of damage is difficult to repair, so do not allow sharp objects to come in contact with this upholstery material. You must also be careful when you vacuum not to scratch the vinyl with sharp-edged attachments.

Vinyl-Upholstery Cleaner

The best way to clean vinyl upholstery is with baking soda on a damp cloth, followed by a light washing with dishwashing liquid.

WOOD
Oiled
Oiled-wood surfaces have a warm, soft glow and require only an occasional application of furniture oil to keep them looking nice. Be careful never to wax an oil finish.

Wet drinking glasses leave white spots or rings on oil-finished furniture. You can rub them with toothpaste on a damp cloth. (Try this on other surface stains as well.) Or rub the white spots with a mild abrasive and oil. Appropriate abrasives are ashes, salt, soda, or pumice; suitable oils are olive oil, petroleum jelly, cooking oil, or lemon-oil furniture polish.

Painted
For painted-wood furniture, the best care is probably the least, since some polishes and waxes can damage the color and decoration.

Oil Finish

*Pour equal parts turpentine and boiled linseed oil into a jar, tighten the lid, and shake the liquid to blend it thoroughly. **Caution:** Wear rubber gloves. Pour a small amount of the mixture onto a soft cloth and rub the surface of the furniture, following the grain of the wood. The wood will appear oily, but within an hour the polish will be completely absorbed, leaving a lovely, soft sheen.*

Vacuum the furniture regularly, using the small-brush attachment on your Eureka vacuum cleaner. Wipe the piece with a damp sponge to remove smudges and fingerprints. If you feel you must wax, use a hard paste wax no more than once a year.

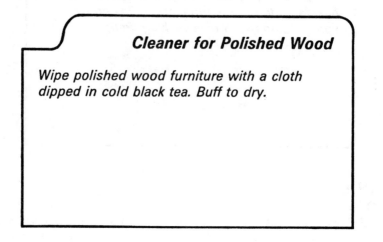

Cleaner for Polished Wood

Wipe polished wood furniture with a cloth dipped in cold black tea. Buff to dry.

Polished

Polished-wood furniture is finished with varnish, lacquer, or wax. Any commercial aerosol polishing/waxing product will clean and polish wood surfaces quickly. Choose a product that is appropriate for the high-gloss or satin finish of your furniture.

Paste wax gives a harder, longer-lasting finish than spray or liquid polish and is recommended for antiques. Although paste wax takes a bit of "elbow grease," the beautiful results are worth the effort.

If you wear cotton gloves while you wax furniture, you will not leave fingerprints. Or you can sprinkle cornstarch over the surface of recently polished furniture and rub it to a high gloss. Cornstarch absorbs excess oil or wax and leaves a glistening surface that is free of fingerprints.

There are several ways to remove white spots, such as those left by wet drinking glasses. You can rub them with toothpaste on a damp cloth, with paste furniture polish, or with a mild abrasive and oil. Appropriate abrasives are ashes, salt, soda, or pumice; suitable oils are olive oil, petroleum jelly, cooking oil, or lemon-oil furniture polish.

Specialty

Specialty-wood furniture is made of wicker, rattan, bamboo, cane, and rush. This kind of furniture usually has a natural finish, but some pieces may have a varnish or shellac coating.

Vacuum specialty-wood furniture regularly with the small-brush attachment of your Eureka vacuum cleaner.

With the exception of rush chair seats that are damaged by moisture, occasionally wet down specialty woods outdoors with a garden hose or in the shower to restore moisture to the fibers to keep them soft. Wetting cane seats tightens them; spray the unvarnished side with water and allow it to air-dry.

If specialty-wood furniture is very dirty, clean it with an all-purpose cleaner. Rinse well and allow it to dry thoroughly before using it again.

Lamp Shades

Since many lamp shades direct a beam light onto their collected cobwebs and dust, they'll need to be cleaned more frequently than less-obvious dirt collectors. Lamp shades are made of many different materials. Some are washable and some are not; keep all the care information from the manufacturer so you know the proper cleaning procedure for your lamp shade.

Remove dust and cobwebs from lamp shades with the small-brush attachment of your Eureka vacuum cleaner.

Wash silk, nylon, and rayon shades only if they are sewn onto their frame. Dry-clean shades that are glued to their frames. Remove spots from nonwashable fabric shades with spot remover.

Clean a washable lamp shade by dunking it in a tub of sudsy water. Rinse it by dunking in clear water.

We recommend that you use your bathtub or a large laundry sink to wash lamp shades. Make a sudsy warm-water solution with liquid dishwashing detergent. Dip the shade in and out of the solution, making sure that the shade is completely covered, and then rinse it in lukewarm water, following the same dipping procedure. Rinse until the water is clear. Take the shade outside and swing it vigorously in a circle to get rid of excess moisture, and then dry it in the sun or with an electric fan or hair dryer.

If your lamp shade is washable but has glued-on trim that prevents your immersing it in water, use the following method for cleaning:

Lamp-Shade Cleaner

Mix ¼ cup dishwashing liquid with 1 cup warm water and whip the mixture with an eggbeater until it makes a stiff foam. Apply the foam to the shade with a sponge, being careful not to wet the trim. Rinse by going over the shade with a clean cloth wrung out in clear water. Allow the shade to dry.

Plastic and fiberglass shades need only be wiped occasionally with a damp cloth to remove soil.

We suggest that you clean lamp shades that are made from parchment or wallpaper with commercial products especially formulated to clean these surfaces. Follow manufacturer's instructions.

Luggage

Clean leather luggage with a soft rag dipped in baby shampoo. Work on a small area at a time. Repeat until the whole bag has been covered, then use the same cloth to buff the luggage to a natural sheen. If black scuffmarks don't come off, remove them with lemon extract.

Mirrors

If you want the mirrors in your home to reflect well on you, you'll have to keep them spotless. This won't take much time, since mirrors are easy to clean, and when mirrors sparkle, the whole room looks brighter.

Mirror Cleaner

Mix ⅓ cup clear ammonia in 1 gallon warm water. Apply the solution with a sponge/ squeegee or pour it into a pump bottle and spray sparingly onto the mirror. Buff with a lint-free cloth, chamois, or paper toweling. Vinegar may be substituted for ammonia.

Mirror Cleaner

Pour vinegar into a shallow bowl or pan, crumple a sheet of newspaper, dip it in the vinegar, and apply to the mirror. Wipe it several times with the same newspaper until the mirror is almost dry, then shine it with a clean, soft cloth or dry newspaper.

Mirror Cleaner

Mix 2 cups isopropyl rubbing alcohol (70-percent), 2 tablespoons liquid dishwashing detergent, and 2 cups water. Stir until the solution is thoroughly mixed and then pour it into a pump bottle. Spray the mixture sparingly on the mirror, and buff it with a lint-free cloth or paper toweling.

If you use a liquid glass cleaner on your mirror, don't allow moisture to collect along the edges or in the corners of the mirror frame. This can cause the glue holding the frame to loosen or the silver backing on the glass to peel, crack, or discolor. We recommend that you keep glass cleaner away from the mirror frame by holding a blotter or towel against the frame while you are cleaning the mirror.

Vacuum ornamental mirrors and frames with the small-brush attachment of your Eureka vacuum cleaner between and before thorough cleanings.

Pianos

A piano is a valuable instrument, made with expert craftsmanship, and a major investment for most households. Your piano should be treated with respect and care. Whether or not your piano is being played regularly, we recommend that you have it tuned frequently by a licensed piano tuner. Have this done approximately four times during the first year you own a new piano, semiannually for an older instrument, and whenever your piano is moved from one location to another.

Pianos should be protected from changes of temperature, drafts, and humidity. Direct sunlight can also damage a piano. For these reasons, an upright piano should be placed against an inside wall of your home and a grand piano should sit away from windows and heating units.

Dust the piano case regularly with a soft cloth and vacuum the interior occasionally with the small-brush attachment and crevice tool of your Eureka vacuum cleaner. Keeping the top of a grand piano closed when the instrument is not being played protects it from potentially damaging dust buildup. Also cover the keyboard when it is not in use if the keys are plastic; ivory keys need to be exposed to light to prevent them from yellowing.

Use a nonsilicone furniture polish or wax on the case of a piano that has a varnish or lacquer finish. A piano that has a high-gloss, polyester epoxy finish can be cleaned with a damp cloth or chamois and buffed dry; it should never be waxed or rubbed with furniture polish.

Dust the keyboard regularly with a soft cloth treated with a spray-on dusting aid. Wrap the cloth around the eraser end of a pencil to get between the keys. Some smudges on the keys can be eliminated by rubbing them with the eraser. To remove stubborn stains from ivory or plastic keys use a damp cloth dipped in baking soda, being careful not to let the soda fall between the keys. Wipe the keys with a soft, clean cloth.

Pictures

Paintings, whether oil, acrylic, or watercolor, and photographs, whether framed behind glass or dry-mounted, require a minimum amount of care.

If the painting or photograph is damaged, we recommend that you have it repaired or cleaned professionally. If the frame or glass over a picture is damaged, you may be able to make the repairs yourself or simply reframe your picture.

Vacuum the painting, frame, and glass regularly, using the small-brush attachment of your Eureka vacuum cleaner.

When you clean the glass over a painting, be careful not to allow any moisture to get behind the glass. Also, do not spray furniture polish directly on picture frames. Spray it on a cloth and then carefully apply the polish to the frame, making sure that it does not get on the painting or under the glass.

To make a tarnished gilt frame gleam again, wipe it with a rag dampened with turpentine.

Slipcovers

Slipcovers usually are washable. Refer to the manufacturer's care instructions or the fabric-care label for cleaning information.

We recommend that you use your Eureka vacuum cleaner to remove lint and dust from slipcovers before washing them. Mend any ripped seams, close all zippers and fasteners, and pretreat heavy soil and spots before washing.

Machine wash slipcovers whenever possible. Hand washing is suitable only for small pieces. Select the appropriate water temperature for the fabric, but never use hot water if there is any possibility of shrinking or fading.

Machine-dry the slipcover until it is slightly damp, not completely dry. Press pleats or ruffles if necessary before refitting the slipcover on the furniture. We recommend that you put a slipcover back on the furniture while it is still damp for a smooth fit.

Television Sets

Television sets attract dust and airborne particles. We recommend you vacuum the TV screen and cabinet regularly, using the small-brush attachment of your Eureka vacuum cleaner. When all the shows on your television begin to look as though they're taking place in a fog, remove film from the TV screen with a sponge dampened in dishwashing detergent; then rinse, and buff to dry.

Wipe plastic TV cabinets with a damp sponge or a cloth moistened with a commercial plastic cleaner or rubbing alcohol. Use furniture polish for wood cabinets. But use as little moisture as possible when washing the screen or cleaning the cabinet to prevent seepage behind the screen or into the crevices around the controls.

Window Coverings

When you shut the shades to block the view or draw the drapes to hide the windows you didn't have time to wash, you end up looking at smudgy shades or dusty drapes. When light filters through your miniblinds or shutters, eventually the slats appear to be flocked with gray fluff. Then it's time to do something about your window coverings. As with all the other dirt catchers in your home, regular use of your Eureka vacuum cleaner will keep your curtains and blinds from disappearing in a cloud of dust. When more than dust is obscuring your drapes and shutters, we also know what to do.

BLINDS

The best way to clean blinds is to vacuum them regularly with the small-brush attachment of your Eureka vacuum cleaner. Close adjustable slats when vacuuming so that you reach more of their surface.

You can remove finger marks with a damp sponge. But when blinds require a thorough cleaning, immerse them in water. Wash them in the bathtub or outdoors by hanging them on the clothesline for scrubbing. Natural wood blinds with decorative yarn tapes should not be immersed, but plastic, metal, and painted wood blinds can be cleaned in this way.

Pour a low-sudsing, all-purpose cleaner into a bathtub filled with warm water, or for outdoor cleaning mix a solution of ½ cup cleaner in 1 gallon warm water and apply with a brush. If you wear cotton gloves when you wash blinds, you can use your fingers to rub the slats. Rinse the blinds with clean water; allow them to drip-dry either on the clothesline or on the shower-curtain rod, placing towels underneath them to catch drips. Rehang the blinds on the window when the dripping has stopped; stretch the tapes or cords to full length to prevent shrinking. Leave the slats in the open position until the blinds are completely dry.

CURTAINS

Carefully read the care label attached to new curtains, and follow the manufacturer's instructions for cleaning. Using the upholstery attachment on your Eureka vacuum cleaner, regularly go over curtain panels for quick cleaning. Vacuuming is almost all the cleaning that fiberglass curtains ever need.

We recommend that you vacuum curtains to remove excess dust before washing. Also disconnect curtain rings and clips (unless they are permanently attached) to prepare your curtains for washing.

Fiberglass curtains should be washed and never dry-cleaned. You must wear rubber gloves when hand washing them to protect your hands from glass filaments. Thoroughly rinse the washing machine after washing fiberglass to ensure that no fine glass fragments remain in the tub.

Handle cotton curtains gently if they have been hanging in a sunny window; sunlight may have weakened the fabric. Machine wash sheers, open weave, and other delicate fabrics in a mesh bag or hand wash so that the fabric does not stretch or tear.

Tumble or drip-dry curtains, according to their fabric. Use curtain stretchers for drying lace or net curtains, and iron curtains that need to be pressed before they are completely dry.

DRAPERIES

Draperies are often lined and are usually made of fabrics that are much heavier than those used for curtains. It is usually best to dry-clean draperies, but some drapery fabric is washable; check the care label.

Dust draperies with the upholstery attachment on your Eureka vacuum cleaner. Also vacuum drapes before you wash them or send them out to be cleaned. Don't forget to dust the tops of the drapes, the valances, and the drapery hardware. Occasionally air draperies on a clothesline on a breezy day to refresh them between cleanings.

Remove all hooks and pins unless they are permanently attached before washing or dry-cleaning. If you plan to wash your draperies, test a corner of the fabric in a bowl of warm water and detergent to see if it bleeds. Use only the gentle cycle to wash draperies.

SHADES

Light-diffusing or opaque shades usually are made of fabrics that are washable, and some shades have a protective vinyl coating that makes them very easy to clean. Other shades are not washable and must be dry-cleaned.

Vacuum shades regularly, using the small-brush attachment of your Eureka vacuum cleaner. Lower the shades completely before vacuuming to clean the full length. Don't forget the tops of the shades and the valances.

Remove finger marks with a damp sponge or a quick spray of all-purpose cleaner. To thoroughly clean the shades, remove them from the window and spread them out on a flat surface. Test a corner of the shade with a detergent solution to see if the color bleeds.

Make a mild soapsuds solution using a liquid dishwashing detergent, and apply it to a rolled-out shade with a sponge. Rinse with a clean sponge dipped in clear water, and allow the shade to dry before rerolling.

Some spots on nonwashable shades can be removed with an art gum eraser. Use it as though you were erasing a pencil mark. You can also clean grease spots on shades that can't be washed by thoroughly rubbing the surface with a rough, absorbent cloth dipped in cornmeal. The secret of this treatment is that the abrasiveness of the cloth and the absorbency of the cornmeal work together to pick up soil and grease. Terry cloth is good for this job, but an old sweatshirt turned inside out is even better. Dry kitchen flour can be substituted for cornmeal.

SHUTTERS

We recommend that you vacuum all shutters regularly with the small-brush attachment of your Eureka vacuum cleaner. Wipe them occasionally with a damp sponge to remove smudges and fingerprints.

For painted shutters, the best care is probably the least, since some polishes and waxes can damage the color and/or decoration. Use warm, soapy water with a damp cloth to wash painted shutters; wash each louver separately on both sides. If you feel you must wax, use a hard paste wax only once a year.

Shutters finished with varnish, lacquer, or wax can be cleaned with commercial aerosol polishing/waxing products. Choose a product that is appropriate for the high-gloss or satin finish of your shutters, but do not spray any cleaner directly onto the shutters because it can seep into the dowels and clog the louvers.

DOING
LAUNDRY

(continued)

DOING LAUNDRY

(continued)

W hen we think about laundry, we often imagine snow-white sheets billowing in the breeze, shirts with no telltale stains or rings around the collars, glimmering little-league uniforms, and baby-soft, sweet-smelling piles of neatly folded clothes. When we think about *doing* the laundry, we may see heavy baskets of dirty clothes with a black sock sticking out of one side and a lacy blouse falling off the top, a confusion of products, and a pair of machines that we may not be able to control. The reality of laundry is somewhere in between these two views.

If you don't want to wash dishes, you can eat out. If you don't want to polish brass candlesticks, you can put away the wedding presents. But if you don't keep up with the laundry, you won't have anything to wear. Since you have to do it, make it as easy as you can. We're here to help speed you through piles of laundry, with guidelines and tips on how to care for everything from your favorite sweatshirt to your best shirt.

Understanding Fabric Care Labels

The first step toward doing your laundry quickly and efficiently is to know what an item is made of and the best way to care for it. Most garments and many other fabric items manufactured and sold in the United States have permanently attached care labels. These labels are also required on garments made of suede and leather. They can be of enormous help in determining exactly how you should remove stains and clean an item.

Certain information is not included on care labels. Neither the manufacturer nor the retailer is required to inform a consumer that a certain fabric will shrink. The label assumes that the purchaser knows that an item labeled "hand wash" should be washed in lukewarm water and that *all* nonwhite articles should not be treated with chlorine bleach. Therefore, care labels do not have to specify such information. The chart that follows explains the instructions found on care labels.

Another important piece of information contained on fabric care labels is the fiber content of the material. This is especially important with blends. These fabrics are combinations of fibers, such as cotton and wool, cotton and polyester, or wool and acrylic. Blends should be cared for in the same way as the fiber with the *highest percentage in the blend*. For example, a blend of 60 percent cotton and 40 percent polyester should be cleaned as though it were 100 percent cotton. However, when you remove spots and stains, you should follow procedures recommended for the *most delicate fiber in the blend.* For example, to remove stains from a blend of cotton and silk, use the procedure recommended for silk. If after such treatment the stain is still apparent, follow the procedure for cotton, the most durable fiber in this blend.

MACHINE WASHABLE

When label reads:	It means:
Machine wash	Wash, bleach, dry, and press by any customary method, including commercial laundering and dry-cleaning.
Home launder only	Same as above, but do not use commercial laundering.
No chlorine bleach	Do not use chlorine bleach. Oxygen bleach may be used.
No bleach	Do not use any type of bleach.
Cold wash/cold rinse	Use cold water or cold washing machine setting.
Warm wash/warm rinse	Use warm water or warm washing machine setting.
Hot wash	Use hot water or hot washing machine setting.
No spin	Remove wash load before final machine spin cycle.
Delicate cycle/gentle cycle	Use appropriate machine setting; otherwise wash by hand.
Durable press cycle/permanent press cycle	Use appropriate machine setting; otherwise use warm wash, cold rinse, and short spin cycle.
Wash separately	Wash alone or with like colors.

NONMACHINE WASHABLE

When label reads:	It means:
Hand wash	Launder only by hand in lukewarm (hand-comfortable) water. May be bleached. May be dry-cleaned.
Hand wash only	Same as above, but do not dry-clean.
Hand wash separately	Hand wash alone or with like colors.
No bleach	Do not use bleach.
Damp wipe	Surface clean with damp cloth or sponge.

HOME DRYING

When label reads:	It means:
Tumble-dry	Dry in tumble dryer at specified setting—high, medium, low, or no heat.
Tumble-dry/remove promptly	Same as above, but in absence of cool-down cycle remove at once when tumbling stops.
Drip-dry	Hang wet and allow to dry with hand shaping only.
Line-dry	Hang damp and allow to dry.
No wring	Hang dry, drip-dry, or dry flat only.
No twist	Handle to prevent wrinkles.
Dry flat	Lay garment on flat surface.

Reprinted with permission of the Consumer Affairs Committee, American Apparel Manufacturers Association

IRONING OR PRESSING

When label reads:	It means:
Cool iron	Set iron at lowest setting.
Warm iron	Set iron at medium setting.
Hot iron	Set iron at hot setting.
Do not iron	Do not iron or press with heat.
Steam iron	Iron or press with steam.
Iron damp	Dampen garment before ironing.

MISCELLANEOUS

When label reads:	It means:
Dry-clean only	Garment should be dry-cleaned only, including self-service.
Professionally dry-clean only	Do not use self-service dry-cleaning.
No dry-clean	Use recommended care instructions. No dry-cleaning materials to be used.

Natural Fabrics

COTTON

Cotton fabric is strong, long-wearing, and absorbent. It will shrink and wrinkle unless it is given special treatment. Cotton is often blended with other fibers or treated with a finish to make it wrinkle-resistant. It is available in a wide variety of weights and textures, from denim or corduroy to percale.

Machine wash and tumble-dry cotton fabrics, using a water temperature ranging from cold to hot, depending on the manufacturer's care instructions, and an all-purpose detergent. If needed, a chlorine bleach can be used on white or colorfast cotton unless a fabric finish has been applied.

Do not use more than the recommended amount of bleach; this can damage the fibers.

We recommend that you use fabric softener to improve softness and to reduce wrinkling. But fabric softener makes cotton less absorbent and should not be used on towels, washcloths, or diapers.

Pretreat oil-based spots and stains with a prewash.

Wash and shrink cotton fabrics before using them for home sewing.

Iron cotton with a hot iron for best results and use spray starch or spray sizing to restore its crisp appearance.

LINEN

Pure linen fabric wrinkles easily, so many manufacturers make linen blends or add wrinkle-resistant finishes to overcome this problem. Linen is absorbent and comfortable to wear, but it can crack or show wear at the seams, along the creases, and at the finished edges of the garment.

Machine wash and tumble-dry linen. An all-purpose detergent is the best cleaning agent, and chlorine bleach can be used on white linen, following the manufacturer's recommended amount so as not to damage the fabric.

Linen can also be dry-cleaned. It should be pressed with a hot iron while it is still slightly damp for the best results.

SILK

Silk is a delight to wear, but it requires special care. Most silk garments are marked "dry-clean only." However, some silk can be washed by hand. A piece of silk fabric that you are going to make into a garment should first be washed by hand.

We suggest that you always test a corner of the fabric for colorfastness before washing a whole piece of silk. Some dyed silk will bleed.

Use a hair shampoo containing protein and warm or cool water for hand washing; the protein in the shampoo feeds the protein in the silk. Handle washable silk gently during washing; never twist or wring it. Hang silk out of direct sunlight to drip-dry.

Press silk while it is still damp with a warm iron (below 275 degrees Fahrenheit) or use a steam iron.

To remove stains from washable white or light-colored silk, use only oxygen bleach or mix 1 part hydrogen peroxide (3 percent) to 8 parts water.

WOOL

Wool fabric is highly resilient, absorbent, and sheds wrinkles well, but wool will shrink and mat if it's exposed to heat and rubbing. Popular in both knit and woven fabrics, the textures of wool fabrics range from fine wool crepe and jersey to felt and mohair.

We recommend that you treat spots and stains on wool fabrics with solvent-based spot removers. Clean felt by wiping it with a dry sponge. For

To clean felt at home, first steam it and then brush away the soil with a dry sponge.

a more thorough treatment, hold the material over steam from a teakettle, and brush lightly with a dry sponge or lint-free cloth to smooth the surface.

Wool should always be dry-cleaned unless it is specifically marked "washable."

Use light-duty detergent in cold water to wash wool. Allow the article to soak for a few minutes before starting the washing process. Handle woolens carefully when they are wet to avoid stretching. Machine washing is appropriate only if the care label indicates that it is, and then use only cold water and the gentle cycle.

Remove excess moisture by rolling a wool article in a towel, then block it into shape and dry it on a flat surface. Only machine-dry woolens if the manufacturer's instructions recommend it.

Press wool with a hot iron, using lots of steam. Cover the article with a damp cloth or chemically treated press cloth. Allow the garment to dry thoroughly before storing it.

Using a press cloth allows you to iron delicate fabrics on the right side.

Synthetic Fabrics

ACETATE

Acetate is made from cellulose and has a silklike appearance. Closely related to rayon, it has good body and drapes well. Taffeta, satin, crepe, brocade, and double knits often contain acetate. It is not very absorbent or colorfast, and acetate loses its strength when it is wet.

Hand wash acetate carefully in warm water, using a light-duty detergent, if the care label specifies that the article is washable; otherwise have it dry-cleaned. Do not soak colored items or wash them with white articles. We suggest that you add fabric softener to the rinse water to reduce wrinkles.

Line-dry acetate away from heat or direct sunlight. Press at the coolest setting, on the wrong side, while the article is damp. Use a press cloth when pressing the right side of the fabric.

Nail-polish remover and perfumes will permanently damage acetate.

ACRYLIC

Many acrylic weaves resemble wool's softness, bulk, and fluffiness. Acrylics are wrinkle-resistant and usually are machine washable. Often acrylic fibers are blended with wool or polyester fibers. Acrylic's biggest drawback is its tendency to pill. Blends will do this less than pure acrylic.

Dry-clean acrylic garments or wash them by hand or in the machine. Pretreat oil-based stains, and turn garments inside out before laundering to reduce pilling. Wash delicate items by hand in warm water, gently squeezing out the water. Machine wash sturdy articles with an all-purpose detergent, and tumble-dry at low temperatures.

If the fabric is labeled "colorfast," it can be bleached with either chlorine or oxygen bleach. We've found that adding fabric softener to the rinse water every third or fourth time an article is washed reduces static electricity.

Press at a moderate temperature setting, using steam.

FIBERGLASS

Fiberglass fabrics are wrinkle- and soil-resistant, but they have poor resistance to abrasion. They are not absorbent but stand up well to sun and weather. This makes fiberglass fabrics ideal for curtains and draperies. Fiberglass is never made into wearing apparel because it sheds small glass fibers.

Dust fiberglass periodically with the upholstery brush of your Eureka vacuum cleaner.

Hand wash for best results, using an all-purpose detergent. Wear rubber gloves to protect your hands from glass fibers. If you wash machine-washable fiberglass in your washing machine, rinse out the tub to remove the glass fibers. Never wash fiberglass articles with items made of anything else.

Drip-dry fiberglass articles and do not iron them.

MODACRYLIC

Modacrylic is a fiber often used in fake furs, fleece robes, blankets, stuffed toys, and wigs. It is resilient, soft, and warm, and it resists moths, mildew, sunlight damage, and wrinkling.

Hand wash delicate modacrylic items, such as wigs, and machine wash sturdy items in warm water with a gentle cycle and light-duty detergent. We recommend that you use fabric softener to reduce static electricity.

Use a low-heat setting on the dryer, and remove modacrylic articles as soon as the tumbling stops. If pressing is needed, use a cool iron.

NYLON

Nylon fabrics are extremely strong, lightweight, smooth, and lustrous. They are also nonabsorbent and have excellent abrasion- and wrinkle-resistance. Often combined with spandex, nylon knits are very stretchy but hold and recover their original shape. Available in many textures, nylon is used to make all kinds of items, including lingerie, carpets, rainwear, and tents.

Always follow the manufacturer's cleaning instructions. Pretreat oil-based stains on nylon. Machine wash sturdy articles in warm water with an all-purpose detergent. Hand wash lingerie and hosiery, using warm water and light-duty detergent, or machine wash in a mesh bag to prevent stretching or tearing. Do not launder white nylon with colored fabrics of any kind.

Use a chlorine bleach only if a nylon article is colorfast, and use fabric softener to reduce static electricity. Tumble-dry nylon at a low temperature setting. Press at a cool temperature setting.

OLEFIN

Olefin fabrics are nonabsorbent and hold in body warmth. But they are also very heat sensitive and melt immediately upon contact with heat. Olefin is used as a filling for outerwear and upholstery. The fabric is bulky but lightweight.

Machine wash olefin in warm water, using an all-purpose detergent. We recommend adding fabric softener to the final rinse.

Tumble-dry at the lowest temperature setting. Ironing olefin is not recommended, since even the slightest amount of heat will melt the fabric.

POLYESTER

Polyester fabrics are strong, resilient, wrinkle-resistant, colorfast, and crisp. They hold pleats and creases well, but they are also nonabsorbent, attract and hold oil-based stains, may pill when rubbed, and may yellow with age. Polyester is used for clothing and filling; some bed linens and towels are also made from polyester blends.

Polyester can be safely dry-cleaned or machine washed. Pretreat oil-based stains with prewash or all-purpose liquid detergent. We recommend that you turn polyester-knit garments inside out before washing to prevent snags. Machine wash polyester in warm water using an all-purpose detergent, and tumble-dry at a low temperature setting. Use a chlorine bleach if necessary. Using a fabric softener will reduce static electricity.

Do not overdry polyester; this will cause gradual shrinkage. Press polyester fabrics at a moderate temperature setting or use steam.

RAYON

Rayon is a strong, absorbent fabric, but it tends to lose its strength when it is wet. It is used for drapery and upholstery fabrics as well as for clothing.

Dry-clean rayon or wash it by hand unless it is labeled "machine washable." For hand wash, use lukewarm water with a light-duty detergent. Machine wash rayon in warm water on a gentle cycle with a light-duty detergent. Squeeze moisture out gently when washing rayon fabrics by hand. Chlorine bleach can be used on rayon unless it has been treated with a resin finish.

Drip-dry and press rayon on the wrong side with an iron at a medium temperature setting while the fabric is damp.

Trademarks of Synthetic Fibers

Trademark	Generic Name	Trademark	Generic Name
A		**E**	
A.C.E	nylon or polyester	Eloquent Luster	nylon
		Eloquent Touch	nylon
Acetate by Avtex	acetate	Encron	polyester
Absorbit	rayon	Enka 10-10	nylon
Acrilan	acrylic or modacrylic	Enkaire	rayon
		Enkaloft	nylon
Anso	nylon	Enkalure	nylon
Antron	nylon	Enkasheer	nylon
Ariloft	acetate	Enkrome	rayon
Arnel	triacetate	Estron	acetate
Avlin	polyester		
Avril	rayon	**F**	
Avsorb	rayon	Fibro	rayon
		Fina	acrylic
B		Fortel	polyester
Beau-Grip	rayon		
Bi-Loft	acrylic	**G**	
Blue "C"	nylon or polyester	Golden Glow	polyester
		Golden Touch	polyester
C		**H**	
Cadon	nylon	Herculon	olefin
Cantrece	nylon	Hollofil	polyester
Caprolan	nylon		
Celanese	nylon or acetate	**K**	
		Kodel	polyester
Chromspun	acetate	KodOfill	polyester
Coloray	rayon	KodOsoff	polyester
Cordura	nylon		
Courtaulds Nylon	nylon	**L**	
		Lanese	acetate/ polyester
Crepeset	nylon		
Crepesoft	polyester	Loftura	acetate
Creslan	acrylic	Lusteroff	nylon
Cumuloft	nylon	Lycra	spandex
D		**M**	
Dacron	polyester	Marquesa	olefin

Trademark	Generic Name	Trademark	Generic Name
M *(continued)*		**S** *(continued)*	
Marvess	olefin	Silver Label	nylon
Multisheer	nylon	Softalon	nylon
		So-Lara	acrylic
N		Spectran	polyester
Natura Luster	nylon	Strialine	polyester
O		**T**	
Orlon	acrylic	Trevira	polyester
		Twisloc	polyester
P			
Patlon	olefin	**U**	
Plyloc	polyester	Ulstron	nylon
Polyextra	polyester	Ultron	nylon
Polyloom	olefin		
		V	
Q		Vectra	olefin
Qiana	nylon	Verel	modacrylic
		Vive La Crepe	nylon
R			
Rayon by Avtex	rayon	**Z**	
		Zantrel	rayon
S		Zeflon	nylon
SEF	modacrylic	Zefran	acrylic or
Shareen	nylon		nylon
Silky Touch	polyester		

Reprinted with permission of the Man-Made Fiber Producers Association, Inc.

SPANDEX

Spandex is a lightweight fiber that resembles rubber in durability. It has good stretch and recovery, and it is resistant to damage from sunlight, abrasion, and oils. Always blended with other fibers, spandex provides the stretch in waistbands, foundation garments, swimwear, and dancewear.

Pretreat oil-based stains. Hand or machine wash spandex-blend garments in warm water using an all-purpose detergent. Do not wash white spandex with colored fabrics of any kind. Use only oxygen or sodium-perborate bleach. Rinse thoroughly.

Line-dry or tumble-dry garments made with spandex at a low temperature setting. Press clothing that contains spandex rapidly, if needed, using a low temperature setting.

TRIACETATE

Triacetate resembles acetate, but it is less sensitive to heat. This allows triacetate to be creased and crisply pleated. Triacetate is often a component in jersey, textured knits, and taffeta.

Pleated garments can be hand or machine washed in cold water. Set the gentle cycle to agitate for 3 minutes. Drip-dry permanently pleated garments, or air-dry them in dryer.

Most triacetate articles can be machine washed with an all-purpose detergent in hot or warm water. Tumble- or line-dry triacetate. Press, if necessary, using a hot temperature setting.

Laundry Techniques

When you can no longer force shut the lid of your laundry hamper or when the pile of dirty clothes in your laundry room has grown almost as high as the top of the washer, it's time to do the wash. You could jam all your dirty laundry in the washing machine, run it through whatever wash cycle happens to be programmed, and hope for the best. This method may leave your sweater doll-sized or turn your white silk shirt pink, but it's quick—if you don't count the time you'll spend replacing your ruined clothes. Doing your laundry properly will take more time. If this is too much of a hassle for you, we seriously suggest you consider sending your laundry out. When you do your own laundry, your clothes will last longer and look better if you pay careful attention to sorting, pretreating, water temperature, machine cycle, and the right laundry products for each particular fabric.

SORTING

Properly sorting the laundry is the first step to a clean wash and helps to keep your clothes, linens, and other household items looking their best through repeated washings.

Color: First sort the laundry by color. Put all the white or predominantly white articles in one pile, the light colors and pastels in another pile, and the bright and dark-colored items into a third. Then separate the dark pile into two piles: one for colorfast items and one for noncolorfast items.

Degree of soil: Separate each pile into three smaller piles: lightly soiled, moderately soiled, and heavily soiled.

Compatible loads: Now you have up to 12 various-sized piles of laundry. Combine or divide the piles to come up with compatible, washer-sized loads. The following hints will help you with your final sorting:

- Combine white and light-colored items that have similar degrees of soil into the same pile.
- Combine noncolorfast items with similarly colored colorfast items with the same degree of soil.
- Create a separate pile for delicate items that must be hand washed.
- Separate white synthetic articles, and wash them only with other white fabrics.
- Separate synthetics, blends, and permanent-press fabrics from natural-fiber fabrics without special finishes.
- Separate items made from fabrics that produce lint, such as chenille robes and bath towels, from fabrics that attract lint, such as corduroy, knits, synthetics, and permanent press.

PREPARING THE WASH

Follow these hints to minimize damage to the articles you are washing and to help clean them thoroughly:

- Know the fiber content and finishes of fabrics so you can select the proper water temperature and cleaning products.
- Save care information so you can follow the recommended cleaning procedures.
- Close all zippers, hook all hooks, and button all buttons.
- Turn pockets inside out to get rid of debris.
- Remove nonwashable trim or decorations and pins or buckles that might make holes or snag other articles in the wash.
- Tie or buckle all belts and sashes to prevent tangling.
- Mend seams, tears, holes, or loose hems to prevent further damage during the wash cycle.
- Turn sweaters and corduroy garments inside out to prevent pilling and to combat their tendency to collect lint.
- Pretreat spots, stains, and heavily soiled items with prewash spot-and-stain remover, liquid detergent, a paste made from granular soap or detergent, a bar of soap, or a presoak solution.

PREWASH SPOT–AND–STAIN REMOVERS

While soaps and detergents can be worked directly into spots and heavily soiled areas before you put the laundry into the washer, a special product designed just for removing spots and stains is more convenient to use. Called prewash spot-and-stain removers, these aerosols or pump sprays are excellent for spot treating stubborn soil, especially grease marks on synthetic fabrics.

Treat the stain while it is still fresh. Saturate the soiled area completely, then lightly rub the fabric together to work the prewash product into the fibers.

Some prewash products can damage the exterior finish of your washer and dryer, so be careful where you spray them.

PRESOAKS

Granular presoak products containing enzymes break down some stubborn stains such as milk, blood, baby formula, chocolate, gravy, fruits and vegetables, and grass. Presoaks are not effective on rust, ink, oil, or grease.

Following the manufacturer's directions, mix a solution in a large sink or in the washer. Before adding the soiled laundry, make sure that the presoak has dissolved thoroughly. Soak clothes for the recommended length of time; an overnight soak is suitable for articles that look dull and dingy. Do not soak dark- and light-colored fabrics together for long periods of time; this can cause colors to run. Wash the laundry as usual after using a presoak.

You can use presoaks for diaper-pail solutions and as detergent boosters.

LAUNDRY PRODUCTS

Most commercial laundry preparations are designed to be used in washing machines, but some can be used for both hand and machine washing. Read the label carefully before purchasing any product to make sure it is the right one for the job you want it to do. When you use a laundry product, follow the directions precisely and measure accurately.

Water Conditioners

The amount and type of chemicals and minerals dissolved in water determines whether it is hard or soft. The condition of the water affects the cleaning potential of laundry products: The softer the water, the more effective it is for cleaning. Determine the hardness of your water so you will know if you need to condition it for effective cleaning.

Hard water leaves a residue on articles you launder; this is known as *washing film.* To soften water, the minerals must be removed or chemically locked up. Water that measures under four grains hardness per gallon will probably clean effectively, especially if a detergent rather than soap is used. You can soften hard water with a mechanical water softener that attaches to your home's water tank or by adding a water-conditioning product to the wash and rinse water.

Follow the directions on product labels precisely.

Wash flame-retardant items only in soft water.

Use a water conditioner to remove previously formed washing film or soap/detergent buildup. You can also remove hard-water washing film from diapers, towels, or fabrics by soaking them in a solution of 1 cup white vinegar and 1 gallon water in a plastic container.

Use a water softener if you use soap in hard water or if you use a phosphate-free detergent.

Detergents and Soaps

Soap is a mixture of alkalies and fats that is a good cleaner in soft water, breaks down well in city sewer systems, and does not harm the environment. Soap is less effective in hard water, however, because it reacts with the high mineral content to form soap curd, which leaves a gray scum on clothing.

Detergents are synthetic washing products derived from petroleum and other nonfatty materials. They are less affected by hard water than soap and have excellent cleaning power. Since detergents contain a wetting agent that lifts off dirt and agents that help to make hard water minerals inactive, they do not create scum.

Most detergents contain phosphates, which are harmful to the environment because they promote an overgrowth of algae in water, but some detergents are phosphate-free. The cleaning ability of phosphate-free detergents is less effective in hard water and in cold-water washes than detergents that contain phosphates, and these detergents may cause excessive wear to some fabrics.

Always follow the manufacturer's instructions for the amount of detergent to use, the proper wash cycle, and the recommended water temperature. Measure carefully, but use extra detergent for heavy and/or greasy soil, larger-than-normal loads, and warm- or cold-water washes. You may also need more than the manufacturer's recommended amount of detergent if you have hard water and when you use phosphate-free detergent. Adding 1 cup ammonia to the wash water will boost detergent effectiveness for heavily soiled or greasy wash loads.

Use liquid detergents in cold-water washes for best results, or dissolve powder or granular detergents in 1 quart hot water, then add the solution to the cold wash water.

Bleach

Bleach works with detergent or soap to remove stains and soil, whiten white items, and brighten the colors of some fabrics. It also acts as a mild disinfectant. The two basic types of laundry bleach are chlorine and oxygen. Common liquid chlorine bleach is the most effective and least expensive, but it cannot be used on all fabrics. Oxygen bleach is safer for all washable fabrics, resin-finished fibers, and most washable colors, but it is much less strong than chlorine bleach.

Always give colored fabrics a colorfastness test before using any bleach by mixing 1 tablespoon chlorine bleach with ¼ cup warm water or 1 tablespoon oxygen bleach with 2 quarts hot water. Apply the solution to an inconspicuous place; wait a few minutes and check for a color change. If the color does not bleed, use the bleach according to the manufacturer's directions.

Add diluted chlorine bleach to the wash water about five minutes after the wash cycle has begun or use the automatic bleach dispenser if your washer is equipped with one. Bleach clothes only in the wash cycle so the bleach can be completely removed during the rinse cycle. Hot water improves the performance of bleach.

Fabric Softeners

Fabric softeners add softness and fluffiness, reduce static electricity on synthetics so they will not cling, help decrease lint, and make pressing easier. They are available in liquid, sheet, or solid form. Liquid fabric softener is added to the wash or rinse cycle; sheet and solid products are used in the dryer.

Read the instructions for using a fabric softener to determine at what time in the laundering cycle to add it. Dilute liquid fabric softeners with water before adding them to the automatic fabric-softener dispenser or to the rinse.

Fabric softener can stain fabric if it is poured or sprayed directly onto clothes or if it is used with a water conditioner. Sheet fabric softeners will stain polyester articles if they are used in the dryer when these fabrics are drying. If you stain an item with fabric softener, rub the stained area with liquid detergent or a prewash spot-and-stain remover and rewash the article.

USING AN AUTOMATIC CLOTHES WASHER

When you consider the alternative of a washtub in the backyard, the automatic clothes washer is a great time saver. But for the best results from your washing machine, you must know how to combine multiple load capacities, water levels, temperature settings, and cycles properly.

Loading the Machine

Read the washer manufacturer's instruction booklet thoroughly, put it away in a safe place for reference, and follow the recommended laundry procedures.

Do not overload the machine; garments should not pile up past the top of the agitator. Mix small and large items in each load for the best circulation, and distribute the load evenly around the wash basket. Loading the washer to full capacity each time you wash will save time and energy. But don't be tempted to throw your dark bath towels in a bleach load or your sweaters in a permanent-press load just to fill it.

Water Temperature

The correct water temperature(s) for a load of wash varies according to the kinds of fabric being washed and the amount of soil. Use the following chart to help you select the proper wash and rinse temperature settings. Be aware of the actual temperature of the water in your washing machine; it can vary during the year. If the water temperature is below 80 degrees Fahrenheit, it is too cold to do a good job even if you use a cold-water detergent. Adjust the amounts of cold and hot water flowing into your machine to get the water within the correct temperature range for each temperature setting.

Type of Load	Wash Temperature	Rinse Temperature
White and light-colored cottons and linens Diapers Heavily soiled permanent-press and wash-and-wear fabrics All other greasy or heavily soiled wash	130° F. –150° F. (hot)	warm or cold
Dark colors Lightly and moderately soiled permanent-press and wash-and-wear fabrics Some woven or knit synthetic fabrics (see care label) Some washable woolens (see care label) Any other moderately soiled wash	100° F. –110° F. (warm)	cold
Noncolorfast fabrics Some washable woolens (see care label) Some woven or knit synthetic fabrics (see care label) Fragile items Bright colors Any lightly soiled wash	80° F. –100° F. (cold)	cold

Water Level

Use enough water to provide good circulation, but do not use so much that you waste water and energy. Most machines have a water-level control, and you should adjust this control to match each load you wash. Refer to the manufacturer's instructions for this information.

Machine Cycles

Select the type of cycle and the length of washing time according to the kind of load and the degree of soil. Follow these guidelines, using a longer cycle for heavily soiled laundry.

Type of Load	Cycle	Wash Time
Sturdy white and and colorfast items	Normal	10-12 minutes
Sturdy noncolorfast items	Normal	6-8 minutes
Sturdy permanent-press and wash-and-wear fabrics	Permanent-press	6-8 minutes
Delicate fabrics and knits	Gentle or delicate	4-6 minutes

HAND WASHING

Most washable fabrics can be put into the machine, but some items are marked "hand wash only." We recommend that you never disregard this label even when you're in a hurry. We've also found that even though the washing machine is usually the fastest and best way to do your wash, hand washing is quicker and cheaper than using the machine when you have only a few items to clean.

Sort hand wash in the same way you sort machine wash. Separate the clothes into piles by color, putting white and light colors together, dark and noncolorfast items into separate piles. Pretreat stains and heavily soiled areas with prewash spot-and-stain remover or by rubbing liquid detergent into the area.

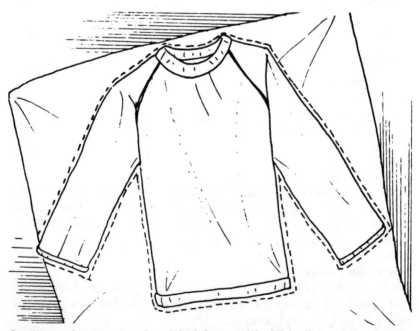

Gently stretch a sweater to its original shape and dry it lying flat on a towel.

Use light-duty soap or detergent and dissolve it in warm or cool wash water before adding the clothes. Submerge the articles in the water and let them soak for 3 to 5 minutes. Gently squeeze the suds through the fabric, being careful not to rub, twist, or wring excessively. Rinse articles thoroughly in cool water until the water runs clear. Add a few drops of fabric softener to the last rinse if desired.

Hang blouses, dresses, scarves, and lingerie to drip-dry. The shower is a good place for this. Use towels to blot excess moisture from sweaters, stockings, panties, and bras. Hang these items to dry only if the weight of the water will not stretch them out of shape; otherwise, dry them on a towel on a flat surface.

DRYING CLOTHES

Most clothes dried in an automatic dryer come out soft and almost wrinkle-free. If you have time and a backyard, you may prefer to dry your laundry on the clothesline on sunny days, reserving the dryer for inclement weather and for your permanent-press fabrics.

Machine Drying

Read the manufacturer's instruction booklet to familiarize yourself with your dryer's operating procedures and recommended cycles.

Shake out each article before placing it in the dryer to speed the drying time and cut down on wrinkles. Do not overload the dryer; this will cause uneven drying and excessive wrinkling. Remove items from the dryer as soon as it stops, and hang or fold them to keep them from getting wrinkled. Dry clothes until they are "almost dry" rather than "bone dry" if you are going to iron them. Clean the lint filter after each use of the dryer.

Line-Drying

If you are going to the trouble to hang your clothes outside to dry, make sure that your clothespins and clotheslines are clean and free of rust. You can wash plastic clothespins in mild soap and warm water in an automatic clothes washer, using a mesh bag. Wash wooden clothespins in a hot dish-washing-detergent solution. Use plastic rope or plastic-coated wire for your clothesline, and wipe it with a damp cloth before using it.

Attach items to the clothesline by their most sturdy edges. Smooth the clothes as you hang them, running your fingers down seams and along the front, collar, and cuff edges. Dry white and light-colored items in the sun and bright-colored items in the shade.

USING A COIN-OPERATED LAUNDRY

The basic techniques for doing laundry at a coin-operated laundry are exactly the same as those you use if you have a washing machine and dryer at home. First sort the laundry, then make up compatible loads. But rather than putting the loads into the washer one after another, put each load in a laundry bag. When you get to the laundromat, your wash is already sorted.

We recommend that you buy a laundry tote that will hold all your supplies. Check your supplies before you leave home, so that once you're at the laundromat, you won't have to go out and buy more bleach.

Take plenty of change along with you. During the week as change builds up in your pocket or purse, put it aside in a special place, and you never have to scrounge for change on laundry day.

Most coin-operated laundries post full instructions for operating their machines. Read these and follow their advice to get the best service from commercial washers and dryers.

Not all laundromats are created equal; shop around for the best one in your neighborhood. Look for one that is clean and well-lighted, and has most of its machines in working order. Also look for rolling baskets, clean work tables, hanging racks, change machines, and laundry-product dispensers. An attendant who is on duty whenever the laundry is open is usually an assurance that a laundromat is well-run.

Solving Laundry Problems

Here are some of the most common laundry problems and simple, quick ways to solve them. To find out more about cleaning stains, turn to the Stain-Removal Guide later in this book.

Brown Stains
Cause: Soap, detergent, or bleach reacting with iron or manganese in the water.
Solution: Install an iron filter on your water system. Do not use chlorine bleach in the wash. Use a water conditioner in both the wash and rinse water.

Excessive Wear
Cause: Improper use of bleach.
Solution: Always dilute chlorine bleach before adding it to the washer.
Cause: Tears, holes, snags, split seams, and loose hems.
Solution: Make all repairs before washing an item and hook all hooks, close zippers, and remove pins or other sharp objects before putting articles in the washer.

Gray and Dingy Fabric
Cause: Incorrect sorting, insufficient detergent, or water temperature too low.
Solution: Follow our suggestions for sorting and proper washing techniques.

Greasy Spots
Cause: Undiluted liquid fabric softener coming into contact with fabric.
Solution: Dilute liquid fabric softeners before adding them to the rinse or softener dispenser.
Cause: Fabric softener sheets in the dryer with lightweight fabrics.
Solution: Use liquid softener in the washing machine when cleaning delicate fabrics. Greasy spots can be removed by rubbing in liquid detergent and then washing again. Also use a lower temperature setting on the dryer.
Cause: Hard water.
Solution: Use a water conditioner appropriate for your detergent or install a mechanical water softener.
Cause: Overloaded washer.
Solution: Reduce the load size so the clothes can circulate more freely.

Harsh-Feeling Fabrics
Cause: Spin speed not adequate.
Solution: Increase the spin speed or check to make sure the load is balanced so the spin can reach its maximum speed.
Cause: Hard water.
Solution: Increase the amount of detergent, install a mechanical water softener, or use a water-conditioning product.
Cause: Using soap in hard water.
Solution: Switch to a detergent, install a mechanical water softener, or use a water conditioner.

Linting
Cause: Incorrect sorting.
Solution: Read and follow our suggestions for sorting.
Cause: Not enough detergent.
Solution: Increase the amount of detergent to help hold lint in suspension so it can be flushed down the drain.
Cause: Overloaded washer.
Solution: Reduce load size or increase the water level so the wash can circulate freely.
Cause: Improper use of fabric softener.
Solution: Do not add softener directly to wash water unless specifically directed to do so.
Cause: Debris in cuffs or pockets.
Solution: Remove any tissues, paper, or loose dirt before washing.

Scorching During Ironing
Cause: Iron temperature setting too high.
Solution: Check recommended heat on garment tag and reduce the temperature setting on the iron accordingly.

Cause: Heat of iron reacting with a buildup of laundry products.
Solution: Run clothes through one or two complete washing cycles with 1 cup water conditioner and no other laundry product, then wash as usual.

Static Electricity
Cause: Synthetic fabrics tend to produce static electricity.
Solution: Use a fabric softener in your washer or dryer.

Yellowing
Cause: Incomplete removal of soil, especially body oils.
Solution: Pretreat heavily soiled areas, increase the amount of detergent, use hotter water, and use bleach.
Cause: Iron in the water.
Solution: Install an iron filter, use extra detergent, and use water conditioner.
Cause: Aging of some fabrics.
Solution: No solution except the above suggestions for routine washing to slow the aging process.

CLEANING YOUR CAR

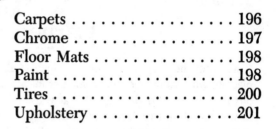

M any of us who are otherwise quite tidy treat our cars as though they were traveling dustbins. In the backseat, the debris from fast-food meals gets piled on top of autumn leaves, comic books, broken toys, and you name it. The outside of the car has an allover greasy film of road dirt and mud spatters on the fenders. The car already looks like a clunker, and you're still paying for it.

Cleaning and maintaining the original appearance of your car may not be high on your list of favorite ways to spend your weekend, but we've found that it is time well spent. You can expect to obtain at least several hundred dollars more at trade-in time or when you sell your car if you've helped your car to keep its good looks. Your car is a very large investment, and keeping it looking as new as possible protects that investment. In this chapter, we'll show you how to clean your car—inside and out.

Carpets

Keeping the carpet in your car clean is almost impossible: There's no place to wipe your feet before you get in. Mats offer some protection from dirt and grime, and we suggest that you install them in a new car as soon as you buy it and replace them when they become worn. But even when you use mats to protect the carpeting, dirt and grime inevitably accumulate in the carpet fibers.

Vacuum the carpeting in your car frequently to remove the grit and soil that can break down carpet fibers and cause unnecessary wear. A cordless

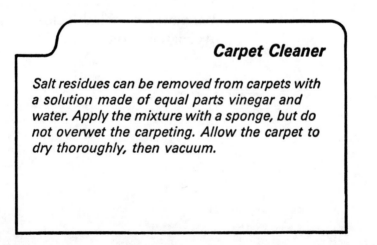

Carpet Cleaner

Salt residues can be removed from carpets with a solution made of equal parts vinegar and water. Apply the mixture with a sponge, but do not overwet the carpeting. Allow the carpet to dry thoroughly, then vacuum.

Eureka Mini Mite® is especially good for vacuuming your car, and its recharging stand can be mounted right in your garage so it's conveniently at hand. Your full-sized Eureka vacuum cleaner with the upholstery brush and crevice tool will also get into hard-to-reach places and do an excellent cleaning job. We recommend that every time you vacuum the car, you remove the mats, shake them thoroughly, and vacuum them as well.

Spills in the car are not like spills in the house. When you turn a corner too fast and spill your morning coffee, you can't stop in the middle of traffic and clean up the mess. But you should try to wipe up spills soon after they occur. We suggest that you keep paper towels and a whisk broom in the car and accessible for emergency cleanups.

Make it your habit to roll up your car windows whenever you park your car outside. If rain or water from the neighbor's lawn sprinkler leaks into your car and soaks the carpet, it is difficult to dry it out, and mildew can set in quickly.

When the carpeting in your car needs to be cleaned, use a spray or spray-foam carpet cleaner. Some manufacturers make carpet-cleaning products especially for cars. Read and follow the instructions for the best results. Vacuum the carpet after cleaning only when it is completely dry.

Chrome

Shiny chrome adds sparkle to a car's appearance, and chrome must be cleaned and polished regularly to prevent rust and corrosion. Polish chrome after the car has been washed. Remove rust spots with a steel-wool pad or a piece of crumpled aluminum foil. Wax chrome trim when you wax the car's body. Use a different cloth to polish the chrome than you use for the body.

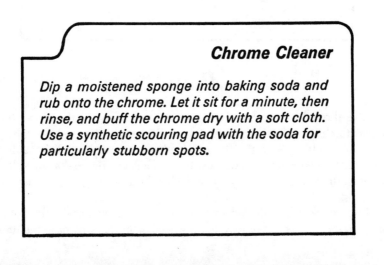

Chrome Cleaner

Dip a moistened sponge into baking soda and rub onto the chrome. Let it sit for a minute, then rinse, and buff the chrome dry with a soft cloth. Use a synthetic scouring pad with the soda for particularly stubborn spots.

Residues of salt will pit chrome. Have your car washed frequently during the winter when the roads have been salted, and hose off salt residues when the temperature is above freezing.

Many commercial chrome cleaners and polishes are available. If you use one, follow the manufacturer's instructions for the best results.

Floor Mats

Rubber mats give your automobile's carpet essential protection from excessive wear. We recommend that you clean the mats every time you wash your car. Even though it may take a bit of extra effort, you should clean car mats frequently in the winter, because they accumulate salt and sand when it's snowy. Use a stiff-bristled brush and scrub them with a detergent solution. Do not use harsh chemicals, solvents, or steel wool to clean the mats; these cleaners will damage the rubber. After washing the mats, apply a rubber protectant or liquid-wax shoe polish.

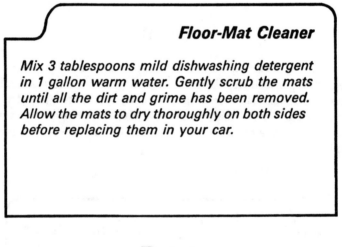

Floor-Mat Cleaner

Mix 3 tablespoons mild dishwashing detergent in 1 gallon warm water. Gently scrub the mats until all the dirt and grime has been removed. Allow the mats to dry thoroughly on both sides before replacing them in your car.

Paint

Drive-through car washes are convenient and many use the proper techniques to clean and protect a car's finish. But some use strong detergents that can eventually ruin the finish. Washing your car yourself is a safe alternative to high-priced car washes. You can achieve professional results by washing, drying, and waxing your car by hand with the right equipment and methods.

Move your car to a shaded spot; washing or waxing a car in the hot sun or when the surface is hot may cause streaking and may damage the finish.

Use mild dishwashing detergent or car shampoo and a soft sponge to wash your car.

Close all the car windows tightly before starting to wash your car. Then thoroughly hose off the dust and loose dirt; brushing it off with a cloth or even with your hand may scratch the finish. Use a garden nozzle on the hose that provides strong water pressure. Spray the wheels, hubcaps, undersurface of the fenders (avoid wetting the engine compartment), bumpers, and as far under the chassis as possible, using a hard stream of water to remove dirt, mud, and salt.

We recommend that you use mild dishwashing liquid or commercial car shampoo to clean your car. Remember that you are using cold water and will need to use plenty of detergent. Apply the cleaning solution with a clean, soft sponge, mitt, or cloth, scrubbing *lightly* where necessary. Work from the top down. Wash one area at a time, but keep water running over the entire car so that the dirt slides off rather than being scrubbed in.

Use a cleaner, automotive rubbing compound, or cleaner/wax on older cars to help remove the oxidized layer. Remove tar deposits with special tar remover. You can also remove tar, as well as bird droppings and insects, with a cloth saturated with vegetable oil. Hold the cloth on the dirty area until the material lifts off with gentle rubbing.

Polish your car, using a circular motion with overlapping strokes.

Rinse the car before the suds dry. You may have to work quickly to do this on hot days and in dry climates.

Dry the car with a soft, absorbent terry-cloth towel or a chamois to prevent water spots. Paper toweling can scratch automobile finishes. It should not be used to dry the exterior of the car except the windows.

When water no longer beads up on the car's surface, apply wax or polish, following the manufacturer's instructions. After the wax has dried, sprinkle baking soda or cornstarch on the surface. Either powder will pick up the wax and help bring out surface luster. If dried wax remains around the chrome trim, remove it with a soft-bristled brush.

Tires

Wash tires and hubcaps after the rest of the car has been washed. Hose them with a hard stream of water to remove loose dirt before scrubbing.

Use a special tire brush or a sponge to remove soil and pebbles from the tires and the spokes of the hubcaps. Tires can be cleaned with all-purpose cleaners, steel-wool soap pads, and special whitewall cleaners. A synthetic scouring pad should be used to remove black scuff marks from whitewalls. Alloy hubcaps must be treated especially gently because their surfaces are easily damaged.

Coat the cleaned tires with a rubber protectant to help maintain a shiny appearance and to minimize rubber deterioration. Self-polishing floor wax will also make tires shine.

Upholstery

CLOTH

Care should be taken to avoid spots and spills on cloth upholstery because it is not easy to clean. Mop up all spills as soon as possible, and spot treat them to avoid stains. Always carry paper toweling in your car to absorb spills.

Vacuum cloth upholstery, using your Eureka vacuum cleaner with an upholstery brush or your Mini Mite®. We recommend that you use a crevice tool to pick up dirt from hard-to-reach places.

Any commercial upholstery shampoo can be used to clean automobile upholstery. Follow the manufacturer's instructions, and vacuum thoroughly when the product is completely dry.

Put a cordless Eureka Mini Mite® in its recharging stand in your garage and use it often to vacuum your car's upholstery.

Upholstery Cleaner

Make a stiff foam by mixing ¼ cup white liquid dishwashing detergent in 1 cup warm water and beating the mixture with an eggbeater. Spread the foam over the upholstery with a sponge, using circular, overlapping strokes. Let it dry, then vacuum the soil away.

VINYL AND LEATHER

Vinyl upholstery is cold in winter and hot in summer, but it's durable and easy to care for. Leather upholstery is a luxury-car option, but the care for both kinds of upholstery is the same.

Vacuum the creases and crevices of your car's upholstery as part of your routine, general car care, but be especially careful not to scratch the upholstery with sharp-edged attachments or by exerting too much pressure. Use a whisk broom to remove loose soil or debris when you are unable to vacuum. Clean upholstery with a commercial product or a homemade solution. Use a leather or vinyl conditioner periodically to prevent cracking, drying out, and fading. When you use a commercial product, read and follow the manufacturer's instructions

Leather or Vinyl Upholstery Cleaner

Make a warm, soapy solution using soap flakes and water. Apply the suds to the upholstery with a soft-bristled brush, working the cleaner gently into the grain. Wipe the upholstery clean with a damp sponge, and buff it dry with a soft cloth.

Use a soft-bristled brush and a mild cleaner to scrub your vinyl car top.

Cleaner for Vinyl Car Tops

Pour ⅛ cup dishwashing detergent into a pail, and add a hard stream of about 1 gallon warm water to make lots of suds. Apply the solution with a sponge and scrub with a brush. Rinse well, wipe dry, and apply a vinyl dressing for protection.

Vinyl Car Tops

Some cars have decorative vinyl tops, which require special cleaning products to keep them looking good for a long time. Scrub the vinyl top with a soft-bristled brush and a mild cleaner to get soil out of the grain. Then apply a protective coating for vinyl to the car top to guard against damage from sun, pollutants, and extreme weather. Do not use ordinary car wax.

Many commercial products are available to clean and protect vinyl car tops. If you use one of these products, read and follow the manufacturer's instructions.

Windows and Windshields

Before self-service gas stations, shining car windows was one cleaning task that most people didn't do for themselves. But now that many of us pump our own gas, we also clean our own windshields, car windows, headlights, and taillights. Keeping them clear is essential to safe driving.

Clean all exterior glass and plastic windows each time you refuel your car. Use a synthetic scouring pad to remove stubborn street grime and bugs. Make sure that the cloth with which you wipe the windows is free of grit that can scratch the surface. Ideally, you should use only a full-skin chamois; it will not streak and is unlikely to scratch your car windows.

Each time you wash the car, clean the glass and plastic windows inside and out with a glass-cleaning product or windshield-washer fluid. Clean the inside of the windows with strokes in one direction and the outside with strokes in another direction; this makes it easy to find and correct streaks.

To properly care for your windshield, always use specially formulated windshield-washer fluid. Keep the washer jets clear and adjusted so that they spray onto the windshield correctly. Replace windshield-wiper blades when they begin to smear or skip on the windshield. We've found that the blades will last longer if you always wet the windshield before using the wipers.

Car-Window Cleaner

Mix ¼ cup vinegar in 1 gallon warm water. Wipe the windows inside and out with a cloth dipped in the solution. Then wipe with a clean, dry cloth. This solution also cleans plastic car windows.

HOW TO BEAT SPOTS AND STAINS

W hen you walk into some homes, it's like entering an archaeological site: faint crayon marks on the wallpaper record the toddler age, grease spots on the carpet in front of the door to the garage recall the period of do-it-yourself car maintenance, sauce splatters and wine stains in the dining room remember the gourmet-cooking fad, and the discolored spots on the living room carpet will never forget Fido. Most of us don't want our houses to say quite so much about us.

For years, we at Eureka have been helping you deal with the usual dust and dirt of daily living; and in this chapter and the next, we'll help you deal with the unusual and not-so-unusual spots and stains that find their way onto your carpeting, your clothes, your furniture, and the other surfaces in your home.

Grass stains on jeans, wine spots on tablecloths, oil spills on the floor of the garage—the variety of potential stains in your home is mind-boggling. Each stain requires its own special treatment, or you may end up with a worse mess than you started with. Catsup on your carpet just cannot be treated in the same way as the cat's paw-prints on your comforter. That's where the Stain-Removal Guide comes in.

The guide explains the quickest and most effective ways to remove almost any stain from almost any surface. All you have to do to beat stains is to go after them as soon as they happen, before they have time to set, following the methods you'll find in the next chapter.

Before you get into the Stain-Removal Guide, which tells you how to clean up specific spots and stains, we want to share with you some basic information about stains and stain-removal. We'll give you a comprehensive shopping list of cleaning tools and products that you will want to have in your stain-removal kit to combat stains, and we'll teach you the eight basic techniques of stain-removal.

Three Kinds of Stains

GREASY STAINS

When the extra-gigantic popcorn bucket gets dumped in your lap at the movies or you inadvertently wipe the dipstick across your sleeve when you're checking the oil level in your car, the result is a greasy stain. You can sometimes remove grease spots from washable fabrics by laundering. Pre-treating by rubbing detergent directly into the spot often helps, as does using dry-cleaning solution on the stain. If you are treating an old stain or one that has been ironed, a yellow stain may remain after treatment with a solvent. Bleach can sometimes remove this yellow residue.

To remove grease spots from nonwashable fabrics, sponge the stain with dry-cleaning solution. Elimination of the stain may require several applications. Allow the spot to dry completely between spongings. Greasy stains may also be removed from nonwashable fabrics by using an absorbent, such as cornstarch, cornmeal, French chalk, or fuller's earth (mineral clay available at most drug stores). Dust the absorbent on the greasy spot. When it begins to look caked, it should be shaken or brushed off.

Absorbents are easy to use and will not harm fabrics. However, other stain-removal agents, such as detergents, dry-cleaning solvents, and bleach, can damage fibers. Before using any of these products, you should carefully read the care label on the stained item and the label on the product container. If you do not have either one of these labels, we recommend that you test the cleaning product on the fabric in an inconspicuous area.

NONGREASY STAINS

Fruit juice on your collar, black coffee on your lapel, tea on your pocket flap, food coloring on your cuff, ink on your pant leg—nongreasy stains are easy to acquire, but not impossible to remove. If you are treating a nongreasy stain on a washable fabric, we recommend that you sponge the stain with cool water as soon as possible. If this doesn't remove the stain, try soaking the fabric in cool water. The stain may soak out within half an hour, or you may need to leave the item in water overnight. If some of the stain still remains after this treatment, try gently rubbing liquid detergent into it, then rinse with cool water. The very last resort is to use bleach, but always read the fabric-care label before you bleach. If the stain is old or has already been ironed, it may be impossible to remove it completely.

A nongreasy stain on fabric that cannot be washed can be sponged with cool water. Place an absorbent pad under the stained area and slowly drip water through the fabric with an eye dropper or pump/trigger spray bottle. This method of flushing the stain lets you control the amount of water and the rate at which it flows through the fabric so that you don't inadvertently spread the stain. If you treat a nongreasy stain with water while it is still fresh, you often can remove it entirely. If water alone fails to remove the stain, work liquid detergent into the stain and rinse it by sponging or flushing with cool water. Sponge the spot with rubbing alcohol after you've rinsed it to remove detergent residue and to speed drying. (**Caution:** If you're treating acetate, acrylic, modacrylic, rayon, triacetate, or vinyl, be sure to dilute the alcohol with water, 1 part alcohol to 2 parts water.)

COMBINATION STAINS

Some stains are double trouble. Coffee with cream, Thousand Island salad dressing, and lipstick leave a trail of combination stains behind them;

they're both greasy and nongreasy. Getting rid of combination stains is a two-part operation. First get rid of the nongreasy stain and then attack the greasy residue. On most fabrics, you'll need to sponge the stain with cool water, then work liquid detergent into the stain and rinse thoroughly. After the fabric has dried, apply dry-cleaning solution to the greasy part of the stain. Allow the fabric to dry.

Taking the Stress Out of Stains

There's a surefire strategy for beating stains. You'll save time by doing it right the first time rather than wasting time experimenting with various cures for the problem and possibly making the stain worse than it was to start with.

Here are the basic rules; precise instructions for handling specific kinds of stains can be found in the Stain-Removal Guide.

- **The quicker the better.** The best time to treat a stain is the moment after it occurs. The longer it sets, the more likely it is that a stain will become permanent.
- **Know what you're cleaning.** Identify both the staining agent and the stained surface. Both will affect the way in which you treat the stain.
- **Clean it off before you clean it.** Remove as much of the staining agent as you possibly can before you begin the stain-removal process.
- **Be gentle.** Rubbing, folding, wringing, and squeezing cause stains to penetrate more deeply and may damage delicate fibers.
- **Keep it cool.** Avoid using hot water, high-heat clothes dryers, and irons on stains; heat makes some stains impossible to remove.
- **Pretest stain removers.** Even clear water can damage some fabrics, so test every cleaner you plan to use in an inconspicuous place before you use it on the stain.
- **Follow directions.** Read manufacturers' care labels, directions on product containers, and the directions in our Stain-Removal Guide before you start to clean a stain.
- **Work from the edges into the center.** You won't spread the stain or leave a ring.

Your Stain-Removal Kit

To beat stains, you have to be prepared. Your well-stocked stain-removal kit, like a first-aid kit, should be ready to help you handle cleaning emergencies whenever they occur.

Here are the tools you'll need to have in your kit:
- Clean, white cotton cloths
- Disposable diapers for absorbing flushed cleaning solutions
- White blotting paper
- White paper toweling
- A spoon, blunt knife, or spatula for scraping
- An eyedropper or trigger spray bottle
- A small brush
- Several colorfast weights

Your kit will also need to include a variety of stain-removal agents. What you need depends on what you are likely to have to clean. We suggest that you check through the list of stains in our Stain-Removal Guide. Find the stains that occur most frequently in your house, and also look up the stains that would be most disastrous if they did occur. Read through the treatment for the stain to learn which of the following stain-removing agents you're likely to need. You will be able to purchase most of them at your local hardware store, grocery store, or pharmacy.

ABSORBENTS

Absorbents "soak up" grease stains. We consider cornmeal the best absorbent for light colors, and fuller's earth the best for dark colors. Spread the absorbent on the stained areas and allow it to work. As the grease is soaked up, the absorbent material will cake or become gummy. It should then be shaken or brushed off. You should repeat the process until the stain has been removed. This may take as long as eight hours or more.

BLEACHES

Chlorine

Commonly used to bleach white cotton, linen, and synthetic fabrics, chlorine bleach is a powerful stain remover, which can weaken fibers if it is allowed to stay on fabric for too long a time. Never use chlorine bleach on silk, wool, or fabrics that are exposed to sunlight, such as curtains. Always test chlorine bleach in an inconspicuous place before bleaching an entire item. **Caution:** Chlorine bleach is poisonous. If it comes in contact with skin or eyes, it will cause burns and irritation.

Color Remover

Hydrosulfite, the active chemical compound in color removers, lightens the color of fabric before it is redyed a lighter color. This chemical also removes some stains from colorfast fibers. Always pretest color remover. If the product causes a distinct color change instead of fading the fabric, you may be able to restore the original color by rinsing immediately with cool water. If the color fades when color remover is applied, the original color cannot be restored. Color remover should not be used in a metal container.

Caution: Color removers are poisonous. Avoid prolonged contact with skin. Observe all precautions on the label.

Hydrogen Peroxide
The 3-percent solution of hydrogen peroxide that is sold as a mild antiseptic is a safe bleach for most fibers. A stronger solution used for lightening hair is too strong to use on fabric and other household surfaces. Buy peroxide in small quantities and store it in a cool, dark place; it loses strength quickly after it is opened and if it is exposed to light.

Sodium Perborate
You may purchase sodium perborate in crystal form at pharmacies under trade names or generically. It is safe for all fabrics and surfaces. This oxygen bleach is slower-acting than hydrogen peroxide. When you use this bleach, be sure that you rinse the treated articles thoroughly in clear water.

CHEMICALS
Acetic acid
You can buy acetic acid in a 10-percent solution at pharmacies. White vinegar is a 5-percent acetic acid and can be used as a substitute for the stronger solution. Acetic acid is a clear fluid, used full strength to remove stains on silk and wool. It must be diluted with 2 parts water for use on cotton and linen. (We recommend that you test for colorfastness.) Never use this chemical on acetate. If acetic acid causes a color change, try sponging the affected areas with ammonia; this may restore the color.

Acetone
Fingernail-polish remover and household-cement thinner are acetone based, but they should not be substituted for pure acetone because they contain other ingredients that may worsen the stain. You can purchase acetone at pharmacies and paint stores. The colorless liquid smells like peppermint, and it can be used on stains caused by substances such as fingernail polish or household cement. Although acetone will damage neither natural fibers nor most synthetics, it should be tested to make sure that dyed fabrics will not be harmed. Acetone should not be used on fabrics containing acetate; it will dissolve them. **Caution:** Acetone is flammable and evaporates rapidly, producing toxic fumes. When using acetone, work outside or in a well-ventilated area. Avoid inhaling the fumes. Store acetone in a tightly capped container in a cool place.

Alcohol
Isopropyl alcohol in a 70-percent solution is sufficient for most stain-removal jobs that call for alcohol. Stronger, denatured alcohol (90-percent solution) can also be used. Be sure you do not buy alcohol with added color

or fragrance. Since alcohol will fade some dyes, we recommend that you test it on the fabric you will be cleaning. Alcohol will damage acetate, triacetate, modacrylic, and acrylic fibers. If you must use it on fibers in the acetate family, dilute the alcohol with 2 parts water. **Caution:** Alcohol is poisonous and flammable.

Ammonia

Use plain household ammonia without added color or fragrance for stain removal. Because ammonia affects some dyes, we recommend that you test it on the stained article. To restore color changed by ammonia, rinse the affected area in water and apply a few drops of white vinegar, then rinse with clear water. Ammonia damages silk and wool; if you must use it on these fibers, dilute it with an equal amount of water and use as sparingly as possible. **Caution:** Ammonia is poisonous. Avoid inhaling its fumes. It will cause burns or irritation if it comes in contact with skin or eyes.

Amyl Acetate

Chemically pure amyl acetate, or banana oil, is available in drugstores; it's safe for use on fibers that could be damaged by acetone, but it should not be allowed to come in contact with plastics or furniture finishes. **Caution:** Amyl acetate is poisonous and flammable. Avoid contact with skin.

Coconut Oil

You can buy coconut oil in drug and health-food stores. It is used in the preparation of dry spotter that is used to remove many kinds of stains. If you cannot obtain coconut oil, you may substitute mineral oil, which is almost as effective.

To make **dry spotter,** combine 1 part coconut oil and 8 parts liquid dry-cleaning solvent. Store this solution in a tightly capped container to prevent evaporation.

Glycerine

Use glycerine in the preparation of wet spotter that is used to remove many kinds of stains.

To make **wet spotter,** mix 1 part glycerine, 1 part white dishwashing detergent, and 8 parts water. Store the solution in a plastic squeeze bottle, and shake well before each use.

Oxalic Acid

Effective in treating ink and rust stains, oxalic acid crystals are sold in many pharmacies. The crystals must be dissolved in water (1 tablespoon crystals to 1 cup warm water). Test the solution on a hidden corner of the spotted item before using it on the stain. Moisten the stained area with the solution. Allow it to dry, then reapply. Be sure all traces of the solution are rinsed out. **Caution:** Oxalic acid is poisonous. Avoid contact with skin and eyes, and wear rubber gloves when working with this chemical.

Sodium Thiosulfate
Also known as photographic "hypo" or "fixer," sodium thiosulfate is available in crystal form at drugstores and photo-supply houses. Although considered safe for all fibers and harmless to dyes, this chemical should be tested on an inconspicuous area before use.

Turpentine
Most often used as a thinner for oil-based paints, turpentine is effective on paint and grease stains. **Caution:** Turpentine is flammable and poisonous. Observe all the precautions stated on the label.

Vinegar
When we suggest that you use vinegar on a stain, we always want you to use white (clear) vinegar. Cider and red-wine vinegar have color that can leave a stain. Vinegar is a 5-percent acetic acid solution and should be diluted if you use it on cotton or linen. Vinegar is safe for all other colorfast fibers, but it can change the color of some dyes, so always test it on an inconspicuous area first. If an article changes color, rinse the affected area with water to which you've added a few drops of ammonia. Rinse thoroughly with clear water. This may restore the color.

DRY-CLEANING SOLVENTS
Perchloroethylene, trichlorethane, and trichloroethylene are three of the most common and effective ingredients in dry-cleaning solvents. Most solvents are nonflammable, but their fumes are toxic and should not be inhaled. Not all dry-cleaning solvents can be used on all surfaces and not all of these products remove all stains, so be sure to read the label before using a solution.

WASHING AGENTS
Detergents
When our stain-removal directions call for a mild detergent, choose a white dishwashing liquid; the dyes in nonwhite detergents may worsen the stain. When instructions call for a pretreating paste made of detergent and water, use a powdered detergent that does not contain bleach. When the stain-removal directions specify that you should apply a liquid laundry detergent directly to the spot or stain, be sure to read the directions on the product's label carefully. Some products cannot safely be used in this manner. Other detergent products, such as those used in automatic dishwashers or for heavy-duty household cleaning, and certain laundry products may contain alkalies. They can set stains caused by ammonia, soap, and oven cleaner and should not be used for spot removal.

Enzyme Presoaks

Most effective on protein stains, such as those caused by meat juices, eggs, and blood, enzyme presoaks may harm silk and wool. Make sure you have exhausted every alternative before you use enzyme presoaks on these two fabrics. Use a presoak as soon as possible after mixing with water; enzyme-presoak solutions become inactive in storage. Be sure to read and observe all the directions on the product label.

Powdered Cleansers

Scouring powders and baking soda can be used to remove stains on surfaces that will not be harmed by abrasives. However, you should be aware that prolonged or overly vigorous scrubbing with these products can scratch even the most durable surface. Make sure you rinse away all the powder when the job is completed.

Pretreaters

Use pretreaters on spots and stains when you think that a stain might not respond to normal laundering procedures. Pretreaters start the cleaning process before the stained item is put in the washer. They must be used in conjunction with the rest of the laundering process; do not try to use a pretreater alone, as though it were a spot remover. After applying a pretreater, you should not allow the fabric to dry out before you begin washing.

Soaps

Bath soaps with added moisturizers, fragrance, dyes, or deodorant should not be used to treat spots. Purchase either laundry soap or pure white soap.

Safety Precautions

In order to treat stains and spots as soon as they occur, you have to be prepared. But many of the products you stock in your stain-removal kit are flammable or toxic, and certain safety tips should be kept in mind when storing and using these products.

- Store stain-removing products carefully and out of the reach of children. The storage area should be cool, dry, and separate from food storage areas. Keep bottles tightly capped and boxes closed.
- Do not transfer cleaning products to new containers. Keep them in their original containers so that you never have to search for directions for their proper use and so that they are always clearly labeled.
- Follow the directions on the product label and heed all warnings.
- Glass and unchipped porcelain containers are preferable to metal or plastic when working with stain-removal agents. Never use plastic with sol-

If any kind of cleaning solution splashes in your eye, rinse the eye with clear water for 15 minutes.

vents. Never use any container that is rusty. Clean all containers thoroughly after use.

• Protect your hands with rubber gloves. Don't touch your eyes or skin while handling stain-removal chemicals. If you do accidentally touch your eyes or spill chemicals on your skin, flush immediately with clear water.

• Remember that the fumes of solvents are toxic; work in a well-ventilated area.

• Do not use chemicals near an open flame or electrical outlet. Do not smoke while using chemicals.

• Do not use a solvent as a laundry additive.

• When using a solvent on a washable fabric, be sure to rinse all traces of the solvent out of the fabric.

• Do not experiment with mixtures of stain-removal agents. Never combine products unless specifically directed to do so in the recipes for homemade cleaning solutions or the Stain-Removal Guide in this book. Many combinations can be dangerous.

• If the cleaning process requires the use of more than one stain-removal agent, rinse out each product thoroughly before applying the next.

Eight Ways to Beat Stains

We would all like to be able to squirt a little dab of the right solution on a stain, stand back, and watch the spot fade away forever. Unfortunately, stain removal has not yet become quite that simple. Until someone comes up with a spray for the common mustard stain, you can go around with a yellow streak down your shirt or you can beat the stain with a combination of the right techniques and the right cleaning solutions. We have already discussed the cleaning supplies you need to have on hand in your stain-removal kit, but you also need to know how these tools and products are used to remove stains quickly and effectively.

There are eight basic techniques for stain removal: brushing, flushing, freezing, presoaking, pretreating, scraping, sponging, and tamping. The right technique for a particular spot or stain depends on what was spilled and where it fell. So read through the cleaning methods, and then use these techniques when our Stain-Removal Guide calls for them in the treatment of a particular stain.

BRUSHING

Use brushing to remove dried stains. Some kinds of spots, such as dried mud, can be removed completely by brushing. For other kinds of stains, brushing is only a step in the cleaning process.

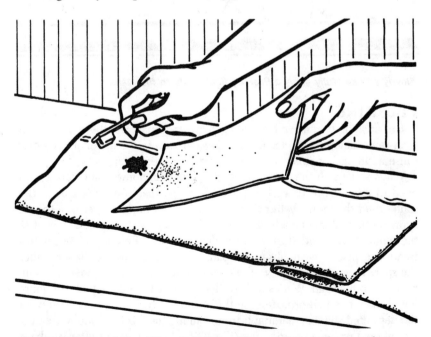

A stiff-bristled brush should be used for brushing a stain up and onto a sheet of paper.

We recommend a small, stiff-bristled brush for this technique. When you're working on fabric, stretch the piece on a firm, clean surface. Hold a sheet of paper next to the stain, and brush the staining material onto the paper. A gentle motion with the brush pulls the stain up off the surface and onto the paper.

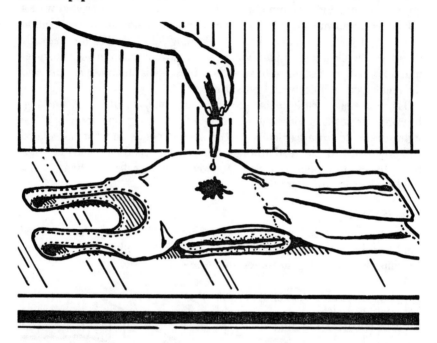

Slowly and carefully apply a flushing liquid only to the stain.

FLUSHING

Use flushing to remove loosened staining materials and the residue from stain-removal agents. If cleaning products are left in the material, they may cause additional staining or even damage the treated article.

When you are flushing a stain, especially one on nonwashable fabric, you need to control the flow of water carefully so that you don't spread the stain or get the fabric wetter than you need to. An eyedropper or a trigger spray bottle that can be adjusted to a fine stream lets you precisely control the amount of liquid flushed through the fabric. Before you begin this treatment, place a clean absorbent pad, such as a disposable diaper, under the spot. Then slowly and carefully apply water or the recommended stain remover to the stain. Work slowly so that you don't flood the pad with more liquid than it can absorb. Replace the absorbent pad frequently to prevent the deposited staining material from restaining the fabric. If you're treating a stain on a washable fabric, rinse the article in warm water after you have flushed the stain.

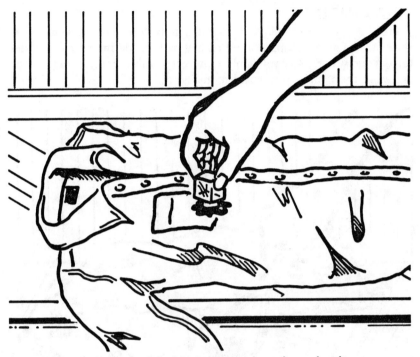

Freezing a stain is accomplished by holding an ice cube against it.

FREEZING

Candle wax, chewing gum, and other gooey substances are easier to remove when they are cold and hard. Hold an ice cube against the stain to freeze it. If the stained item is not washable, place the ice in a plastic bag. You can put a small stained item in a plastic bag and place the whole thing in the freezer. After the stain has solidified, it can usually be gently lifted or scraped from the surface.

PRESOAKING

When your wash is grayed, yellowed, or heavily soiled, washing alone will not get it clean and bright—you will have to presoak. Sort the soiled items before presoaking; items that are not colorfast should be presoaked separately from colorfast items because their colors may bleed.

You may add bleach, laundry detergent, or an enzyme presoak to the soaking water. But don't use chlorine bleach and an enzyme product at the same time. You can leave colorfast, stained articles in a presoak for as long as it takes to get them clean, but for most stains, 30 minutes is long enough. Items that aren't colorfast should be soaked only briefly.

Before you wash a load of presoaked laundry, make sure that it has been thoroughly rinsed and that no residue of the presoak is left on the items.

PRETREATING

Pretreat oily, greasy stains with liquid laundry detergent, a soil-and-spot-removing spray, bar soap, or a pretreating paste made from powdered detergent and water. After you apply a pretreater, rub it into the stain gently, and wash the item as you would normally.

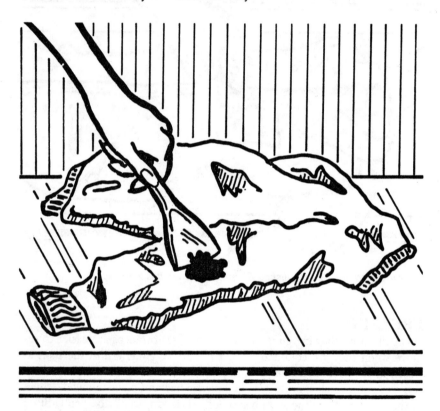

Scraping is used to lift off excess solid or caked-on stains.

SCRAPING

Scrape away solid staining material with a dull knife, spoon, or spatula before you apply stain remover. Don't press too hard; move the edge of your scraping tool back and forth across the stain in short strokes.

SPONGING

Put an absorbent pad, such as a disposable diaper, under the stain before you sponge it. On a carpet you will have to work without an absorbent pad, so be especially careful not to use excessive amounts of cleaning solution or water. Use another pad or a sponge to apply the stain-removing agent.

Sponge the stain gently using light strokes. Change either pad as soon as any of the stain is deposited on it.

Some fabrics, such as acetate, triacetate, and rayon, are likely to develop rings when they are sponged. When you work on stains on these fabrics, barely wet the pad with stain remover and touch the fabric lightly so that the stain remover is absorbed as slowly as possible. Blot the treated area between absorbent pads. Allow it to air-dry. Ironing or drying with heat may cause the stain remover itself to stain the fabric.

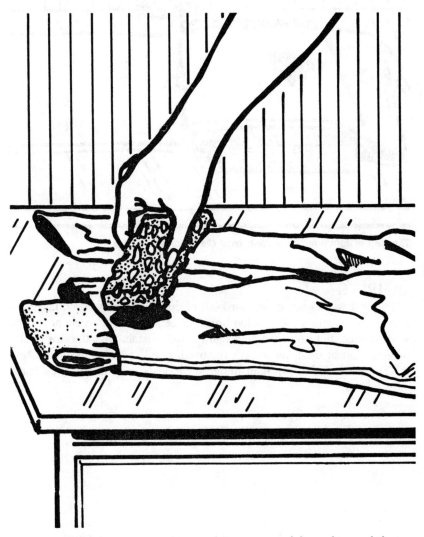

When you're sponging on a stain-removing agent, work inward toward the center, using light strokes.

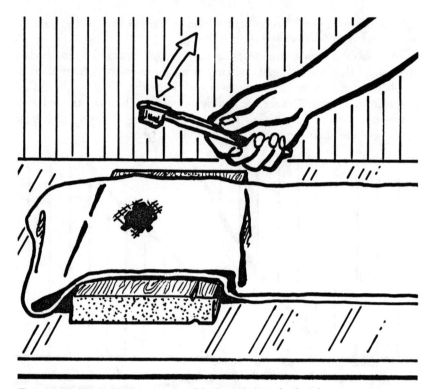

Tamping is lightly hitting a stain with the bristles of a brush.

TAMPING

The best way to get some stains out of durable, tightly woven fabrics is to tamp them with a soft-bristled brush. Place the stained article on a hard work surface, not on a pad, and lightly rap the stain with the tips of the bristles. Repeat until the stain is removed. Use this technique only when it is recommended in our Stain-Removal Guide, because tamping will harm most fabrics.

STAIN-REMOVAL GUIDE

(continued)

STAIN-REMOVAL GUIDE

(continued)

STAIN-REMOVAL GUIDE

(continued)

Y ou try to be careful to keep greasy spots off clothes and winter slush off carpet: You put on an apron over your dress-for-success suit before packing the kids' lunches, and there's a set of slippers in all sizes in a basket by your front door so no one has to wear their shoes in the house. But no matter what you do to guard against stains, they happen. Spots and stains are an inevitable part of life, but you don't have to live with them forever. If you act quickly, using the proper technique, you can clean up almost any stain.

Each stain has its own unique personality that's a combination of the staining potential of the ingredients in what has been spilled and the stain-absorbing qualities of the surface that was spilled on. Some techniques will work only on certain kinds of stains and fabrics, and the use of an improper cleaning method can make some stains worse. We don't want to scare you away from cleaning, but we do want to caution you to use this Stain-Removal Guide. When stains occur in your home, look them up, read the information about them, and follow the instructions carefully. All the procedures and products listed in this guide have been thoroughly tested, and you can be sure that they all work.

How to Use This Guide

This could happen to any of us: The boss is over for dinner. You give the puppy a bone to keep him quiet in the kitchen. When you open the kitchen door to bring out a tray of hors d'oeuvres, the little dog dashes between your legs and heads straight for the boss, who is sitting on the couch, drink in hand, and jumps in her lap. Here you have the potential for many kinds of stains—cheese on the carpet, Scotch on the upholstery, damp bone on wool serge. Assess the damage, then look up the "staining agent" (that's the spilled substance not the puppy). These staining agents are listed in alphabetical order. Next, find the kind of surface that has been stained. Then read the procedure for removing the staining agent from the target it hit, such as your boss's *wool* suit.

Most of us are afraid we may make a stain worse if we try to do anything about it. Take the additional precaution of testing cleaning products on a hidden portion of the stained item. If you know a surface is colorfast and can accurately identify the stain, testing isn't necessary, but it can't hurt, so we suggest that you make it a practice to test.

You will find that in almost all cases the first few steps listed in our Stain-Removal Guide will remove a fresh stain. You may not have to use the remaining steps. But the procedures work best in sequence. Always start with the first step and go on to the next until the stain is removed. Skipping steps can have disastrous results. If you follow the recommended methods, you should be able to restore an item that might otherwise have been ruined, saving yourself the time and expense of buying a new one.

We have listed all fabrics by generic fiber. If you're not sure which fibers a blend or a synthetic fabric is made of, the following chart lists the fiber content of many common trademark fabrics.

Trademarks of Synthetic Fibers

Trademark	Generic Name	Trademark	Generic Name
A		**C** *(continued)*	
A.C.E	nylon or polyester	Cordura	nylon
Acetate by Avtex	acetate	Courtaulds Nylon	nylon
Absorbit	rayon	Crepeset	nylon
Acrilan	acrylic or modacrylic	Crepesoft	polyester
		Creslan	acrylic
Anso	nylon	Cumuloft	nylon
Antron	nylon		
Ariloft	acetate	**D**	
Arnel	triacetate	Dacron	polyester
Avlin	polyester		
Avril	rayon	**E**	
Avsorb	rayon	Eloquent Luster	nylon
		Eloquent Touch	nylon
B		Encron	polyester
Beau-Grip	rayon	Enka 10-10	nylon
Bi-Loft	acrylic	Enkaire	rayon
Blue "C"	nylon or polyester	Enkaloft	nylon
		Enkalure	nylon
		Enkasheer	nylon
C		Enkrome	rayon
Cadon	nylon	Estron	acetate
Cantrece	nylon		
Caprolan	nylon	**F**	
Celanese	nylon or acetate	Fibro	rayon
		Fina	acrylic
Chromspun	acetate	Fortel	polyester
Coloray	rayon		

(continued)

Trademarks of Synthetic Fibers *(continued)*

Trademark	Generic Name	Trademark	Generic Name
G		**Q**	
Golden Glow	polyester	Qiana	nylon
Golden Touch	polyester		
		R	
H		Rayon by Avtex	rayon
Herculon	olefin		
Hollofil	polyester	**S**	
		SEF	modacrylic
K		Shareen	nylon
Kodel	polyester	Silky Touch	polyester
KodOfill	polyester	Silver Label	nylon
KodOsoff	polyester	Softalon	nylon
		So-Lara	acrylic
L		Spectran	polyester
Lanese	acetate/ polyester	Strialine	polyester
Loftura	acetate	**T**	
Lusteroff	nylon	Trevira	polyester
Lycra	spandex	Twisloc	polyester
M		**U**	
Marquesa	olefin	Ulstron	nylon
Marvess	olefin	Ultron	nylon
Multisheer	nylon		
		V	
N		Vectra	olefin
Natura Luster	nylon	Verel	modacrylic
		Vive La Crepe	nylon
O			
Orlon	acrylic	**Z**	
		Zantrel	rayon
P		Zeflon	nylon
Patlon	olefin	Zefran	acrylic or nylon
Plyloc	polyester		
Polyextra	polyester		
Polyloom	olefin		

ADHESIVE TAPE

Acetate	Rayon
Carpet/Synthetic	Silk
Carpet/Wool	Triacetate
Fiberglass	Wool

Scrape gummy matter from the material very gently. Use dry-cleaning solvent. If stain persists, apply dry spotter to the stain and cover with an absorbent pad dampened with spotter. Change the pad as it picks up the stain. Let it stand as long as any stain is being removed, keeping both the stain and pad moist. Sponge the area with dry-cleaning solvent. Allow the surface to dry completely.

Acrylic Fabric	Olefin
Burlap	Polyster
Nylon	Spandex

Gently scrape up the tape. Very carefully, apply cleaning fluid to the stain. If any adhesive remains, apply wet spotter, with a few drops of ammonia added, to the stain. Tamp and blot occasionally with an absorbent pad. Flush with water and dry thoroughly.

Acrylic Plastic	Marble
Alabaster	Pewter
Asphalt	Platinum
Chromium	Plexiglas
Copper	Vinyl Clothing
Enamel	Vinyl Tile
Glass	Vinyl Wallcovering
Linoleum	

Scrape to remove the tape. Do not use an abrasive product. Dip a clean sponge or cloth into warm, sudsy water and rub the gummy matter. The warm water will soften the tape so it can be removed with the sponge or cloth. Rinse with warm water and wipe dry with a clean cloth.

Aluminum	Stainless Steel
Iron	

Pick off as much tape as possible with your fingertips or tweezers. If possible, soak the stain in warm to hot, sudsy water. This should loosen the sticky substance enough that it can be wiped off. Should any remain, gently rub the area in one direction only with a soft scouring pad to remove any traces.

Adhesive Tape *(continued)*

Bamboo	**Ceramic Glass/Tile**
Cane	**Polyurethane**

Rub the gummy area with a cloth or sponge dipped in warm, soapy water to which a few drops of ammonia have been added. Rinse with clear water. Dry thoroughly.

Bluestone	**Limestone**
Brick	**Masonry Tile**
Concrete	**Sandstone**
Flagstone	**Slate**
Granite	**Terrazzo**

Mix a solution of washing soda or laundry detergent and warm water. Do not use soap; it will leave a hard-to-remove scum. With a soft-bristled brush—a toothbrush is good for small areas—gently spread the solution over the gummy portion until it is removed. Rinse with clear, warm water.

Brass	**Porcelain**
Bronze	**Tin**
Ivory	**Zinc**
Jade	

Remove tape with your fingertips or tweezers. Mix a solution of hot water and mild soap. With a soft cloth dipped in the solution, rub until the gummy substance is softened and removed. Rinse with clear water.

Cork

Scrape to remove tape, taking care not to gouge the soft surface. Gently rub any remaining gummy matter with fine-grade (000) steel wool dipped in liquid or paste wax. Wipe away soiled wax as you work.

Cotton	**Linen**

Scrape to remove tape. Place the fabric stained side down on an absorbent pad and sponge the area with spot remover or cleaning fluid. Allow fluid to dry thoroughly; launder soon to remove all traces of fluid.

Felt

Remove tape carefully to avoid shredding the fiber. Freeze to harden remainder and gently brush with a sponge or soft-bristled brush. This should

Adhesive Tape *(continued)*

remove any remaining adhesive. In extreme cases, rub the surface carefully with a razor blade; however, this removes some felt fiber.

Fur/Natural   **Fur/Synthetic**

Take care not to remove the fur when removing adhesive. With ice cubes in a plastic bag, freeze to harden gummy residue. Gently brush with a fine-bristled brush or a damp sponge. Take care not to soak pelt or backing. If a gummy residue remains, scrape it carefully in the direction of the nap with a razor blade. In extreme cases, the gummy matter can be carefully cut away with a pair of scissors if it is at the very tips of the hairs.

Gold

Add a few drops of ammonia to hot, sudsy water. Immerse the stained object if it is small, or use a brush, such as a toothbrush, to apply the solution. Rinse in clear, hot water and dry with a soft cloth.

Grout

Remove as much of the gummy matter as possible. Apply grout cleaner. Or dip a wet toothbrush in powdered cleanser and gently scrub. Rinse with clear water and dry.

Leather

Carefully scrape to remove tape. Dip a cloth or sponge into mild soap-suds and gently scrub until the remaining matter is removed. Dry with a clean cloth. Condition the leather with saddle soap.

Paint/Flat   **Paint/Gloss**

Remove excess gum carefully to avoid removing any paint. Mix dish-washing detergent in hot water and swish to make a great volume of suds. Dip a cloth in only the foam and apply to the stain. Do not allow the water to run off as it will cause hard-to-remove streaks. Rinse with clear water. Dry thoroughly.

Photographs

With your fingertip and a very gentle touch, rub the gummy matter in one direction toward the edge of the photo. It should ball up as you rub and should roll off the photo. Continue until all the adhesive is removed.

Adhesive Tape *(continued)*

Silver

Pick off as much tape as possible with your fingertips or tweezers. Rub the remaining portion using hot suds and a soft cloth. Rinse with hot water and dry immediately and thoroughly to prevent tarnish.

Suede

Carefully pick off as much tape as possible with your fingertips. Gently rub an art gum eraser over the remaining gummy surface, or apply suede cleaner. If that doesn't work, cautiously rub the spot with an emery board or very fine-grade (6/0 to 8/0) sandpaper. You are attempting to remove only a thin layer of suede, so work carefully.

Wallpaper

Put a white blotter against the tape and press through the blotter with a warm iron. Repeat, if necessary, with a clean portion of the blotter.

Wood

Remove tape gently so the finish will not be marred. Rub gently with a cloth dipped in the suds of hot, soapy water. Rub only the stained portion. Rinse with clear water, wipe dry immediately, and polish.

ALCOHOLIC BEVERAGES

Acetate	**Rope**
Burlap	**Silk**
Felt	**Triacetate**
Fiberglass	**Wool**
Rayon	

Blot up liquid. Spray on fabric spot cleaner, or flush area with cool water. Apply wet spotter and a few drops of white vinegar. Cover with an absorbent pad dampened with wet spotter and let stand as long as any stain is being removed. Keep the stain and pad moist, changing the pad as it picks up the stain. Flush with cool water, blotting excess liquid with a clean absorbent pad. Dry thoroughly.

Alcoholic Beverages *(continued)*

Acrylic Fabric	Olefin
Cotton	Polyester
Linen	Spandex
Nylon	

Apply fabric spot cleaner, or sponge the stain promptly with cool water. If possible, soak the stain in cool water for at least 30 minutes or overnight. Work undiluted dishwashing or liquid laundry detergent into stain. Rinse well. Launder as soon as possible. Old or ironed-in stains may be impossible to remove.

Acrylic Plastic	Paint/Flat
Aluminum	Paint/Gloss
Asphalt	Pearls
Chromium	Platinum
Copper	Plexiglas
Cork	Polyurethane
Enamel	Stainless Steel
Glass	Tin
Iron	Vinyl Clothing
Ivory	Vinyl Tile
Jade	Vinyl Wallcovering
Linoleum	Zinc

Wipe spill immediately with a cloth or sponge moistened with warm, sudsy water. Rinse well and wipe dry.

Alabaster	Marble

Wipe immediately and thoroughly with a damp cloth. If a stain remains, make a thick paste of water, chlorine bleach, and a mild powdered laundry detergent and put it on the stain. Cover with a damp cloth. Let it stand until the stain is bleached out. Rinse thoroughly and wipe dry with a soft cloth.

Bamboo	Ceramic Glass/Tile
Cane	Gold

Wipe up spill immediately. Wash with a cloth dipped in a solution of warm water and mild pure soap with a few drops of ammonia added. Rinse with clear water and dry thoroughly.

Alcoholic Beverages *(continued)*

Bluestone	Limestone
Brick	Masonry Tile
Concrete	Sandstone
Flagstone	Slate
Granite	Terrazzo

Wipe spill immediately. Clean any residue with a solution of washing soda or all-purpose laundry detergent (do not use soap) and water. Rinse well. Allow to dry thoroughly.

Brass	**Bronze**

Wipe up spill immediately. Wash with a cloth dipped in a solution of hot water and mild soap. Rinse with clear water and wipe thoroughly dry.

Carpet/Synthetic	**Foam Rubber**
Carpet/Wool	

After blotting the spill, apply carpet stain remover. An alternate technique is to blot up excess moisture, working from the outside of the spill inward. Spray with rug shampoo or mix 1 teaspoon of mild, nonalkali detergent in ½ pint lukewarm water. Add a small amount to the stain and blot until no more is removed. Mix 1 part white vinegar to 2 parts lukewarm water. Apply a small amount of the mixture and blot to neutralize the remaining stain. Place an absorbent pad over the stained area and weight it down for several hours. Allow to dry thoroughly.

Fur/Natural	**Fur/Synthetic**

For quick spot removal, use disposable cleaning cloths. Or blot up spill immediately with a clean, dry cloth. Try to prevent the hide or backing from getting wet. Mix dishwashing detergent in hot water and swish to make a great volume of suds. Dip a cloth in only the foam and gently rub with the nap. Rinse with another cloth dipped in clear water and wrung nearly dry. Allow to air-dry away from heat.

Grout

Wipe spill immediately. This should be all that is needed, but if the sealer on the grout is worn away or old, dip a wet toothbrush in powdered cleanser and apply, or use grout cleaner. Gently scrub. Rinse thoroughly and allow to dry.

Alcoholic Beverages *(continued)*

Leather   Suede

Blot up spill immediately. Mix a solution of mild soap in lukewarm water. Swish to make a great volume of suds. Apply only the suds with a slightly damp cloth. Rub gently but with vigor. Rub dry with a clean cloth. On leather only, condition with saddle soap.

Silver

Wipe up the spill immediately. Wash silver in hot, sudsy water with a soft cloth. Rinse well in hot, clear water. Wipe dry immediately to prevent tarnish.

Wallpaper

Blot up the spill immediately. Wipe stained area very gently with warm, clear water—do not use detergent or soap—without overwetting the paper. Strokes should overlap or the wall may become streaked. Carefully pat dry.

Wood

Wipe up the spill immediately. Rub stained area with liquid or paste wax, boiled linseed oil, or a cloth dampened in water and a few drops of ammonia. Rewax the stained area.

ALKALIES

(See Ammonia, Oven Cleaner, Soap.)

AMMONIA

Acetate	Polyester
Acrylic Fabric	Rayon
Burlap	Silk
Carpet/Synthetic	Spandex
Carpet/Wool	Triacetate
Nylon	Wool
Olefin	

(continued)

Ammonia *(continued)*

Sponge with cool water. If stain persists, thoroughly flush it with cool water. If the color has been altered, or to prevent fading or bleeding, neutralize the spot with a few drops of a mild acid such as lemon juice, white vinegar, or 10-percent acetic acid solution. Sponge thoroughly with cool water. Silk and wool are weakened and sometimes destroyed by alkalies such as ammonia, so be especially prompt in treatment.

Acrylic Plastic	**Jade**
Alabaster	**Linoleum**
Aluminum	**Marble**
Asphalt	**Opal**
Bamboo	**Paint/Flat**
Brass	**Paint/Gloss**
Bronze	**Pearls**
Cane	**Pewter**
Ceramic Glass/Tile	**Platinum**
Chromium	**Plexiglas**
Copper	**Polyurethane**
Coral	**Porcelain**
Cork	**Rope**
Fiberglass	**Stainless Steel**
Glass	**Tin**
Gold	**Vinyl Clothing**
Grout	**Vinyl Tile**
Iron	**Vinyl Wallcovering**
Ivory	**Zinc**

Rinse well with a sponge dipped in cool water. Wipe dry with a clean, soft cloth. Treat pearls stained with ammonia immediately; they are permanently damaged by ammonia and other alkalies.

Bluestone	**Limestone**
Brick	**Masonry Tile**
Concrete	**Sandstone**
Flagstone	**Slate**
Granite	**Terrazzo**

Scrub with a solution of washing soda or detergent—not soap—and water. Rinse well and dry.

Cotton	**Linen**

Flush area with cool water until all trace of ammonia is gone. Launder

Ammonia *(continued)*

as soon as possible. The acid treatment recommended for other fabrics cannot be used on cotton or linen because they may be permanently damaged by acids.

Felt

With a sponge dipped in cool water and wrung out, gently brush in the direction of the nap. If any stain remains, neutralize it with a few drops of lemon juice, white vinegar, or 10-percent acetic acid solution. Sponge thoroughly with cool water. Since felt is composed mainly of wool fibers, an ammonia stain may damage it permanently.

Fur/Natural   Fur/Synthetic

Dip a cloth or sponge in cool water and wring out as much of the water as possible. Gently rub with the nap; do not overwet the pelt or backing. Air-dry away from heat.

Leather   Suede

Mix dishwashing detergent in hot water and swish to make a great volume of suds. Dip a cloth in only the foam and gently wipe away any ammonia residue. Wipe with a clean, dry cloth. Dry away from heat. On leather only, condition with saddle soap.

Silver

Wash silver in hot, sudsy water with a soft cloth. Rinse in hot water and dry immediately with a soft cloth.

Wallpaper

Take special care here because ammonia may dissolve the adhesive behind the paper. Dip a sponge in clear, warm water. Wring until sponge is damp, then gently stroke the stain, overlapping strokes. Pat dry with a clean cloth.

Wood

Ammonia may dissolve wood polishes. With a sponge dipped in cool water then wrung out until damp, wipe the area, making sure not to spread the stain. Wipe dry with a soft cloth. Polish or wax immediately to prevent permanent wood damage.

ANTIPERSPIRANT

(Follow procedures for Deodorant.)

APPLE/APPLE JUICE

Acetate	Rayon
Carpet/Synthetic	Silk
Carpet/Wool	Triacetate
Fiberglass	Wool

Spray on fabric spot cleaner. If stain remains, sponge area with cool water, then apply wet spotter and a few drops of white vinegar. Cover stain with an absorbent pad dampened with wet spotter. Let stand as long as any stain is being removed. Keep both the stain and pad moist with wet spotter and vinegar. Flush with water and repeat if necessary. If stain persists, moisten the area with a solution of 1 cup warm water and 1 teaspoon enzyme presoak product—do not use on silk or wool. Cover with a clean pad moistened with the solution. Let it stand 30 minutes. Add more solution, if needed to keep the area warm and moist, but do not allow the wet area to spread. When no more stain is being lifted, flush with water.

Acrylic Fabric	Nylon
Cotton	Olefin
Linen	Polyester
Modacrylic	Spandex

Spray on fabric spot cleaner. If stain remains, soak in a solution of 1 quart warm water, ½ teaspoon liquid dishwashing or laundry detergent, and 1 tablespoon white vinegar for 15 minutes. Rinse with water and launder if possible. If not, soak in a solution of 1 quart warm water and 1 tablespoon enzyme presoak product for 30 minutes. Rinse well with water and launder as soon as possible.

Acrylic Plastic	Linoleum
Aluminum	Masonry Tile
Asphalt	Paint/Flat
Brass	Paint/Gloss
Bronze	Plexiglas
Ceramic Glass/Tile	Polyurethane
Copper	Porcelain Dishes
Cork	Stainless Steel
Enamel	Tin
Glass	Vinyl Clothing

Apple/Apple Juice *(continued)*

Grout	**Vinyl Tile**
Iron	**Vinyl Wallcovering**

Wipe up the spill. Then wipe the surface with a cloth or sponge dipped in warm, sudsy water. Rinse well and wipe dry.

Bluestone	**Limestone**
Brick	**Sandstone**
Concrete	**Slate**
Flagstone	**Terrazzo**
Granite	

Wipe up the spill. Wash with a solution of washing soda or detergent (never soap) and water. Use a soft cloth or soft-bristled brush. Rinse thoroughly with clear water and allow to dry.

Leather	**Suede**

Blot up the spill. Mix a solution of mild soap in lukewarm water. Swish to create a great volume of suds. Apply only the foam with a sponge. Wipe with a clean, dry cloth. On leather only, condition with saddle soap.

Silver

Wash as soon as possible in hot, sudsy water. Rinse in hot water and dry immediately with a soft cloth.

Wood

Mix dishwashing detergent in hot water and swish to make a great volume of suds. Dip a cloth in only the foam and wipe up the excess spill. Rinse with a clean cloth dampened with clear water. Polish or wax as soon as possible.

BABY FOOD/FORMULA

Acetate	**Rayon**
Burlap	**Rope**
Carpet/Synthetic	**Silk**
Carpet/Wool	**Triacetate**
Fiberglass	**Wool**

(continued)

Baby Food/Formula *(continued)*

Blot up baby formula or scrape solid baby food from fabric. Sponge with a dry-cleaning solvent, or apply dry spotter to the stain and cover with an absorbent pad dampened with dry spotter. Let stand as long as any stain is being removed. Keep pad and stain moist, changing the pad as it picks up the stain. Allow to dry completely.

Acrylic Fabric	Olefin
Cotton	Polyester
Linen	Spandex
Nylon	

Blot up or scrape baby-food spills and rinse stain in cool water. Soak for 30 minutes in an enzyme presoak. Launder immediately if possible. If not, flush with cool water and allow to dry thoroughly. If stain has dried, repeated laundering may be necessary.

Acrylic Plastic	Marble
Aluminum	Paint/Flat
Asphalt	Paint/Gloss
Bamboo	Plexiglas
Cane	Polyurethane
Ceramic Glass/Tile	Porcelain
Chromium	Stainless Steel
Cork	Tin
Enamel	Vinyl Clothing
Glass	Vinyl Tile
Iron	Vinyl Wallcovering
Linoleum	

Wipe up spilled formula or baby food immediately with a sponge dipped in warm, sudsy water. Rinse with clear water. Some baby foods contain dyes that will stain if allowed to remain on these surfaces.

Grout

Wipe up spills from grout. If any stain remains, dip a wet toothbrush in powdered cleanser or apply grout cleaner. Gently scrub the grout. Rinse with clear water.

Leather	Suede

Carefully blot up liquid or scrape solid baby-food spills from the surface immediately. Mix a solution of mild soap and lukewarm water. Swish to

Baby Food/Formula (continued)

create a great volume of suds. Apply only the foam with a sponge. Blot dry with a clean cloth. If stain persists, file gently with an emery board or very fine-grade (6/0 to 8/0) sandpaper. Work slowly and carefully, because the procedure removes a thin layer of the hide. On leather only, condition with saddle soap.

Silver

Wash silver immediately in hot, sudsy water. Rinse in hot water and dry immediately with a soft cloth or silver-polishing cloth to prevent tarnish.

Wallpaper

Carefully blot up spilled formula or scrape up baby-food spills. Try wiping with a cool, damp cloth in even, overlapping strokes. Pat dry. If stain persists, try rubbing very gently with an art gum eraser or a stale piece of rye bread to soak up the oily residue.

Wood

Immediately wipe excess liquid or solids with a damp sponge. Follow with a coat of wood cleaner, then apply polish or wax.

BEER

(Follow procedures for Alcoholic Beverages.)

BEETS

(Follow procedures for Berries.)

BERRIES (BLUEBERRY, CRANBERRY, RASPBERRY, STRAWBERRY)

Acetate	Rayon
Carpet/Synthetic	Rope
Carpet/Wool	Triacetate
Fiberglass	Wool

Spray on fabric spot cleaner. If stain remains, sponge with cool water.

Berries *(continued)*

Then sponge the area with lemon juice or rub a slice of lemon over the stain. Flush with clear water. Blot as much excess liquid as possible and allow to dry. If stain still persists, apply wet spotter. Cover with an absorbent pad moistened with wet spotter. Let stand as long as any stain is being removed. Change the pad as it picks up the stain. Keep the pad and stained area moist with wet spotter. Flush with water. If any trace of stain still appears, moisten the area with a solution of 1 cup warm water and 1 teaspoon enzyme presoak product—do not use on silk or wool. Cover with a clean, absorbent pad that has been dipped in the solution and wrung almost dry. Let it stand for 30 minutes. Add enough solution to keep the stain and pad moist, but do not allow the wet area to spread. When no more stain is visible, flush thoroughly with water and allow to air-dry.

Acrylic Fabric	Olefin
Modacrylic	Polyester
Nylon	Spandex

Spray on fabric spot cleaner. If stain remains, sponge with cool water immediately. Then sponge with lemon juice or rub a lemon slice over the stain. Flush with water. Blot as much excess liquid as possible and allow to dry. If any trace of stain remains, soak in a solution of 1 quart warm water, ½ teaspoon liquid dishwashing or laundry detergent, and 1 tablespoon white vinegar for 15 minutes. Rinse with water and launder if possible. If not, soak in a solution of 1 quart warm water and 1 tablespoon enzyme presoak product for 30 minutes. Rinse well with water and launder soon.

Acrylic Plastic	Grout
Aluminum	Iron
Asphalt	Paint/Flat
Bamboo	Paint/Gloss
Brass	Plexiglas
Bronze	Polyurethane
Cane	Porcelain Dishes
Ceramic Glass/Tile	Porcelain Fixtures
Copper	Stainless Steel
Enamel	Vinyl Clothing
Glass	Vinyl Wallcovering

Wipe up the spill with a cloth or sponge dipped in warm, sudsy water. Rinse well and wipe dry.

Bluestone	Granite
Brick	Masonry Tile

Berries *(continued)*

Concrete	Slate
Flagstone	Terrazzo

Wipe up the spill. Wash area with a solution of washing soda or detergent (not soap) and water. Use a soft cloth or soft-bristled brush. Rinse thoroughly with clear water and allow to dry.

Cork	Linoleum
Vinyl Tile	

Wipe up the spill and wash the area with a solution of washing soda or detergent and water. Use a soft-bristled brush or cloth to scrub gently. Rinse thoroughly with clear water and allow to dry. If stain persists, wipe area with a cloth dampened in a solution of 1 tablespoon oxalic acid and 1 pint water. Rinse well and wipe dry. Polish the surface if necessary.

Cotton	Linen

Test fabric for colorfastness. If color doesn't change, stretch the stain over a bowl; fasten in place with a rubber band. Pour boiling water through the fabric from a height of 2 or 3 feet. Avoid splatters. This procedure must be done immediately. If stain persists, soak in a solution of 1 quart warm water and ½ teaspoon detergent for 15 minutes. Rinse with water. Sponge the area with rubbing alcohol and launder if possible. If not, soak in a solution of 1 quart warm water and 1 tablespoon enzyme presoak product for 30 minutes. Rinse well and launder.

Leather	Suede

Blot up excess liquid and scrape away solid stains. Mix a solution of mild soap and lukewarm water. Swish to create a great volume of suds. Apply only the foam with a sponge. Wipe with a clean, dry cloth. On leather only, condition with saddle soap.

Marble

After wiping up excess liquid, wipe surface with a cloth or sponge dipped in warm, sudsy water. Rinse well and wipe dry. If any stain or discoloration remains, mix a thick paste of water, powdered detergent, and chlorine bleach. Apply a thick paste to the stain and cover with a damp cloth to retard evaporation. When the stain is bleached out, rinse thoroughly and dry.

Berries *(continued)*

Silver

Wash silver as soon as possible in hot, sudsy water. Rinse in hot water and dry immediately with a soft cloth to prevent tarnish.

Wood

Mix dishwashing detergent in hot water and swish to make a great volume of suds. Dip a cloth in only the foam and apply to berry stain. Rinse with a clean cloth dampened with clear water. If any stain remains, rub the area with a cloth dampened in a solution of 1 tablespoon oxalic acid to 1 pint water. Rinse well and wipe dry. Wax or polish as soon as possible.

BLOOD

Acetate	Rope
Burlap	Silk
Fiberglass	Triacetate
Rayon	Wool

Treat the stain as soon as possible; set bloodstains can be extremely difficult to remove. Sponge the stain with cold water. If the blood is still wet, this step should remove it. If any stain remains, apply wet spotter and a few drops of ammonia. (Do not use ammonia on silk and wool.) Cover with an absorbent pad dampened with wet spotter and ammonia. Let it stand as long as any stain is being removed, changing the pad as it picks up the stain. Keep the stain and pad moist with the wet spotter and ammonia. Flush thoroughly with cool water, making sure to remove all traces of the ammonia. If stain persists, moisten it with a solution of ½ teaspoon enzyme presoak—except on silk or wool—and ½ cup warm water. Cover the stain with an absorbent pad dampened slightly with the enzyme solution. Let it stand for 30 minutes. Add more solution to keep the stain moist and warm, but do not let the wet area spread. Flush with water and dry thoroughly.

Acrylic Fabric	Olefin
Cotton	Polyester
Linen	Spandex
Nylon	

Fresh bloodstains usually can be removed by a thorough laundering in cold water. If any stain remains, soak in a solution of 1 quart warm water, ½ teaspoon dishwashing or liquid laundry detergent, and 1 tablespoon am-

Blood *(continued)*

monia for 15 minutes. Tamp or scrape the stain, blotting occasionally with an absorbent pad. Continue as long as any stain is being removed. Rinse well with water, making sure to remove all trace of the ammonia. If the stain persists, soak in a solution of 1 quart warm water and 1 tablespoon enzyme presoak product. After 30 minutes, rinse well, then dry or launder.

Acrylic Plastic	Linoleum
Aluminum	Opal
Asphalt	Paint/Flat
Brass	Paint/Gloss
Bronze	Pearls
Ceramic Glass/Tile	Pewter
Chromium	Platinum
Copper	Plexiglas
Coral	Polyurethane
Cork	Porcelain
Enamel	Stainless Steel
Glass	Tin
Gold	Vinyl Clothing
Iron	Vinyl Tile
Ivory	Vinyl Wallcovering
Jade	Zinc

Wipe up stain with a sponge or cloth dipped in cool water or warm, sudsy water. Dry with a clean cloth.

Alabaster	Marble

Wipe up stain with a sponge dipped in cold water. If stain remains, mix a thick paste of water, powdered detergent, and chlorine bleach. Apply it thickly to the stain and cover with a damp cloth to retard drying. When the stain is bleached out, rinse thoroughly and dry.

Bamboo	Cane

Wash with a cloth or brush dipped in warm, soapy water to which a few drops of ammonia have been added. Rinse with clear water and dry.

Bluestone	Limestone
Brick	Masonry Tile
Concrete	Sandstone
Flagstone	Slate
Granite	Terrazzo

(continued)

Blood *(continued)*

Try wiping up the stain with a sponge dipped in cool water. If any stain remains, wash or brush stain with a solution of washing soda or detergent in warm water. Rinse well and allow to dry.

Carpet/Synthetic Carpet/Wool	Foam Rubber

Squirt carpet stain remover on the stained area. Another way to remove blood is to mix 1 teaspoon of mild, nonalkali detergent with ½ pint lukewarm water. Add a small amount to the stain and blot the liquid. Do not force the stain further into the fibers. Continue blotting until no more stain is removed. If stain remains, add 1 tablespoon ammonia to 1 cup water (do not use on wool), sponge stain, and blot liquid. Continue until no more stain is removed. Place an absorbent pad over the damp area and weight it down. When no more liquid is drawn out, remove the pad and allow to air-dry thoroughly.

Fur/Natural	Fur/Synthetic

Blot up excess. Dampen a cloth in the suds of a mild detergent solution to which a few drops of ammonia have been added. Rub with the nap, taking care not to overwet the pelt or backing. To rinse, dip a cloth in cool water, wring almost dry, and stroke with the nap. Air-dry away from heat.

Grout

Wipe the stain with a sponge dipped in cool water. If any bloodstain remains, dip a wet toothbrush in baking soda or powdered cleanser, or apply grout cleaner and gently scrub the grout. Rinse thoroughly and dry.

Leather	Suede

Mix a solution of mild soap and lukewarm water. Swish to create a great volume of suds. Apply only the foam with a sponge and gently rub the stained area, taking care not to spread the stain. Wipe dry with a clean, soft cloth. On leather only, condition with saddle soap.

Silver

Wash silver in hot, sudsy water. Rinse in hot water and wipe dry immediately with a soft cloth to prevent tarnish.

Wallpaper

Blood *(continued)*

Blood can permanently stain wallpaper. Try dipping a cloth in cool water, wringing until damp, and gently sponging the area, taking care not to spread the stain. Overlap the strokes slightly to prevent streaking. Gently pat dry.

Wood

Wipe the stain with a cloth dipped in cool water. Wipe dry immediately and polish or wax as usual.

BLUING

(Follow procedures for Fabric Softener.)

BLUSHER

Acetate	Rayon
Carpet/Synthetic	Silk
Carpet/Wool	Triacetate
Fiberglass	Wool

Brush or blot up excess, taking care not to spread the stain. Flush with dry-cleaning solvent. Apply dry spotter to the stain and cover with an absorbent pad dampened with dry spotter. Check the stain every 5 minutes. Before changing pads, press hard against the stain. Continue the alternate soaking and pressing until no more stain is being removed. Flush with dry-cleaning solvent and allow to dry. If any stain remains, flush it with water and apply wet spotter with a few drops of ammonia. (Do not use ammonia on silk or wool.) Cover with an absorbent pad dampened with wet spotter. Let it stand as long as any stain is being removed. Change the pad as it picks up the stain. Keep the stain and pad moist. Flush well with water. Repeat if necessary; allow to dry.

Acrylic Fabric	Nylon
Cotton	Olefin
Linen	Polyester
Modacrylic	Spandex

Brush or blot up as much blusher as you can, taking care not to spread the stain. Flush with dry-cleaning solvent. Apply dry spotter to the stain and cover with a cloth dampened with dry spotter. Check the stain often,

Blusher *(continued)*

tamping before changing the pad. Continue alternate soaking and tamping until no more stain is lifted. Flush with dry-cleaning solvent and allow to dry. If any stain remains, try the same procedure of soaking and tamping using wet spotter and a few drops of ammonia. When the stain is gone, be sure to flush the area with water to remove all trace of ammonia. Launder as soon as possible.

Acrylic Plastic	Jade
Alabaster	Linoleum
Asphalt	Marble
Bamboo	Paint/Flat
Cane	Paint/Gloss
Ceramic Glass/Tile	Plexiglas
Cork	Polyurethane
Enamel	Stainless Steel
Glass	Vinyl Clothing
Gold	Vinyl Tile
Ivory	Vinyl Wallcovering

Wipe up spills or brush away powders. With a cloth or sponge dipped in warm, sudsy water, wash the surface. Rinse well with water and wipe dry with a clean cloth.

Bluestone	Slate
Masonry Tile	Terrazzo
Sandstone	

Remove excess. Mix a solution of washing soda or detergent (not soap) and water. Wash the stained area. Rinse well with clear water and allow to dry.

Leather	Suede

Gently remove as much blusher as you can. Mix a solution of mild soap and lukewarm water. Swish to create a great volume of suds. Apply only the foam with a sponge. Wipe dry with a clean cloth. If a greasy or oily stain remains, powder it with an absorbent, such as cornmeal. Give the absorbent plenty of time to work. Gently brush or shake the absorbent from the surface. Repeat if necessary. On leather only, follow with saddle soap to condition. On suede, apply suede cleaner.

Wood

Blusher *(continued)*

Mix dishwashing detergent in hot water and swish to make a great volume of suds. Dip a cloth in only the foam and apply to the stain. Rinse with clear water. Wipe dry immediately with a soft cloth and polish or wax as usual.

BUTTER

Acetate	Rayon
Burlap	Rope
Carpet/Synthetic	Silk
Carpet/Wool	Triacetate
Fiberglass	Wool

Scrape up as much of the solid butter as you can without driving any of it further into the fibers. Apply an absorbent (cornmeal for light colors, fuller's earth for dark colors) but do not press it in. Give the absorbent plenty of time to work. Remove the absorbent and, if needed, repeat the application. If any residue remains, sponge the spot with cleaning fluid or spot remover.

Acrylic Fabric	Nylon
Cotton	Olefin
Linen	Polyester
Modacrylic	Spandex

Scrape solid butter. Pretreat with stain remover, blot the stained area, and launder as usual. If the stain remains or if immediate laundering is impossible, place the fabric stained side down on an absorbent pad. Flush with cleaning fluid through the back of the stain and blot with a clean, absorbent pad. Pretreat again and rinse well or launder.

Acrylic Plastic	Grout
Alabaster	Iron
Aluminum	Linoleum
Asphalt	Marble
Bamboo	Paint/Gloss
Brass	Pewter
Bronze	Plexiglas
Cane	Polyurethane
Ceramic Glass/Tile	Porcelain
Chromium	Stainless Steel

(continued)

Butter *(continued)*

Copper	Tin
Cork	Vinyl Clothing
Enamel	Vinyl Tile
Glass	Vinyl Wallcovering
Gold	Zinc

Scrape to remove as much butter as possible. Wipe with a clean sponge or cloth dipped in warm, sudsy water. Rinse with clear water and wipe dry.

Bluestone	Limestone
Brick	Masonry Tile
Concrete	Sandstone
Flagstone	Slate
Granite	Terrazzo

Wipe up butter. Mix a solution of washing soda or detergent and water. Scrub any remaining stain. Rinse well and allow to dry.

Felt

Scrape to remove butter without forcing any of it further into the fibers. Dust the stain with an absorbent (cornmeal for light colors or fuller's earth for dark colors). Allow plenty of time for the grease to be absorbed. Gently brush off absorbent in the direction of the nap. If any stain remains, re-apply fresh absorbent. Allow absorbent to work, then gently brush off.

Leather	Suede

Gently scrape to remove as much butter as you can. Rub the stain with a thick paste of fuller's earth and water. Let it dry and gently brush off the powder. Repeat if necessary. Then, for leather only, apply saddle soap.

Paint/Flat	Wallpaper

Scrape away solid butter. Rub the stain with a thick paste of fuller's earth (on dark surfaces) or cornmeal (on light surfaces) and water, and press the paste onto the stain with the palm of your hand. Allow to dry, then carefully brush off with a clean cloth.

Silver

Wash silver in hot, soapy water. Rinse in hot water and wipe dry immediately with a clean soft cloth.

Butter *(continued)*

Wood

Wipe up excess with a clean, dry cloth. Dip a cloth into warm, sudsy water and wipe away any greasy residue. Rinse well and polish or **wax**.

CANDLE WAX

Acetate	Rope
Burlap	Silk
Fiberglass	Triacetate
Rayon	Wool/Nonwashable

Freeze to harden the wax. Carefully scrape up as much wax as you can, then place an absorbent pad under the stain and flush with spot remover. Allow to dry. Repeat if necessary.

Acrylic Fabric	Olefin
Cotton	Polyester
Linen	Spandex
Modacrylic	Wool/Washable
Nylon	

Scrape to remove excess wax. Place the stained area between two pieces of white blotting paper and press with a warm iron. Change the paper as it absorbs the stain. This stain can easily spread, so use care while pressing. On colorfast fabrics, white cotton, or linen, try pouring boiling water through the stain. Allow to dry. If any trace remains, flush with dry-cleaning fluid. If any dye remains, sponge with 1 part rubbing alcohol mixed with 2 parts water. (Do not use on acrylic or modacrylic fabric.) Rinse well with clear water and dry.

Acrylic Plastic	Iron
Alabaster	Ivory
Aluminum	Jade
Bamboo	Limestone
Bluestone	Marble
Brass	Paint/Flat
Bronze	Paint/Gloss
Cane	Pewter
Ceramic Glass/Tile	Plexiglas
Concrete	Polyurethane
Copper	Porcelain

(continued)

Candle Wax *(continued)*

Enamel	**Sandstone**
Flagstone	**Slate**
Glass	**Stainless Steel**
Gold	**Terrazzo**
Granite	**Tin**
Grout	**Vinyl Clothing**

Freeze to harden the wax, then gently scrape the residue from the surface. Take care not to scratch the surface. Wipe with a sponge dipped in a solution of washing soda or detergent and water. Rinse well and wipe dry.

Asphalt	**Linoleum**
Cork	**Vinyl Tile**

Freeze to harden the wax. Gently scrape it off with a metal spatula, taking care not to gouge the stained surface. Dip a clean cloth into rubbing alcohol and wipe stain. Wash and wipe dry. Polish or wax as usual.

Carpet/Synthetic	**Carpet/Wool**

Freeze to harden the wax. Gently scrape to remove it from the surface. To prevent damage to the backing, apply a small amount of cleaning fluid. Blot with an absorbent pad. Continue until no more stain is removed. If any dye remains, dilute 1 part rubbing alcohol with 2 parts water and apply it to the stain in small amounts, blotting well after each application. Allow to dry thoroughly.

Felt

Freeze to harden the wax. Very carefully scrape the residue, taking care not to shred the felt fibers. If any residue remains, try brushing gently with a stiff-bristled brush. In extreme cases, use a razor blade gently to scrape the excess. Use this as a last resort; it will damage some of the fibers.

Leather	**Suede**

Freeze to harden the wax. Gently scrape. If any stain remains, mix a thick paste of fuller's earth with water and apply it to the stain. Allow the paste to dry, then carefully brush it off with a soft-bristled brush or toothbrush. Repeat if necessary. When the stain has been removed, on leather only, apply saddle soap to condition.

Silver

Candle Wax *(continued)*

Freeze to harden the wax. Carefully scrape with a plastic spatula until no more wax can be removed. Wash the silver in hot, soapy water. Rinse in hot water and wipe dry immediately to prevent tarnish.

Wood

Freeze to harden the wax. Gently scrape it up to avoid gouging the wood. When all wax has been removed, buff the wood with a chamois.

CANDY/CHOCOLATE

(Follow procedures for Chocolate/Cocoa.)

CANDY/NONCHOCOLATE

Acetate	Rayon
Burlap	Rope
Carpet/Synthetic	Silk
Carpet/Wool	Triacetate
Fiberglass	Wool

Scrape to remove as much of the candy as possible. Sponge with warm water. Spray on fabric spot cleaner or wet spotter with a few drops of white vinegar added. Let stand as long as any stain is being removed. Press down on the stain with a clean absorbent pad every 5 minutes. Keep the stain moist with wet spotter and vinegar. When no more stain is being removed, flush with water. If any stain remains, repeat the process, using rubbing alcohol instead of the wet spotter and vinegar. (Do not use alcohol on acetate or triacetate.) When the stain is removed, rinse well with water to remove all of the sugar. On carpeting, blot the excess liquid with an absorbent pad. Then apply carpet stain remover. Allow to dry.

Acrylic Fabric	Nylon
Cotton	Olefin
Linen	Polyester
Modacrylic	Spandex

Usually, soaking or laundering in warm, sudsy water will remove the stain. If the stain persists, spray on fabric spot cleaner or soak the fabric,

Candy/Nonchocolate *(continued)*

adding a few drops of ammonia to the soaking solution. Let the fabric soak for 30 minutes and rinse thoroughly with water. Next, soak in a solution of 1 quart warm water and 1 tablespoon white vinegar for 1 hour (30 minutes for cotton and linen). Rinse well and dry. If stain persists, apply rubbing alcohol (do not use on acrylic or modacrylic) to the stain and tamp gently. Keep the stain moist with alcohol and blot occasionally. Continue as long as any stain is being removed. Rinse well with water. Dry or launder as soon as possible.

Acrylic Plastic	**Linoleum**
Aluminum	**Paint/Flat**
Asphalt	**Paint/Gloss**
Bamboo	**Pewter**
Brass	**Plexiglas**
Bronze	**Polyurethane**
Cane	**Porcelain**
Ceramic Glass/Tile	**Sandstone**
Copper	**Stainless Steel**
Cork	**Tin**
Enamel	**Vinyl Clothing**
Glass	**Vinyl Tile**
Gold	**Vinyl Wallcovering**
Iron	**Zinc**
Ivory	

With a cloth dipped in warm, sudsy water, wipe stain from the surface. Rinse thoroughly and wipe dry.

Bluestone	**Limestone**
Brick	**Masonry Tile**
Concrete	**Sandstone**
Flagstone	**Slate**
Granite	**Terrazzo**

Scrape any candy from the surface, taking care not to gouge the softer stones. Wash or scrub any remainder with a solution of washing soda or detergent and water (never use soap—it leaves a scum impossible to remove). Rinse well and dry.

Leather	**Suede**

Gently scrape candy from the hide. Mix a solution of mild soap and lukewarm water. Swish to create a great volume of suds. Apply only the

Candy/Nonchocolate *(continued)*

foam with a sponge, stroking with the nap on suede. Wipe dry with a clean cloth. On leather only, follow with saddle soap to condition.

Silver

Wash the silver in hot, sudsy water. This should dissolve any candy residue. Rinse in hot water and wipe dry with a soft clean cloth to prevent tarnish.

Wood

Wipe the stain with a cloth dipped in warm, sudsy water. Then wipe with a clean, damp cloth. Wipe dry and polish or wax as usual.

CARBON PAPER/TYPEWRITER RIBBON

Acetate	Linen
Burlap	Rope
Carpet/Synthetic	Silk
Carpet/Wool	Triacetate
Cotton	Wool
Fiberglass	

Apply dry spotter to the stain and cover it with an absorbent pad dampened with dry spotter. Keep the stain and pad moist. Let stand as long as any stain is being removed. Change the pad as it picks up the stain. When no more stain is being picked up, flush with cleaning fluid. Scrape or tamp to help loosen the stain. When not working on the stain, keep it covered to minimize evaporation. Flush the stain with the cleaning fluid. Allow to dry. On carpets, blot liquid, then apply carpet stain remover. Work undiluted liquid detergent into the stain, then rinse. If stain persists, apply amyl acetate to the stain and cover with an absorbent pad dampened with amyl acetate. Keep moist for 15 minutes, blot with a clean, absorbent pad.

Acrylic Plastic	Paint/Flat
Bamboo	Paint/Gloss
Cane	Plexiglas
Glass	Polyurethane
Linoleum	Vinyl Clothing

Wipe the stain with a cloth dipped in warm, sudsy water to which a few drops of ammonia have been added. Rinse well and wipe dry.

CATSUP

Acetate	Rayon
Burlap	Rope
Carpet/Synthetic	Silk
Carpet/Wool	Triacetate
Fiberglass	Wool

Gently scrape catsup from fabric. Sponge with cleaning fluid or treat silk by applying spot remover. Apply dry spotter to the stain and cover with an absorbent pad dampened with dry spotter. Keep the stain and pad moist. Continue this treatment as long as any stain is being removed. Change the pad as it picks up the stain. When no more stain is being removed, flush with cleaning fluid or reapply spot remover on silk. Allow to dry. If any stain remains, moisten it with a solution of ½ teaspoon enzyme presoak product and ½ cup warm water. (Do not use on silk and wool.) Cover with a clean pad that has been dipped in the enzyme presoak solution and squeezed nearly dry. Let stand for 30 minutes, adding more solution as needed to keep the area warm and moist, but do not let the wet area spread. Flush with water and allow to dry. On carpets, place a clean dry pad over the area and weight it down. When no more liquid is being absorbed, allow to air-dry thoroughly.

Acrylic Fabric	Nylon
Cotton	Olefin
Linen	Polyester
Modacrylic	Spandex

Scrape up as much catsup as possible. Apply wet spotter and work into the fabric. Rinse thoroughly with water and launder. If laundering must wait and any stain remains, apply an enzyme presoak paste and let it work a while, keeping the paste moist. Thoroughly rinse area to remove all trace of enzyme presoak paste. Allow to dry, and launder as soon as possible.

Acrylic Plastic	Ivory
Aluminum	Linoleum
Asphalt	Paint/Flat
Bamboo	Paint/Gloss
Bronze	Pewter
Cane	Plexiglas
Ceramic Glass/Tile	Polyurethane
Chromium	Porcelain Dishes
Copper	Stainless Steel
Cork	Tin
Enamel	Vinyl Clothing

Catsup *(continued)*

Glass	**Vinyl Tile**
Gold	**Vinyl Wallcovering**
Iron	**Zinc**

Wipe up spills as soon as possible—the tomato in catsup can permanently stain many of these surfaces. Use a cloth or sponge dipped in warm, sudsy water. Rinse with clean water and wipe dry.

Alabaster	**Marble**
Bluestone	**Masonry Tile**
Concrete	**Sandstone**
Flagstone	**Slate**
Granite	**Terrazzo**
Limestone	

Remove excess catsup. Wipe with a cloth dipped in a solution of washing soda or detergent and warm water. If any stain remains, mix a thick paste of water, bleach, and a powdered detergent and apply to the stained area. Cover with a damp cloth to retard evaporation. When stain is gone, rinse well and wipe dry.

Leather	**Suede**

Mix a solution of mild soap and lukewarm water. Swish to create a great volume of suds. Apply only the foam with a sponge. Wipe dry with a clean cloth. On leather only, follow with saddle soap to condition.

Silver

Take care of silver as soon as possible; tomato can pit the metal. Wash silver in hot, soapy water. Rinse in hot water and wipe dry with a clean, soft cloth.

Wallpaper

Wipe immediately, as catsup often permanently stains wallpaper. Use a damp cloth or sponge, overlapping strokes to prevent streaks. Gently pat dry with a soft cloth.

Wood

Catsup spills usually occur on wood tabletops that have a treated surface—such as polyurethane sealer. Wiping these surfaces with a damp

Catsup *(continued)*

cloth is sufficient to remove the spill. Nontreated surfaces should be wiped immediately with a cloth dipped in warm, sudsy water, rinsed with a clean, damp cloth, wiped dry, and polished or waxed as usual.

CEMENT/CONTACT

Acetate	Olefin
Acrylic Fabric	Polyester
Burlap	Rayon
Carpet/Synthetic	Silk
Carpet/Wool	Spandex
Cotton	Triacetate
Linen	Wool
Nylon	

Carefully scrape contact cement from fabric. Sponge stain with dry-cleaning solvent. Apply dry spotter and cover with an absorbent pad dampened with dry spotter. Let stand as long as any stain is being removed. Change pad as it picks up any stain, keeping stain and pad moist with dry spotter. Flush with dry-cleaning solvent. If any stain remains, repeat the above process using amyl acetate. (Do not use on cotton and linen.) Flush with dry-cleaning solvent. If stain persists on cotton and linen only, try flushing it with a few drops of acetone, then rinse with dry-cleaning solvent.

Acrylic Plastic	Paint/Gloss
Aluminum	Plexiglas
Ceramic Glass/Tile	Polyurethane
Cork	Vinyl Clothing
Glass	Vinyl Tile
Linoleum	Vinyl Wallcovering
Paint/Flat	

Remove any matter before it has a chance to set. Try wiping with a cloth dipped in warm, sudsy water to which a few drops of amyl acetate have been added. Rinse well and wipe dry. Contact cement can eventually damage the surface beyond repair, so work promptly.

CEMENT/EPOXY

All Surfaces

This stain cannot be removed.

CEMENT/HOUSEHOLD

Acetate	Nylon
Acrylic Fabric	Olefin
Burlap	Polyester
Carpet/Synthetic	Rayon
Carpet/Wool	Silk
Cotton	Spandex
Linen	Triacetate
Modacrylic	Wool

Carefully scrape household cement from fabric. Sponge stain with dry-cleaning solvent. Apply dry spotter and cover with an absorbent pad dampened with dry spotter. Let stand as long as any stain is being removed. Change pad as it picks up stain, keeping both stain and pad moist with dry spotter. Flush with dry-cleaning solvent. If any stain remains, repeat the above procedure using amyl acetate (do not use this step on cotton and linen), and flush with dry-cleaning solvent. If stain persists on cotton and linen only, try flushing it with a few drops of acetone, then rinse with dry spotter.

Acrylic Plastic	Paint/Gloss
Aluminum	Plexiglas
Ceramic Glass/Tile	Polyurethane
Cork	Vinyl Clothing
Glass	Vinyl Tile
Linoleum	Vinyl Wallcovering
Paint/Flat	

Before household cement has a chance to set, wipe up the stain with a cloth dipped in warm, sudsy water to which a few drops of amyl acetate have been added. Rinse well and wipe dry. Cement can eventually damage the surface beyond repair, so work promptly.

CEMENT/RUBBER

Acetate	Nylon
Acrylic Fabric	Olefin
Burlap	Polyester
Carpet/Synthetic	Rayon
Carpet/Wool	Silk
Cotton	Spandex
Fiberglass	Triacetate
Linen	Wool
Modacrylic	

Rub away as much cement as possible. If stain remains, place a clean, absorbent pad under the stain, if possible. Apply dry-cleaning solvent, and cover the stain with an absorbent pad dampened with dry-cleaning solvent. Change the pads as they pick up the stain. Keep stain and pads moist. Apply dry spotter. Cover with a pad dampened with dry spotter. Remove pad every 5 minutes. Press the pad hard into the stain—don't rub. Continue with the alternate soaking and pressing until all the stain has been removed. Flush with dry-cleaning solvent and allow to dry.

Acrylic Plastic	Paint/Gloss
Aluminum	Plexiglas
Ceramic Glass/Tile	Stainless Steel
Cork	Suede
Glass	Vinyl Clothing
Leather	Vinyl Tile
Linoleum	Vinyl Wallcovering
Paint/Flat	Wood

Scrape to remove liquid. Use a rubber-cement pickup, available at most art or stationery stores, to gently rub away any remaining cement. This should remove any trace of the stain.

CHEESE

Acetate	Rayon
Burlap	Silk
Carpet/Synthetic	Triacetate
Carpet/Wool	Wool
Fiberglass	

Scrape to remove cheese. Sponge the stain with dry-cleaning solvent. Apply dry spotter to the stain and cover with an absorbent pad dampened

Cheese *(continued)*

with dry spotter. Let stand as long as any stain is being removed. Change the pad as it picks up the stain. Keep the stain and pad moist with dry spotter. Flush with dry-cleaning solvent. If any stain remains, moisten it with a solution of 1 teaspoon of enzyme presoak and 1 cup water (not for use on silk or wool). Cover with a clean pad that has been dipped in the solution and wrung almost dry. Let it stand for 30 minutes. Add more solution if needed to keep the area warm and moist, but do not allow the wet area to spread. When no more stain is being lifted, flush thoroughly.

Acrylic Fabric	**Nylon**
Cotton	**Olefin**
Linen	**Polyester**
Modacrylic	**Spandex**

Scrape to remove cheese. Sponge the area with dry-cleaning solvent. Apply dry spotter to the stain and cover with an absorbent pad dampened with dry spotter. Continue this treatment as long as any stain is being removed. Change the pad as it picks up the stain. Keep the stain and pad moist with dry spotter. Flush with liquid dry-cleaning solvent. If any stain remains, apply a few drops of dishwashing detergent and a few drops of ammonia to the stain, then tamp or scrape. Keep the stain moist with detergent and ammonia and blot occasionally with an absorbent pad. Flush well with water to remove all trace of ammonia. Allow to dry.

Acrylic Plastic	**Linoleum**
Alabaster	**Marble**
Aluminum	**Paint/Flat**
Asphalt	**Paint/Gloss**
Brass	**Pewter**
Bronze	**Plexiglas**
Ceramic Glass/Tile	**Polyurethane**
Copper	**Porcelain**
Cork	**Stainless Steel**
Enamel	**Tin**
Glass	**Vinyl Clothing**
Grout	**Vinyl Tile**
Iron	**Vinyl Wallcovering**
Ivory	**Zinc**

Scrape to remove cheese. Wipe the surface with a cloth or sponge dipped in warm, sudsy water. Rinse well and wipe dry with a soft cloth.

Bamboo	**Cane**	*(continued)*

Cheese *(continued)*

Scrape up as much cheese as you can without gouging the fibers. Wipe with a cloth dipped in a solution of mild soapsuds and water. Rinse thoroughly and allow to dry.

Bluestone	**Limestone**
Brick	**Masonry Tile**
Concrete	**Sandstone**
Flagstone	**Slate**
Granite	**Terrazzo**

Scrape to remove cheese. Wash the area with a solution of washing soda or detergent (never use soap) and water. Use a cloth or soft-bristled brush. Rinse thoroughly with clear water and allow to dry.

Leather	**Suede**

Gently scrape up cheese. Mix a solution of mild soap and lukewarm water. Swish to create a great volume of suds. Apply only the foam with a sponge. Wipe dry with a clean cloth. If a grease stain remains, powder the stain with an absorbent, such as cornmeal. Give it plenty of time to work. Gently brush it off. Repeat if necessary. On leather only, follow with saddle soap to condition.

Silver

Wash the silver as soon as possible in hot, sudsy water. Rinse in hot water and dry immediately with a soft cloth to prevent tarnish.

Wallpaper

Carefully remove cheese. Make a paste of equal parts cornstarch and water. Apply it to the stain and allow it to dry. Brush it off, repeating if necessary.

Wood

Mix dishwashing detergent in hot water and swish to make a great volume of suds. Dip a cloth in only the foam and apply. Rinse with a clean cloth dipped in clear water and wrung until damp. Dry immediately. Polish or wax as soon as possible.

CHERRY

Acetate	Rayon
Carpet/Synthetic	Rope
Carpet/Wool	Triacetate
Fiberglass	Wool

Spray on fabric spot cleaner. If stain remains, sponge with cool water. Then sponge the area with lemon juice or rub the cut sides of a slice of lemon over the stain. Flush with water. Blot as much excess liquid as possible and allow to dry. If stain persists, apply wet spotter. Cover with an absorbent pad moistened with wet spotter. Let stand as long as any stain is being removed. Change the pad as it picks up the stain. Keep the pad and stained area moist with wet spotter. Flush with water. If any trace of stain still appears, moisten the area with a solution of 1 cup warm water and 1 teaspoon enzyme presoak product—do not use on silk or wool. Cover with a clean, absorbent pad that has been dipped in the solution and wrung almost dry. Let it stand for 30 minutes. Add enough solution to keep the stain and pad moist, but do not allow the wet area to spread. When no more stain is visible, flush thoroughly with water and allow to dry.

Acrylic Fabric	Olefin
Modacrylic	Polyester
Nylon	Spandex

Spray on fabric spot cleaner. If stain remains, sponge with cool water immediately. Then sponge with lemon juice or rub a lemon slice over the stain. Flush with water. Blot as much excess liquid as possible and allow to dry. If any trace of stain still exists, presoak in a solution of 1 quart warm water, ½ teaspoon liquid dishwashing or laundry detergent, and 1 tablespoon white vinegar for 15 minutes. Rinse with water and launder if possible. If not, soak in a solution of 1 quart water and 1 tablespoon enzyme presoak product for 30 minutes. Rinse well with water and launder as soon as possible.

Acrylic Plastic	Grout
Aluminum	Iron
Asphalt	Paint/Flat
Bamboo	Paint/Gloss
Brass	Plexiglas
Bronze	Polyurethane
Cane	Porcelain Dishes
Ceramic Glass/Tile	Porcelain Fixtures
Copper	Stainless Steel

(continued)

Cherry *(continued)*

Enamel	**Vinyl Clothing**
Glass	**Vinyl Wallcovering**

Wipe up the spill with a cloth or sponge dipped in warm, sudsy water. Rinse well and wipe dry.

Bluestone	**Granite**
Brick	**Masonry Tile**
Concrete	**Slate**
Flagstone	**Terrazzo**

Wipe up the spill. Wash the area with a solution of washing soda or detergent (not soap) and water. Use a soft cloth or soft-bristled brush. Rinse thoroughly with clear water and allow to dry.

Cork	**Vinyl Tile**
Linoleum	

Wipe up the spill and wash the area with a solution of washing soda or detergent and water. Use a soft-bristled brush or cloth to scrub gently. Rinse thoroughly with clear water and allow to dry. If stain persists, wipe area with a cloth dampened in a solution of 1 tablespoon oxalic acid and 1 pint water. Rinse well and wipe dry. Polish the surface if necessary.

Cotton	**Linen**

Test fabric for colorfastness. If color doesn't change, stretch the stain over a bowl; fasten in place with a rubber band. Pour boiling water through the fabric from a height of 2 or 3 feet. Avoid splatters. This procedure must be done immediately. If stain persists, soak in a solution of 1 quart warm water and ½ teaspoon detergent for 15 minutes. Rinse with water. Sponge area with rubbing alcohol and launder if possible. If not, soak in a solution of 1 quart warm water and 1 tablespoon enzyme soak product for 30 minutes. Rinse well and launder.

Leather	**Suede**

Blot up the spill. Mix a solution of mild soap and lukewarm water. Swish to create a great volume of suds. Apply only the foam with a sponge. Wipe with a clean, dry cloth. On leather only, follow with saddle soap to condition.

Cherry *(continued)*

Marble

After wiping up as much of the spill as possible, wipe the surface with a cloth or sponge dipped in warm, sudsy water. Rinse well and wipe dry. If any stain or discoloration remains, mix a thick paste of water, powdered detergent, and chlorine bleach. Apply the thick paste to the stain and cover with a damp cloth to retard evaporation. When the stain is bleached out, rinse thoroughly and dry.

Silver

Wash silver as soon as possible in hot, sudsy water. Rinse in hot water and dry immediately with a soft cloth to prevent tarnish.

Wood

Mix dishwashing detergent in hot water and swish to make a great volume of suds. Dip a cloth in only the foam and apply to the stain. Rinse with a clean cloth dampened with clear water. If any stain remains, rub the area with a cloth dampened in a solution of 1 tablespoon oxalic acid and 1 pint water. Rinse well and wipe dry. Wax or polish as soon as possible.

CHEWING GUM

Acetate	Nylon
Acrylic Fabric	Olefin
Burlap	Polyester
Carpet/Synthetic	Rayon
Carpet/Wool	Silk
Cotton	Spandex
Fiberglass	Triacetate
Linen	Wool
Modacrylic	

Freeze until gum gets hard. Carefully scrape or rub it from the fabric. Sponge with dry-cleaning solvent. Apply dry spotter to the stain and cover with an absorbent pad dampened with dry spotter. Continue this treatment as long as any stain is being removed. Change the pad as it picks up the stain. Keep the stain and pad moist with dry spotter. Flush with dry-cleaning solvent. If stain remains, reapply dry spotter and cover. Check the stain

Chewing Gum *(continued)*

every 5 minutes and press hard against the stain. Continue the alternate soaking and pressing until all the stain has been removed. Flush with dry-cleaning solvent. Dry.

Acrylic Plastic	**Paint/Gloss**
Aluminum	**Plexiglas**
Asphalt	**Polyurethane**
Paint/Flat	**Vinyl Clothing**

Freeze until gum gets hard. Carefully scrape or rub the substance from the surface. With a clean cloth dipped in warm, sudsy water, wipe the surface until all trace of the gum has been removed. Rinse well and wipe dry with a soft cloth.

Bamboo	**Cane**

Freeze until the gum gets hard. Carefully scrape away as much gum as you can. Wipe with a cloth dipped in a solution of warm, sudsy water to which a few drops of ammonia have been added. Rinse well and air-dry.

Felt

Since felt is not woven but rather fused together, take every precaution in removing gum because chunks of the felt may come with it. Freeze to harden the gum and gently brush with a sponge or soft-bristled brush, such as a toothbrush. This should remove any excess that remains on the surface. In extreme cases, very carefully rub the stain with a razor blade. This will remove stubborn stains, but it will also remove some of the felt fibers. If stain persists, make a paste of cornmeal and water and apply it to the stain. Give it plenty of time to work. When it is dry, carefully brush it off.

Fur/Natural	**Fur/Synthetic**

Take care not to remove the fur when removing the gum. Freeze to harden the gum and gently rub it with a dry sponge or soft-bristled brush. Dampen a sponge or cloth in the suds of a mild detergent and wipe in the direction of the nap to remove any sugary residue. Take care not to overwet the pelt or backing. Allow to air-dry.

Leather

Carefully scrape excess gum. Mix a solution of mild soap in lukewarm water. Swish to create a great volume of suds. Apply only the foam with a

Chewing Gum *(continued)*

sponge and scrub gently until the gum is removed. Dry with a clean cloth. Follow with saddle soap to condition.

Linoleum   **Vinyl Wallcovering**
Vinyl Tile

Freeze the gum to harden it. Use a dull tool, such as a metal spatula, to scrape the brittle gum without gouging the surface. If there is any residue, try rubbing it with a cloth dipped in spot remover or cleaning fluid. Wipe gingerly, then rub with fine-grade (000) steel wool. Wash the area and wax when dry.

Suede

Very carefully scrape to remove gum. Gently rub an art gum eraser over the residue. If any stain remains, apply suede cleaner. If there is still some stain remaining, cautiously rub the spot with an emery board or very fine-grade (8/0) sandpaper. Since you are removing a thin layer of the hide, work slowly and carefully.

Wood

Take special precautions in removing gum so as not to remove any of the finish. Rub gently with a cloth dipped in the suds of hot, soapy water. Rub only on the portion that is stained. Rinse by wiping with a cloth dipped in clear water. Wipe dry immediately and polish or wax as usual.

CHLORINE

Acetate   **Olefin**
Acrylic Fabric   **Polyester**
Burlap   **Rayon**
Cotton   **Silk**
Linen   **Spandex**
Modacrylic   **Wool**
Nylon

Immediately flush the stain with a solution of 1 teaspoon sodium thiosulfate in 1 quart water. When the stain has been neutralized, flush well with water to remove chemicals. If stain remains, mix ¼ teaspoon color remover with ½ cup cool water. Sponge the stain with the solution, and flush well with water. Chlorine stains are often permanent.

Chlorine *(continued)*

Acrylic Plastic	Masonry Tile
Asphalt	Plexiglas
Cork	Vinyl Tile
Linoleum	

Because chlorine may bleach out surface color, treat immediately. Wipe up the spill, then sponge the surface with a cloth dipped in warm, sudsy water. Rinse well and wipe dry.

Leather	Vinyl Clothing
Suede	Vinyl Wallcovering

Chlorine will change the color of these materials on contact. There is no way to remove the stain.

CHOCOLATE/COCOA

Acetate	Rope
Burlap	Silk
Fiberglass	Triacetate
Rayon	Wool

Blot or scrape up any chocolate from the surface. Flush the stain with club soda to prevent setting. Sponge the stain with dry-cleaning solvent. Then apply dry spotter to the stain and cover with an absorbent pad dampened with dry spotter. Keep the stain and pad moist with dry spotter. Let it stand as long as any stain is being removed. Change the pad as it picks up the stain. Flush with dry-cleaning solvent. If a stain remains, moisten it with a solution of 1 cup warm water and 1 teaspoon enzyme presoak product—but do not use on silk or wool. Cover with a clean pad that has been dipped in the solution and wrung almost dry. Let it stand at least 30 minutes. Add more solution if needed to keep the stain warm and moist, but do not allow the wet area to spread. When the stain is lifted, flush thoroughly with water and allow to dry.

Acrylic Fabric	Modacrylic
Cotton	Olefin
Linen	Polyester
Nylon	Spandex

Wipe up as much chocolate as possible without driving the stain further into the fibers. Flush the stain with club soda. Sponge the area with dry-

On cotton - Ossengal stick

Chocolate/Cocoa *(continued)*

cleaning solvent. Apply dry spotter to the stain and cover with an absorbent pad dampened with dry spotter. Keep the stain moist with dry spotter. Let it stand as long as any stain is being lifted. Change the pad as it picks up the stain. Flush with dry-cleaning solvent. If any stain remains, apply a few drops of dishwashing detergent and a few drops of ammonia to the stain, then tamp or scrape. Keep the stain moist with detergent and ammonia and blot occasionally with an absorbent pad. Flush well with water to remove all trace of ammonia. Allow to dry, or launder as usual.

Acrylic Plastic	**Ivory**
Aluminum	**Jade**
Asphalt	**Paint/Flat**
Bamboo	**Paint/Gloss**
Brass	**Pewter**
Bronze	**Plexiglas**
Cane	**Polyurethane**
Ceramic Glass/Tile	**Porcelain**
Copper	**Stainless Steel**
Cork	**Tin**
Enamel	**Vinyl Clothing**
Glass	**Vinyl Tile**
Gold	**Vinyl Wallcovering**
Iron	**Zinc**

Scrape to remove chocolate. Wipe the surface with a cloth dipped in warm, sudsy water. Rinse well and wipe dry.

Alabaster	**Marble**

Carefully scrape chocolate. Wipe with a clean cloth dipped in a solution of washing soda or detergent and water. Rinse well and wipe dry. If any stain remains, mix a few drops of ammonia with 1 cup 3-percent hydrogen peroxide. Soak a white blotter with the solution and place it over the stain. Weight it down with a heavy object. Continue applying the solution until the oil has been drawn out and any remaining stain is bleached out.

Bluestone	**Limestone**
Brick	**Masonry Tile**
Concrete	**Sandstone**
Flagstone	**Slate**
Granite	**Terrazzo**

Scrape to remove chocolate, taking care not to gouge the surface. Wash

Chocolate/ Cocoa *(continued)*

with a solution of washing soda or detergent (never use soap) and water. Use a cloth or a soft-bristled brush. Rinse thoroughly with clear water and allow to dry.

Carpet/Synthetic   **Carpet/Wool**

Blot up or scrape as much of the chocolate as possible. To prevent the stain from setting, flush with club soda. Try an application of carpet stain remover or a concentrated solution of a nonalkali carpet shampoo. After drying and vacuuming, if stain remains, mix 1 tablespoon ammonia with 1 cup water and carefully drop small amounts of the solution onto the stain. (On wool carpets, test in an inconspicuous corner first; ammonia can harm wool.) Blot with an absorbent pad. Flush area rugs or sponge carpeting with clear water. It is important to remove all trace of ammonia. Place a clean absorbent pad over the area and weight it down. When no more liquid is being absorbed, allow it to air-dry thoroughly.

Felt   **Fur/Synthetic**
Fur/Natural

Gently scrape to remove chocolate. Mix mild soap in hot water and swish to make a great volume of suds. Dip a cloth in only the foam and apply. Rinse by wiping with a clean cloth dampened with clear water. If a grease stain remains, powder the stain with an absorbent, such as cornmeal. Give it plenty of time to work. Gently brush it out. Take care not to force the absorbent further into the hairs. Repeat if necessary.

Grout

Wipe up chocolate with a cloth dipped in warm, sudsy water. If any stain remains, dip a wet toothbrush in baking soda or powdered cleanser, or apply tile-and-grout cleaner and gently scrub the spot. Rinse well and wipe dry with a soft cloth.

Leather   **Suede**

Gently scrape chocolate from the surface. Mix a solution of mild soap and lukewarm water. Swish to create a great volume of suds. Apply only the foam with a sponge. Wipe dry with a clean cloth. If a stain remains, powder it with an absorbent, such as cornmeal. Give it plenty of time to work. Gently brush it off. Repeat if necessary; on leather only, follow with saddle soap to condition.

Chocolate/Cocoa *(continued)*

Silver

Wash silver in hot, sudsy water. Rinse thoroughly in hot water. Wipe dry immediately with a clean, soft cloth to prevent tarnish.

Wood

Mix dishwashing detergent in hot water and swish to make a great volume of suds. Dip a cloth in only the foam and apply. Rinse with a clean cloth dampened with clear water. Polish or wax as usual.

COFFEE

Acetate	**Rayon**
Fiberglass	**Triacetate**

Blot up coffee with a clean cloth. Sponge the stain with water. Apply fabric spot cleaner or wet spotter and a few drops of white vinegar. Cover with an absorbent pad dampened with wet spotter. Keep the stain and pad moist with wet spotter and vinegar. Continue this treatment as long as any stain is being removed. Change the pad as it picks up the stain. Flush with water. Repeat until no more stain is removed. If any stain remains, moisten it with a solution of 1 teaspoon enzyme presoak product and 1 cup warm water. Cover with a clean pad that has been dipped in the solution and wrung almost dry. Let it stand for at least 30 minutes. Add more solution if needed to keep the area warm and moist, but do not allow the wet area to spread. When the stain is removed, or no more is being lifted, flush thoroughly with water and allow to dry. (If coffee contained cream and any greasy stain remains, follow procedures for Cream.)

Acrylic Fabric	**Olefin**
Modacrylic	**Polyester**
Nylon	**Spandex**

Blot up coffee with a clean cloth. Soak the stain in a solution of 1 quart warm water, ½ teaspoon dishwashing detergent, and 1 tablespoon white vinegar for 15 minutes. Rinse with water. Sponge the remaining stain with rubbing alcohol and launder if possible. If not, soak in a solution of 1 quart warm water and 1 tablespoon enzyme presoak product for 30 minutes. Rinse well with water. Allow to dry, but launder as soon as possible. (If coffee contained cream and any greasy stain remains, follow procedures for Cream.)

Coffee (continued)

Acrylic Plastic	**Ivory**
Aluminum	**Jade**
Asphalt	**Linoleum**
Bamboo	**Paint/Flat**
Brass	**Paint/Gloss**
Bronze	**Pewter**
Cane	**Plexiglas**
Ceramic Glass/Tile	**Polyurethane**
Copper	**Stainless Steel**
Cork	**Tin**
Enamel	**Vinyl Clothing**
Glass	**Vinyl Tile**
Gold	**Vinyl Wallcovering**
Grout	**Zinc**
Iron	

Blot up coffee. Wipe the surface with a cloth or sponge dipped in warm, sudsy water. Rinse well and wipe dry.

Alabaster	**Marble**

Blot up coffee. Wipe the surface with a cloth dipped in a solution of washing soda or detergent and water. Rinse well and wipe dry. If a stain remains, mix a few drops of ammonia with 1 cup 3-percent hydrogen peroxide. Soak a white blotter with the solution and place it over the stain. Weight it with a heavy object. Continue applying the solution until the oil has been drawn out and any remaining stain is bleached out.

Bluestone	**Limestone**
Brick	**Masonry Tile**
Concrete	**Sandstone**
Flagstone	**Slate**
Granite	**Terrazzo**

Mix a solution of washing soda or detergent in water. Gently brush stain away. Wash with clear water and allow to dry.

Burlap	**Wool**
Silk	

Blot up coffee. Sponge the stain with water. Apply fabric spot cleaner or wet spotter and a few drops of white vinegar. Cover with an absorbent pad dampened with wet spotter. Continue this treatment as long as any stain

Coffee *(continued)*

is being lifted. Change the pad as it picks up the stain. Keep the stain and pad moist with wet spotter and vinegar. Flush with water. Repeat until no more stain is being removed. If any stain remains, apply rubbing alcohol to the stain and cover with an absorbent pad dampened with alcohol. Let stand as long as it is picking up stain, changing the pad as it does. Keep the stain and pad moist with alcohol. Flush with water. For a stubborn or old stain, try moistening the stain with a solution of 1 teaspoon enzyme presoak product and 1 cup warm water—use only on burlap. Cover with a clean pad dipped in the solution and squeezed almost dry. Let it stand for at least 30 minutes. Add more solution as needed to keep the area warm and moist, but do not allow the wet area to spread. When the stain is lifted, flush thoroughly with water. (If the coffee contained cream and any greasy stain remains, follow procedures for Cream.)

Carpet/Synthetic   **Foam Rubber**
Carpet/Wool

Blot up what you can. Apply carpet stain remover. Flush the stain with a solution of 1 quart warm water, ½ teaspoon liquid laundry detergent or dishwashing detergent, and 1 tablespoon white vinegar. Blot with a clean pad and rinse well with water. If the stain remains, try flushing it with a solution of 1 quart warm water and 1 tablespoon enzyme presoak product. (Do not use on wool.) Blot and flush alternately until no more stain is left. Sponge the area well with water. Blot all excess liquid and place a clean pad over the area and weight it down. When no more stain is being absorbed, allow the area to air-dry thoroughly. (If coffee contained cream and any greasy stain remains, follow procedures for Cream.)

Cotton   **Linen**

Blot up coffee. Pretreat with prewash spot-and-stain remover, then launder immediately. If that is not possible, soak the stain in a solution of 1 quart warm water and ½ teaspoon dishwashing detergent for 15 minutes. Rinse well with clear water. Next, sponge the stain with rubbing alcohol. Rinse and allow to dry. If the stain remains, soak it in a solution of warm water and enzyme presoak product for 30 minutes. Rinse well with water and dry. Launder as soon as possible. Another method is to stretch the stained area over a bowl and secure with a rubber band. Pour boiling water through the stain from a height of 2 to 3 feet. Stand back to avoid splatters. Although cotton and linen can withstand boiling water, some of the finishes and colors used on the fabrics might be damaged by such harsh treatment. Be sure to test on an inconspicuous corner first. (If coffee contained cream and any greasy stain remains, follow procedures for Cream.)

Coffee *(continued)*

Felt   **Fur/Synthetic**
Fur/Natural

Blot up what you can without forcing the stain further into the fibers. Mix mild soap in hot water and swish to make a great volume of suds. Dip a cloth in only the foam and apply. Rinse with a cloth dipped in clear water and wrung nearly dry. If an oily residue remains, powder the stain with an absorbent, such as cornmeal. Don't push the powder into the fibers or pelt. Give it plenty of time to work. Gently brush or shake it out. Repeat if necessary. Make sure the material is dry before applying powder. (If coffee contained cream and any greasy stain remains, follow procedures for Cream.)

Leather   **Suede**

Carefully blot up coffee. Mix a solution of mild soap and lukewarm water. Swish to create a great volume of suds. Apply only the foam with a sponge. Wipe dry with a clean, dry cloth. If an oily stain remains, powder the stain with an absorbent, such as cornmeal. Give it plenty of time to work. Gently brush it off. Repeat if necessary. On leather only, condition with saddle soap. (If coffee contained cream and any greasy stain remains, follow procedures for Cream.)

Porcelain Dishes   **Porcelain Fixtures**

Clean the stain by washing it in warm, sudsy water or wiping it with a cloth dipped in warm, sudsy water. Rinse well and wipe dry. To remove an old stain from the bottom of a cup, dip a soft, damp cloth into baking soda and wipe stain. Rinse well and dry.

Silver

Wash silver in hot, soapy water. Rinse in hot water and wipe dry immediately with a soft cloth.

Wood

Gently wipe the surface with a cloth dipped in suds made of mild detergent and water. Rinse well with a clean cloth dampened with clear water. Polish or wax the wood as soon as possible.

COLOGNE

Acetate	Silk
Fiberglass	Triacetate
Rayon	

Flush the stain with water. Spray on fabric spot cleaner. An alternate method is to flush, then add a few drops of glycerine. Rinse well with water. If some stain remains, cautiously try a diluted solution of white vinegar. Make sure you work the stain inward toward the center to avoid leaving a ring. Flush with clear water to remove the vinegar, and allow to dry.

Acrylic Fabric	Nylon
Burlap	Olefin
Carpet/Synthetic	Polyester
Carpet/Wool	Rope
Cotton	Spandex
Linen	Wool
Modacrylic	

Sponge the stain with water. Spray on fabric spot cleaner. If stain remains, apply wet spotter and cover with an absorbent pad dampened with wet spotter. Continue this treatment as long as any stain is being removed. Change the pad as it picks up the stain. Keep the stain and pad moist with wet spotter. Flush well with water. Repeat until no more stain is being lifted. If any stain remains, apply rubbing alcohol to the stain and cover it with an absorbent pad dampened with alcohol. (Do not use this on acrylic or modacrylic.) Let stand as long as any stain is being lifted. Change the pad as it picks up the stain. Keep the stain and pad moist with alcohol. Flush well with water and allow to dry.

Acrylic Plastic	Marble
Alabaster	Paint/Flat
Asphalt	Paint/Gloss
Ceramic Glass/Tile	Plexiglas
Cork	Polyurethane
Glass	Stainless Steel
Gold	Vinyl Tile
Ivory	Vinyl Clothing
Jade	Vinyl Wallcovering
Linoleum	

Wash spill with a solution of warm, sudsy water. Rinse well and wipe dry with a clean cloth.

Cologne *(continued)*

Bluestone	Limestone
Brick	Masonry Tile
Concrete	Sandstone
Flagstone	Slate
Granite	Terrazzo

Wash stained area with a solution of washing soda or detergent and water. Use a cloth or soft-bristled brush to scrub the stain. Rinse thoroughly and allow to dry.

Leather   **Suede**

Gently blot up the spill. Mix a solution of mild soap and lukewarm water. Swish to create a great volume of suds. Apply only the foam with a sponge. Wipe with a clean, dry cloth. If an oily stain remains, powder the stain with an absorbent, such as cornmeal. Give it plenty of time to work. Gently brush it off. Repeat if necessary. On leather only, follow with saddle soap to condition.

Wallpaper

Cologne often permanently stains paper, so treat the stain immediately. Carefully wipe with a sponge dipped in clear, warm water and wrung out until damp. Strokes should be overlapped to prevent streaking. Gently pat dry with a clean cloth.

Wood

Rub the stain with denatured alcohol immediately if possible. Follow this with a liberal application of boiled linseed oil. If the stain persists, leave some oil on the surface for 24 hours, then wipe with a clean, soft cloth and polish or wax as usual.

COSMETICS

(See Blusher; Eyeliner/Eye Pencil/Eye Shadow; Face Powder; Lipstick; Liquid Foundation; Lotion/Body, Facial, Foot, Hair; Lotion/Hand; Lotion/Suntan; Mascara; Rouge.)

COUGH SYRUP

Acetate	**Silk**
Fiberglass	**Triacetate**
Rayon	**Wool**

Sponge the area with water. Spray on fabric spot cleaner. Then apply wet spotter and a few drops of white vinegar. Cover with an absorbent pad dampened with wet spotter. Let it stand as long as any stain is being removed. Change the pad as it picks up the stain. Keep stain and pad moist with wet spotter and vinegar. Repeat until no more stain is removed. If any stain remains, soak in a solution of 1 quart warm water, ½ teaspoon liquid detergent, and 1 tablespoon white vinegar for 15 minutes. Rinse with water.

Acrylic Fabric	**Spandex**

Sponge the area with water. Spray on fabric spot cleaner. Then apply wet spotter and a few drops white vinegar. Cover with an absorbent pad dampened with wet spotter. Let it stand as long as any stain is being removed. Tamp occasionally and change the pad as it picks up the stain. Flush with water. If stain remains, soak in a solution of 1 quart warm water, ½ teaspoon liquid detergent, and 1 tablespoon white vinegar for 15 minutes. Launder if possible. If not, soak in a solution of 1 quart warm water and 1 tablespoon enzyme presoak product for 30 minutes. Rinse well with water and launder as soon as possible.

Acrylic Plastic	**Linoleum**
Alabaster	**Marble**
Aluminum	**Paint/Flat**
Asphalt	**Paint/Gloss**
Bamboo	**Plexiglas**
Cane	**Polyurethane**
Ceramic Glass/Tile	**Stainless Steel**
Cork	**Vinyl Tile**
Glass	**Vinyl Wallcovering**

Wipe up cough syrup immediately because it contains not only alcohol, but also food coloring, which can permanently stain and damage the surface. Wipe surface with a cloth or sponge dipped in warm, sudsy water. Rinse well and wipe dry.

Bluestone	**Flagstone**
Concrete	**Slate**

(continued)

Cough Syrup *(continued)*

Wipe up cough syrup. Wash with a solution of washing soda or detergent (never use soap) and water. Use a cloth or soft-bristled brush. Rinse thoroughly with clear water and allow to dry.

Carpet/Synthetic	Nylon
Carpet/Wool	Olefin
Cotton	Polyester
Linen	

Sponge area with water. Apply fabric spot remover, or carpet stain remover. Then apply wet spotter and a few drops of white vinegar. (Do not use vinegar on cotton and linen.) Cover with an absorbent pad dampened with wet spotter. Continue this treatment as long as stain is being removed. Change the pad as it picks up the stain. Keep stain and pad moist with wet spotter and vinegar. Flush with water. Repeat until no more stain is removed. If the stain persists, apply rubbing alcohol and cover with an absorbent pad dampened with alcohol. Let stand as long as any stain is being removed. Change the pad as it picks up the stain. Keep stain and pad moist with alcohol. If stain still remains, soak in a solution of 1 quart warm water, ½ teaspoon liquid detergent, and 1 tablespoon white vinegar for 15 minutes. Rinse with water. Sponge with alcohol. Launder if possible. If not, soak in a solution of 1 quart warm water and 1 tablespoon enzyme presoak product for 30 minutes (not for use on wool carpets). Rinse well with clear water. Launder as soon as possible. For carpets, thoroughly dampen the area with the solution and cover with an absorbent pad moistened with the solution. Keep covered for 30 minutes. Using absorbent pads, remove as much moisture as possible. Allow the area to air-dry thoroughly.

Grout

Wipe excess immediately with a cloth dipped in warm, sudsy water. If any stain remains, dip a wet toothbrush into powdered cleanser or apply tile-and-grout cleaner and gently scrub spot. Rinse well and wipe dry.

| Leather | Suede |

Gently remove any cough syrup. Mix a solution of mild soap and lukewarm water. Swish to create a great volume of suds. Apply only the foam with a sponge. Wipe with a clean, dry cloth. If a grease stain remains, powder the stain with an absorbent, such as cornmeal. Allow plenty of time for absorbent to work, and then gently brush stain off. Repeat if necessary. On leather only, follow with saddle soap to condition.

CRAYON

Acetate	Rope
Burlap	Silk
Fiberglass	Triacetate
Rayon	Wool/Nonwashable

Gently scrape to remove crayon. Place an absorbent pad under the stain and flush with dry-cleaning solvent. Allow to dry. Repeat if necessary until all trace of the stain has been removed.

Acrylic Fabric	Olefin
Cotton	Polyester
Linen	Spandex
Modacrylic	Wool/Washable
Nylon	

Scrape to remove crayon. Place the stain between two pieces of white blotting paper and press with a warm iron. Change the blotter as the stain is absorbed. This stain can easily spread, so use care while pressing. On colorfast and white cotton or linen, try pouring boiling water through the stain. Allow fabric to dry. If any crayon remains, flush it with dry-cleaning solvent. If any dye remains, sponge it with 1 part rubbing alcohol in 2 parts water. (Do not use this solution on acrylic or modacrylic.) Rinse well with clear water and allow to dry.

Acrylic Plastic	Iron
Alabaster	Ivory
Aluminum	Jade
Bamboo	Limestone
Bluestone	Marble
Brass	Paint/Flat
Brick	Paint/Gloss
Bronze	Pewter
Cane	Plexiglas
Ceramic Glass/Tile	Polyurethane
Concrete	Porcelain
Copper	Sandstone
Enamel	Slate
Flagstone	Stainless Steel
Glass	Terrazzo
Gold	Tin
Granite	Vinyl Clothing
Grout	Vinyl Tile

(continued)

Crayon *(continued)*

Gently scrape crayon from the surface. Take care not to scratch the surface. This should be sufficient to remove the stain. Wipe with a sponge dipped in a solution of washing soda or detergent (not soap) and water. Rinse well and wipe dry. On flat or gloss paint, grout, or marble, rub a mildly abrasive pumice bar lightly over the crayon marks. Remove any shine left on flat paint by sponging lightly with hot water.

Asphalt   **Linoleum**
Cork

On linoleum floors, a mildly abrasive pumice bar rubbed lightly on the surface removes crayon marks. Polish or wax as usual. You can also remove crayon from all of these surfaces by using a metal spatula to gently scrape up the mark; take care not to gouge the surface.

Carpet/Synthetic   **Carpet/Wool**

Gently scrape as much crayon as you can from the surface. Add a small amount of dry-cleaning solvent, and blot with an absorbent pad. (Overwetting may damage the carpet's backing.) Continue until no more stain is removed. If any dye remains, dilute 1 part rubbing alcohol with 2 parts water and test on an inconspicuous place. If the carpet proves to be colorfast, apply the solution to the stain in small amounts, blotting well after each application. Allow to dry.

Felt

Very carefully scrape off the residue, taking care not to pull out the fibers. If any residue remains, try brushing gently with a stiff-bristled brush. In extreme cases, use a razor blade to gently scrape the excess. Use this as a last resort; it will remove some of the fibers.

Leather   **Suede**

With a dull knife or your fingernail, gently scrape up the crayon. If any stain remains, mix a thick paste of fuller's earth and water and apply it to the stain. Carefully brush it off when dry. Repeat if necessary. When the stain has been removed, on leather only, follow with saddle soap to condition.

Silver

Crayon *(continued)*

Scrape up crayon with your fingernail or a nonmetal utensil until no more can be removed. Wash the silver in hot, soapy water. Rinse in hot water and wipe dry.

Wallpaper

Rub the crayon marks lightly with the edge of a mildly abrasive pumice bar, rubbing in several directions if the wallpaper is textured. An alternate method is to spray aerosol spotlifter onto the stain, or lightly rub the stain with a dry, soap-filled steel-wool pad. If the stain persists, rub it very gently with baking soda sprinkled on a damp cloth. Wipe away any residue with a damp cloth and dry.

Wood

Rub the crayon marks with a mildly abrasive pumice bar, then polish or wax the wood. Or gently remove any material by scraping with a dull knife or your fingernail. Polish with a chamois.

CREAM

Acetate	Rayon
Burlap	Rope
Carpet/Synthetic	Silk
Carpet/Wool	Triacetate
Fiberglass	Wool/Nonwashable

Remove cream immediately. Sponge with dry-cleaning solvent. Then apply dry spotter to the stain and cover with an absorbent pad dampened with dry spotter. Continue this treatment as long as any stain is being removed. Change the pad as it picks up the stain. Keep the pad and stain moist with dry spotter. Flush with dry-cleaning solvent. If any stain remains, moisten the area with a solution of 1 cup warm water and 1 teaspoon enzyme presoak—do not use on silk or wool. Cover with a clean pad that has been dipped in the solution and wrung almost dry. Let stand for 30 minutes. Add more solution if needed to keep the area warm and damp, but do not allow the wet area to spread. When no more stain is being lifted, flush the area thoroughly with clear water and allow to dry.

Acrylic Fabric	Olefin
Cotton	Polyester

(continued)

Cream *(continued)*

Linen	**Spandex**
Modacrylic	**Wool/Washable**
Nylon	

Immediately remove as much cream as you can. Sponge the stain with dry-cleaning solvent. Apply dry spotter and cover with an absorbent pad dampened with dry spotter. Let stand as long as any stain is being removed. Change the pad as it picks up the stain. Keep stain and pad moist with dry spotter. Flush with liquid dry-cleaning solvent. If any stain remains, apply a few drops of dishwashing detergent and a few drops of ammonia to the area, then tamp or scrape. Keep the stain moist with detergent and ammonia and blot occasionally with an absorbent pad. Flush well with clear water to remove all trace of ammonia and allow to dry.

Acrylic Plastic	**Linoleum**
Aluminum	**Paint/Flat**
Asphalt	**Paint/Gloss**
Bamboo	**Pewter**
Brass	**Platinum**
Bronze	**Plexiglas**
Cane	**Polyurethane**
Ceramic Glass/Tile	**Porcelain Dishes**
Copper	**Stainless Steel**
Cork	**Tin**
Enamel	**Vinyl Clothing**
Glass	**Vinyl Tile**
Gold	**Vinyl Wallcovering**
Iron	**Zinc**
Ivory	

Wipe up the cream immediately. Wipe the surface with a cloth or sponge dipped in warm, sudsy water. Rinse well and wipe dry.

Alabaster	**Marble**

Wipe up cream. Mix a few drops of ammonia with 1 cup of rubbing alcohol. Soak a white blotter (about the size of the stain) in the solution and place it over the area. Cover it with a heavy object. Continue applying the solution until the oil has been drawn out and any remaining stain is bleached out. If any stain persists, make a thick paste of bleach, water, and powdered detergent. Apply it to the stain. Cover with a damp cloth to minimize drying. Remove when the stain is bleached out.

Cream *(continued)*

Bluestone	Limestone
Brick	Masonry Tile
Concrete	Sandstone
Flagstone	Slate
Granite	Terrazzo

Remove cream. Wash the stained area with a solution of washing soda or detergent (never use soap) and water. Use a cloth or soft-bristled brush. Rinse the area thoroughly with clear water and allow to dry.

Fur/Natural   **Fur/Synthetic**

Wipe up any excess cream. Mix dishwashing detergent in hot water and swish to make a great volume of suds. Dip a cloth in only the foam and apply. Wipe again with a clean, dry cloth. If a grease stain remains, powder the stain with an absorbent, allowing plenty of time for it to work. Gently brush off the powder and wipe the area with a damp cloth. Allow fur to air-dry.

Grout

Wipe up cream with a cloth dipped in warm, sudsy water. If any stain remains, apply tile-and-grout cleaner or dip a wet toothbrush in powdered cleanser and gently scrub the spot. Rinse well and wipe dry with a clean cloth.

Leather

Wipe up excess cream from the surface. Mix a solution of mild soap in lukewarm water. Swish to create a great volume of suds. Apply only the foam with a sponge. Wipe with a clean, dry cloth. If a grease stain remains, powder the stain with an absorbent, such as cornmeal. Give it plenty of time to work. Gently brush it off. Repeat if necessary. Follow with saddle soap to condition. If after applying the absorbent and brushing it off, any stain persists, use liquid leather cleaner. Rub it in with a clean soft cloth and allow to dry. Condition with saddle soap.

Silver

Remove cream with a cloth. Wash as soon as possible in hot, sudsy water. Rinse in hot water and dry immediately with a soft cloth.

Cream *(continued)*

Suede

Blot up cream from the surface of fabric. Mix a solution of mild soap in lukewarm water. Swish to create a great volume of suds. Apply only the foam with a sponge. Wipe with a clean, dry cloth. If a grease stain remains, powder the area with an absorbent, allowing plenty of time for it to work. Gently brush off the stain.

Wallpaper

Carefully blot up the cream. With a cloth or sponge dipped in cool, clear water and squeezed almost dry, wipe the stained area. Overlap strokes to prevent streaking. Gently pat dry.

Wood

Mix dishwashing detergent in hot water and swish to make a great volume of suds. Dip a cloth in only the foam and apply. Rinse with a clean cloth dipped in clear water and squeezed almost dry. Polish or wax as soon as possible.

DEODORANT

Acetate	Linen
Burlap	Rayon
Carpet/Synthetic	Silk
Carpet/Wool	Triacetate
Cotton	Wool
Fiberglass	

Spray on fabric spot cleaner. Another method is to apply rubbing alcohol to the stain and cover with an absorbent pad dampened with alcohol. (Dilute alcohol with 2 parts water for acetate, rayon, and triacetate; test silk for colorfastness before using alcohol.) Keep both the stain and the pad moist. Allow to stand as long as any stain is being removed. If the stain remains (and as a last resort), flush with a solution of warm, sudsy water with a few drops of ammonia added. (Use special care on silk and wool.) Rinse with clear water. Apply a solution of warm water with a few drops of white vinegar added, taking special care with this solution on cotton and linen. Rinse again with clear water. Dry thoroughly. (If the color of the fabric has been changed, it may possibly be restored by sponging lightly with a solution of 2 parts water and 1 part ammonia.) **Caution:** Never iron material

Deodorant (continued)

with a deodorant stain. The interaction of chemicals and heat will ruin most fabrics.

Acrylic Fabric	**Olefin**
Modacrylic	**Polyester**
Nylon	**Spandex**

Most deodorant stains can be removed by treating with liquid detergent or prewash spot-and-stain remover and laundering as usual. If the stain doesn't seem to be loosening with this treatment, rinse out the detergent and flush with white vinegar. Rinse in clear water. If the stain remains, flush the area with denatured alcohol. Rinse with clear water, let dry.

Acrylic Plastic	**Iron**
Aluminum	**Linoleum**
Asphalt	**Marble**
Bamboo	**Masonry Tile**
Brass	**Paint/Flat**
Bronze	**Paint/Gloss**
Cane	**Plexiglas**
Ceramic Glass/Tile	**Polyurethane**
Chromium	**Stainless Steel**
Cork	**Tin**
Enamel	**Vinyl Clothing**
Glass	**Vinyl Tile**
Gold	**Vinyl Wallcovering**
Grout	

Wipe the area with a cloth dipped in warm, sudsy water. Rinse well and wipe dry with a clean cloth.

Leather	**Suede**

Mix a solution of mild soap in lukewarm water. Swish to create a great volume of suds. Apply only the foam with a sponge. Wipe dry with a clean cloth. On leather only, follow with saddle soap to condition.

Wallpaper

Carefully wipe the wallpaper with a sponge dampened with clear, warm water. Do this immediately after spilling deodorant on the wallpaper; deodorant can permanently stain paper. Strokes should overlap to prevent streaking. Gently pat dry with a clean cloth.

Deodorant *(continued)*

Wood

Wipe spills or deodorant-sprayed areas as soon as possible with a sponge or soft cloth dipped in sudsy water. Wipe dry and apply wax or polish as soon as possible.

DYE (EXCEPT RED AND YELLOW)

Acetate	**Rayon**
Carpet/Synthetic	**Triacetate**
Fiberglass	

Sponge with water. Spray on fabric spot cleaner. Then apply wet spotter and a few drops of white vinegar. Use an absorbent pad dampened with wet spotter to blot occasionally. Keep the stain moist with wet spotter and vinegar. When no more stain can be blotted, flush with water. If stain persists, apply more wet spotter and a few drops of ammonia. Cover the stain this time with an absorbent pad and allow it to remain as long as any stain is being lifted. Keep stain and pad moist with wet spotter and ammonia. Flush with water and allow to dry.

Acrylic Fabric	**Olefin**
Modacrylic	**Polyester**
Nylon	**Spandex**

Presoak in a solution of 1 quart warm water, ½ teaspoon liquid dishwashing detergent or liquid laundry detergent, and 1 tablespoon white vinegar for 15 minutes. Rinse well and launder if possible. If not, soak in solution of 1 quart warm water and 1 tablespoon enzyme presoak for 30 minutes. Rinse well and launder as soon as possible. If stain still remains, mix a solution of 1 tablespoon ammonia and 1 cup water. Be sure to test on a hidden seam first, then carefully drop solution onto stain, using an eyedropper. Blot with an absorbent pad. Flush with clear water. Place an absorbent pad over the stain and weight it down. When no more liquid is absorbed, allow to dry thoroughly.

Acrylic Plastic	**Paint/Flat**
Aluminum	**Paint/Gloss**
Bamboo	**Plexiglas**
Cane	**Polyurethane**
Ceramic Glass/Tile	**Vinyl Clothing**
Glass	**Vinyl Wallcovering**

Dye *(continued)*

Immediately wipe up the spill with a cloth or sponge dipped in warm, sudsy water. Rinse well and wipe dry.

Alabaster   **Marble**

Immediately wipe up the spill with a cloth or sponge dipped in warm, sudsy water. Rinse well and wipe dry. If the stain persists, soak an absorbent pad in rubbing alcohol, wring almost dry, and place over the stain. Wait 5 minutes and apply an absorbent pad soaked in ammonia and squeezed nearly dry. Alternate alcohol and ammonia pads until stain has been removed. Wipe surface with a cloth moistened with cool, clear water and wipe dry with a clean cloth.

Asphalt   **Linoleum**
Cork   **Vinyl Tile**

Wipe up any dye with a cloth or sponge dipped in warm, sudsy water. Rinse well and wipe dry. If stain persists, cover with an absorbent pad soaked in rubbing alcohol. Let it remain in place for several minutes, then wipe the area with a cloth dampened with ammonia. Rinse well with a cloth dipped in warm, sudsy water and rewipe with a cloth dampened with clear water. Allow to dry and polish or wax the surface.

Bluestone   **Limestone**
Brick   **Masonry Tile**
Concrete   **Sandstone**
Flagstone   **Slate**
Granite   **Terrazzo**

Wipe up the excess dye. Wash with a solution of washing soda or detergent (not soap) and water. Gently scrub with a cloth or soft-bristled brush. Rinse thoroughly with clear water and allow to dry.

Carpet/Wool   **Wool**
Silk

Sponge with water, then apply wet spotter and a few drops of white vinegar. Blot frequently as the stain is loosened. Keep the stain moist with wet spotter and vinegar. Flush with water when no more stain is removed. If stain remains, apply rubbing alcohol to the stain and cover with an absorbent pad moistened with alcohol. Let it remain as long as stain is being removed. Change the pad as it picks up the stain. Keep the stain and pad moist with alcohol. Allow to air-dry.

Dye *(continued)*

Cotton   **Linen**

Soak in a solution of 1 quart warm water, ½ teaspoon dishwashing detergent, and 1 tablespoon ammonia for 30 minutes. Rinse with water. Apply rubbing alcohol and tamp or scrape. Keep the stain moist with alcohol and blot occasionally. Continue as long as stain is being removed. Flush with water and allow to dry. Launder as soon as possible.

Grout

Wipe up dye with a cloth dipped in warm, sudsy water. If any stain persists, apply tile-and-grout cleaner or dip a wet toothbrush in baking soda or powdered cleanser. Gently scrub the spot. Rinse well and wipe dry.

Leather   **Suede**

Dye will immediately change the color of these materials. Once contact has been made, there is no way to remove the stain.

Wood

Mix dishwashing detergent in hot water and swish to make a great volume of suds. Dip a cloth in only the foam and apply. Rinse with a clean cloth moistened with clear water. Polish or wax.

DYE/RED

Acetate   **Rayon**
Carpet/Synthetic   **Silk**
Carpet/Wool   **Triacetate**
Fiberglass   **Wool**

Sponge the area immediately with water to dilute the spill. Apply wet spotter and a few drops of ammonia. (Use ammonia sparingly on silk and wool.) Cover with an absorbent pad dampened with wet spotter. Let the pad remain as long as any stain is being removed. Change the pad as it picks up the stain. Keep both the stain and pad moist with wet spotter and ammonia. Flush well with water and repeat if necessary. If, after allowing to dry, a stain still persists, mix color remover according to package direction. After testing on an inconspicuous place, flush it through the stain onto an absorbent pad. When dealing with carpet, sponge color remover on the stain and blot with an absorbent pad. Rinse well with clear water.

Dye/Red *(continued)*

Acrylic Fabric	**Nylon**
Cotton	**Olefin**
Linen	**Polyester**
Modacrylic	**Spandex**

Soak the item in a solution of 1 quart warm water, ½ teaspoon liquid dishwashing detergent or liquid laundry detergent, and 1 tablespoon ammonia for 30 minutes. Rinse well. If stain persists, soak in a solution of 1 quart warm water and 1 tablespoon white vinegar for 1 hour. Use white vinegar with care on cotton and linen. Rinse well with water and allow to dry. If stain is set, try applying rubbing alcohol to the area and tamping. As stain loosens, blot liquid and stain with an absorbent pad. Keep both the stain and pad moist with alcohol and change the pad as it picks up stain. Allow to dry. As a last resort for any remaining trace of stain, mix color remover according to package directions and apply to stain. After testing on a hidden place, flush the solution through the stain. Rinse well with clear water and allow to dry thoroughly.

Acrylic Plastic	**Paint/Flat**
Aluminum	**Paint/Gloss**
Bamboo	**Plexiglas**
Cane	**Polyurethane**
Ceramic Glass/Tile	**Vinyl Clothing**
Glass	**Vinyl Wallcovering**

Immediately wipe up the spill with a cloth or sponge dipped in warm, sudsy water. Rinse well and wipe dry.

Alabaster	**Marble**

Immediately wipe up the spill with a cloth or sponge dipped in warm, sudsy water. Rinse well and wipe dry. If a stain persists, soak an absorbent pad in rubbing alcohol, wring dry, and place over the stain. Wait 5 minutes and apply an absorbent pad soaked in ammonia and wrung out. Alternate the alcohol and ammonia pads until stain has been removed. Wipe surface with a cloth dampened with clear water, then wipe with a clean, dry cloth.

Asphalt	**Linoleum**
Cork	**Vinyl Tile**

Wipe up spill with a cloth or sponge dipped in warm, sudsy water. Rinse well and wipe dry. If a stain remains, cover it with an absorbent pad soaked in rubbing alcohol. Let it remain in place for several minutes, then wipe

Dye/Red *(continued)*

the area with a cloth dampened with ammonia. Wipe with cloth dipped in warm, sudsy water and rinse with a cloth dipped in clear water. Allow to dry.

Bluestone	**Limestone**
Brick	**Masonry Tile**
Concrete	**Sandstone**
Flagstone	**Slate**
Granite	**Terrazzo**

Wipe up excess dye. Wash with a solution of washing soda or detergent (not soap) and water. Scrub with a cloth or soft-bristled brush. Rinse thoroughly with clear water and allow to dry.

Grout

Wipe up dye with a cloth dipped in warm, sudsy water. If any stain persists, dip a wet toothbrush in baking soda or powdered cleanser, or apply tile-and-grout cleaner and gently scrub the stain. Rinse well with clear water and wipe dry.

Leather	**Suede**

Dye will immediately act on the color of the hide. Once contact has been made, there is no way to remove the stain.

Wood

Mix dishwashing detergent in hot water and swish to make a great volume of suds. Dip a cloth in only the foam and apply. Rinse with a clean cloth dipped in clear water and wrung out. Polish or wax as soon as possible.

DYE/YELLOW

Acetate	**Rayon**
Carpet/Synthetic	**Silk**
Carpet/Wool	**Triacetate**
Fiberglass	**Wool**

Sponge the area with dry-cleaning solvent. Then apply dry spotter and tamp or scrape to loosen the stain. Flush with liquid dry-cleaning solvent.

Dye/Yellow *(continued)*

If stain persists, apply amyl acetate and tamp again. Flush with dry-cleaning solvent and allow to dry. If any trace still remains, sponge stain with water and apply a few drops of white vinegar. Tamp or scrape again. Apply wet spotter and a few drops of ammonia, then tamp again. Allow to dry. Sponge with rubbing alcohol and pat with a pad dampened with alcohol. (Do not use alcohol on acetate, rayon, or triacetate.) Allow to dry away from heat.

Acrylic Fabric	**Nylon**
Cotton	**Olefin**
Linen	**Polyester**
Modacrylic	**Spandex**

Cover the stain with a pad dampened with rubbing alcohol. (Dilute alcohol with 2 parts water for acrylic and modacrylic and pretest its effects.) Let the pad remain on the stain for a few minutes, then wipe with a cloth dampened with ammonia. If stain persists, sponge area with spot remover or dry-cleaning fluid. Then apply dry spotter. Tamp or scrape to loosen the stain. Flush with liquid dry-cleaning solvent. If stain persists, apply amyl acetate and tamp again. Flush with the dry-cleaning solvent. If the stain remains, sponge with clear water and apply wet spotter and a few drops of white vinegar—do not use vinegar on cotton or linen. Tamp again, then apply wet spotter and a few drops of ammonia. Flush with dry-cleaning solvent and allow to dry.

Acrylic Plastic	**Paint/Flat**
Aluminum	**Paint/Gloss**
Bamboo	**Plexiglas**
Cane	**Polyurethane**
Ceramic Glass/Tile	**Vinyl Clothing**
Glass	**Vinyl Wallcovering**

Immediately wipe up the spill with a cloth or sponge dipped in warm, sudsy water. Rinse well and wipe dry.

Alabaster	**Marble**

Immediately wipe up the spill with a cloth or sponge dipped in warm, sudsy water. Rinse well and wipe dry. If a stain persists, soak an absorbent pad in rubbing alcohol and place it over the stain. Wait 5 minutes, then apply an absorbent pad soaked with ammonia. Alternate pads until stain has been removed. Rinse surface with cloth dampened with clear water. Wipe dry with a clean cloth.

Dye/Yellow *(continued)*

Asphalt	**Linoleum**
Cork	**Vinyl Tile**

Wipe up any excess with a cloth or sponge dipped in warm, sudsy water. Rinse well and wipe dry. If stain remains, cover with an absorbent pad soaked in rubbing alcohol. Let it remain in place for several minutes, then wipe the area with a cloth dampened with ammonia. Rinse with a cloth dipped in warm, sudsy water and follow with a cloth dampened with clear water. Allow to dry.

Bluestone	**Limestone**
Brick	**Masonry Tile**
Concrete	**Sandstone**
Flagstone	**Slate**
Granite	**Terrazzo**

Wipe up excess dye. Wash with a solution of washing soda or detergent (not soap) and water. Scrub with a cloth or soft-bristled brush. Rinse thoroughly with clear water and allow to dry.

Grout

Wipe up spill with a cloth dipped in warm, sudsy water. If any stain persists, dip a wet toothbrush in baking soda or powdered cleanser or use tile-and-grout cleaner. Gently scrub the stain. Rinse thoroughly and wipe dry.

Leather	**Suede**

Dye will discolor these materials on contact. There is no way to remove this discoloration, because it is absorbed into the hide.

Wood

Mix dishwashing detergent in hot water and swish to make a great volume of suds. Dip a cloth in only the foam and apply. Rise with a clean cloth dampened with clear water. Polish or wax as soon as possible.

EGG

Acetate	**Rayon**
Burlap	**Rope**
Carpet/Synthetic	**Silk**

Egg *(continued)*

Carpet/Wool	Triacetate
Fiberglass	Wool

Remove the egg, then sponge with dry-cleaning solvent. Then apply dry spotter to the stain and cover with an absorbent pad dampened with dry spotter. Let stand as long as any stain is being removed. Change the pad as it picks up the stain. Keep the pad and stain moist with dry spotter. Flush with liquid dry-cleaning solvent. If any stain remains, moisten it with a solution of 1 cup warm water and 1 teaspoon enzyme presoak—do not use on silk or wool. Cover with a clean pad that has been dipped in the solution and wrung almost dry. Let it stand 30 minutes. Add more solution if needed to keep the area warm and moist, but do not allow the wet area to spread. When no more stain is being lifted, flush with clear water.

Acrylic Fabric	Nylon
Cotton	Olefin
Linen	Polyester
Modacrylic	Spandex

Scrape to remove the egg and sponge the stain with dry-cleaning solvent. Then apply dry spotter to the stain and cover with an absorbent pad dampened with dry spotter. Let stand as long as any stain is being removed. Change the pad as it picks up the stain. Keep both stain and pad moist with dry spotter. Flush with liquid dry-cleaning solvent. If any stain persists, apply a few drops of dishwashing detergent and a few drops of ammonia to the stain, then tamp or scrape. Keep the stain moist with detergent and ammonia and blot occasionally with an absorbent pad. Flush well with clear water to remove all of the ammonia. Allow to dry. If any stain remains, moisten it with a solution of 1 cup warm water and 1 teaspoon enzyme presoak. Cover with a clean pad that has been dipped in the solution and wrung almost dry. Let it stand 30 minutes. Add more solution if needed to keep the area warm and moist, but do not allow the wet area to spread. When no more stain is being lifted, thoroughly flush the area with water.

Acrylic Plastic	Jade
Alabaster	Linoleum
Aluminum	Marble
Asphalt	Paint/Flat
Bamboo	Paint/Gloss
Brass	Pewter
Bronze	Plexiglas
Cane	Polyurethane
Ceramic Glass/Tile	Porcelain Dishes

(continued)

Egg *(continued)*

Copper	Porcelain Fixtures
Cork	Stainless Steel
Enamel	Tin
Glass	Vinyl Clothing
Gold	Vinyl Tile
Iron	Vinyl Wallcovering
Ivory	

Scrape up excess egg with a dull knife. Wipe the area with a cloth or sponge dipped in warm, sudsy water. Rinse well and wipe dry.

Bluestone	Limestone
Brick	Masonry Tile
Concrete	Sandstone
Flagstone	Slate
Granite	Terrazzo

Wipe up egg. Wash with a solution of washing soda or detergent (never soap) and water. Use a cloth or soft-bristled brush. Rinse thoroughly with clear water and allow to air-dry.

Felt	Fur/Synthetic
Fur/Natural	

Very gently scrape the egg from the surface. Mix dishwashing detergent in hot water and swish to make a great volume of suds. Dip a cloth in only the foam and apply. Wipe with a clean, dry cloth. If a grease stain remains, powder the area with an absorbent, such as cornmeal. Give it plenty of time to work, then gently brush it off. Repeat if necessary. Using a damp cloth, gently remove any remaining powder.

Grout

Wipe up the egg with a cloth dipped in warm, sudsy water. If any stain remains, apply tile-and-grout cleaner or dip a wet toothbrush in powdered cleanser and gently scrub the spot. Rinse well with clear water and wipe dry with a soft cloth.

Leather	Suede

Very gently scrape the spilled egg. Mix a solution of mild soap in lukewarm water. Swish to create a great volume of suds. Apply only the foam with a sponge. Dry with a clean cloth. If a grease stain remains, pow-

Egg *(continued)*

der the area with an absorbent, such as cornmeal, allowing enough time for it to work. Gently brush it off and repeat if necessary. On leather only, follow with saddle soap to condition.

Silver

Remove the spill. Wash as soon as possible in hot, sudsy water. Rinse in hot water and dry immediately with a soft cloth to prevent tarnish. Buff to bring up the shine.

Wallpaper

Carefully wipe up the egg. With a cloth or sponge moistened with cool, clear water, wipe the area. Overlap strokes to prevent streaking. Gently pat dry with a soft cloth.

Wood

Mix dishwashing detergent in hot water and swish to make a great volume of suds. Dip a cloth in only the foam and wipe off egg residue. Rinse with a clean cloth moistened with clear water. Polish or wax as soon as possible.

EYELINER/EYE PENCIL/ EYE SHADOW

Acetate	**Rayon**
Carpet/Synthetic	**Silk**
Carpet/Wool	**Triacetate**
Fiberglass	**Wool**

Brush or blot up any eye makeup, taking care not to spread the stain. Flush with dry-cleaning solvent. Apply dry spotter to the stain and cover with an absorbent pad dampened with dry spotter. Check the stain every 5 minutes. Press the pad hard against the stain. Continue the alternate soaking and pressing until no more stain is being removed. Flush with dry-cleaning solvent and allow to dry. If any stain remains, flush it with water and apply wet spotter with a few drops of ammonia. (Do not use ammonia on silk or wool.) Cover with an absorbent pad dampened with wet spotter. Let stand as long as any stain is being removed. Change the pad as it picks up the stain. Keep the stain and pad moist. Flush well with clear water. Repeat if necessary; allow to dry.

Eyeliner/Eye Pencil/Eye Shadow *(continued)*

Acrylic Fabric	**Nylon**
Cotton	**Olefin**
Linen	**Polyester**
Modacrylic	**Spandex**

Brush or blot away any spilled eye makeup, taking care not to spread the stain. Flush with dry-cleaning solvent. Apply dry spotter to the stain and cover with a cloth dampened with dry spotter. Check the stain often, tamping before changing the pad. Continue alternate soaking and tamping until no more stain is lifted. Flush with dry-cleaning solvent and allow to dry. If any stain remains, try the same procedure of soaking and tamping, using wet spotter and a few drops of ammonia. When the stain is gone, be sure to flush the area with water to remove all trace of ammonia. Launder as soon as possible.

Acrylic Plastic	**Jade**
Alabaster	**Linoleum**
Asphalt	**Marble**
Bamboo	**Paint/Flat**
Cane	**Paint/Gloss**
Ceramic Glass/Tile	**Plexiglas**
Cork	**Polyurethane**
Enamel	**Stainless Steel**
Glass	**Vinyl Clothing**
Gold	**Vinyl Tile**
Ivory	**Vinyl Wallcovering**

Wipe up spills or brush away any excess makeup. With a cloth or sponge dipped in warm, sudsy water, wash the surface. Rinse well with water and wipe dry with a clean cloth.

Bluestone	**Sandstone**
Limestone	**Slate**
Masonry Tile	**Terrazzo**

Wipe up eye makeup. Mix a solution of washing soda or detergent (not soap) and water. Wash the stained area. Rinse well with clear water and allow to dry.

Leather	**Suede**

Gently remove eye makeup. Mix a solution of mild soap and lukewarm water. Swish to create a great volume of suds. Apply only the foam with a

Eyeliner/Eye Pencil/Eye Shadow *(continued)*

sponge. Wipe dry with a clean cloth. If a greasy or oily stain remains, powder it with an absorbent, such as cornmeal. Give it plenty of time to work. Gently brush or shake the absorbent from the surface. Repeat if necessary. On leather only, follow with saddle soap to condition.

Wood

Mix dishwashing detergent in hot water and swish to make a great volume of suds. Dip a cloth in only the foam and apply to the stain. Rinse with clear water. Wipe dry immediately with a soft cloth and polish or wax as usual.

FABRIC SOFTENER

Acetate	Rayon
Carpet/Synthetic	Silk
Carpet/Wool	Triacetate
Fiberglass	Wool

Dampen the stain with water and rub gently with bar soap. (Do not use deodorant soap.) Or rub the area with liquid laundry detergent. Rinse thoroughly with clear water, then blot the excess liquid and allow to dry.

Acrylic Fabric	Nylon
Cotton	Olefin
Linen	Polyester
Modacrylic	Spandex

Dampen the area with water and gently rub with bar soap. (Do not use deodorant soap.) Or, rub the area with liquid laundry detergent. Rinse thoroughly. Blot the excess liquid and launder as soon as possible.

Acrylic Plastic	Paint/Gloss
Aluminum	Plexiglas
Asphalt	Polyurethane
Ceramic Glass/Tile	Porcelain Dishes
Cork	Porcelain Fixtures
Glass	Vinyl Clothing
Linoleum	Vinyl Tile
Paint/Flat	Vinyl Wallcovering

Wipe up fabric softener immediately; the chemicals can damage the sur-

Fabric Softener *(continued)*

face. Wipe the area with a cloth or sponge dipped in warm, sudsy water. Rinse well and wipe dry.

FACE POWDER

Acetate	Rayon
Carpet/Synthetic	Silk
Carpet/Wool	Triacetate
Fiberglass	Wool

Brush or blot up face powder, taking care not to spread the stain. Flush with dry-cleaning solvent. Apply dry spotter to the stain and cover with an absorbent pad dampened with dry spotter. Check the stain every 5 minutes. Before changing pads, press hard against the stain. Continue the alternate soaking and pressing until no more stain is being removed. Flush with dry-cleaning solvent and allow to dry. If any stain remains, flush it with water and apply wet spotter with a few drops of ammonia. (Do not use ammonia on silk or wool.) Cover with an absorbent pad dampened with wet spotter. Let stand as long as any stain is being removed. Change the pad as it picks up the stain. Keep the stain and pad moist. Flush well with water. Repeat if necessary; allow to dry.

Acrylic Fabric	Nylon
Cotton	Olefin
Linen	Polyester
Modacrylic	Spandex

Brush away or blot face powder, taking care not to spread the stain. Flush with dry-cleaning solvent. Apply dry spotter to the stain and cover with a cloth dampened with dry spotter. Check the stain often, tamping before changing the pad. Continue alternate soaking and tamping until no more stain is lifted. Flush with dry-cleaning solvent and allow to dry. If any stain remains, try the same procedure of soaking and tamping using wet spotter and a few drops of ammonia. When the stain is gone, be sure to flush the area with clear water to remove all traces of ammonia. Launder as soon as possible.

Acrylic Plastic	Jade
Alabaster	Linoleum
Asphalt	Marble
Bamboo	Paint/Flat
Cane	Paint/Gloss

Face Powder *(continued)*

Ceramic Glass/Tile	Plexiglas
Cork	Polyurethane
Enamel	Stainless Steel
Glass	Vinyl Clothing
Gold	Vinyl Tile
Ivory	Vinyl Wallcovering

Wipe spills or brush away face powder. With a cloth or sponge dipped in warm, sudsy water, wash the surface. Rinse well with clear water and wipe dry with a clean cloth.

Bluestone	Slate
Masonry Tile	Terrazzo
Sandstone	

Remove face powder. Mix a solution of washing soda or detergent (not soap) and water. Wash the stained area. Rinse well with clear water and allow to dry.

Leather	Suede

Gently remove face powder. Mix a solution of mild soap in lukewarm water. Swish to create a great volume of suds. Apply only the foam with a sponge. Wipe dry with a clean cloth. If a greasy or oily stain remains, powder it with an absorbent, such as cornmeal. Give it plenty of time to work. Gently brush or shake the absorbent from the surface. Repeat if necessary. On leather only, follow with saddle soap to condition.

Wood

Mix dishwashing detergent in hot water and swish to make a great volume of suds. Dip a cloth in only the foam and apply. Rinse with clean water. Wipe dry immediately with a soft cloth and polish or wax as usual.

FINGERNAIL POLISH

Acetate	Silk
Fiberglass	Triacetate
Rayon	Wool

Immediately scrape away fingernail polish with a dull knife or spatula. Apply dry spotter to the stain and cover with an absorbent pad dampened

Fingernail Polish *(continued)*

with dry spotter. Let stand as long as any stain is being removed. Keep the pad and stain moist. Flush with dry-cleaning solvent. Allow to dry.

Acrylic Fabric	**Nylon**
Burlap	**Olefin**
Cotton	**Polyester**
Linen	**Rope**
Modacrylic	**Spandex**

Scrape up the fingernail polish. Test acetone on an inconspicuous place. If fiber color doesn't change, flush acetone through the stain to an absorbent pad. When no more stain is being removed, change pads and flush well with dry-cleaning solvent. Allow to dry thoroughly.

Acrylic Plastic	**Polyurethane**
Asphalt	**Vinyl Clothing**
Cork	**Vinyl Tile**
Linoleum	**Vinyl Wallcovering**
Plexiglas	

Fingernail polish contains chemicals that can quickly ruin the surface. Immediately scrape up any excess spill. Dab the area with a cloth dipped in amyl acetate and rinse. This stain may be permanent.

Alabaster	**Marble**

Wipe up the fingernail polish immediately. Wipe the area with a cloth dampened with acetone. Rinse with a cloth dipped in clear water and wipe dry. If any stain remains, make a thick paste of water, 3-percent hydrogen peroxide, and mild powdered detergent. Apply to the stain and cover with a damp cloth. When the stain is bleached out, rinse thoroughly and dry.

Aluminum	**Stainless Steel**
Iron	**Tin**

Wipe up fingernail polish immediately. Since these surfaces aren't porous, there shouldn't be a stain, only a mild discoloration. To remove this discoloration, scrub gently with a steel-wool soap pad, rinse thoroughly, and dry.

Bamboo	**Cane**

Fingernail Polish (continued)

Remove the fingernail polish and wipe the area with a cloth dipped in mild soapsuds to which a few drops of ammonia have been added. If any stain remains, dip a clean cloth in acetone and gently dab at the stain—be careful not to force the stain into the plant fibers. If not treated immediately, this could be a permanent stain.

Bluestone	**Limestone**
Brick	**Masonry Tile**
Concrete	**Sandstone**
Flagstone	**Slate**
Granite	**Terrazzo**

Remove the fingernail polish as soon as possible. With a cloth dipped in acetone, dab at the remaining stain until no more is picked up. Wash the area using a soft-bristled brush with a solution of washing soda or detergent and water. Rinse with clear water and allow to dry.

Carpet/Synthetic	**Carpet/Wool**

Scrape up as much of the fingernail polish as you can without forcing it into the pile. Apply amyl acetate to the stain and cover with an absorbent pad dampened with amyl acetate. Keep the area moist and let stand for about 15 minutes, blotting occasionally. Scrape to help loosen the stain. Flush carefully with dry-cleaning solvent. Allow to dry thoroughly.

Ceramic Glass/Tile	**Platinum**
Enamel	**Porcelain**
Glass	**Rhinestones**
Gold	**Silver**

Wipe up excess polish as soon as possible. Wash with a cloth dipped in a solution of washing soda, water, and a few drops of ammonia. Rinse well with clear water and wipe dry. Hardened polish on ceramic tile, enamel, and glass can sometimes be carefully scraped away with a razor blade.

Grout

With a sponge, blot up as much fingernail polish as possible. Apply a tile-and-grout cleaner or dip a wet toothbrush in powdered cleanser and scrub gently. Rinse well with clear water and wipe dry.

Jade	**Pearls (except simulated)**
Opal	

(continued)

Fingernail Polish *(continued)*

Blot up excess polish. Fingernail polish may permanently damage pearls and mother-of-pearl. A cotton swab moistened with oily fingernail-polish remover (not acetone-based polish remover) and gently dabbed on the stain may be effective. Blot with a dry cotton swab.

Leather	Suede

Carefully scrape up fingernail polish with a dull knife or spatula. Mix a solution of mild soap in lukewarm water. Swish to create a great volume of suds. Apply only the foam with a sponge, but avoid spreading the stain. Dry with a clean cloth. If the polish has hardened, try gently rubbing an art gum eraser across it. As a last resort, cautiously file the area with an emery board or a piece of very-fine-grade (6/0 to 8/0) sandpaper. Because a thin layer of hide is removed, work carefully.

Paint/Flat	Paint/Gloss

Wipe away the excess, being careful not to spread the polish. Wipe the stain with a cloth dipped in ⅓ quart warm, sudsy water to which 1 teaspoon borax has been added. Rinse with clear water and dry thoroughly.

FLOOR WAX

Acetate	Silk
Carpet/Synthetic	Triacetate
Carpet/Wool	Wool
Rayon	

Sponge the area with dry-cleaning solvent. Then apply dry spotter to the stain and cover with an absorbent pad dampened with dry spotter. Let it stand as long as any stain is being picked up. Change the pad as it removes the stain. Keep both the stained area and the pad moist with dry spotter. Flush with dry-cleaning solvent and allow to dry. If any stain remains, sponge with water and apply a few drops of ammonia. (Take care when using ammonia on silk and wool.) Cover with an absorbent pad dampened with wet spotter. Let stand as long as any stain is being removed. Change the pad as it picks up the stain. Keep stain and pad moist with wet spotter and ammonia. Flush with water. Repeat until no more stain is removed.

Acrylic Fabric	Nylon
Cotton	Olefin

Floor Wax *(continued)*

Linen	**Polyester**
Modacrylic	**Spandex**

Remove excess wax, then sponge the area with dry-cleaning solvent. Apply dry spotter to the stain and cover with an absorbent pad dampened with dry spotter. Let stand as long as any stain is being removed. To help remove stubborn wax, tamp the area, adding dry spotter as needed to keep it moist. Flush the area with liquid dry-cleaning solvent and allow to dry. If a stain persists, sponge it with clear water and apply a few drops of ammonia along with wet spotter. Cover the area with an absorbent pad and let it remain as long as any stain is being removed. Change the pad as it picks up the stain. Keep the stain and pad moist with wet spotter and ammonia. Tamping again will help break up the stain. Flush with water. Repeat if necessary.

Acrylic Plastic	**Paint/Gloss**
Alabaster	**Plexiglas**
Asphalt	**Polyurethane**
Bamboo	**Porcelain Dishes**
Cane	**Porcelain Fixtures**
Ceramic Glass/Tile	**Vinyl Clothing**
Cork	**Vinyl Wallcovering**
Paint/Flat	

Remove excess wax. Wipe the surface with a cloth or sponge dipped in warm, sudsy water to which a few drops of ammonia have been added. Rinse well and wipe dry with a clean cloth.

Leather	**Suede**

Blot up wax. Apply liquid leather cleaner on leather or suede cleaner on suede. Rub it in with a soft cloth and allow it to dry. If any waxy residue remains, test dry-cleaning solvent on an inconspicuous place; if no color change occurs, gingerly apply. Allow to dry. On leather only, follow with saddle soap to condition.

Wood

Gently wipe up the floor wax with a cloth dipped in the suds of mild detergent and water to which a small amount of ammonia has been added. Rinse well with a clean cloth moistened with the solution. Polish or wax as soon as possible.

FLOWERS

(Follow procedures for Grass.)

FOOD COLORING

(See Dye, Dye/Red, Dye/Yellow.)

FRUITS

(See Apple/Apple Juice, Berries, Cherry, Grape, Orange, Prune.)

FURNITURE POLISH

Acetate	Silk
Fiberglass	Triacetate
Rayon	Wool

Blot up furniture polish. Sponge with dry-cleaning solvent or spray on fabric spot cleaner. Apply dry spotter and cover with an absorbent pad dampened with dry spotter. Check the stain every 5 minutes and change pads as they absorb the stain. Press hard against the stain. Continue the alternate soaking and pressing until all the stain has been removed. Flush with dry-cleaning solvent and allow to dry. If any stain remains, sponge the stain with clear water and apply wet spotter and a few drops of white vinegar. Cover with an absorbent pad dampened with wet spotter. Let stand as long as any stain is being removed. Change the pad as it picks up the stain. Keep the stain and pad moist with wet spotter and vinegar. Flush with water and repeat until no more stain is visible. Flush with water and allow to dry.

Acrylic Fabric	Nylon
Cotton	Olefin
Linen	Polyester
Modacrylic	Spandex

Blot up the spilled polish. Apply dry spotter and cover with an absorbent pad dampened with dry spotter. Tamp the stain, then press the pad into the stained area to absorb any loosened material. Continue tamping and pressing until the stain has been removed. Flush with dry-cleaning solvent and allow to dry. If any stain remains, spray on fabric spot cleaner or sponge

Furniture Polish *(continued)*

the area with clear water, then apply wet spotter and a few drops of white vinegar. (Do not use vinegar on cotton or linen.) Tamp the area and blot with a clean, dry absorbent pad. Keep the stain moist with wet spotter and vinegar. When no more stain is visible, flush well with water and allow to dry.

Aluminum	**Porcelain Dishes**
Asphalt	**Stainless Steel**
Cork	**Vinyl Clothing**
Glass	**Vinyl Tile**
Linoleum	**Vinyl Wallcovering**

Wipe up the spilled polish with a cloth or sponge dipped in warm, sudsy water. Rinse well with clear water and wipe dry. If a waxy residue still exists, wipe again with a cloth dipped in warm, sudsy water to which a few drops of ammonia have been added. Rinse again and wipe dry with a clean cloth.

Bluestone	**Concrete**
Brick	**Flagstone**

Wipe up the furniture polish. Wash with a solution of washing soda or detergent (never soap) and water. Use a soft-bristled brush or soft cloth to scrub the area. Rinse thoroughly with clear water and allow to dry.

Carpet/Synthetic	**Carpet/Wool**

Scrape to remove furniture polish, then apply carpet stain remover. Or powder the stained area with an absorbent, such as cornmeal. Let stand, then brush. If a stain still remains, spray on foam rug shampoo or apply dry spotter. Cover with an absorbent pad dampened with dry spotter. Check the stain every 5 minutes, changing pads as the stain is absorbed. Press the pads hard against the stain. Continue to alternate applying dry spotter and pressing until all the stain has been removed. Gently sponge the area with dry-cleaning solvent. Allow to dry. If a stain persists, sponge with clear water and apply wet spotter and a few drops of white vinegar. Cover with an absorbent pad dampened with wet spotter. Let the pad remain as long as any stain is being removed. As the pad picks up the stain, change it. Keep the pad and stain moist with wet spotter and vinegar, but avoid soaking the carpet. Sponge with water and blot up excess liquid. Repeat until no more stain is removed and air-dry.

Leather	**Suede**	*(continued)*

Furniture Polish (continued)

Mix a solution of mild soap and lukewarm water. Swish to create a great volume of suds. Apply only the foam with a sponge. Wipe with a clean, dry cloth. If a greasy or waxy stain remains, powder the area with an absorbent, such as fuller's earth or cornmeal, allowing plenty of time for it to work. Gently brush off the absorbent. Repeat if necessary. On leather only, follow with saddle soap to condition.

Silver

Wash the item as soon as possible in hot, sudsy water. Rinse in hot water and dry immediately with a soft cloth to prevent tarnish.

GELATIN

Acetate	**Rayon**
Carpet/Synthetic	**Silk**
Carpet/Wool	**Triacetate**
Fiberglass	**Wool**

Scrape to remove gelatin. Make a paste with an enzyme presoak product and water—do not use on silk or wool. Let it stand on the stain for 15 minutes. Rinse thoroughly with water. For carpets, blot the excess water and allow to air-dry. Be certain that all the sugar has been removed. If any discoloration remains, treat it as a dye. (See Dye.)

Acrylic Fabric	**Nylon**
Cotton	**Olefin**
Linen	**Polyester**
Modacrylic	**Spandex**

Remove any spilled gelatin. Soak in a solution of prewash soil-and-stain remover and water as directed, and launder as soon as possible.

Acrylic Plastic	**Marble**
Aluminum	**Paint/Flat**
Asphalt	**Paint/Gloss**
Bamboo	**Plexiglas**
Brass	**Polyurethane**
Bronze	**Porcelain Dishes**
Cane	**Porcelain Fixtures**
Ceramic Glass/Tile	**Stainless Steel**
Copper	**Tin**

Gelatin *(continued)*

Cork	**Vinyl Clothing**
Glass	**Vinyl Tile**
Iron	**Vinyl Wallcovering**
Linoleum	

Remove gelatin immediately, before it sets. Wipe the surface with a cloth dipped in warm, sudsy water. Rinse well and wipe dry.

Bluestone	**Slate**
Brick	**Terrazzo**
Concrete	

Carefully remove excess gelatin. Wash with a solution of washing soda or detergent (not soap) and water, using a cloth or soft-bristled brush. Rinse thoroughly with clear water and allow to dry.

Felt	**Suede**
Leather	

Gently scrape to remove gelatin. Mix a solution of mild soap and lukewarm water. Swish to create a great volume of suds. Apply only the foam with a sponge. Wipe with a clean, dry cloth. If the surface remains sticky, wipe again and dry. On leather only, follow with saddle soap to condition.

Silver

Wash the item as soon as possible in hot, sudsy water. Rinse in hot water and dry immediately with a soft cloth to prevent tarnish.

Wood

Gently wipe up gelatin. Mix dishwashing detergent in hot water and swish to make a great volume of suds. Dip a cloth in only the foam and apply to the stain. Rinse with a clean cloth dipped in clear water and wrung out. Polish or wax.

GLUE

Acetate	**Silk**
Fiberglass	**Triacetate**
Rayon	**Wool**

(continued)

Glue *(continued)*

Immediately sponge the area with water. Spray on fabric spot remover. Then apply wet spotter and a few drops of white vinegar. Cover with an absorbent pad dampened with wet spotter. Let it stand as long as any stain is being picked up. Change the pad as it removes the stain. Keep both the stain and pad moist with wet spotter and vinegar. Flush with water and repeat until no more stain is removed. For a lingering stain, moisten the area with a solution of 1 cup warm water and 1 teaspoon enzyme presoak product—do not use on silk or wool. Cover with a clean pad that has been dipped in the solution and wrung dry. Let it stand 30 minutes. Keep the area and pad moist and warm, but do not let the wet area spread. When no more stain is removed, flush thoroughly with water and allow to dry.

Acrylic Fabric	**Olefin**
Cotton	**Polyester**
Linen	**Rayon**
Modacrylic	**Spandex**

Soak in a solution of 1 quart warm water, ½ teaspoon liquid dishwashing detergent or liquid laundry detergent, and 1 tablespoon white vinegar. (Omit vinegar when treating cotton and linen.) Let soak for 15 minutes and rinse well with water. Sponge cotton or linen only with rubbing alcohol. Launder if possible. If not, soak in a solution of 1 quart warm water and 1 tablespoon enzyme presoak product for 30 minutes. Rinse well and launder as soon as possible.

Acrylic Plastic	**Paint/Gloss**
Aluminum	**Plexiglas**
Asphalt	**Polyurethane**
Ceramic Glass/Tile	**Porcelain Dishes**
Cork	**Vinyl Clothing**
Glass	**Vinyl Tile**
Linoleum	**Vinyl Wallcovering**
Paint/Flat	

Remove as much glue as possible with a dull knife or spatula. Wipe surface with a cloth or sponge dipped in warm, sudsy water. Rinse well and wipe dry.

Bluestone	**Granite**
Brick	**Limestone**
Concrete	**Slate**
Flagstone	**Terrazzo**

Glue *(continued)*

Carefully scrape to remove excess glue. Wash with a solution of washing soda or detergent (not soap) and water. Use a cloth or soft-bristled brush to scrub. Rinse thoroughly with clear water and allow to air-dry.

Grout

Wipe up glue with a cloth dipped in warm, sudsy water. To remove any dried material, apply tile-and-grout cleaner or dip a wet toothbrush in powdered cleanser and gently scrub the stain. Rinse well with clear water and wipe dry with a clean cloth.

Leather　　　　　　　　**Suede**

Very gently scrape to remove excess glue. Mix a solution of mild soap and lukewarm water. Swish to create a great volume of suds. Apply only the foam with a sponge. Wipe with a clean, dry cloth. Repeat if necessary to remove any stickiness. If suede needs conditioning, apply suede cleaner. On leather, follow with saddle soap.

Wallpaper

Gently rub the glue with an art gum eraser. Use small, gentle strokes so you won't tear the paper. When the glue has been removed, wipe the area with a cloth dampened with clear water to remove any eraser particles.

Wood

Mix dishwashing detergent in hot water and swish to make a great volume of suds. Dip a cloth or sponge in only the foam and apply. Rinse with a clean cloth dampened with clear water. Polish or wax as soon as possible.

GRAPE

Acetate	Rayon
Carpet/Synthetic	Rope
Carpet/Wool	Triacetate
Fiberglass	Wool

Spray on fabric spot cleaner. If stain remains, sponge with cool water. Then sponge the area with lemon juice or rub a slice of lemon over the stain. Flush with water. Blot as much excess liquid as possible and allow to

Grape *(continued)*

dry. If stain persists, apply wet spotter. Cover with an absorbent pad moistened with wet spotter. Let stand as long as any stain is being removed. Change the pad as it picks up the stain. Keep the pad and stained area moist with wet spotter. Flush with clear water. If any trace of stain remains, moisten the area with a solution of 1 cup warm water and 1 teaspoon enzyme presoak product—do not use on silk or wool. Cover with a clean, absorbent pad that has been dipped in the solution and wrung almost dry. Let it stand for 30 minutes. Add enough solution to keep the stain and pad moist, but do not allow the wet area to spread. When no more stain is visible, flush thoroughly with water and allow to air-dry.

Acrylic Fabric	**Olefin**
Modacrylic	**Polyester**
Nylon	**Spandex**

Spray on fabric spot cleaner. If stain remains, sponge with cool water immediately. Then sponge with lemon juice or rub a lemon slice over the stain. Flush with water. Blot as much excess liquid as possible and allow to dry. If any trace of stain still exists, presoak in a solution of 1 quart warm water, ½ teaspoon liquid dishwashing or laundry detergent, and 1 tablespoon white vinegar for 15 minutes. Rinse with clear water and launder if possible. If not, soak in a solution of 1 quart water and 1 tablespoon enzyme presoak product for 30 minutes. Rinse well with water and launder as soon as possible.

Acrylic Plastic	**Grout**
Aluminum	**Iron**
Asphalt	**Paint/Flat**
Bamboo	**Paint/Gloss**
Brass	**Plexiglas**
Bronze	**Polyurethane**
Cane	**Porcelain Dishes**
Ceramic Glass/Tile	**Porcelain Fixtures**
Copper	**Stainless Steel**
Enamel	**Vinyl Clothing**
Glass	**Vinyl Wallcovering**

Wipe up the spill with a cloth or sponge dipped in warm, sudsy water. Rinse well and wipe dry.

Bluestone	**Granite**
Brick	**Masonry Tile**

Grape *(continued)*

Concrete   **Slate**
Flagstone   **Terrazzo**

Wipe up the spill. Wash area with a solution of washing soda or deter-gent (not soap) and water. Use a soft cloth or soft-bristled brush. Rinse thoroughly with clear water and allow to dry.

Cork   **Vinyl Tile**
Linoleum

Wipe up the grape spill and wash the area with a solution of washing soda or detergent and water. Use a soft-bristled brush or cloth to scrub gently. Rinse thoroughly with clear water and allow to dry. If stain persists, wipe area with a cloth dampened in a solution of 1 tablespoon oxalic acid and 1 pint water. Rinse well and wipe dry. Polish the surface if necessary.

Cotton   **Linen**

Test fabric for colorfastness. If color doesn't change, stretch the stain over a bowl; fasten in place with a rubber band. Pour boiling water through the fabric from a height of 2 or 3 feet. Avoid splatters. This procedure must be done immediately. If the stain persists, soak in a solution of 1 quart warm water and ½ teaspoon detergent for 15 minutes. Rinse with water. Sponge area with rubbing alcohol and launder immediately if possible. If not, soak in a solution of 1 quart warm water and 1 tablespoon enzyme presoak product for 30 minutes. Rinse well and launder.

Leather   **Suede**

Blot up excess liquid. Mix a solution of mild soap and lukewarm water. Swish to create a great volume of suds. Apply only the foam with a sponge. Wipe with a clean, dry cloth. On leather only, follow with saddle soap to condition.

Marble

After wiping up the spill, wipe the surface with a cloth or sponge dipped in warm, sudsy water. Rinse well and wipe dry. If any stain or discoloration remains, mix a thick paste of water, powdered detergent, and chlorine bleach. Apply the thick paste to the stain and cover with a damp cloth to retard evaporation. When the stain is bleached out, rinse thoroughly and dry.

Grape *(continued)*

Silver

Wash silver as soon as possible in hot, sudsy water. Rinse in hot water and dry immediately with a soft cloth to prevent tarnish.

Wood

Mix dishwashing detergent in hot water and swish to make a great volume of suds. Dip a cloth in only the foam and apply to the grape stain. Rinse with a clean cloth dampened with clear water. If a stain remains, rub the area with a cloth dampened in a solution of 1 tablespoon oxalic acid and 1 pint water. Rinse well and wipe dry. Wax or polish as soon as possible.

GRAPHITE

(Follow procedures for Pencil Lead.)

GRASS

Acetate	Silk
Carpet/Synthetic	Triacetate
Carpet/Wool	Wool
Rayon	

Sponge the area with dry-cleaning solvent. Apply dry spotter to the stain and cover with an absorbent pad dampened with dry spotter. Let it stand as long as any stain is being removed. Change the pad as it picks up the stain. Keep both the stain and pad moist with dry spotter. Flush with dry-cleaning solvent and allow to dry thoroughly. When working on carpets, be sure to blot up the excess liquid during the procedure and before drying.

Acrylic Fabric	Nylon
Cotton	Olefin
Linen	Polyester
Modacrylic	Spandex

Work liquid dishwashing or laundry detergent into the stain and rinse well with clear water. If any stain remains, soak in a solution of enzyme presoak product and water. Rinse thoroughly and launder as soon as possible. If any stain still remains, test for colorfastness in an inconspicuous

Grass *(continued)*

place, then use a mild sodium perborate bleach or 3-percent hydrogen peroxide. Thoroughly rinse with clear water, then launder as usual.

Acrylic Plastic	**Linoleum**
Aluminum	**Vinyl Clothing**
Ceramic Glass/Tile	**Vinyl Tile**
Cork	**Vinyl Wallcovering**

Remove grass stains by wiping with a cloth dipped in warm, sudsy water. Rinse well with clear water and wipe dry with a clean cloth.

Bluestone	**Limestone**
Brick	**Masonry Tile**
Concrete	**Slate**
Flagstone	**Terrazzo**
Granite	

Wash stain with a solution of washing soda or detergent (not soap) and water. Use a cloth or soft-bristled brush gently to scrub the grass stain. Rinse thoroughly with clear water and allow to dry

Leather	**Suede**

Mix a solution of mild soap and lukewarm water. Swish to create a great volume of suds. Apply only the foam with a sponge. Wipe with a clean, dry cloth. If an oily stain remains, powder the area with an absorbent, such as cornmeal. Allow plenty of time for the absorbent to work, then brush off the stain and powder. Repeat if necessary. On leather only, follow with saddle soap to condition.

GRAVY

Acetate	**Silk**
Fiberglass	**Triacetate**
Rayon	**Wool**

Gently scrape up spilled gravy. Sponge the area with dry-cleaning solvent. Apply dry spotter to the stain and cover with an absorbent pad dampened with dry spotter. Let it stand as long as any stain is being removed. Change the pad as it begins to pick up the stain. Keep both the stain and pad moist with dry spotter. Flush with liquid dry-cleaning solvent. If any

Gravy *(continued)*

stain persists, moisten the stain with a solution of 1 cup warm water and 1 teaspoon enzyme presoak product—do not use on silk or wool. Cover with a clean pad that has been dipped in the solution and wrung dry. Let it remain on the stain for 30 minutes. Add enough solution to keep the area warm and moist, but do not let the stained area spread. When no more stain is being lifted, flush thoroughly with clear water and let dry.

Acrylic Fabric	**Nylon**
Cotton	**Olefin**
Linen	**Polyester**
Modacrylic	**Spandex**

Gently scrape up gravy. Sponge the area with dry-cleaning solvent. Then apply dry spotter to the stain and cover it with an absorbent pad dampened with dry spotter. Let stand as long as any stain is being removed. Change the pad as it picks up the stain. Flush the area with liquid dry-cleaning solvent and allow to dry. If any stain persists, apply a few drops of dishwashing detergent and a few drops of ammonia to the stain, then gently tamp or scrape to loosen the material. Keep the stain moist with detergent and ammonia and blot occasionally with an absorbent pad. Flush with water to remove all trace of ammonia. Allow to dry. If the stain remains, moisten it with a solution of 1 cup warm water and 1 teaspoon enzyme presoak product. Cover with a clean pad that has been dipped in the solution and wrung almost dry. Let it stand for 30 minutes. Add enough solution to keep the stained area warm and moist. When no more stain is being lifted, flush thoroughly with clear water and allow to dry.

Acrylic Plastic	**Paint/Gloss**
Aluminum	**Pewter**
Asphalt	**Plexiglas**
Bamboo	**Polyurethane**
Cane	**Porcelain Dishes**
Ceramic Glass/Tile	**Stainless Steel**
Cork	**Vinyl Clothing**
Glass	**Vinyl Tile**
Linoleum	**Vinyl Wallcovering**
Paint/Flat	

Scrape to remove excess gravy. Wash the surface with a cloth dipped into warm, sudsy water. Rinse well and wipe dry.

Alabaster	**Marble**

Gravy *(continued)*

Scrape to remove excess gravy. Wash the surface with a cloth dipped in warm, sudsy water. Rinse well and wipe dry. If any stain remains, mix a thick paste of water, detergent, and bleach. Apply the paste to the surface, cover with a damp cloth to retard evaporation, and let it stand. When the stain is bleached out, rinse well with clear water and wipe dry.

Bluestone	**Masonry Tile**
Brick	**Sandstone**
Concrete	**Slate**
Flagstone	**Terrazzo**
Granite	

Wipe up the spill. Wash with a solution of washing soda or detergent (not soap) and water. Use a cloth or soft-bristled brush to scrub the surface. Rinse thoroughly with clear water and allow to dry.

Carpet/Synthetic	**Carpet/Wool**

Scrape to remove as much of the spill as possible. Apply carpet stain remover. Then apply an absorbent, such as cornmeal. Allow plenty of time for it to absorb the gravy. Gently brush it off the pile. If a stain still exists, carefully sponge the area with dry-cleaning solvent. Apply dry spotter to the stain and cover with an absorbent pad dampened with dry spotter. Let it stand as long as any stain is being removed. Change the pad as it picks up the stain and remember to keep both the pad and stain moist with dry spotter. Sponge with dry-cleaning solvent and let dry. If any trace of the stain still remains, moisten the area with a solution of 1 cup warm water and 1 teaspoon enzyme presoak product, but do not use on wool carpets. Cover with a clean pad that has been dipped into the solution and wrung almost dry. Let it stand for 30 minutes. Add enough solution to keep the stained area warm and moist. When no more stain is being lifted, sponge with clear water, let dry, and vacuum.

Felt

Gently scrape to remove excess gravy. Mix dishwashing detergent in hot water and swish to make a great volume of suds. Dip a cloth in only the foam and wipe the stain. Wipe the area with a clean, dry cloth. If a grease stain remains, powder the area with an absorbent, such as cornmeal. Allow plenty of time for it to work, then brush it off the felt. Repeat if necessary.

Gravy *(continued)*

Leather   **Suede**

Gently scrape away excess gravy. Mix a solution of mild soap and lukewarm water. Swish to create a great volume of suds. Apply only the foam with a sponge. Wipe with a clean, dry cloth. If a grease stain remains, powder the area with an absorbent, such as cornmeal. Give it plenty of time to work. Gently brush off the powder. Repeat if necessary. On leather only, follow with saddle soap to condition.

Silver

Wash as soon as possible in hot, sudsy water. Rinse in hot water and dry immediately with a soft cloth to prevent tarnish.

Wood

Mix dishwashing detergent in hot water and swish to make a great volume of suds. Dip a cloth in only the foam and gently scrub the spill. Wipe with a clean cloth moistened with clear water. Polish or wax when dry.

GREASE/AUTOMOTIVE, COOKING

Acetate	**Silk**
Carpet/Synthetic	**Triacetate**
Carpet/Wool	**Wool**
Rayon	

Blot up as much grease as possible and apply an absorbent, such as cornmeal. After letting the absorbent work, brush it off the fabric. If a stain remains, sponge with dry-cleaning solvent. Then apply dry spotter to the area. Cover the stain with an absorbent pad dampened with dry spotter. Let it remain in place as long as any stain is being lifted. Change the pad as it picks up the stain. Keep both the stain and pad moist with dry spotter. Flush with dry-cleaning solvent. If a stain still persists, sponge stain with water and apply wet spotter with a few drops of white vinegar. Cover the area with an absorbent pad moistened with wet spotter. Let it stand as long as any stain is being removed. Change the pad as it picks up the stain. Keep both the stain and pad moist with wet spotter and vinegar. Flush the area with water and repeat the above procedure until no more stain is removed. Allow to dry.

Grease/Automotive, Cooking *(continued)*

Acrylic Fabric	**Olefin**
Cotton	**Polyester**
Linen	**Spandex**
Modacrylic	

Blot up the excess grease as soon as possible. Apply an absorbent and let it soak up the spill. After brushing off the powder, sponge the area with dry-cleaning solvent. Then apply dry spotter to any remaining stain. Cover the stain with an absorbent pad dampened with dry spotter and let it remain in place until no more stain is lifted. Change the pad as it picks up the stain. To help loosen the stain, occasionally tamp the area, blotting up any loosened material. Flush with liquid dry-cleaning solvent. If any trace of stain remains, sponge stain with water and apply wet spotter and a few drops of ammonia. Tamp the stain again, blotting with an absorbent pad to remove any loosened material. Flush the area with clear water and repeat until no more stain is removed. Allow to dry.

Acrylic Plastic	**Paint/Gloss**
Aluminum	**Pewter**
Asphalt	**Plexiglas**
Bamboo	**Polyurethane**
Cane	**Porcelain Dishes**
Ceramic Glass/Tile	**Stainless Steel**
Cork	**Vinyl Clothing**
Glass	**Vinyl Tile**
Linoleum	**Vinyl Wallcovering**
Paint/Flat	

Blot up excess grease. Wipe the surface with a cloth or sponge dipped in warm, sudsy water. Rinse well with clear water and wipe dry.

Bluestone	**Limestone**
Brick	**Masonry Tile**
Concrete	**Sandstone**
Flagstone	**Slate**
Granite	**Terrazzo**

Pour a strong solution of washing soda and boiling water onto the surface. Cover the stain with a paste made of fuller's earth and hot water. Leave overnight. Rinse with clear water. Repeat if necessary.

Leather *(continued)*

Grease/Automotive, Cooking *(continued)*

Rub the stain with a thick paste of fuller's earth and water. Allow the paste to dry, then brush off the powder. Repeat if necessary. Follow with saddle soap to condition the leather.

Marble

Wipe up spilled grease, then gently scrub the surface with a cloth or sponge dipped in warm, sudsy water. Rinse well with clear water and buff dry with a clean cloth. If any residue remains, mix a thick paste of water, detergent, and bleach. Apply to the stain and cover with a dampened cloth to retard evaporation. After the stain is bleached out, rinse the area thoroughly with water and allow to dry.

Silver

Immediately wash in hot, sudsy water. Rinse thoroughly in hot water and dry with a soft, clean cloth to prevent tarnish.

Suede

Dip a clean cloth into ground cornmeal and rub in a circular motion into the stain. Gently brush off all the powder with a wire brush. Repeat if necessary. If stain persists, test lemon juice in an inconspicuous place, then brush stain with the juice and wire brush. Hold in the steam of a boiling kettle for a few minutes. Brush with a wire brush.

Wallpaper

Make a paste of cornstarch and water. Apply it to the stain and allow to dry. Brush off the powder and repeat if necessary. If the stain persists, make a paste of fuller's earth and trichloroethane. Apply and allow to dry. Brush it off.

Wood

Mix dishwashing detergent in hot water and swish to make a great volume of suds. Dip a cloth in only the foam and gently wipe. Rinse with a clean cloth moistened with clear water. Polish or wax as soon as possible.

HAIR DYES

(See Dye, Dye/Red, Dye/Yellow.)

HAIR SPRAY

Acetate	Nylon
Acrylic Fabric	Olefin
Carpet/Synthetic	Polyester
Carpet/Wool	Rayon
Cotton	Silk
Fiberglass	Spandex
Linen	Triacetate
Modacrylic	Wool

Wipe up excess spray. Sponge the stain with dry-cleaning solvent. For silk, apply paste spotlifter. Apply dry spotter to the area and cover with an absorbent pad dampened with dry spotter. Let the pad stay in place as long as any stain is being removed. Change the pad as it picks up the stain. Keep both the pad and stained area moist with dry spotter. On stronger fabrics, tamp dried spray to help loosen it. Flush the area with liquid dry-cleaning solvent or reapply spotlifter on silk. If any stain remains, sponge the stain with clear water and apply wet spotter and a few drops of ammonia. (Do not use ammonia on silk or wool.) Cover the stain with an absorbent pad moistened with wet spotter. Continue this treatment as long as any stain is being removed. Change the pad as it picks up the stain. Keep both the stain and pad moist with the dry spotter and ammonia mixture. Flush with water when stain has disappeared.

Acrylic Plastic	Marble
Alabaster	Paint/Flat
Aluminum	Paint/Gloss
Bamboo	Plexiglas
Cane	Polyurethane
Ceramic Glass/Tile	Porcelain Fixtures
Cork	Vinyl Clothing
Glass	Vinyl Tile
Grout	Vinyl Wallcovering
Linoleum	

Wipe up the hair spray with a cloth or sponge dipped in warm, sudsy water. Rinse well and wipe dry.

Leather	Suede

Carefully test the effects of dry-cleaning solvent in an inconspicuous place. Using a clean cloth, carefully dab a small amount of dry-cleaning solvent on the stain. Allow it to air-dry and then condition leather with saddle soap.

Hair Spray *(continued)*

Wallpaper

Carefully wipe up spray with a cloth or sponge dampened with cool, clear water. Be sure to overlap strokes to prevent streaking. Use a soft, dry cloth to pat dry.

Wood

Mix dishwashing detergent in hot water and swish to make a great volume of suds. Dip a cloth in only the foam and apply. Wipe with a clean cloth moistened with clear water. Polish or wax as soon as possible.

HEEL MARKS

Asphalt	Vinyl Tile
Linoleum	

Use superfine-grade (0000) steel wool dipped in a liquid wax and rub gently in a circular motion. Wipe with a damp cloth, dry with a clean cloth, and apply a coat of floor wax or polish.

Paint/Flat	Paint/Gloss

Rub a nontoxic dry-chemical cleaning bar on the marks. On flat paint, a shiny mark may be left; sponge the shiny spot with a cloth moistened with hot water. Wipe the scuff marks from painted furniture legs with a cloth dipped in warm, soapy water. If marks remain on furniture, use a light application of liquid wax. Rub well to remove excess wax.

Wood

On woodwork, rub a nontoxic dry-chemical cleaning bar on the marks. On other wood, mix dishwashing detergent in hot water and swish to make a great volume of suds. Dip a cloth in only the foam and apply to the heel marks. Rinse with a clean cloth moistened with clear water. If any marks remain, use superfine-grade (0000) steel wool and gently remove the stain with small circular motions. **Caution:** The steel wool will actually remove a thin layer of the wood finish, so be gentle. Polish or wax as soon as possible to seal the exposed wood.

ICE CREAM/CHOCOLATE

(Follow procedures for Chocolate/Cocoa.)

ICE CREAM/NONCHOCOLATE

Acetate	Rayon
Burlap	Rope
Carpet/Synthetic	Silk
Carpet/Wool	Triacetate
Fiberglass	Wool/Nonwashable

Scrape to remove any excess immediately. Sponge the area with dry-cleaning solvent. Apply dry spotter to the stain and cover with an absorbent pad moistened with dry spotter. Let it stand as long as any stain is being removed. Change the pad as it picks up the stain. Keep the pad and stain moist with dry spotter. Flush with dry-cleaning solvent. If any stain remains, moisten the area with a solution of 1 cup warm water and 1 teaspoon enzyme presoak product—do not use on silk or wool. Cover with a clean pad that has been dipped in the solution and wrung almost dry. Let it stand for 30 minutes. Add enough solution to keep the area warm and moist, but do not allow the wet area to spread. When no more stain is being lifted, flush the area with clear water and allow to dry.

Acrylic Fabric	Olefin
Cotton	Polyester
Linen	Spandex
Modacrylic	Wool/Washable
Nylon	

Immediately scrape to remove any excess ice cream. Sponge the area with dry-cleaning solvent. Then apply dry spotter and cover with an absorbent pad moistened with dry spotter. Let stand as long as any stain is being removed. Change the pad as it picks up the stain and keep the stain and pad moist with dry spotter. Flush with liquid dry-cleaning solvent. If any stain remains, apply a few drops of liquid dishwashing or laundry detergent and a few drops of ammonia to the area. Tamp or scrape to loosen the stain. Keep the stain moist with the detergent and ammonia solution. Blot occasionally with an absorbent pad. Flush well with water to remove all of the ammonia and allow to dry.

Acrylic Plastic	Linoleum
Aluminum	Paint/Flat

(continued)

Ice Cream/Nonchocolate *(continued)*

Asphalt	Paint/Gloss
Bamboo	Pewter
Brass	Plexiglas
Bronze	Polyurethane
Cane	Porcelain Dishes
Ceramic Glass/Tile	Porcelain Fixtures
Copper	Stainless Steel
Cork	Tin
Enamel	Vinyl Clothing
Glass	Vinyl Tile
Gold	Vinyl Wallcovering
Iron	Zinc
Ivory	

Wipe up excess ice cream immediately. Wipe the surface with a cloth or sponge dipped in warm, sudsy water. Rinse well with clear water and dry with a clean cloth.

Alabaster	Marble

Wipe up spilled ice cream. Mix a few drops of ammonia with 1 cup rubbing alcohol. Soak a white blotter (about the size of the stain) in the solution and place it over the area. Weight it down with a heavy object. Continue applying the solution until the grease is drawn out and any remaining stain is bleached out. If the stain persists, make a thick paste of bleach, water, and powdered detergent. Apply it to the stain. Cover with a damp cloth to retard evaporation. Remove when the stain is bleached out.

Bluestone	Limestone
Brick	Masonry Tile
Concrete	Sandstone
Flagstone	Slate
Granite	Terrazzo

Wipe up excess ice cream. Wash the stained area with a solution of washing soda or detergent (never soap) and water. Use a soft-bristled brush or cloth to scrub the stain. Rinse the area thoroughly with clear water and allow to dry.

Fur/Natural	Fur/Synthetic

Wipe up the spill. Then wipe the surface with a cloth dipped in the suds of a mild detergent and water. Wipe again with a clean, dry cloth. If a

Ice Cream/Nonchocolate *(continued)*

grease stain persists, powder the area with an absorbent, such as cornmeal, allowing plenty of time for it to work. Gently brush off the powder and sponge the area with a damp cloth. Allow the fur to air-dry.

Grout

Wipe up the spill with a cloth dipped in warm, sudsy water. If any stain remains, apply tile-and-grout cleaner or dip a wet toothbrush in powdered cleanser or baking soda and gently scrub the stain. Rinse well with water and wipe dry with a clean cloth.

Leather

Gently scrape excess ice cream from the leather. Mix a solution of mild soap and lukewarm water. Swish to create a great volume of suds. Apply only the foam with a sponge. Wipe with a clean, dry cloth. If a grease stain remains, powder the area with an absorbent, such as cornmeal. Give it plenty of time to work. Gently brush off the stain. If after using the cornmeal absorbent any trace still remains, try a leather cleaner. Rub it in with a clean, soft cloth and allow to dry. After the stain is removed, condition the leather with saddle soap.

Silver

Remove the spill with a cloth. Wash as soon as possible in hot, sudsy water. Rinse in hot water and dry immediately with a soft cloth to prevent tarnish.

Suede

Very gently scrape to remove the excess ice cream from the suede. Wipe the stain with a cloth dipped in the suds of mild detergent and water. Wipe with a clean, dry cloth. If a grease stain remains, powder the area with an absorbent, allowing plenty of time for it to work. Gently brush off the absorbent.

Wallpaper

Carefully remove the spill. With a cloth or sponge moistened with cool, clear water, wipe the stained area. Overlap strokes to prevent streaking. Gently pat the area dry with an absorbent pad.

Wood

(continued)

Ice Cream/Nonchocolate *(continued)*

Wipe up the ice cream. Mix dishwashing detergent in hot water and swish to make a great volume of suds. Dip a cloth in only the foam and apply to the stain. Rinse with a clean cloth moistened with clear water. Polish or wax as soon as possible.

INK/BALLPOINT, STAMP PAD (EXCEPT RED)

Acetate	Rayon
Burlap	Silk
Carpet/Synthetic	Triacetate
Carpet/Wool	Wool
Fiberglass	

Sponge the ink stain with water. Try spraying hair spray on the spot to loosen the stain, then apply wet spotter and a few drops of white vinegar. Let stand for 30 minutes, blotting every 5 minutes with a clean absorbent pad. Spray on fabric spot cleaner. Add wet spotter and vinegar as needed to keep the stain moist. Flush with clear water. If the stain persists, apply rubbing alcohol and cover with an absorbent pad moistened with alcohol. Let stand as long as any stain is being removed. Change the pad as it picks up the stain. Flush with alcohol. (Do not use alcohol on acetate, rayon, or triacetate.) If any trace of the stain remains, sponge the area with water and apply wet spotter and a few drops of ammonia. Let stand for 30 minutes, blotting every 5 minutes. Add enough wet spotter and ammonia to keep the stain moist. (Do not use ammonia on silk or wool.) Flush with water and allow to dry.

Acrylic Fabric	Nylon
Cotton	Olefin
Linen	Polyester
Modacrylic	Spandex

A light mist of hair spray may loosen the stain. Soak in a solution of 1 quart warm water, ½ teaspoon dishwashing detergent, and 1 tablespoon white vinegar for 30 minutes—use care when using vinegar on cotton and linen. Rinse with clear water and allow to dry. If the stain persists, apply rubbing alcohol and cover with an absorbent pad moistened with alcohol. (Use alcohol sparingly on acrylic and modacrylic.) Let stand as long as any stain is being removed. Change pad as it picks up the stain. Keep both the stain and pad moist with alcohol. Flush with alcohol and allow to dry. If any trace of stain remains, soak in a solution of 1 quart warm water, ½ teaspoon

Ink/Ballpoint, Stamp Pad *(continued)*

dishwashing detergent, and 1 tablespoon ammonia for 30 minutes. Rinse thoroughly with water and allow to dry.

Acrylic Plastic	**Polyurethane**
Ceramic Glass/Tile	**Porcelain Dishes**
Cork	**Porcelain Fixtures**
Glass	**Vinyl Clothing**
Plexiglas	**Vinyl Wallcovering**

Apply an all-purpose spray cleaner, following label directions. If any trace of the ink stain remains, cover the area with a pad sprinkled with ammonia. Rinse well and wash with a cloth dipped in warm, sudsy water. Rinse again and allow to dry.

Alabaster	**Marble**

Wipe the surface with a cloth or sponge dipped in warm, sudsy water. Rinse well and wipe dry. If any trace of stain persists, apply an absorbent pad dampened with rubbing alcohol. After several minutes, replace the pad with one moistened with ammonia. Continue alternating alcohol and ammonia pads until stain is removed. Rinse well and wipe dry.

Asphalt	**Flagstone**
Bluestone	**Sandstone**
Brick	**Slate**
Concrete	**Terrazzo**

Wash with a solution of washing soda or detergent (not soap) and water. Use a cloth or soft-bristled brush to scrub the stain. Rinse thoroughly with clear water and allow to dry.

Bamboo	**Paint/Flat**
Cane	**Paint/Gloss**

Wipe with a cloth dipped in a solution of mild soap and water to which a few drops of ammonia have been added. Rinse well and dry thoroughly.

Grout

Wipe stain with a cloth dipped in warm, sudsy water. If the stain remains, apply tile-and-grout cleaner or dip a wet toothbrush in baking soda or powdered cleanser and gently scrub. Rinse well with clear water and wipe dry.

Ink/Ballpoint, Stamp Pad *(continued)*

Leather   Suede

On leather, apply a leather cleaner. On suede, apply suede cleaner. Rub in the cleaner with a clean, soft cloth and let it dry. If any stain still remains, try applying dry-cleaning solvent. Dab it on with a clean cloth, after testing on a hidden seam. Allow to air-dry. On leather only, follow with saddle soap to condition. **Caution:** There is no guaranteed way to remove this stain from these materials.

Linoleum   Vinyl Tile

First, apply an all-purpose spray cleaner according to package directions. If any stain remains, cover the area with a pad dampened with rubbing alcohol. Rinse with clear water. If the stain persists, rub the area with superfine-grade (0000) steel wool dipped in liquid floor wax. Wash the area with soapy water, dry, then wax as usual.

Wallpaper

Try removing the ink with a soft eraser. Work in small movements to avoid tearing the paper. If the stain persists, wipe the area with a cloth or sponge moistened with cool, clear water. Overlap the strokes to avoid streaking. Use a clean cloth to pat dry.

Wood

Mix dishwashing detergent in hot water and swish to make a great volume of suds. Dip a cloth in only the foam and gently wipe the stain. Rinse with a clean cloth moistened with clear water. If a stain remains, rub the area with superfine-grade (0000) steel wool dipped in liquid wax. Rub lightly, because steel wool will remove a fine layer of the surface. Polish or wax as soon as possible.

INK/BALLPOINT, STAMP PAD/RED

Acetate	Rayon
Carpet/Synthetic	Silk
Carpet/Wool	Triacetate
Fiberglass	Wool

Sponge the area immediately with water to dilute the ink. Spraying on fabric spot cleaner may help to remove the stain. Apply wet spotter and a

Ink/Ballpoint, Stamp Pad/Red *(continued)*

few drops of ammonia. (Use ammonia with care on silk and wool.) Cover
with an absorbent pad dampened with wet spotter. Continue this treatment
as long as any stain is being removed. Change the pad as it picks up the
stain. Flush well with clear water and repeat if necessary. After drying if
a stain persists, mix color remover according to package directions. After
testing on a hidden seam, flush it through the stain to an absorbent pad beneath. When dealing with carpeting, sponge the color remover on the stain
and blot with an absorbent pad. Rinse well with water and allow to dry
thoroughly.

Acrylic Fabric	**Nylon**
Cotton	**Olefin**
Linen	**Polyester**
Modacrylic	**Spandex**

Soak the item in a solution of 1 quart warm water, ½ teaspoon dishwashing detergent, and 1 tablespoon ammonia for 30 minutes. Rinse well. If
stain remains, soak in a solution of 1 quart warm water and 1 tablespoon
white vinegar for 1 hour. (Take care when using vinegar on cotton and
linen.) Rinse well and allow to dry. If the stain has set, apply rubbing alcohol to the area (dilute with 2 parts water for acrylic or modacrylic) and
tamp. As the stain loosens, blot liquid and stain with an absorbent pad.
Keep both the stain and pad moist with alcohol and change the pad as it
picks up the stain. Allow to dry. As a last resort for any remaining stain, test
color remover in an inconspicuous place, then apply to the stain. Flush the
solution through the stain and onto an absorbent pad beneath. Rinse well
with clear water and allow to dry.

Acrylic Plastic	**Paint/Flat**
Aluminum	**Paint/Gloss**
Bamboo	**Plexiglas**
Cane	**Polyurethane**
Ceramic Glass/Tile	**Vinyl Clothing**
Glass	**Vinyl Wallcovering**

Immediately wipe up the spill with a cloth or sponge dipped in warm,
sudsy water. Rinse well and wipe dry.

Alabaster	**Marble**

Immediately wipe up the spill with a cloth or sponge dipped in warm,
sudsy water. Rinse well and wipe dry. If a stain remains, soak an absorbent
pad in rubbing alcohol, wring almost dry, and place over the stain. Wait 5

Ink/Ballpoint, Stamp Pad/Red *(continued)*

minutes and apply an absorbent pad soaked with ammonia and squeezed until damp. Alternate pads until stain has been removed. Wipe the surface with a cloth moistened with clear water and dry with a clean cloth.

Asphalt	**Linoleum**
Cork	**Vinyl Tile**

Wipe up excess ink with a cloth or sponge dipped in warm, sudsy water. Rinse well and wipe dry. If a stain remains, cover it with an absorbent pad soaked in rubbing alcohol. Leave the pad in place for several minutes, then wipe the area with a cloth dampened with ammonia. Wipe with a cloth dipped in warm, sudsy water. Rinse with a cloth moistened with clear water and allow to dry.

Bluestone	**Masonry Tile**
Brick	**Sandstone**
Concrete	**Slate**
Flagstone	**Terrazzo**
Granite	

Wipe up the red ink. Wash with a solution of washing soda or detergent (not soap) and water. Use a cloth or soft-bristled brush to scrub the stain. Rinse thoroughly with clear water and allow to dry.

Grout

Wipe up the spilled ink with a cloth dipped in warm, sudsy water. If any stain remains, apply tile-and-grout cleaner or dip a wet toothbrush in baking soda or powdered cleanser and gently scrub the stain. Rinse well with clear water and wipe dry.

Leather	**Suede**

Ink spilled on these materials will act immediately on the hide. Once contact has been made, it is impossible to remove.

Wood

Mix dishwashing detergent in hot water and swish to make a great volume of suds. Dip a cloth in only the foam and gently wipe up the ink. Rinse with a clean cloth moistened with clear water. Polish or wax as soon as possible.

INK/FELT TIP, INDIA

Acetate	Rope
Burlap	Silk
Fiberglass	Triacetate
Rayon	Wool

Sponge the area with dry-cleaning solvent, and then apply dry spotter to the stain. Cover with an absorbent pad moistened with dry spotter. Be sure to keep the stain from bleeding. Change the pad as it picks up the stain. Keep the stain and pad moist with dry spotter. Flush with liquid dry-cleaning solvent. If the stain persists, sponge with water and apply wet spotter and a few drops of ammonia. (Do not use ammonia on silk or wool.) Cover the stain with an absorbent pad moistened with wet spotter. Change the pad as it picks up the stain. Keep both the pad and stain moist with wet spotter and white vinegar. Flush with water and repeat as necessary. Allow to dry. **Note:** Permanent inks are almost impossible to remove.

Acrylic Fabric	Linen
Cotton	Modacrylic

Sponge the area with dry-cleaning solvent. If stain remains, mix a paste of equal parts powdered detergent and water and add a few drops of ammonia. Apply to the stain. Place an absorbent pad under the stain. When no more stain is being removed, flush thoroughly with clear water and launder. **Note:** Permanent inks are almost impossible to remove.

Acrylic Plastic	Paint/Gloss
Aluminum	Plexiglas
Asphalt	Polyurethane
Bamboo	Porcelain Dishes
Cane	Porcelain Fixtures
Ceramic Glass/Tile	Stainless Steel
Enamel	Vinyl Clothing
Glass	Vinyl Wallcovering
Paint/Flat	

Wipe the surface with a cloth or sponge dipped in warm, sudsy water to which a few drops of ammonia have been added. Rinse well with clear water and wipe dry. **Note:** Permanent inks are almost impossible to remove.

Alabaster	Marble

(continued)

Ink/Felt Tip, India *(continued)*

Wipe the surface with a cloth or sponge dipped in warm, sudsy water to which a few drops of ammonia have been added. Rinse well and wipe dry. If stain persists, apply a cloth soaked in rubbing alcohol; allow it to stand for 15 minutes. Next, apply a cloth soaked with ammonia for 15 minutes. Alternate alcohol and ammonia applications until stain is removed. Rinse thoroughly and wipe dry.

Bluestone	**Limestone**
Brick	**Masonry Tile**
Concrete	**Sandstone**
Flagstone	**Slate**
Granite	**Terrazzo**

Wash the stain with a solution of washing soda or detergent (never soap) and water. Use a cloth or soft-bristled brush to scrub the stain. Rinse thoroughly with clear water and allow to dry.

Carpet/Synthetic	**Carpet/Wool**

Blot as much of the stain as possible without forcing it deeper into the pile. Sponge the stain with a concentrated solution of carpet spot remover. **Caution:** Never rub ink stains on carpet. Continue to sponge the area, rinsing the sponge as it picks up the stain. Repeat until no more stain is removed. If the stain persists, have the rug professionally cleaned. Repeated applications of a liquid all-purpose cleaning solution also will help remove the ink. **Note:** Permanent inks are almost impossible to remove.

Cork	**Vinyl Tile**
Linoleum	

Cover the stain with a pad moistened with rubbing alcohol. Let the pad remain in place for 5 minutes. Wipe the area with a cloth dampened with ammonia. Rinse well with clear water and allow to dry. **Note:** Permanent inks are almost impossible to remove.

Felt	**Leather**
Fur/Natural	**Suede**
Fur/Synthetic	

Due to the nature of the material involved, this stain can only be removed professionally.

Grout

Ink/Felt Tip, India *(continued)*

Wipe the stain with a cloth dipped in warm, sudsy water. If the stain remains, apply tile-and-grout cleaner or dip a wet toothbrush in baking soda or powdered cleanser. Gently scrub the spot. Rinse and wipe dry.

Nylon	**Polyester**
Olefin	**Spandex**

Sponge the stain with detergent solution immediately. Then apply dry-cleaning solution. Sprinkle lemon juice and salt over the stain and leave for 1 hour. Rinse well, repeat if necessary, and launder as soon as possible.

Wallpaper

Try erasing light ink marks with an art gum eraser. Remember not to push hard. If stain remains, rub the area lightly with a dry steel-wool soap pad. If the stain persists, rub very gently with baking soda sprinkled on a damp cloth. Then wipe the area with a cloth or sponge moistened in cool, clear water. Overlap strokes to prevent streaking. Use a clean, absorbent pad to pat dry.

Wood

Dilute oxalic acid in warm water and apply with an artist's brush to the stained area. **Caution:** Oxalic acid is poisonous, so wear rubber gloves when applying it. On painted surfaces, wipe with a cloth moistened with detergent suds. For unpainted or stripped surfaces, after applying the oxalic acid, neutralize the area with white vinegar and rinse with rubbing alcohol. Allow to dry. **Note:** Permanent inks are impossible to remove.

INSECTICIDE

Acetate	**Rayon**
Carpet/Synthetic	**Silk**
Carpet/Wool	**Triacetate**
Fiberglass	**Wool**

Sponge the area with dry-cleaning solvent. Then apply dry spotter to the stain and cover with an absorbent pad moistened with dry spotter. Let stand as long as any stain is being removed. Change the pad as it picks up the stain. Keep the stain and pad moist with dry spotter. Flush with liquid dry-cleaning solvent. If any stain persists, sponge it with clear water and apply wet spotter and a few drops of ammonia. Cover with a pad damp-

Insecticide *(continued)*

ened with wet spotter. Let stand as long as any stain is being removed. Change the pad as it picks up the stain. Keep the stain and pad moist with wet spotter and ammonia—do not use ammonia on silk or wool. Flush with water and allow to dry.

Acrylic Fabric	Olefin
Cotton	Polyester
Linen	Spandex
Nylon	

Sponge the area with dry-cleaning solvent. Apply dry spotter to the stain and cover with an absorbent pad moistened with dry spotter. Let stand as long as any stain is being removed. Change the pad as it picks up the stain. Keep the stain and pad moist with dry spotter. Flush with liquid dry-cleaning solvent. If any stain remains, sponge it with clear water and apply wet spotter and a few drops of ammonia. Cover with a pad dampened with wet spotter. Let stand as long as any stain is being removed. Change the pad as it picks up the stain. Keep the stain and pad moist with wet spotter and ammonia. Flush with water and allow to dry.

Acrylic Plastic	Paint/Gloss
Aluminum	Plexiglas
Bamboo	Polyurethane
Cane	Porcelain Dishes
Cork	Stainless Steel
Glass	Vinyl Clothing
Linoleum	Vinyl Tile
Paint/Flat	Vinyl Wallcovering

Wipe the surface with a cloth or sponge dipped in warm, sudsy water to which a few drops of ammonia have been added. Rinse well and wipe dry.

Asphalt	Granite
Bluestone	Masonry Tile
Brick	Sandstone
Concrete	Slate
Flagstone	Terrazzo

Wash stain with a solution of washing soda or detergent (never soap) and water. Use a cloth or soft-bristled brush. Rinse thoroughly with clear water and allow to dry.

Insecticide *(continued)*

Leather	Suede

Mix a solution of mild soap and lukewarm water. Swish to create a great volume of suds. Apply only the foam with a sponge or cloth. Wipe with a clean, dry cloth. If a grease stain remains, powder the area with an absorbent, such as cornmeal. Give it plenty of time to work, then gently brush it off. Repeat if necessary. On leather only, follow with saddle soap to condition.

Wallpaper

Wipe the area with a cloth or sponge moistened with cool, clear water. Overlap the strokes to prevent streaking. With a clean cloth, gently pat dry.

Wood

Mix dishwashing detergent in hot water and swish to make a great volume of suds. Dip a cloth in only the foam and apply to the stain. Rinse with a clean cloth moistened with clear water. Polish or wax as soon as possible.

IODINE

Acetate	Nylon
Acrylic Fabric	Olefin
Carpet/Synthetic	Polyester
Carpet/Wool	Rayon
Cotton	Silk
Fiberglass	Spandex
Linen	Triacetate
Modacrylic	Wool

Since iodine is a dye, it must be treated immediately to prevent a permanent stain. Sponge the area thoroughly with clear water. Add 1 teaspoon sodium thiosulfate (available at drug stores) to ½ cup warm water and stir until the crystals are completely dissolved. Test the fabric with the solution; if the color doesn't change, wet the stain with this solution, blotting with an absorbent pad. Flush well with clear water and repeat if necessary.

Acrylic Plastic	Plexiglas
Ceramic Glass/Tile	Polyurethane

(continued)

Iodine *(continued)*

Glass	Porcelain Fixtures
Paint/Flat	Vinyl Clothing
Paint/Gloss	Vinyl Wallcovering

Wipe the stain with a cloth or sponge dipped in warm, sudsy water to which a few drops of ammonia have been added. Rinse well and wipe dry.

Alabaster	**Marble**

Mix a few drops of ammonia with 1 cup of 3-percent hydrogen peroxide. Soak a white blotter (about the size of the stain) with the solution and place it over the stain. Weight it down with a heavy object. Continue applying the solution until the stain is bleached out. For tougher stains, make a thick paste of powdered detergent, bleach, and water. Apply this paste to the stain and cover with a damp pad to retard evaporation. Leave overnight. Then remove the dried paste, rinse the area with clear water, and dry with a clean, dry cloth.

Asphalt	**Linoleum**
Cork	

Rub the stain with a cloth dampened in a solution of ammonia and water. If any stain remains, saturate the cloth in the solution and place it over the stain until no more stain is being lifted. Wash the area and wax as usual.

Bluestone	**Granite**
Brick	**Masonry Tile**
Concrete	**Slate**
Flagstone	**Terrazzo**

Wash the stained area with a solution of washing soda or detergent (not soap) and water. Use a cloth or soft-bristled brush to scrub the stain. Rinse thoroughly with clear water and allow to dry.

Grout

Wipe the area with a cloth dipped in warm, sudsy water. If any stain remains, apply tile-and-grout cleaner or dip a wet toothbrush in baking soda or powdered cleanser and gently scrub the spot. Rinse well and wipe dry.

Leather	**Suede**

Iodine *(continued)*

Because iodine contains a dye, it affects these materials on contact. Therefore, it cannot be removed.

Wood

Mix dishwashing detergent in hot water and swish to make a great volume of suds. Dip a cloth in only the foam and apply to the iodine stain. Rinse with a clean cloth moistened with clear water. Polish or wax as soon as possible.

IRON

(Follow procedures for Rust.)

JAM/JELLY

(See Apple/Apple Juice, Berries, Cherry, Grape, Orange, Prune.)

JUICE

(See Apple/Apple Juice, Berries, Cherry, Grape, Orange, Prune, Tomato.)

KETCHUP

(See Catsup.)

LACQUER

Acetate	Silk
Fiberglass	Triacetate
Rayon	Wool

Scrape to remove as much lacquer as you can. Apply dry spotter to the stain and cover with an absorbent pad moistened with dry spotter. Let stand as long as any stain is being removed. Keep the pad and stain moist. Flush with dry-cleaning solvent and allow to dry.

Lacquer *(continued)*

Acrylic Fabric	Nylon
Burlap	Olefin
Cotton	Polyester
Linen	Rope
Modacrylic	Spandex

Scrape to remove excess lacquer immediately. Flush acetone through the stain to an absorbent pad underneath. When no more stain is being removed, change pads and flush well with dry-cleaning solvent. Allow to dry thoroughly.

Acrylic Plastic	Polyurethane
Asphalt	Vinyl Clothing
Cork	Vinyl Tile
Linoleum	Vinyl Wallcovering
Plexiglas	

Lacquer can quickly damage or ruin these surfaces, so act immediately. Scrape to remove excess lacquer with a dull knife. Dab the area with a cloth dipped in amyl acetate. Rinse with clear water. **Note:** This stain may be permanent.

Alabaster	Marble

Wipe up excess lacquer immediately. Wipe the area with a cloth dampened with acetone. Rinse with a damp cloth and wipe dry. If any stain remains, make a thick paste of water, 3-percent hydrogen peroxide, and mild powdered detergent. Apply to the stain and cover with a damp cloth to retard evaporation. When the stain is bleached out, rinse thoroughly with water and wipe dry.

Aluminum	Stainless Steel
Iron	Tin

Wipe the spilled lacquer immediately. To remove discoloration, gently scrub with a steel-wool soap pad. Rinse thoroughly with clear water and wipe dry.

Bamboo	Cane

Remove the excess and wipe the area with a cloth dipped in mild soapsuds to which a few drops of ammonia have been added. If any stain remains, try dipping a clean cloth in acetone and gently dabbing at the

Lacquer *(continued)*

stain—be careful not to force any staining material into the surface. **Note:** If not treated immediately, this could become a permanent stain.

Bluestone	**Limestone**
Brick	**Masonry Tile**
Concrete	**Sandstone**
Flagstone	**Slate**
Granite	**Terrazzo**

Remove excess lacquer as soon as possible. With a cloth dipped in acetone, dab at the remaining stain until no more is picked up. Wash the area with a soft-bristled brush, using a solution of washing soda or detergent (not soap) and water. Rinse with clear water and allow to dry.

Carpet/Synthetic   **Carpet/Wool**

Scrape up as much of the stain as you can without forcing the lacquer deeper into the fiber. Apply amyl acetate to the stain and cover with an absorbent pad dampened with amyl acetate. Keep moist and let stand for about 15 minutes, blotting occasionally. Scrape to help loosen the stain. Carefully apply carpet stain remover and allow to dry.

Ceramic Glass/Tile   **Glass**
Enamel   **Porcelain Fixtures**

Wipe up excess lacquer as soon as possible. Wash with a cloth dipped in a solution of washing soda, water, and a few drops of ammonia. Rinse well with clear water and wipe dry. Hardened lacquer can sometimes be carefully scraped with a razor blade on all surfaces except porcelain.

Grout

Wipe up as much lacquer as possible. Apply tile-and-grout cleaner or dip a wet toothbrush in baking soda or powdered cleanser and scrub gently. Rinse well with clear water and wipe dry.

Leather   **Suede**

Carefully scrape to remove excess lacquer. Mix a solution of mild soap in lukewarm water. Swish to create a great volume of suds. Apply only the foam with a sponge. Dry with a clean cloth. If the lacquer has hardened, gently rub it with an emery board or a piece of fine sandpaper. A thin layer of hide will also be removed, so work slowly and carefully.

Lacquer *(continued)*

Paint/Flat	Paint/Gloss

Wipe away excess lacquer, being careful not to spread the stain. Wash with a cloth dipped in 1 pint warm water mixed with 1 tablespoon borax. Rinse with clear water and dry thoroughly.

LIPSTICK

Acetate	Rayon
Carpet/Synthetic	Silk
Carpet/Wool	Triacetate
Fiberglass	Wool
Modacrylic	

Sponge the area with dry-cleaning solvent. Then apply dry spotter and blot immediately with an absorbent pad. Continue sponging and blotting until no more stain is removed. If the stain begins to spread, flush immediately with liquid dry-cleaning solvent. Let all the solvent evaporate, then sponge the area with clear water. Apply wet spotter and a few drops of ammonia. (Do not use ammonia on silk or wool.) Blot frequently with an absorbent pad. Flush with water to remove all the ammonia. Apply wet spotter and a few drops of white vinegar. Blot frequently with an absorbent pad. Flush with water and allow to dry.

Acrylic Fabric	Olefin
Cotton	Polyester
Linen	Spandex
Nylon	

Treat with a laundry prewash product used as directed and rinse in warm water. If dye from the lipstick remains, soak in 1 quart warm water and 1 tablespoon enzyme presoak for 1 hour. Launder immediately, if possible. If not, rinse well and dry thoroughly. If any stain remains, apply dry-cleaning solvent and dry spotter. Blot immediately with an absorbent pad. If the stain begins to spread, flush immediately with liquid dry-cleaning solvent. Let the solvent evaporate. If stain still remains, sponge with clear water and apply wet spotter with a few drops of ammonia. Tamp and blot frequently with an absorbent pad. Flush well with water. Allow to dry. Launder as soon as possible.

Acrylic Plastic	Polyurethane
Ceramic Glass/Tile	Porcelain Dishes

Lipstick *(continued)*

Glass	Porcelain Fixtures
Paint/Flat	Stainless Steel
Paint/Gloss	Vinyl Clothing
Plexiglas	Vinyl Wallcovering

Wipe stain with a cloth dipped in warm, sudsy water. Rinse well and wipe dry. If stain remains, add a few drops of ammonia to warm, sudsy water and wipe the area. Rinse well, then dry with a clean cloth.

Alabaster	Marble

Mix a few drops of ammonia in 1 cup rubbing alcohol. Soak a white blotter with this solution and place it over the stain. Weight it down with a heavy object. Continue applying the solution until the grease is drawn out and any remaining stain is bleached out. If any color remains, make a thick paste of bleach, powdered detergent, and water. Apply to the stain and cover with a damp cloth to retard drying. Leave until stain is bleached out.

Asphalt	Linoleum
Cork	Vinyl Tile

Mix a solution of warm, sudsy water and a few drops of ammonia. Dip a plastic scouring pad (do not use steel wool) into the solution and rub gently. Rinse well and wipe dry.

Fur/Natural	Leather
Fur/Synthetic	Suede

Gently scrape to remove excess lipstick. Wipe the stain with a cloth dipped in the suds of mild detergent and water. Wipe with a clean, dry cloth. If a grease stain remains, powder the stain with an absorbent, such as cornmeal. Give it plenty of time to work. Gently brush it off. Repeat if necessary. As a last resort, dip a cloth in cleaning fluid and dab gently at stain. Do not rub. On leather only, follow with saddle soap to condition.

LIQUID FOUNDATION

Acetate	Rayon
Carpet/Synthetic	Silk
Carpet/Wool	Triacetate
Fiberglass	Wool

(continued)

Liquid Foundation *(continued)*

Brush or blot up excess liquid foundation, taking care not to spread the stain. Flush with dry-cleaning solvent. Apply dry spotter to the stain and cover with an absorbent pad dampened with dry spotter. Check the stain every 5 minutes. Before changing pads, press hard against the stain. Continue the alternate soaking and pressing until no more stain is being removed. Flush with liquid dry-cleaning solvent and allow to dry. If any stain remains, flush with clear water and apply wet spotter with a few drops of ammonia. (Do not use ammonia on silk or wool.) Cover with an absorbent pad dampened with wet spotter. Let it stand as long as any stain is being removed. Change the pad as it picks up the stain. Keep the stain and pad moist. Flush well with water. Repeat if necessary; allow to dry.

Acrylic Fabric	Nylon
Cotton	Olefin
Linen	Polyester
Modacrylic	Spandex

Brush or blot up foundation, taking care not to spread the stain. Flush with dry-cleaning solvent. Apply dry spotter to the stain and cover with a cloth dampened with dry spotter. Check the stain often, tamping before changing the pad. Continue to alternate soaking and tamping until no more stain is lifted. Flush with dry-cleaning solvent and allow to dry. If any stain remains, try the same procedure of soaking and tamping using wet spotter and a few drops of ammonia. When the stain is gone, be sure to flush the area with clear water to remove all trace of ammonia. Launder as soon as possible.

Acrylic Plastic	Jade
Alabaster	Linoleum
Asphalt	Marble
Bamboo	Paint/Flat
Cane	Paint/Gloss
Ceramic Glass/Tile	Plexiglas
Cork	Polyurethane
Enamel	Stainless Steel
Glass	Vinyl Clothing
Gold	Vinyl Tile
Ivory	Vinyl Wallcovering

Wipe up spills or brush away excess liquid foundation. Wash the surface with a cloth or sponge dipped in warm, sudsy water. Rinse well with water and wipe dry with a clean cloth.

Liquid Foundation *(continued)*

Bluestone	**Slate**
Masonry Tile	**Terrazzo**
Sandstone	

Remove as much liquid foundation as you can. Mix a solution of washing soda or detergent (not soap) and water. Wash the stained area. Rinse well with clear water and allow to dry.

Leather	**Suede**

Gently remove excess liquid foundation. Mix a solution of mild soap and lukewarm water. Swish to create a great volume of suds. Apply only the foam with a sponge. Wipe dry with a clean cloth. If a greasy or oily stain remains, powder it with an absorbent, such as cornmeal. Give it plenty of time to work. Gently brush or shake the absorbent from the surface. Repeat if necessary. On leather only, follow with saddle soap to condition.

Wood

Mix dishwashing detergent in hot water and swish to make a great volume of suds. Dip a cloth in only the foam and apply to the stain. Rinse with clear water. Wipe dry immediately with a soft cloth and polish or wax as usual.

LOTION/BODY, FACIAL, FOOT, HAIR

Acetate	**Rayon**
Carpet/Synthetic	**Silk**
Carpet/Wool	**Triacetate**
Fiberglass	**Wool**

Blot up excess lotion, taking care not to spread the stain. Flush with dry-cleaning solvent and apply dry spotter to the stain. Cover with an absorbent pad dampened with dry spotter. Check the stain every 5 minutes. Before changing pads, press hard against the stain. Continue the alternate soaking and pressing until no more stain is being removed. Flush with liquid dry-cleaning solvent and allow to dry. If any stain remains, flush with clear water and apply wet spotter with a few drops of ammonia added. (Do not use ammonia on silk or wool.) Cover with an absorbent pad moistened with wet spotter. Let stand as long as any stain is being removed. Change the pad as it picks up the stain. Keep the stain and pad moist with wet spotter. Flush well with water and allow to dry. Repeat if necessary.

Lotion/Body, Facial, Foot, Hair *(continued)*

Acrylic Fabric	Nylon
Cotton	Olefin
Linen	Polyester
Modacrylic	Spandex

Blot as much excess lotion as possible. Flush the stain with dry-cleaning solvent and apply dry spotter. Cover with an absorbent pad dampened with dry spotter. Check the stain often, tamping before changing the pad. Continue to alternate soaking and tamping until no more stain is removed. Flush with liquid dry-cleaning solvent and allow to dry. If any stain remains, try the same soaking/tamping procedure, using wet spotter and a few drops of ammonia. After the stain has been removed, flush area with clear water to remove all trace of ammonia. Launder as soon as possible.

Acrylic Plastic	Linoleum
Alabaster	Marble
Asphalt	Paint/Flat
Bamboo	Paint/Gloss
Cane	Platinum
Ceramic Glass/Tile	Plexiglas
Cork	Polyurethane
Enamel	Stainless Steel
Glass	Vinyl Clothing
Gold	Vinyl Tile
Ivory	Vinyl Wallcovering
Jade	

Wipe any spills immediately with a cloth dipped in warm, sudsy water. Rinse well with clear water and wipe dry with a clean cloth.

Bluestone	Sandstone
Brick	Slate
Masonry Tile	Terrazzo

Remove the spill. Mix a solution of washing soda or detergent (not soap) and water. Wash the stained area using a cloth or soft-bristled brush. Rinse well with clear water and allow to dry.

Leather	Suede

Very gently scrape to remove excess lotion. Mix a solution of mild soap and lukewarm water. Swish to create a great volume of suds. Apply only the foam with a sponge. Wipe dry with a clean cloth. If a greasy or oily residue

Lotion/Body, Facial, Foot, Hair *(continued)*

remains, powder it with an absorbent, such as cornmeal. Allow plenty of time for the absorbent to work. Then gently brush the powder off. Repeat the powdering procedure if necessary. On leather only, follow with saddle soap to condition.

Wood

Mix dishwashing detergent in hot water and swish to make a great volume of suds. Dip a cloth in only the foam and apply. Rinse with clear water. Wipe dry with a soft cloth and polish or wax as usual.

LOTION/HAND

Acetate	Rayon
Carpet/Synthetic	Silk
Carpet/Wool	Triacetate
Fiberglass	Wool

Sponge the area with dry-cleaning solvent. Apply dry spotter to the stain and cover with an absorbent pad dampened with dry spotter. Let pad remain as long as it picks up any stain. Change the pad as it absorbs the stain. Keep both the stain and pad moist with dry spotter. To help loosen stubborn stains on stronger fabrics, tamp or scrape the area. Flush with liquid dry-cleaning solvent. Repeat if necessary. If stain persists, sponge with clear water and apply wet spotter and a few drops of ammonia. (Do not use ammonia on silk or wool.) Keep the stain moist and occasionally blot with an absorbent pad. Again, if the fabric is sturdy, tamp or scrape to help loosen the stain. Flush with water and allow to dry.

Acrylic Fabric	Nylon
Cotton	Olefin
Linen	Polyester
Modacrylic	Spandex

Gently scrape to remove excess lotion. Moisten the spot with clear water and apply a solution of 1 cup warm water and 1 tablespoon enzyme presoak. Wait for 30 minutes, then flush the area with water. If possible, launder immediately. If not, allow fabric to air-dry.

Acrylic Plastic	Paint/Gloss
Aluminum	Pearls
Asphalt	Platinum

(continued)

Lotion/Hand *(continued)*

Ceramic Glass/Tile	Plexiglas
Chromium	Polyurethane
Copper	Porcelain Fixtures
Cork	Silver
Glass	Stainless Steel
Gold	Tin
Ivory	Vinyl Clothing
Jade	Vinyl Tile
Linoleum	Vinyl Wallcovering
Paint/Flat	Zinc

Wipe up excess lotion with a cloth or sponge dipped in warm, sudsy water. Rinse well with clear water and wipe dry.

Bluestone	Concrete
Brick	

Wipe up the spill. Wash with a solution of washing soda or detergent (not soap) and water. Use a cloth or soft-bristled brush to scrub the stain. Rinse thoroughly with clear water and allow to dry.

Leather	Suede

Mix a solution of mild soap and lukewarm water. Swish to create a great volume of suds. Apply only the foam with a sponge. Wipe with a clean, dry cloth. If any stickiness remains, test dry-cleaning solvent on an inconspicuous place. Then dab solvent on the spot with a soft cloth. Allow the area to dry thoroughly. On leather only, follow with saddle soap to condition.

Wood

Mix dishwashing detergent in hot water and swish to make a great volume of suds. Dip a cloth in only the foam and apply. Rinse with a clean cloth moistened with clear water. Polish or wax as soon as possible.

LOTION/SUNTAN

Acetate	Rayon
Carpet/Synthetic	Silk
Carpet/Wool	Triacetate
Fiberglass	Wool

Lotion/Suntan *(continued)*

Scrape to remove as much suntan lotion as you can. Sponge the area with dry-cleaning solvent. Apply dry spotter to the stain and cover it with an absorbent pad dampened with dry spotter. Let the pad remain as long as it picks up any stain. Keep both the pad and stain wet with dry spotter. Flush the area with dry-cleaning solvent. If the stain persists, sponge with water and apply wet spotter and a few drops of ammonia. (Do not use the ammonia on silk or wool.) Keep the stain moist and occasionally blot with an absorbent pad. Flush with clear water to make sure all trace of ammonia is out of the fabric. Allow to dry.

Acrylic Fabric	Nylon
Cotton	Olefin
Linen	Polyester
Modacrylic	Spandex

Gently scrape to remove excess lotion. Moisten the spot with water and apply a mixture of 1 tablespoon enzyme presoak and 1 cup warm water. Let the stain soak for 30 minutes. Flush the area with water. If possible, launder immediately. If not, allow the fabric to air-dry.

Acrylic Plastic	Paint/Flat
Aluminum	Paint/Gloss
Asphalt	Platinum
Ceramic Glass/Tile	Plexiglas
Copper	Polyurethane
Cork	Porcelain
Glass	Silver
Gold	Stainless Steel
Ivory	Vinyl Clothing
Jade	Vinyl Tile
Linoleum	Vinyl Wallcovering

Wipe up excess suntan lotion with a cloth or sponge dipped in warm, sudsy water to which a few drops of ammonia have been added. Rinse well to remove all ammonia and wipe dry.

Bluestone	Granite
Brick	Limestone
Concrete	Slate
Flagstone	Terrazzo

Wipe up spilled lotion. Wash with a solution of washing soda or deter-

Lotion/Suntan *(continued)*

gent (never soap) and water. Use a sponge or soft-bristled brush. Rinse thoroughly with clear water and allow to dry.

Leather	**Suede**

Mix a solution of mild soap and lukewarm water. Swish to create a great volume of suds. Apply only the foam with a sponge. Wipe dry with a clean cloth. If any stickiness remains, test spot remover on an inconspicuous place. If safe to use, gently dab the solvent onto the spot with a clean cloth. Allow the area to dry thoroughly. On leather only, follow with saddle soap to condition.

Wood

Wipe up excess suntan lotion, then wash the spot with a cloth dipped in warm, sudsy water. Rinse with a damp, clean cloth and wipe dry. Polish or wax the wood as soon as possible.

MAKEUP

(See Blusher; Eyeliner/Eye Pencil/Eye Shadow; Face Powder; Lipstick; Liquid Foundation; Lotion/Body, Facial, Foot, Hair; Lotion/Hand; Lotion/Suntan; Mascara; Rouge.)

MARGARINE

(Follow procedures for Butter.)

MASCARA

(Follow procedures for Eyeliner/Eye Pencil/Eye Shadow.)

MAYONNAISE

Acetate	Rayon
Burlap	Rope
Carpet/Synthetic	Silk
Carpet/Wool	Triacetate
Fiberglass	Wool

Mayonnaise *(continued)*

Gently scrape to remove excess mayonnaise. Sponge the area with dry-cleaning solvent. Apply dry spotter to the stain and cover with an absorbent pad moistened with dry spotter. Let it stand as long as any stain is being removed. Change the pad as it picks up the stain. Keep the stain and pad moist with dry spotter. When no more stain is removed, flush with dry-cleaning solvent. Allow to dry. If any stain persists, moisten with a solution of ½ teaspoon enzyme presoak and ½ cup warm water—do not use on silk or wool. Cover with a clean pad that has been dipped in the solution and wrung almost dry. Let stand for 30 minutes; add enough solution to keep the area moist. Flush area with water and allow to dry. On carpets, place a clean, dry pad over the area and weight it down. When no more liquid is being absorbed, allow the area to air-dry thoroughly.

Acrylic Fabric	**Nylon**
Cotton	**Olefin**
Linen	**Polyester**
Modacrylic	**Spandex**

Scrape to remove as much mayonnaise as possible. Apply wet spotter and work it into the fabric. Rinse thoroughly with water and launder. If laundering must wait and there is any trace of stain remaining, try applying a paste made with water and enzyme presoak. Let the paste work a while and keep it moist. Thoroughly rinse the area to remove all trace of the enzymes. Allow to dry and launder as soon as possible.

Acrylic Plastic	**Linoleum**
Aluminum	**Paint/Flat**
Asphalt	**Paint/Gloss**
Bamboo	**Pewter**
Bronze	**Plexiglas**
Cane	**Polyurethane**
Ceramic Glass/Tile	**Porcelain Dishes**
Chromium	**Porcelain Fixtures**
Copper	**Stainless Steel**
Cork	**Tin**
Enamel	**Vinyl Clothing**
Glass	**Vinyl Tile**
Gold	**Vinyl Wallcovering**
Iron	**Zinc**
Ivory	

Wipe up the spill as soon as possible with a cloth or sponge dipped in warm, sudsy water. Rinse with clear water and allow to dry.

Mayonnaise *(continued)*

Alabaster	Marble
Bluestone	Masonry Tile
Concrete	Sandstone
Flagstone	Slate
Granite	Terrazzo
Limestone	

Remove excess mayonnaise. Wipe with a cloth dipped in a solution of washing soda or detergent (not soap) and warm water. If any stain remains, mix a thick paste of water, mild bleach, and powdered detergent and apply to the stain. Cover with a damp cloth to retard evaporation. When stain is gone, rinse well with clear water and wipe dry.

Leather	**Suede**

Mix a solution of mild soap and lukewarm water. Swish to create a great volume of suds. Apply only the foam with a sponge. Wipe dry with a clean cloth. On leather only, follow with saddle soap to condition.

Silver

Remove mayonnaise from silver by washing in hot, soapy water. Rinse in hot water and wipe dry with a soft cloth to prevent tarnish.

Wallpaper

Wipe up mayonnaise immediately with a damp cloth or sponge. Overlap strokes to avoid streaking. Use a clean, dry cloth to pat dry.

Wood

Wipe the surface with a cloth dipped in warm, sudsy water. Rinse with a clean, damp cloth and wipe dry. Polish or wax as usual.

MERCUROCHROME/MERTHIOLATE

Acetate	Silk
Fiberglass	Triacetate
Rayon	Wool

Sponge the area immediately with clear water to dilute the spill. Spray on fabric spot cleaner. Then apply wet spotter and a few drops of ammonia.

Mercurochrome/Merthiolate *(continued)*

(Do not use ammonia on silk and wool.) Cover with an absorbent pad dampened with wet spotter. Let the pad remain in place as long as any stain is being removed, changing it as it picks up the stain. Keep both the stain and pad moist with wet spotter and ammonia. Flush well with water and repeat if necessary. Allow to dry. If the stain persists, mix color remover according to package directions. After testing on an inconspicuous place, flush the color remover through the stain into an absorbent pad beneath. Rinse well with water and allow to dry.

Acrylic Fabric	**Nylon**
Cotton	**Olefin**
Linen	**Polyester**
Modacrylic	**Spandex**

Spray on fabric spot cleaner. Then soak the item in a solution of 1 quart warm water, ½ teaspoon dishwashing detergent, and 1 tablespoon ammonia for 30 minutes. Rinse well with clear water. If the stain persists, soak in a solution of 1 quart warm water and 1 tablespoon white vinegar. Use vinegar with care on cotton and linen. Rinse well with water and allow to dry. If stain has set, apply rubbing alcohol to the area and tamp. As stain loosens, blot liquid and stain with an absorbent pad. Keep both the stain and pad moist with alcohol and change the pad as it picks up stain. Allow to dry. As a last resort, mix color remover according to package directions and test its action on a hidden place. If the color of the fabric doesn't change, flush color remover through the stain. Flush well with clear water and allow to dry thoroughly.

Acrylic Plastic	**Paint/Flat**
Aluminum	**Paint/Gloss**
Bamboo	**Plexiglas**
Cane	**Polyurethane**
Ceramic Glass/Tile	**Vinyl Clothing**
Glass	**Vinyl Wallcovering**

Immediately wipe up the spill with a cloth or sponge dipped in warm, sudsy water. Rinse well and wipe dry.

Alabaster	**Marble**

Immediately wipe up the spill with a cloth or sponge dipped in warm, sudsy water. Rinse well with clear water and wipe dry. If a stain remains, soak an absorbent pad in rubbing alcohol, wring almost dry, and place over stain. Wait several minutes, then apply an absorbent pad moistened with

Mercurochrome/Merthiolate *(continued)*

ammonia. Alternate alcohol and ammonia pads until the stain has been re-moved. Wipe surface with a cloth dampened with clear water and wipe dry with a clean cloth.

Asphalt	**Linoleum**
Cork	**Vinyl Tile**

Wipe up the spill with a cloth dipped in warm, sudsy water. Rinse well with clear water and wipe dry. If a stain remains, cover with an absorbent pad soaked in rubbing alcohol. Let it remain in place for several minutes, then wipe stain with a cloth dampened with ammonia. Wipe with a cloth moistened with warm, sudsy water, then rewipe with a cloth dampened with clear water. Allow to dry.

Bluestone	**Masonry Tile**
Brick	**Sandstone**
Concrete	**Slate**
Flagstone	**Terrazzo**
Granite	

Wipe up the spill and wash with a solution of washing soda or detergent (not soap) and water. Use a cloth or soft-bristled brush to scrub. Rinse thoroughly with clear water and allow to dry.

Carpet/Synthetic	**Carpet/Wool**

Carpet stain remover should take care of the stain. If not, sponge color remover on the stain and blot with an absorbent pad. Rinse with clear water and blot up excess liquid.

Grout

Wipe up the spill with a cloth dipped in warm, sudsy water. If any stain persists, apply tile-and-grout cleaner or dip a wet toothbrush in baking soda or powdered cleanser and gently scrub. Rinse well with clear water and wipe dry.

Leather	**Suede**

Mercurochrome or merthiolate will immediately discolor leather and suede. Once contact has been made, there is no way to remove the discoloration.

Mercurochrome/Merthiolate *(continued)*

Wood

Mix dishwashing detergent in hot water and swish to make a great volume of suds. Dip a cloth in only the foam and apply to the stain. Rinse with a clean cloth dampened with clear water. Polish or wax as soon as possible.

MILDEW

Acetate	Rayon
Carpet/Synthetic	Silk
Carpet/Wool	Triacetate
Fiberglass	Wool

Gently brush off mildew. Flush with dry-cleaning solvent. Then apply dry spotter and amyl acetate. Very gently scrape the stain or pat it with an absorbent pad dampened with dry spotter. Flush with dry-cleaning solvent and allow to dry. If stain persists, sponge with clear water and apply wet spotter and a few drops of white vinegar. Scrape or use an absorbent pad dampened with wet spotter to work on the stain. Flush with water and allow to dry. Apply rubbing alcohol and pat the stain with a pad dampened with alcohol. Flush with alcohol and allow to dry. (Do not use alcohol on acetate, rayon, or triacetate.) To remove all trace of the stain, use an oxygen bleach as directed on the package label. When treating carpets, blot all excess liquid, apply an absorbent pad, and weight it down until no more moisture is absorbed.

Acrylic Fabric	Nylon
Cotton	Olefin
Linen	Polyester
Modacrylic	Spandex

Most mildew stains can be removed during regular laundering if they are moistened beforehand. If any stain remains, test fabric for colorfastness. If the color doesn't change, cover the stain with a paste of lemon juice and salt. On cotton and linen, use a paste of oxygen bleach, water, and a few drops of ammonia. Let the paste cover stain for 15 to 30 minutes. Flush thoroughly with clear water and launder again.

Bamboo	Vinyl Clothing
Cane	Vinyl Tile
Cork	Vinyl Wallcovering
Linoleum	

(continued)

Mildew *(continued)*

Wipe the stain with a cloth dipped in warm, sudsy water to which a few drops of ammonia have been added. Rinse well with clear water and wipe dry. If the stain is stubborn, test mildew-stain remover on an inconspicuous place, then apply according to package directions. Do not use the product on fabric or flocked wallcoverings.

Ceramic Tile   **Grout**

Apply tile cleaner or mildew-stain remover. Another effective method is to dampen the stain with water and rub gently with bar soap—not a deodorant soap. Rinse with clear water. Blot excess liquid and allow to dry.

Leather   **Suede**

Rub the stain with petroleum jelly. If stain remains, sponge the area gently with equal parts water and rubbing alcohol. (Be sure to test for colorfastness first.) Condition suede with suede cleaner. Condition leather with saddle soap.

Wood

Gently remove mildew with a cloth dipped in a solution of 5 tablespoons washing soda and 1 gallon water. Rinse with a clean cloth moistened with clear water and polish or wax as soon as possible.

MILK

(Follow procedures for Cream.)

MUD/DIRT

Acetate	Rope
Burlap	Silk
Fiberglass	Triacetate
Rayon	Wool

Let mud dry, then brush off the excess. This should remove the stain, but if any remains, sponge the area with clear water and apply a few drops wet spotter and a few drops white vinegar. Cover with an absorbent pad dampened with wet spotter. Let stand as long as any stain is being re-

Mud/Dirt *(continued)*

moved. Change the pad as it picks up the stain. Keep stain and pad moist with wet spotter and vinegar. Flush with water and repeat the treatment, applying wet spotter and flushing with water until no more stain is removed. If stain remains, apply rubbing alcohol to the area and cover with an absorbent pad dampened with alcohol. (Do not use alcohol on acetate, rayon, or triacetate.) Continue this treatment as long as any stain is being removed. Change the pad as it picks up the stain. Keep the stain and pad moist with alcohol. If stain persists, moisten the area with a solution of 1 cup warm water and 1 teaspoon enzyme presoak, but do not use on silk or wool. Cover with a clean pad that has been dipped in the solution and wrung almost dry. Let stand for 30 minutes. Add enough solution to keep the area warm and moist. When no more stain is being lifted, flush thoroughly with water and allow to dry.

Acrylic Fabric	**Nylon**
Cotton	**Olefin**
Linen	**Polyester**
Modacrylic	**Spandex**

Let mud dry, then brush off excess. Laundering should remove any remaining stain. If more treatment is needed, sponge the stain with rubbing alcohol. (Do not use alcohol on acrylic or modacrylic.) Flush with water. If stain persists, sponge it with dry-cleaning solvent. Allow to air-dry, then launder.

Acrylic Plastic	**Iron**
Alabaster	**Linoleum**
Aluminum	**Marble**
Asphalt	**Paint/Flat**
Bamboo	**Paint/Gloss**
Brass	**Plexiglas**
Bronze	**Polyurethane**
Cane	**Porcelain Dishes**
Ceramic Glass/Tile	**Porcelain Fixtures**
Chromium	**Stainless Steel**
Copper	**Tin**
Cork	**Vinyl Clothing**
Enamel	**Vinyl Tile**
Glass	**Vinyl Wallcovering**
Grout	**Zinc**

Scrape up excess mud with a dull knife or spatula. Wipe the surface with a cloth or sponge dipped in warm, sudsy water. Rinse well and wipe dry.

Mud/Dirt *(continued)*

Bluestone	**Limestone**
Brick	**Masonry Tile**
Concrete	**Sandstone**
Flagstone	**Slate**
Granite	**Terrazzo**

Carefully remove excess mud. Wash with a solution of washing soda (not soap) and water. Use a cloth or soft-bristled brush to scrub the stain. Rinse thoroughly with clear water and allow to dry.

Carpet/Synthetic	**Carpet/Wool**

To avoid forcing mud further into pile, allow it to dry before treating it. Gently brush loose soil, then vacuum as usual. If a stain remains, spray with carpet shampoo. When the shampoo has dried, vacuum.

Felt	**Leather**
Fur/Natural	**Suede**
Fur/Synthetic	

Allow mud to dry, then gently brush it off. Mix a solution of mild soap and lukewarm water. Swish to create a great volume of suds. Apply only the foam with a sponge. Wipe the area with clean, dry cloth.

Silver

Wash as soon as possible in hot, sudsy water. Rinse in hot water and dry immediately with a soft cloth to prevent tarnish.

Wallpaper

Brush off any excess dirt. With a cloth or sponge dampened with cool, clear water, wipe the stained area. Overlap strokes to avoid streaking. Gently pat dry.

Wood

Remove excess dirt with a brush. Mix dishwashing detergent in hot water and swish to make a great volume of suds. Dip a cloth in only the foam and apply to the stain. Rinse with a clean cloth dampened with clear water. Polish or wax as soon as possible.

MUSTARD

Acetate	Rayon
Burlap	Silk
Carpet/Synthetic	Triacetate
Carpet/Wool	Wool
Fiberglass	

Note: Mustard contains turmeric, a yellow dye. If not treated immediately, it can be impossible to remove. Use a dull knife or spatula to lift off as much spilled mustard as you can. Flush the area with dry-cleaning solvent. If the fabric is strong enough, tamp or scrape to loosen the stain. Flush with dry-cleaning solvent. While tamping stain, blot excess material with an absorbent pad. If stain remains, sponge with clear water and apply wet spotter and a few drops of white vinegar. Tamp again to loosen stain. Flush with water. If stain persists, moisten area with 3-percent hydrogen peroxide and add a drop of ammonia (except on silk and wool). Do not let the bleaching solution remain on the stain any longer than 15 minutes, then flush with water and allow to dry. When treating carpets, blot all excess liquid, then weight down an absorbent pad with a heavy object. When all liquid has been absorbed, allow to dry.

Acrylic Fabric	Nylon
Cotton	Olefin
Linen	Polyester
Modacrylic	Spandex

Note: Mustard contains turmeric, a yellow dye. If not treated immediately, it can be impossible to remove. If the stain has just occurred, spray on fabric spot cleaner. If stain is older, scrape as much of the spill as possible. Flush with water, apply liquid detergent to the stain, and flush again. If the stain remains, soak for several hours or overnight in a warm-to-hot solution of detergent and water. Rinse and launder as soon as possible.

Acrylic Plastic	Vinyl Tile
Asphalt	Vinyl Wallcovering
Vinyl Clothing	

Note: Mustard contains turmeric, a yellow dye. If not treated immediately, it can be impossible to remove. Wipe up spilled mustard with a cloth or sponge dipped in warm, sudsy water. Rinse thoroughly and wipe dry with a soft cloth.

Mustard *(continued)*

Aluminum	**Paint/Gloss**
Bamboo	**Plexiglas**
Cane	**Polyurethane**
Ceramic Glass/Tile	**Porcelain Dishes**
Cork	**Stainless Steel**
Glass	**Tin**
Linoleum	**Zinc**
Paint/Flat	

Scrape to remove excess mustard (except on ceramic glass rangetops). Wipe the area with a cloth or sponge dipped in warm, sudsy water. Rinse well with water and wipe dry with a soft cloth.

Bluestone	**Limestone**
Brick	**Masonry Tile**
Concrete	**Sandstone**
Flagstone	**Slate**
Granite	**Terrazzo**

Remove excess mustard. Wash the stain with a solution of washing soda and water. Use a cloth or soft-bristled brush to scrub the stain. Rinse thoroughly with clear water and allow to air-dry.

Grout

Wipe up excess mustard with a cloth dipped in warm, sudsy water. If any stain remains, apply tile-and-grout cleaner or dip a wet toothbrush in baking soda or powdered cleanser and gently scrub the spot. Rinse thoroughly and wipe dry with a soft cloth.

Leather	**Suede**

Note: Mustard contains turmeric, a yellow dye. If not treated immediately, it can be impossible to remove. Although mustard usually causes permanent stains on these materials, try mixing a solution of mild soap and lukewarm water, swishing to create a great volume of suds, and applying only the foam with a sponge. Wipe with a clean cloth dampened with clear water. Dry with a soft cloth. Condition leather with saddle soap.

Silver

Wash in hot, soapy water as soon as possible. Rinse in hot, clear water and dry with a soft cloth.

Mustard *(continued)*

Wallpaper

The turmeric in mustard usually permanently stains wallpaper. If the stain is fresh, gently wipe it with a cloth dipped in the suds of mild detergent and water. Rinse with a clean cloth moistened with cool, clear water. Gently pat dry.

Wood

Immediately mix dishwashing detergent in hot water and swish to make a great volume of suds. Dip a cloth in only the foam and apply to the mustard. Rinse with a clean cloth dampened with cool, clear water. Polish or wax when dry.

NICOTINE/CIGAR, CIGARETTE, PIPE SMOKE

Acetate	**Rayon**
Fiberglass	**Triacetate**

Spray on fabric spot cleaner. Sponge the stain with water and apply wet spotter and a few drops of white vinegar. Cover with an absorbent pad dampened with wet spotter. Let stand as long as it picks up the stain. Keep the stain and pad moist with wet spotter and vinegar. Flush with water and repeat until no more stain is removed. If the stain persists, moisten with a solution of 1 cup warm water and 1 teaspoon enzyme presoak. Cover with a clean pad that has been dipped in the solution and wrung almost dry. Let stand for at least 30 minutes. Add enough solution to keep the stain warm and damp. When the stain is removed or no more is being lifted, flush thoroughly with water and allow to dry.

Acrylic Fabric	**Olefin**
Modacrylic	**Polyester**
Nylon	**Spandex**

Soak the stain in a solution of 1 quart warm water, ½ teaspoon liquid detergent, and 1 tablespoon white vinegar for 15 minutes. Rinse with clear water. Sponge the remaining stain with rubbing alcohol and launder if possible. If not, soak in a solution of 1 quart warm water and 1 tablespoon enzyme presoak for 30 minutes. Rinse well with water, allow to dry, and launder as soon as possible.

Nicotine/Cigar, Cigarette, Pipe Smoke *(continued)*

Acrylic Plastic	Ivory
Aluminum	Jade
Asphalt	Linoleum
Bamboo	Opal
Brass	Paint/Flat
Bronze	Paint/Gloss
Cane	Pewter
Ceramic Glass/Tile	Plexiglas
Copper	Polyurethane
Cork	Stainless Steel
Enamel	Tin
Glass	Vinyl Clothing
Gold	Vinyl Tile
Grout	Vinyl Wallcovering
Iron	

Wipe the stained surface with a cloth or sponge dipped in warm, sudsy water. Rinse well and wipe dry.

Alabaster	**Marble**

Wipe the stained surface with a cloth dipped in a solution of washing soda and water. Rinse well with clear water and wipe dry. If a stain persists, mix a few drops ammonia with 1 cup 3-percent hydrogen peroxide. Soak a white blotter in the solution and place over the stain. Weight it down with a heavy object. Continue applying the solution until the stain is bleached out. Wipe dry.

Bluestone	Limestone
Brick	Masonry Tile
Concrete	Slate
Flagstone	Terrazzo
Granite	

Mix a solution of washing soda and water. Gently brush away the stain with a cloth or soft-bristled brush. Rinse with clear water and allow to dry.

Burlap	**Wool**
Silk	

Sponge the stain with water. Spray on spot cleaner. If stain persists, apply wet spotter and a few drops of white vinegar. Cover with an absor-

Nicotine/Cigar, Cigarette, Pipe Smoke *(continued)*

bent pad dampened with wet spotter. Let stand as long as any stain is being lifted. Change the pad as it picks up the stain. Keep the stain and pad moist with wet spotter and vinegar. Flush with clear water. Repeat until no more stain is being removed. If any stain remains, test for colorfastness, then apply rubbing alcohol and cover with an absorbent pad dampened with alcohol. Let stand as long as any stain is being removed. Flush with water.

| Carpet/Synthetic | Foam Rubber |
| Carpet/Wool | |

Sponge the stained area with a solution of 1 quart warm water, ½ teaspoon liquid detergent, and 1 tablespoon white vinegar. Blot with a clean pad and rinse well with clear water. If stain remains, sponge it with a solution of 1 quart warm water and 1 tablespoon enzyme presoak. Blot and sponge alternately until no more stain is left. Sponge the area with water. Blot up all excess water. Place a clean pad over the area and weight it down with a heavy object. When no more liquid is being absorbed, allow the area to dry.

| Cotton | Linen |

Soak the stain for 15 minutes in a solution of 1 quart warm water and ½ teaspoon liquid detergent. Rinse well with water. Next, sponge the area with rubbing alcohol, rinse with water, and allow to dry. If the stain remains, soak for 30 minutes in a solution of 1 quart warm water and 1 tablespoon enzyme presoak. Rinse well, dry, and launder as soon as possible.

| Felt | Fur/Synthetic |
| Fur/Natural | Wood |

Mix dishwashing detergent in hot water and swish to make a great volume of suds. Dip a cloth in only the foam and apply. Rinse the area with a cloth moistened with clear water. Allow felt and fur to air-dry, but wipe wood surfaces dry with a clean cloth and wax or polish.

| Leather | Suede |

Mix a solution of mild soap and lukewarm water. Swish to create a great volume of suds. Apply only the foam with a sponge. Rinse area with a cloth moistened with clear water. Wipe with a clean cloth to dry.

| Porcelain Dishes | Porcelain Fixtures | *(continued)* |

Nicotine/Cigar, Cigarette, Pipe Smoke *(continued)*

Remove the stain by washing in warm, sudsy water or wiping with a cloth dipped in warm, sudsy water. Rinse well and wipe dry. To remove stubborn stains, dampen a cloth and dip it into baking soda. Wipe away any remaining stain, rinse, and dry with a clean cloth.

Silver

Wash in hot, soapy water. Rinse in hot water and wipe dry with a soft cloth to prevent tarnish.

OIL/AUTOMOTIVE, HAIR, LUBRICATING, MINERAL, VEGETABLE

Acetate	**Silk**
Carpet/Synthetic	**Triacetate**
Carpet/Wool	**Wool**
Rayon	

Blot up as much excess as possible and apply an absorbent, such as cornmeal. After letting the absorbent work, brush the powder off the fabric. If a stain remains, sponge with dry-cleaning solvent. Apply dry spotter. Cover with an absorbent pad that has been dampened with dry spotter. Continue this treatment as long as any stain is being removed. Change the pad as it picks up the stain. Keep both the stain and pad moist with dry spotter. Flush the area with dry-cleaning solvent. If the stain persists, sponge the area with clear water and apply wet spotter with a few drops of white vinegar. Cover the stain with an absorbent pad moistened with wet spotter. Continue this treatment as long as any stain is being removed. Change the pad as it picks up the stain. Keep both the stain and pad moist with wet spotter and vinegar. Flush with water and repeat the procedure until no more stain is removed. Allow to dry.

Acrylic Fabric	**Nylon**
Cotton	**Olefin**
Linen	**Polyester**
Modacrylic	**Spandex**

Blot spilled oil as soon as possible. Apply an absorbent and allow it to soak up the remaining spill. After brushing off the powder, sponge the area with dry-cleaning solvent. Apply dry spotter and cover with an absorbent pad moistened with dry spotter. Continue this treatment until no more stain is removed. Change the pad as it picks up the stain. To help loosen

Oil/Automotive, Hair, Lubricating, Mineral, Vegetable *(continued)*

the stain, occasionally tamp the area, blotting any loosened material. Flush with liquid dry-cleaning solvent. If any trace of the stain remains, sponge the stain with water and apply wet spotter and a few drops of ammonia. Tamp the stain again, blotting with an absorbent pad. Flush the area with water and repeat until no more stain is removed. Allow to dry.

Acrylic Plastic	Paint/Gloss
Aluminum	Pewter
Asphalt	Plexiglas
Bamboo	Polyurethane
Cane	Porcelain Dishes
Ceramic Glass/Tile	Stainless Steel
Cork	Vinyl Clothing
Glass	Vinyl Tile
Linoleum	Vinyl Wallcovering

Blot up oil. Wipe the surface with a cloth or sponge dipped in warm, sudsy water. Rinse well and wipe thoroughly dry.

Bluestone	Limestone
Brick	Masonry Tile
Concrete	Sandstone
Flagstone	Slate
Granite	Terrazzo

Wash with a strong solution of washing soda and hot water. If stain remains, make a paste of 1 pound extra-strength powdered cleaner, 2 cups powdered chalk, and 1 gallon water and cover the stain. Or cover oil stain with a paste made from fuller's earth and hot water. Leave the paste on overnight. Rinse with clear water. Repeat if necessary.

Leather

Rub oil stain with a thick paste of fuller's earth and water. Allow the paste to dry, then brush off the powder. Or apply saddle soap. Repeat if necessary. Saddle soap will also condition the leather.

Marble

Remove any excess oil, then wipe with a cloth dipped in warm, sudsy water. Rinse well and wipe dry with a clean cloth. If any residue remains, mix a thick paste of water, powdered detergent, and bleach. Apply to the stain and cover with a dampened cloth to retard evaporation. After

Oil/Automotive, Hair, Lubricating, Mineral, Vegetable *(continued)*

the stain is bleached out and the oil removed, rinse thoroughly with water and allow to dry.

Paint/Flat   **Wallpaper**

Make a paste of cornstarch and water. Apply to the stain and allow to dry. Brush off the powder and repeat if necessary. If the stain persists, make a paste of fuller's earth and trichloroethane. **Caution:** Use trichloroethane with care and wear rubber gloves. Apply to stain and allow to dry. Brush off.

Silver

Immediately wash in hot, soapy water. Rinse thoroughly in hot water and dry with a soft, clean cloth.

Suede

Test any treatment in an inconspicuous place first. On some oil stains, rubbing lightly with suede cleaner will remove any residue. Dip a clean cloth into ground cornmeal and rub into the stain with a circular motion. Gently brush off the powder with a wire brush. Repeat if necessary. If stain persists, brush with lemon juice and hold in the steam of a boiling teakettle for a few minutes. Brush with a wire brush.

Wood

Mix dishwashing detergent in hot water and swish to make a great volume of suds. Dip a cloth in only the foam and apply to the stain. Rinse with a clean cloth dampened with clear water. Polish or wax as soon as possible.

ORANGE

Acetate	Rayon
Carpet/Synthetic	Silk
Carpet/Wool	Triacetate
Fiberglass	Wool

Spray on fabric spot cleaner. If stain remains, sponge area with cool water, then apply wet spotter and a few drops of white vinegar. Cover stain with an absorbent pad dampened with wet spotter. Let stand as long as any stain is being removed. Keep both the stain and pad moist with wet spotter

Orange (continued)

and vinegar. Flush with water and repeat if necessary. If stain persists, moisten the area with a solution of 1 cup warm water and 1 teaspoon enzyme presoak—do not use on silk or wool. Cover with a clean pad moistened with the solution. Let stand for 30 minutes. Add more solution, if needed, to keep the area warm and moist, but do not allow the wet area to spread. When no more stain is being lifted, flush with clear water.

Acrylic Fabric	**Nylon**
Cotton	**Olefin**
Linen	**Polyester**
Modacrylic	**Spandex**

Spray on fabric spot cleaner. If stain remains, soak in a solution of 1 quart warm water, ½ teaspoon liquid dishwashing or laundry detergent, and 1 tablespoon white vinegar for 15 minutes. Rinse with water and launder if possible. If not, soak in a solution of 1 quart warm water and 1 tablespoon enzyme presoak for 30 minutes. Rinse with water and launder.

Acrylic Plastic	**Linoleum**
Aluminum	**Masonry Tile**
Asphalt	**Paint/Flat**
Brass	**Paint/Gloss**
Bronze	**Plexiglas**
Ceramic Glass/Tile	**Polyurethane**
Copper	**Porcelain Dishes**
Cork	**Stainless Steel**
Enamel	**Tin**
Glass	**Vinyl Clothing**
Grout	**Vinyl Tile**
Iron	**Vinyl Wallcovering**

Wipe up the spill. Then wipe the surface with a cloth or sponge dipped in warm, sudsy water. Rinse well and wipe dry.

Bluestone	**Limestone**
Brick	**Sandstone**
Concrete	**Slate**
Flagstone	**Terrazzo**
Granite	

Wipe up excess orange juice. Wash with a solution of washing soda or detergent (never soap) and water. Use a soft cloth or soft-bristled brush. Rinse thoroughly with clear water and allow to dry.

Orange *(continued)*

Leather	**Suede**

Blot up the spill. Mix a solution of mild soap and lukewarm water. Swish to create a great volume of suds. Apply only the foam with a sponge. Wipe with a clean, dry cloth. On leather only, follow with saddle soap to condition.

Silver

Wash as soon as possible in hot, sudsy water. Rinse in hot water and dry immediately with a soft cloth.

Wood

Mix dishwashing detergent in hot water and swish to make a great volume of suds. Dip a cloth in only the foam and wipe up the excess spill. Rinse with a clean cloth moistened with clear water. Polish or wax as soon as possible.

OVEN CLEANER

Acetate	**Polyester**
Acrylic Fabric	**Rayon**
Carpet/Synthetic	**Silk**
Carpet/Wool	**Spandex**
Modacrylic	**Triacetate**
Nylon	**Wool**
Olefin	

Sponge the stain with cool water. If stain persists, neutralize the spot with a few drops of a mild acid, such as lemon juice, white vinegar, or 10-percent acetic acid solution. Thoroughly sponge the area with cool water. Silk and wool must be treated promptly; oven cleaner will destroy these fabrics.

Acrylic Plastic	**Paint/Gloss**
Aluminum	**Plexiglas**
Asphalt	**Polyurethane**
Ceramic Glass/Tile	**Vinyl Clothing**
Cork	**Vinyl Tile**
Linoleum	**Vinyl Wallcovering**
Paint/Flat	

Oven Cleaner *(continued)*

Wipe well with a cloth dipped in cool water. Wipe dry with a clean, soft cloth.

Bluestone   **Masonry Tile**
Brick   **Terrazzo**
Concrete

Because some oven cleaners leave a soap scum that is almost impossible to remove, wash with a strong solution of washing soda and water. Rinse well and wipe dry.

Cotton   **Linen**

Flush the stain with cool water until all trace of stain is gone. Launder as soon as possible. Do not use acids, such as white vinegar or lemon juice, on these fabrics.

Leather   **Suede**

Mix a solution of mild soap and lukewarm water. Swish to create a great volume of suds. Quickly apply only the foam with a sponge to remove oven cleaner. Gently wipe away all trace of the oven cleaner. Rinse in clear water and wipe dry.

Wallpaper

Treat the stain quickly and carefully because the chemicals in oven cleaners can dissolve wallpaper paste. Wipe with a sponge dampened with clear, warm water. Gently rub the sponge over the stain to remove it. Overlapping strokes will prevent streaking. Use a clean, dry cloth to pat dry.

Wood

Some oven cleaners can dissolve wood finishes, so work quickly. Wipe the area with a cloth or sponge dampened with cool water. Wipe dry with a soft cloth. Polish or wax immediately to prevent permanent damage.

PAINT/LATEX

Acetate   **Rayon**
Burlap   **Silk**
Carpet/Synthetic   **Triacetate**   *(continued)*

Paint/Latex *(continued)*

Carpet/Wool　　　　　　**Wool**
Fiberglass

Note: Once latex paint starts to dry, it begins to adhere to fibers and may become permanent. Treat this stain as soon as possible. After scraping to remove excess paint, sponge the stain with dry-cleaning solvent. Then apply dry spotter to the area and cover with an absorbent pad dampened with dry spotter. Let stand as long as any stain is being removed. Change the pad as it picks up the stain. Keep both the pad and stain moist with dry spotter. Flush with dry-cleaning solvent and allow to dry. If any stain remains, sponge the area with water and apply wet spotter and a few drops of ammonia. (Do not use ammonia on silk or wool.) Cover with an absorbent pad dampened with wet spotter. Let stand as long as any stain is being removed. Change the pad as it picks up the stain. Keep both the stain and pad moist with wet spotter and ammonia. Flush with water and repeat if necessary. Allow to dry thoroughly. When treating carpets, be sure to blot excess liquid with a clean, absorbent pad.

Acrylic Fabric　　　　　　**Nylon**
Cotton　　　　　　　　　　**Olefin**
Linen　　　　　　　　　　　**Polyester**
Modacrylic　　　　　　　　**Spandex**

Note: Treat the stain immediately; it may become permanent once the paint has dried. Flush with warm water to remove as much stain as possible, then launder immediately. If paint has dried, moisten area with rubbing alcohol to soften the paint. (For acrylic and modacrylic dilute alcohol with 2 parts water.) Then brush as much paint as possible from the fibers. Launder the fabric.

Acrylic Plastic　　　　　　**Plexiglas**
Bamboo　　　　　　　　　　**Polyurethane**
Cane　　　　　　　　　　　 **Porcelain Dishes**
Ceramic Tile　　　　　　　 **Porcelain Fixtures**
Enamel　　　　　　　　　　**Stainless Steel**
Glass　　　　　　　　　　　**Vinyl Clothing**
Paint/Flat　　　　　　　　　**Vinyl Wallcovering**
Paint/Gloss

Gently scrape up the spill. Wash the surface with a cloth dipped in warm, sudsy water. Rinse thoroughly with clear water and wipe dry. Paint that is absorbed into some of these surfaces may be impossible to remove

Paint/Latex *(continued)*

completely. On hard surfaces, such as glass or ceramic tile, gently scrape off the dried paint with a razor blade.

| **Asphalt** | **Linoleum** |
| **Cork** | **Vinyl Tile** |

Remove spilled paint immediately, then wash with a cloth dipped in warm, sudsy water. If stain remains, cover it with a pad moistened with rubbing alcohol. Let the pad remain in place for a few minutes. Wipe the stain with a cloth dampened with ammonia. To remove any trace of stain, try rubbing the area with superfine-grade (0000) steel wool dipped in liquid wax. Wash thoroughly with soapy water, wipe dry, then wax.

Bluestone	**Masonry Tile**
Ceramic Glass	**Sandstone**
Concrete	**Slate**
Granite	**Terrazzo**

Immediately wipe up spilled paint. Then wash with a solution of washing soda or detergent (not soap) and water. Scrub with a cloth or soft-bristled brush. Rinse thoroughly with clear water and allow to dry.

Brick

Apply a commercial paint remover to the stain and allow it to dry. Use a wire brush to remove paint. Wash the area with clear water and allow to dry thoroughly.

Grout

Wipe up excess paint carefully. Wipe remaining stain with a cloth dipped in warm, sudsy water. If any stain persists, dip a wet toothbrush in baking soda or powdered cleanser and gently scrub the spot. Rinse well with clear water and wipe dry.

| **Leather** | **Suede** |

Note: Paint stains may be impossible to remove entirely. Carefully scrape to remove excess paint. Mix a solution of mild soap and lukewarm water. Swish to create a great volume of suds. Wipe the paint residue with a sponge dipped in only the foam. Wipe with a clean, dry cloth. On leather only, follow with saddle soap to condition.

Paint/Latex *(continued)*

Wood

Wipe up fresh paint or gently scrape dried paint with a paint scraper. Then wipe the stain with a sponge or cloth dipped in warm, sudsy water. Another effective treatment is to mix 1 tablespoon oxalic acid with 1 pint water and to rub the paint with a cloth dampened in the solution. Wipe dry and wax as needed.

PAINT/OIL–BASED

Acetate	**Silk**
Burlap	**Triacetate**
Fiberglass	**Wool**

Gently scrape to remove the excess paint and sponge the stain with dry-cleaning solvent. Apply dry spotter to the area and cover with an absorbent pad dampened with dry spotter. Let stand as long as any stain is being removed. Change the pad as it picks up the stain. Keep both the stain and pad moist with dry spotter. Flush with dry-cleaning solvent and allow to dry. If stain persists, sponge with clear water and apply wet spotter and a few drops of ammonia. (Do not use ammonia on wool or silk.) Cover stain with an absorbent pad moistened with wet spotter. Let stand as long as any stain is being removed. Change the pad as it picks up the stain. Keep both the pad and stain moist with wet spotter and ammonia. Flush well with water and repeat as necessary.

Acrylic Fabric	**Nylon**
Cotton	**Olefin**
Linen	**Polyester**
Modacrylic	**Spandex**

Flush the stain with the solvent indicated as a thinner on the paint container. If none is indicated, use turpentine. Be careful not to spread the stain. Rinse thoroughly with clear water and repeat if necessary. Rub area with bar soap (not deodorant soap) or liquid detergent. Rinse again and launder.

Acrylic Plastic	**Polyurethane**
Plexiglas	**Vinyl Clothing**

Wipe up the spill immediately with a cloth dipped in warm, sudsy water. Rinse thoroughly with warm, clear water and wipe dry. Do not use a thin-

Paint/Oil-Based *(continued)*

ner on these materials; it will destroy them. If necessary, dip a cloth in dry-cleaning solvent, and quickly but gently dab at the remaining stain. Rinse well and wipe dry.

Asphalt	**Linoleum**
Cork	**Vinyl Tile**

Wipe immediately with a damp cloth. Cover the stain with an absorbent pad moistened with rubbing alcohol. Let the pad remain in place for a few minutes. Then wipe the area with a cloth moistened with ammonia. If stain persists, try rubbing very gently with superfine-grade (0000) steel wool dipped in liquid wax. Wash area with warm, soapy water and rinse. Then wax when dry.

Bamboo	**Paint/Gloss**
Cane	**Porcelain Fixtures**
Paint/Flat	**Stainless Steel**

Scrape to remove excess paint. Wipe the area immediately with a cloth or sponge dipped in warm, sudsy water to which a few drops of ammonia have been added. Rinse thoroughly with clear water and wipe dry.

Bluestone	**Masonry Tile**
Concrete	**Sandstone**
Flagstone	**Slate**
Granite	**Terrazzo**
Limestone	

Scrape up the spill. Wash the area with a solution of washing soda or detergent (not soap) and water. Scrub with a cloth or soft-bristled brush. Rinse well with clear water and allow to dry.

Brick

Apply a commercial paint remover to the stain and allow to dry. Use a wire brush to remove the stain, then wash area with clear water. Allow to dry.

Carpet/Synthetic	**Carpet/Wool**

Gently dab at the stain with a cloth dipped in the solvent indicated on the paint container label or in turpentine. Do not soak the stain; the solvent will damage a carpet's rubber backing and pad. Continue to wipe with a

Paint/Oil-Based *(continued)*

clean, solvent-dampened cloth as long as any stain is picked up. Sponge with clear water and wash with a concentrated liquid carpet shampoo. Sponge with water, blot excess liquid, and allow to dry thoroughly.

Ceramic Glass/Tile   Glass

Scrape to remove excess paint. (Do not scrape ceramic glass range-tops—soak to loosen the stain.) Wipe the stain with a cloth or sponge dipped in warm, sudsy water. Rinse thoroughly and wipe dry. If any trace remains, allow to dry, then scrape gently with a razor blade.

Grout

Wipe up excess paint. Then wipe the area with a cloth dipped in warm, sudsy water. If any stain remains, apply tile-and-grout cleaner or dip a wet toothbrush in baking soda or powdered cleanser and gently scrub the spot. Rinse well with water and wipe dry.

Leather   Suede

Gently scrape to remove paint. Mix a solution of mild soap and lukewarm water. Swish to create a great volume of suds. Apply only the foam with a sponge. Wipe with a clean, dry cloth. If any stain remains, try rubbing a leather cleaner into the spot with a clean, soft cloth. Allow it to dry. If stain persists, test dry-cleaning solvent on an inconspicuous place. If safe to use, gingerly apply to the stained area. Allow to dry. On leather only, follow with saddle soap.

Wood

Wipe immediately with a sponge dampened with warm water. Wipe dry, then wax the wood. **Note:** This stain may be impossible to remove if not treated immediately.

PAINT/WATERCOLOR

Acetate	Rayon
Carpet/Synthetic	Silk
Carpet/Wool	Triacetate
Fiberglass	Wool

Sponge the area immediately with water to dilute the paint. Spray on

Paint/Watercolor *(continued)*

fabric spot cleaner or apply wet spotter and a few drops of ammonia. (Take care when using ammonia on silk and wool.) Cover with an absorbent pad dampened with wet spotter. Continue this treatment as long as any stain is being removed. Change the pad as it picks up the stain. Keep both the pad and stain moist with wet spotter and ammonia. Flush well with water and repeat if necessary. Allow to dry thoroughly. If a stain persists, mix color remover according to package directions. Test on an inconspicuous place. If it does not harm the fabric, flush through the stain into an absorbent pad. On carpets, sponge the color remover on the stain and blot with an absorbent pad. Rinse well with clear water and dry.

Acrylic Fabric	**Nylon**
Cotton	**Olefin**
Linen	**Polyester**
Modacrylic	**Spandex**

Soak the stained item in a solution of 1 quart warm water, ½ teaspoon liquid detergent, and 1 tablespoon ammonia for 30 minutes. Rinse well. If the stain persists, soak in a solution of 1 quart warm water and 1 tablespoon white vinegar for 1 hour. (Take care when using vinegar on cotton and linen.) Rinse well with water and allow to dry. If stain is set, apply rubbing alcohol to the area and tamp. (Dilute alcohol with 2 parts water for acrylic and modacrylic.) As stain loosens, blot excess liquid and stain with an absorbent pad. Keep both stain and pad moist with alcohol and change pad as it picks up the stain. Allow to dry. For any remaining trace of stain, mix color remover according to package directions and test on a hidden place. If it does not harm the fabric, flush through the stain. Rinse well with clear water and allow to dry thoroughly.

Acrylic Plastic	**Paint/Flat**
Aluminum	**Paint/Gloss**
Bamboo	**Plexiglas**
Cane	**Polyurethane**
Ceramic Glass/Tile	**Vinyl Clothing**
Glass	

Immediately wipe up the spill with a cloth or sponge dipped in warm, sudsy water. Rinse well and wipe dry.

Alabaster	**Marble**

Immediately wipe up the spill with a cloth dipped in warm, sudsy water. Rinse well and wipe dry. If a stain persists, soak an absorbent pad in rub-

Paint/Watercolor *(continued)*

bing alcohol, wring almost dry, and place over the stain. Wait 5 minutes, then remove the pad and apply a clean, absorbent pad soaked in ammonia and squeezed until damp. Alternate alcohol and ammonia pads until stain has been removed. Wipe surface with a cloth moistened with clear water and wipe dry with a clean cloth.

| Asphalt | Linoleum |
| Cork | Vinyl Tile |

Wipe up the spill with a cloth dipped in warm, sudsy water. Rinse well and wipe dry. If a stain remains, cover with an absorbent pad soaked in rubbing alcohol. Let it remain in place for several minutes, then wipe the area with a cloth dampened with ammonia. Wipe with a cloth dipped in warm, sudsy water and rinse with clear water. Allow to dry.

Bluestone	Masonry Tile
Brick	Sandstone
Concrete	Slate
Flagstone	Terrazzo
Granite	

Wipe up excess paint. Wash with a solution of washing soda or detergent (not soap) and water. Use a cloth or soft-bristled brush to scrub. Rinse thoroughly with clear water and allow to dry.

Grout

Wipe up the spill with a cloth dipped in warm, sudsy water. If any stain persists, apply tile-and-grout cleaner or dip a wet toothbrush in baking soda or powdered cleanser and brush the spot. Rinse well and wipe dry.

| Leather | Suede |

Paint will immediately act to discolor these fabrics. Once contact has been made, immediately wipe the area with a cloth dampened with clear water. If any stain remains, dab it with a cloth dipped in dry-cleaning solvent. Allow to air-dry. On leather only, condition with saddle soap.

Wood

Mix dishwashing detergent in hot water and swish to make a great volume of suds. Dip a cloth in only the foam and apply. Rinse with a cloth dampened with clear water. Polish or wax as soon as possible.

PARAFFIN

(Follow procedures for Candle Wax.)

PEANUT BUTTER

Acetate	Silk
Carpet/Synthetic	Triacetate
Carpet/Wool	Wool
Rayon	

Scrape up excess peanut butter with a dull knife or spatula. Sponge the stain with dry-cleaning solvent. Apply dry spotter. Cover the stain with an absorbent pad dampened with dry spotter. Continue this treatment as long as any stain is being lifted. Change the pad as it picks up the stain. Keep both the pad and stain moist with dry spotter. Flush with dry-cleaning solvent and allow to dry. If the stain persists, sponge the area with water and apply wet spotter and a few drops of white vinegar. Cover the stain with an absorbent pad moistened with wet spotter. Let stand as long as any stain is being removed. Change the pad as it picks up the stain. Keep the stain and pad moist with wet spotter and vinegar. Flush the area with clear water and repeat until no more stain is removed. Allow to dry.

Acrylic Fabric	Olefin
Cotton	Polyester
Linen	Spandex
Modacrylic	

Scrape to remove excess peanut butter. Sponge the area with dry-cleaning solvent. Cover the stain with an absorbent pad dampened with dry spotter. Let it remain in place as long as any stain is being removed. Change the pad as it picks up the stain. To help loosen the stain, tamp and blot the area. Flush with liquid dry-cleaning solvent. To remove a persistent stain, sponge with clear water, apply wet spotter, and tamp occasionally. Blot up any loosened material with an absorbent pad. Flush the area with water and repeat until no more stain is removed. Allow to dry.

Acrylic Plastic	Paint/Flat
Aluminum	Paint/Gloss
Asphalt	Plexiglas
Bamboo	Polyurethane
Cane	Porcelain Dishes
Ceramic Glass/Tile	Stainless Steel
Cork	Vinyl Clothing

(continued)

Peanut Butter *(continued)*

Glass	**Vinyl Tile**
Linoleum	**Vinyl Wallcovering**

Scrape up excess peanut butter with a dull knife. (Do not scrape ceramic glass rangetops—soak to loosen dried peanut butter.) Wipe the surface with a cloth or sponge dipped in warm, sudsy water. Rinse well and wipe dry with a clean cloth.

Bluestone	**Limestone**
Brick	**Masonry Tile**
Concrete	**Sandstone**
Flagstone	**Slate**
Granite	**Terrazzo**

Wash the stained area with a solution of washing soda or a detergent (not soap) and water. Rinse well with clear water and allow to dry.

Leather

Gently scrape to remove peanut butter. Wipe the area with a cloth dipped in warm, sudsy water. Rinse with a cloth dampened with clear water and gently wipe dry. Condition the leather with saddle soap.

Marble

Scrape to remove peanut butter. Wipe the surface with a cloth or sponge dipped in warm, sudsy water. Rinse well and wipe dry with a clean cloth. If any oily residue remains, mix a thick paste of water, powdered detergent, and bleach. Apply to the stain and cover with a damp cloth to retard evaporation. After the oil has been drawn out, rinse thoroughly with clear water and dry.

Silver

Wash immediately in hot, soapy water. Rinse thoroughly in hot, clear water and dry with a soft, clean cloth.

Suede

Mix a solution of mild soap and lukewarm water. Swish to create a great volume of suds. Apply only the foam with a sponge. Wipe dry with a clean cloth. If an oil stain remains, powder the area with an absorbent, such as

Peanut Butter *(continued)*

cornmeal. Allow plenty of time for it to work. Gently brush it off and repeat if necessary.

Wallpaper

Gently scrape to remove excess peanut butter, taking care not to rip the paper. Make a paste of cornstarch and water and apply to the peanut butter residue. After the paste dries, brush off the powder. Repeat paste application if necessary.

Wood

Gently scrape to remove excess peanut butter. Mix dishwashing detergent in hot water and swish to make a great volume of suds. Dip a cloth in only the foam and apply. Rinse with a clean cloth dampened with clear water. Polish or wax as soon as possible.

PENCIL LEAD

Acetate	Rayon
Burlap	Silk
Carpet/Synthetic	Triacetate
Carpet/Wool	Wool

Use a soft eraser to remove the stain, being careful not to distort the fabric. Spray on dry-cleaning solvent or use dry spotter. Rub in dry spotter with an absorbent pad moistened with the solution. Cover the stain with a pad dampened with dry spotter and let stand for 30 minutes. Spray again with dry-cleaning solvent and allow to dry. If any stain remains, sponge the area with clear water and apply wet spotter plus a few drops of ammonia. (Do not use ammonia on silk and wool.) Tamp or scrape the area to loosen the stain. Flush with water and repeat if necessary. Allow fabric to air-dry.

Acrylic Fabric	Nylon
Cotton	Olefin
Linen	Polyester
Modacrylic	Spandex

Use a soft eraser to remove as much of the stain as you can. Rub detergent into the stain and add a few drops of ammonia. Tamp gently, then flush with clear water to remove ammonia. Launder as soon as possible.

Pencil Lead *(continued)*

Acrylic Plastic	Paint/Gloss
Aluminum	Plexiglas
Asphalt	Polyurethane
Bamboo	Porcelain Dishes
Cane	Porcelain Fixtures
Ceramic Glass/Tile	Stainless Steel
Cork	Vinyl Clothing
Ivory	Vinyl Tile
Linoleum	Vinyl Wallcovering
Marble	

Remove pencil marks with a soft eraser. Wipe the surface with a cloth or sponge dipped in warm, sudsy water. Rinse well with water and wipe dry with a soft cloth.

Bluestone	Granite
Brick	Limestone
Concrete	Slate
Flagstone	Terrazzo

Wash the stain with a solution of washing soda or detergent (not soap) and water. Scrub with a cloth or soft-bristled brush. Rinse thoroughly with clear water and allow to dry.

Grout

Wipe the surface with a cloth dipped in warm, sudsy water. If any stain remains, apply tile-and-grout cleaner or dip a wet toothbrush in baking soda or powdered cleanser and gently scrub the spot. Rinse well and wipe dry with a soft cloth.

Leather	**Suede**

Mix a solution of mild soap and lukewarm water. Swish to create a great volume of suds. Apply only the foam with a sponge. Wipe with a clean, dry cloth. On leather only, follow with saddle soap.

Paint/Flat	**Wallpaper**

Rub pencil marks with a nontoxic dry chemical cleaning bar or a soft eraser to remove as many marks as possible. With a clean cloth dampened with clear water, wipe the surface with overlapping strokes. Gently pat dry with another soft cloth.

Pencil Lead *(continued)*

Silver

Wash as soon as possible in hot, sudsy water. Rinse in hot water and dry immediately with a soft cloth to prevent tarnish.

Wood

Use a soft eraser to remove pencil marks. Mix dishwashing detergent in hot water and swish to make a great volume of suds. Dip a cloth in only the foam and apply to the stain. Rinse with a clean cloth dampened with clear water. Polish or wax as soon as possible.

PERFUME

(Follow procedures for Cologne.)

PERSPIRATION

Acetate	**Silk**
Rayon	**Wool**

Sponge the area with water, then spray on fabric spot cleaner. Follow with an application of wet spotter and a few drops of ammonia. (Take care when using ammonia on silk and wool.) Cover with an absorbent pad moistened with wet spotter. Continue this treatment as long as any stain is being removed. Change the pad as it picks up the stain. Keep both the stain and pad moist with wet spotter and ammonia. Flush well with clear water and allow to dry thoroughly.

Acrylic Fabric	**Nylon**
Cotton	**Olefin**
Linen	**Polyester**
Modacrylic	**Spandex**

Soak the stained garment in enzyme presoak according to package directions. After soaking, launder as usual. For older stains, sponge area with a diluted solution of white vinegar and water, then launder. If the fabric color has changed, stretch the stained area over a bowl of ammonia so fumes penetrate while the spot is moist. Prompt treatment of perspiration stains is necessary, as they can weaken most fibers. **Caution:** Never iron a garment with perspiration stains—the heat will set them.

Perspiration *(continued)*

Leather	Suede

Mix a solution of mild soap and lukewarm water. Swish to create a great volume of suds. Apply only the foam with a sponge. Wipe with a clean, dry cloth. On leather only, follow with saddle soap to condition.

Vinyl Clothing

Wipe the stain with a cloth dipped in warm, sudsy water to which a few drops of ammonia have been added. Rinse well and wipe dry with a clean cloth.

PET STAINS/FECES

Acrylic Fabric	Olefin
Modacrylic	Polyester
Nylon	

Quickly and gently scrape to remove the solids. Be careful not to force any stain into the fiber. Sponge the stain with a solution of 1 quart warm water, 1 teaspoon liquid detergent, and 1 tablespoon ammonia. Tamp or scrape to help loosen the stain and blot occasionally with an absorbent pad. Rinse thoroughly with water to remove all trace of ammonia. If a stain persists, soak in a solution of 1 quart warm water and 1 tablespoon enzyme presoak for 30 minutes. Rinse well and launder as soon as possible.

Asphalt	Linoleum
Cork	Vinyl Tile

Gently scrape up the solids as soon as possible. Wash the area with a cloth dipped in warm, sudsy water. Rinse thoroughly with clear water and wipe dry with a soft cloth.

Bluestone	Limestone
Brick	Masonry Tile
Concrete	Sandstone
Flagstone	Slate
Granite	Terrazzo

Scrape to remove the solids, then wash the area with a cloth dipped in a solution of washing soda or detergent (not soap) and water. Rinse well with clear water and allow to dry.

Pet Stains/Feces *(continued)*

Carpet/Synthetic	Carpet/Wool

Scrape to remove the solids, being careful not to push stain into the carpet pile. Apply carpet stain remover. Be sure to follow the label directions for special instructions and any precautions. An alternate method is to sponge the area with a solution of 1 teaspoon nonalkali detergent and 1 pint lukewarm water. Blot the stain with an absorbent pad. Continue sponging and blotting until no more stain is removed. If any stain persists, sponge the area with a solution of 1 tablespoon ammonia and 1 cup warm water. (Do not use ammonia on wool carpet.) Blot excess liquid and continue this treatment until no more stain is removed. Place an absorbent pad over the damp area and weight it down. When no more liquid is absorbed, remove the pad and allow area to dry.

Wood

Gently scrape to remove the solids. Wipe the area with a cloth dipped in warm, sudsy water. Rinse with a cloth dipped in clear, cool water and wipe dry. Wax or polish as usual.

PET STAINS/URINE

(Follow procedures for Urine.)

PRESERVES

(See Apple/Apple Juice, Berries, Cherry, Grape, Orange, Prune.)

PRUNE

Acetate	Rayon
Carpet/Synthetic	Rope
Carpet/Wool	Triacetate
Fiberglass	Wool

Sponge the stain with cool water, then sponge the area with lemon juice or rub a slice of lemon over the stain. Flush with clear water and blot up as much liquid as possible. Let dry. If the stain persists, apply wet spotter and cover with an absorbent pad moistened with wet spotter. Let stand as long as any stain is being removed. Change the pad as it picks up the stain.

Prune *(continued)*

Keep the stain and pad moist with wet spotter. Flush with water. If any trace of the stain remains, moisten the area with a solution of 1 cup warm water and 1 teaspoon enzyme presoak—do not use on silk or wool. Cover with a clean pad that has been dipped in the solution and wrung almost dry. Let it stand for 30 minutes. Keep the stain and pad moist. When no more stain is visible, flush thoroughly with water and air-dry.

Acrylic Fiber	**Olefin**
Modacrylic	**Polyester**
Nylon	**Spandex**

Sponge stain with cool water immediately. Then rub with a lemon slice or sponge lemon juice on stain. Flush with water, blotting as much liquid as possible. Allow to dry. If any trace of stain persists, soak in a solution of 1 quart warm water, ½ teaspoon dishwashing detergent, and 1 tablespoon white vinegar for 15 minutes. Rinse with water and launder if possible. If not, soak in a solution of 1 quart water and 1 tablespoon enzyme presoak. Rinse well with water and launder as soon as possible.

Acrylic Plastic	**Grout**
Aluminum	**Iron**
Asphalt	**Paint/Flat**
Bamboo	**Paint/Gloss**
Brass	**Plexiglas**
Bronze	**Polyurethane**
Cane	**Porcelain Dishes**
Ceramic Glass/Tile	**Porcelain Fixtures**
Copper	**Stainless Steel**
Enamel	**Vinyl Clothing**
Glass	**Vinyl Wallcovering**

Wipe the stain with a cloth or sponge dipped in warm, sudsy water. Rinse well and wipe dry.

Bluestone	**Granite**
Brick	**Masonry Tile**
Concrete	**Slate**
Flagstone	**Terrazzo**

Wipe up the spill and wash the stain with a solution of washing soda or detergent (not soap) and water. Use a cloth or soft-bristled brush to scrub. Rinse thoroughly and allow to dry.

Prune *(continued)*

Cork	Vinyl Tile
Linoleum	

Wipe up the spill and wash the area with a solution of washing soda or detergent (not soap) and water. Scrub with a cloth or soft-bristled brush. Rinse thoroughly with clear water and allow to dry. If stain persists, wipe the area with a cloth dampened in a solution of 1 tablespoon oxalic acid and 1 pint water. Rinse well with clear water and wipe dry. Polish the surface if needed. **Caution:** Oxalic acid is poisonous; use with care and wear rubber gloves.

Cotton	Linen

Test fabric for colorfastness. Stretch the stained fabric over a bowl and fasten in place with a rubber band. Pour boiling water through the fabric from a height of 2 or 3 feet. Avoid splatters. This procedure must be done immediately. If stain persists, soak in a solution of 1 quart warm water and ½ teaspoon detergent for 15 minutes. Then rinse with water. Sponge area with rubbing alcohol and launder if possible. If not, soak for 30 minutes in a solution of 1 quart warm water and 1 tablespoon enzyme presoak. Rinse well with clear water and launder.

Leather	Suede

Wipe up prune juice, then mix a solution of mild soap and lukewarm water. Swish to create a great volume of suds. Apply only the foam with a sponge. Wipe with a clean, dry cloth. On leather only, follow with saddle soap to condition.

Marble

After removing excess prune juice, wipe the surface with a cloth dipped in warm, sudsy water. Rinse well with clear water and wipe dry. If any stain or discoloration remains, mix thick paste of water, powdered detergent, and bleach. Apply the paste to the stain and cover with a damp cloth to retard evaporation. Leave in place. When stain has been removed, rinse thoroughly with water and dry.

Silver

Wash silver in hot, sudsy water as soon as possible. Rinse in hot water and dry immediately with a soft cloth to prevent tarnish.

Prune *(continued)*

Wood

Mix dishwashing detergent in hot water and swish to make a great volume of suds. Dip a cloth in only the foam and apply to the juice. Rinse with a clean cloth moistened with clear water. If any stain remains, rub the area with a cloth dampened with a solution of 1 tablespoon oxalic acid and 1 pint water. Rinse well with clear water and wipe dry. Wax or polish as soon as possible. **Caution:** Oxalic acid is poisonous; use with care and wear rubber gloves.

ROUGE

(Follow procedures for Lipstick.)

RUST

Acetate	Silk
Fiberglass	Triacetate
Rayon	Wool

Because rust stains are very difficult to remove, have them removed professionally from these delicate fabrics.

Acrylic Fabric	Olefin
Modacrylic	Polyester
Nylon	

Apply lemon juice to the stain, but do not let it dry. Rinse thoroughly with clear water. If possible, launder. If not and the stain remains, test a rust remover formulated for fabrics, then apply it according to package directions. After using, flush the area with cool water and launder as soon as possible. **Caution:** Be careful not to spill rust remover on porcelain or enamel finishes (like those on washing machines); this product can ruin the finish.

Asphalt	Vinyl Tile
Linoleum	

Wipe the stain with a cloth or sponge dipped in warm, sudsy water. Rinse well and wipe dry. If any stain remains, use a rust remover that is safe for resilient floors when used according to package directions.

Rust *(continued)*

Brick	**Granite**
Concrete	

Make a paste from 7 parts lime-free glycerine, 1 part sodium citrate (available from drug stores), 6 parts lukewarm water, and enough powdered calcium carbonate (chalk) to create a thick paste. Apply it to the stain and allow to harden. Remove with a wooden scraper and repeat if necessary. Wash stained area thoroughly with clear water and let dry.

Carpet/Synthetic   **Carpet/Wool**

Apply lemon juice and salt to the stain. Flush with clear water and blot well. If any stain remains, test a rust remover formulated for fabric. If the fabric is not damaged, apply the rust remover according to label directions. Flush thoroughly with water; blot excess liquid. Allow to dry.

Ceramic Tile   **Porcelain Fixtures**
Porcelain Dishes

On the tub, sink, ceramic tile, or toilet, wet a pumice bar and rub the rust stain. **Caution:** Do not use this pumice stick on ceramic glass, such as cookware or cooktops; it will scratch the surface. A paste of borax and lemon juice also is effective on rust stains. Rub the paste into the stain and allow it to dry. Rinse with clear water, then repeat if necessary. Rinse again and dry with a clean cloth.

Cotton   **Linen**

Rub liquid dishwashing or laundry detergent into the stain, rinse with water, and launder as soon as possible. If stain remains, test fabric for colorfastness, then use a rust remover for fabric, according to package directions.

Leather   **Suede**

Iron and rust are chemical stains that should be treated by a professional cleaner.

Stainless Steel

Rub stainless steel with a damp piece of fine-grade emery cloth, then rub it with a slice of onion. Rinse well with hot water and dry thoroughly with a soft cloth.

SALAD DRESSING/CREAMY

Acetate	Rayon
Burlap	Rope
Carpet/Synthetic	Silk
Carpet/Wool	Triacetate
Fiberglass	Wool

Blot up the spill and sponge the area with dry-cleaning solvent. Apply dry spotter to the stain and cover with an absorbent pad moistened with dry spotter. Continue this treatment as long as any stain is removed. Change the pad as it picks up the stain and keep both the pad and stain moist with dry spotter. When no more stain is removed, flush with dry-cleaning solvent. Allow to dry. If any stain remains, moisten it with a solution of ½ teaspoon enzyme presoak and ½ cup warm water—do not use on silk or wool. Cover with a clean pad that has been moistened with the solution. Let stand for 30 minutes, adding enough solution to keep the area warm and barely moist. Flush with clear water and allow to dry thoroughly. When treating carpets, blot up excess liquid. Cover the area with an absorbent pad and weight it down. When no more liquid is being absorbed, allow the area to dry. Or after blotting up excess dressing, treat the stain with carpet stain remover.

Acrylic Fabric	Nylon
Cotton	Olefin
Linen	Polyester
Modacrylic	Spandex

Remove as much liquid as possible by blotting. Apply wet spotter to the area and work it into the fiber. Rinse thoroughly with water. If stain remains, apply a paste made from enzyme presoak and water. Allow the paste to cover the stain for at least 15 minutes, keeping it moist. Rinse the area with water and launder as soon as possible.

Acrylic Plastic	Ivory
Aluminum	Linoleum
Asphalt	Paint/Flat
Bamboo	Paint/Gloss
Bronze	Pewter
Cane	Plexiglas
Ceramic Glass/Tile	Polyurethane
Chromium	Porcelain Dishes
Copper	Porcelain Fixtures
Cork	Stainless Steel
Enamel	Tin
Glass	Vinyl Clothing

Salad Dressing/Creamy *(continued)*

Gold	**Vinyl Tile**
Iron	**Vinyl Wallcovering**

Wipe up the spill as soon as possible with a cloth dipped in warm, sudsy water. Rinse with clear water and allow to dry

Alabaster	**Marble**
Bluestone	**Masonry Tile**
Concrete	**Sandstone**
Flagstone	**Slate**
Granite	**Terrazzo**
Limestone	

Wipe up the salad dressing. Then wipe the stain with a cloth dipped in a solution of washing soda or detergent (not soap) and water. Rinse well with water. If any stain remains, mix a thick paste of water, bleach, and powdered detergent. Apply paste to the stain and cover with a damp cloth to retard evaporation. When the stain is removed, rinse well with water and wipe dry.

Leather	**Suede**

Mix a solution of mild soap and lukewarm water. Swish to create a great volume of suds. Apply only the foam with a sponge. Wipe dry with a clean cloth. On leather only, follow with saddle soap to condition.

Silver

Wash in hot, soapy water. Rinse in hot water and wipe dry with a soft, clean cloth.

Wallpaper

Blot up excess salad dressing. Wipe the area with a cloth moistened with cool, clear water. Overlap strokes to prevent streaking. Use a clean cloth to pat dry.

Wood

Note: Wooden salad bowls and utensils should not be washed with dishwashing detergent—merely wipe off the dressing with a dishcloth dampened with clear water. Wipe other wood surfaces with a cloth dipped in warm, sudsy water. Rinse with water, wipe dry, and polish or wax as usual.

SALAD DRESSING/OILY

Acetate	Silk
Carpet/Synthetic	Triacetate
Carpet/Wool	Wool
Rayon	

Blot up spilled salad dressing. Sponge the area with dry-cleaning solvent, or use dry spotter and cover the stain with an absorbent pad moistened with dry spotter. Change the pad as it picks up the stain. Keep the pad and stain moist with dry spotter. Flush the area with dry-cleaning solvent. If the stain persists, sponge the area with clear water and apply wet spotter and a few drops of white vinegar. Cover the stain with an absorbent pad dampened with wet spotter. Continue this treatment as long as any stain is being removed, changing the pad as it picks up the stain. Keep both the pad and stain moist with wet spotter and vinegar. Flush with water. Allow to dry.

Acrylic Fabric	Nylon
Cotton	Olefin
Linen	Polyester
Modacrylic	Spandex

Blot up spilled salad dressing and sponge the area with dry-cleaning solvent. Apply dry spotter and cover with an absorbent pad moistened with dry spotter. Continue this treatment as long as any stain is being removed. Change the pad as it picks up the stain. To help loosen any set stains, tamp the area occasionally, blotting up any loose material. Flush with liquid dry-cleaning solvent. If any trace of the stain remains, sponge with clear water and apply wet spotter. Tamp the stain again, blotting up any loosened particles. Flush with water and repeat if necessary. Allow to dry.

Acrylic Plastic	Paint/Gloss
Aluminum	Pewter
Asphalt	Plexiglas
Bamboo	Polyurethane
Cane	Porcelain Dishes
Ceramic Glass/Tile	Porcelain Fixtures
Cork	Stainless Steel
Glass	Vinyl Clothing
Linoleum	Vinyl Tile
Paint/Flat	Vinyl Wallcovering

Blot up excess dressing. Wipe the surface with a cloth or sponge dipped in warm, sudsy water. Rinse well and wipe dry.

Salad Dressing/Oily *(continued)*

Bluestone	Limestone
Brick	Masonry Tile
Concrete	Sandstone
Flagstone	Slate
Granite	Terrazzo

Wash with a strong solution of washing soda or detergent (not soap) and warm water. If an oily stain remains, cover with a paste made with fuller's earth and hot water. Leave overnight. Rinse with clear water and repeat if necessary.

Leather

Gently blot up the spill. An application of saddle soap will often remove any residue. If this doesn't completely remove the stain, rub a thick paste of fuller's earth and water over the stain. Let it dry, then brush the powder off. Repeat the application of paste if necessary. Follow with saddle soap to condition the leather.

Marble

Remove excess salad dressing, then wipe the stain with a cloth dipped in warm, sudsy water. Rinse well with clear water and wipe dry with a clean cloth. If any residue remains, mix a thick paste of water, powdered detergent, and bleach. Apply to the stain and cover with a damp cloth to retard evaporation. After the stain is bleached out and the oil removed, rinse thoroughly with water and wipe dry.

Silver

Wash immediately after use in hot, sudsy water because silver can be damaged by foods containing acids or egg. Then rinse thoroughly in hot water and wipe dry immediately with a soft cloth to prevent tarnish.

Suede

Blot up excess dressing. Then dip a cloth into ground cornmeal and rub it into the stain, using a circular motion. When dry, gently brush off the powder with a wire brush. Apply cornmeal again if necessary. If stain persists, test lemon juice on an inconspicuous place. If the suede isn't damaged, rub the stained area with lemon juice and hold it in the steam from a boiling teakettle for a few minutes. Brush with a wire brush.

Salad Dressing/Oily *(continued)*

Wallpaper

Make a paste of cornstarch and water. Apply to the stain and allow to dry. Brush off the powder and repeat if necessary. If the stain persists, make a paste of fuller's earth and a small amount of dry-cleaning solvent. Apply to stain and allow to dry. Brush off.

Wood

Note: Wooden salad bowls and utensils should not be washed with dishwashing detergent—merely wipe off the dressing with a dishcloth dampened with clear water. For other wood surfaces, mix dishwashing detergent in hot water and swish to make a great volume of suds. Dip a cloth in only the foam and apply to the stain. Rinse with a clean cloth moistened with clear water. Polish or wax wood furniture, floors, or woodwork as soon as possible.

SAUCE/BARBECUE, SPAGHETTI, STEAK

Acetate	Rayon
Burlap	Rope
Carpet/Synthetic	Silk
Carpet/Wool	Triacetate
Fiberglass	Wool

Gently scrape to remove sauce. Sponge the area with dry-cleaning solvent. Apply dry spotter. Cover the stain with an absorbent pad dampened with dry spotter. Continue this process as long as any stain is being removed. Change the pad as it picks up the stain. Keep the stain and pad moist with dry spotter. When no more stain is being removed, flush dry-cleaning solvent through the area and allow to dry. If any stain remains, moisten it with ½ teaspoon enzyme presoak mixed with ½ cup warm water. Cover with an absorbent pad that has been dipped in this solution and wrung nearly dry. Let stand for 30 minutes, adding enough solution to keep the area warm and barely moist. Flush the area with water and allow to dry. On carpets, sponge with water to remove the enzyme mixture, then place a clean, dry pad over the area and weight it down. When no more liquid is being absorbed, allow the carpet to air-dry completely.

Acrylic Fabric	Nylon
Cotton	Olefin

Sauce/Barbecue, Spaghetti, Steak *(continued)*

Linen	**Polyester**
Modacrylic	**Spandex**

Carefully scrape to remove as much sauce as possible. Spray on fabric spot cleaner. If stain remains, apply wet spotter and work it into the fabric. Rinse thoroughly with clear water and launder. If any stain remains, mix a paste using enzyme presoak and water. Let it work on the stain for a while. Keep the paste moist. After about 30 minutes, thoroughly rinse the area with water to remove all trace of enzyme presoak. Launder as soon as possible.

Acrylic Plastic	**Jade**
Aluminum	**Linoleum**
Asphalt	**Opal**
Bamboo	**Paint/Flat**
Brass	**Paint/Gloss**
Bronze	**Pearls**
Cane	**Pewter**
Ceramic Glass/Tile	**Platinum**
Chromium	**Plexiglas**
Copper	**Polyurethane**
Cork	**Porcelain Dishes**
Enamel	**Stainless Steel**
Glass	**Vinyl Clothing**
Gold	**Vinyl Tile**
Iron	**Vinyl Wallcovering**
Ivory	

Note: The tomato sauce contained in these foods can permanently stain some surfaces. Wipe up the excess immediately with a cloth or sponge dipped in warm, sudsy water. Rinse with clear water and wipe dry.

Alabaster	**Marble**
Bluestone	**Masonry Tile**
Concrete	**Sandstone**
Flagstone	**Slate**
Granite	**Terrazzo**
Limestone	

Carefully remove the spilled sauce. Wipe stain with a cloth dipped in a solution of washing soda or detergent (not soap) and water. If any stain remains, mix a thick paste of water, bleach, and powdered detergent. Apply

Sauce/Barbecue, Spaghetti, Steak *(continued)*

to the stained area and cover with a damp cloth to retard evaporation. When stain has been removed, rinse well and wipe dry with a soft cloth.

Leather   **Suede**

Mix a solution of mild soap and lukewarm water. Swish to create a great volume of suds. Apply only the foam with a sponge. Wipe dry with a clean cloth. On leather only, follow with saddle soap to condition.

Silver

Wash silver immediately in hot, soapy water because the acids in these sauces can damage the silver. Rinse thoroughly in hot water and wipe dry with a soft cloth to prevent tarnish.

Wallpaper

Wipe immediately with a cloth dampened with clear, cool water. Use overlapping strokes to prevent streaking. Gently pat dry with a soft cloth.

Wood

Wipe immediately with a cloth moistened with warm, sudsy water. Rinse with a cloth dampened with clear water, wipe dry, and polish or wax as usual.

SAUCE/SOY, WORCESTERSHIRE

Acetate   **Rayon**
Fiberglass   **Triacetate**

Blot up the sauce. Spray on fabric spot cleaner or sponge the stain with clear water and apply wet spotter and a few drops of white vinegar. Cover with an absorbent pad dampened with wet spotter. Continue this treatment as long as any stain is being removed. Change the pad as it picks up the stain. Keep the stain and pad moist with wet spotter and vinegar. Flush with water and repeat until no more stain can be removed. If the stain still persists, moisten it with a solution of 1 teaspoon enzyme presoak and 1 cup warm water. Cover with a clean pad that has been dipped in this solution and wrung nearly dry. Let stand for at least 30 minutes. Add enough solution to keep the stained area warm and moist. When the stain is removed or no more is being removed, flush with water and allow to dry.

Sauce/Soy, Worcestershire *(continued)*

Acrylic Fabric	**Polyester**
Modacrylic	**Spandex**
Olefin	

Blot up any excess sauce with a clean cloth. Then soak the stain in a solution of 1 quart warm water, ½ teaspoon liquid detergent, and 1 tablespoon white vinegar for 15 minutes. Rinse with water. Sponge the remaining stain with rubbing alcohol and launder if possible. If not, soak in a solution of 1 quart warm water and 1 tablespoon enzyme presoak for 30 minutes. Rinse with clear water and allow to dry. Launder as soon as possible.

Acrylic Plastic	**Ivory**
Aluminum	**Jade**
Asphalt	**Linoleum**
Bamboo	**Paint/Flat**
Brass	**Paint/Gloss**
Bronze	**Pewter**
Cane	**Plexiglas**
Ceramic Glass/Tile	**Polyurethane**
Copper	**Stainless Steel**
Cork	**Tin**
Enamel	**Vinyl Clothing**
Glass	**Vinyl Tile**
Gold	**Vinyl Wallcovering**
Grout	**Zinc**
Iron	

Wipe up spilled sauce, then wipe the area with a cloth or sponge dipped in warm, sudsy water. Rinse well with clear water and dry with a soft cloth.

Alabaster	**Marble**

Blot up excess sauce. Wipe the stain with a cloth dipped in a solution of washing soda or detergent (not soap) and water. If any stain remains, mix a few drops ammonia with 1 cup 3-percent hydrogen peroxide. Soak a white blotter with the solution and place over the stain. Continue applying the solution until all the stain is bleached out and the oil drawn out. Rinse well and wipe dry with a soft cloth.

Bluestone	**Limestone**
Brick	**Masonry Tile**
Concrete	**Sandstone**

(continued)

Sauce/Soy, Worcestershire *(continued)*

Flagstone	Slate
Granite	Terrazzo

Wash the stain with a solution of washing soda or detergent (not soap) and warm water. Scrub with a cloth or soft-bristled brush. Rinse with clear water and allow to dry.

Burlap	**Wool**
Silk	

Blot up excess sauce with a clean pad. Spray on fabric spot cleaner or sponge the stain with clear water. Apply wet spotter and a few drops of white vinegar. Cover with an absorbent pad moistened with wet spotter. Continue this process as long as any stain is being removed. Change the pad as it picks up the stain. Keep both the stain and pad moist with wet spotter and vinegar. Flush with water and repeat until no more stain can be removed. If any stain remains, apply rubbing alcohol to the area and cover with an absorbent pad dampened with alcohol. Continue this treatment as long as any stain is being removed. Change the pad as it picks up the stain and keep both the stain and pad moist with alcohol. Flush with water. For stubborn or old stains, moisten the area with a solution of 1 teaspoon alcohol and 1 cup warm water. Cover with a pad dipped in this solution and wrung nearly dry. Let stand at least 30 minutes. Add enough solution to keep the stained area warm and moist. When the stain is removed, flush thoroughly with clear water and allow to dry.

Carpet/Synthetic	**Foam Rubber**
Carpet/Wool	

Blot up as much spilled sauce as you can with a clean pad. Apply carpet stain remover. Then flush the stain with a solution of 1 quart warm water, ½ teaspoon liquid detergent, and 1 tablespoon white vinegar. Blot with a clean, absorbent pad and rinse well with water. If any stain remains, flush it with a solution of 1 quart warm water and 1 tablespoon enzyme presoak—do not use on wool carpets. Blot and flush alternately until no more stain is left. Rinse well with water. Blot excess liquid and place a clean pad over the area and weight it down. When no more liquid is being absorbed, allow the area to air-dry thoroughly.

Cotton	**Linen**

Blot up the spill, then test enzyme presoak. If it does not discolor the fabric, presoak the stain. Or test soil-and-stain remover on an inconspicuous

Sauce/Soy, Worcestershire *(continued)*

place. Use as directed on the package label. If the fabric isn't damaged or the color doesn't change, pretreat the stain. If you're unable to pretreat or if stain is not removed by the treatment, soak stain in a solution of 1 quart warm water and ½ teaspoon liquid detergent for 15 minutes. Rinse with clear water, then sponge the stain with rubbing alcohol. Rinse and allow to dry. If stain persists, soak in a solution of 1 quart warm water and 1 tablespoon enzyme presoak for 30 minutes. Rinse well with water and allow to dry. Launder as soon as possible.

Leather	Suede

Carefully blot up excess sauce. Mix a solution of mild soap and lukewarm water. Swish to create a great volume of suds. Apply only the foam with a sponge. Wipe dry with a clean, dry cloth. If an oil stain remains, powder the area with an absorbent, such as cornmeal. Allow plenty of time for it to work. Gently brush off the powder. Repeat the application of the absorbent if necessary. On leather only, follow with saddle soap to condition.

Porcelain Dishes	Porcelain Fixtures

Wash the stain in warm, sudsy water. Rinse well and wipe dry. If the fixture cannot be removed for washing, wipe it with a cloth dipped in warm, sudsy water.

Silver

Wash silver in hot, soapy water. Rinse in hot water and wipe dry with a soft cloth to prevent tarnish.

Wood

Mix dishwashing detergent in hot water and swish to make a great volume of suds. Dip a cloth in only the foam and apply to the stain. Rinse with a cloth dampened with clear water. Polish or wax as soon as possible.

SHOE POLISH (EXCEPT WHITE)

Acetate	Rope
Burlap	Silk
Fiberglass	Triacetate
Rayon	Wool

(continued)

Shoe Polish *(continued)*

Sponge the stain with dry-cleaning solvent and apply dry spotter. Cover the stain with an absorbent pad moistened with dry spotter. Continue this treatment as long as any stain is being removed. Change the pad as it picks up the stain. Keep both the pad and stain moist with dry spotter. Flush the stain with dry-cleaning fluid. If the stain persists, sponge it with clear water and apply wet spotter and a few drops of ammonia. (Do not use ammonia on silk or wool.) Cover the stain with an absorbent pad dampened with wet spotter and ammonia. Change the pad as it picks up the stain, keeping both the stain and pad moist with wet spotter and ammonia. Flush the area with water and repeat if necessary. Allow to dry.

Acrylic Fabric	**Linen**
Cotton	**Modacrylic**

Sponge the area with dry-cleaning solvent. If the stain persists, mix a paste of powdered detergent, water, and a few drops of ammonia. Place an absorbent pad beneath the stained area and apply the paste to the stain. When no more stain is being removed, flush the area thoroughly with clear water and launder as soon as possible.

Acrylic Plastic	**Paint/Flat**
Aluminum	**Paint/Gloss**
Asphalt	**Platinum**
Ceramic Glass/Tile	**Plexiglas**
Chromium	**Polyurethane**
Enamel	**Silver**
Glass	**Stainless Steel**
Gold	**Vinyl Clothing**
Ivory	**Vinyl Wallcovering**
Jade	

Wipe the surface with a cloth or sponge dipped in warm, sudsy water to which a few drops of ammonia have been added. Rinse well with clear water and wipe dry.

Alabaster	**Marble**

Wipe the surface with a cloth dipped in warm, sudsy water to which a few drops of ammonia have been added. Rinse well and wipe dry. If a stain persists, mix a thick paste of water, bleach, and powdered detergent. Apply it to the stain and let it remain until the oil has been drawn out and the stain is bleached out. Rinse thoroughly with clear water and wipe dry.

Shoe Polish *(continued)*

Carpet/Synthetic	Carpet/Wool

Scrape to remove as much shoe polish as possible. Sponge the stain with a concentrated solution of carpet shampoo. Continue sponging the area, rinsing the cloth or sponge in clear water as it picks up the stain. Repeat until no more stain is removed.

Cork	Vinyl Tile
Linoleum	

Cover the stain with a pad moistened with rubbing alcohol. Let the pad remain in place for 5 minutes. Wipe the area with a cloth dampened with ammonia. Rinse well and allow to dry.

Felt	Leather
Fur/Natural	Suede
Fur/Synthetic	

Because of the dyes contained in shoe polish, this stain can be removed only by a professional cleaner.

Grout

Wipe the stain with a cloth dipped in warm, sudsy water. If a stain remains, apply tile-and-grout cleaner or dip a wet toothbrush in baking soda or powdered cleanser. Gently scrub the spot. Rinse well and wipe dry with a soft cloth.

Nylon	Polyester
Olefin	Spandex

Immediately sponge the stain with suds made with dishwashing detergent. Sprinkle lemon juice and salt over the area and allow to penetrate for 1 hour. Rinse thoroughly with clear water and launder as soon as possible. Repeat treatment if necessary.

Wallpaper

Note: This stain might permanently dye the paper. Rub the area very gently with a damp cloth sprinkled with baking soda. Wipe the area with a cloth dampened with cool, clear water. Do not let the wet area spread or run. Overlap strokes to prevent streaking. Use a clean cloth to pat dry.

Shoe Polish *(continued)*

Wood

Wipe the stain with a cloth dipped in warm, sudsy water to which a few drops of ammonia have been added. Rinse well with a cloth moistened with clear water and wipe dry. Polish or wax the wood as usual.

SHOE POLISH/WHITE

Acetate	**Rayon**
Burlap	**Silk**
Carpet/Synthetic	**Triacetate**
Carpet/Wool	**Wool**
Fiberglass	

Sponge the stain with dry-cleaning solvent. Apply dry spotter, blotting until no more stain is being lifted. Flush with dry-cleaning solvent. Sponge with amyl acetate until no more stain is being lifted, then flush again with dry-cleaning solvent. Sponge with clear water and add a few drops of white vinegar if the stain persists. When no more stain is being removed, flush the area with water and allow to dry.

Acrylic Fabric	**Nylon**
Cotton	**Olefin**
Linen	**Polyester**
Modacrylic	**Spandex**

Sponge the area with dry-cleaning solvent. Apply dry spotter and tamp. Flush the area with liquid dry-cleaning solvent. If the stain persists, flush the area with amyl acetate. (Dilute amyl acetate with water for cotton and linen.) Tamp occasionally until no more stain is being lifted. Flush again with dry-cleaning solvent and allow to dry. If any stain remains, dampen the area with clear water and add a few drops of white vinegar and tamp until no more stain remains. (Dilute solution for cotton and linen.) Flush out the vinegar with water and either allow to dry or launder.

Acrylic Plastic	**Paint/Flat**
Asphalt	**Paint/Gloss**
Ceramic Glass/Tile	**Platinum**
Chromium	**Plexiglas**
Cork	**Polyurethane**

Shoe Polish/White *(continued)*

Enamel	**Silver**
Glass	**Stainless Steel**
Gold	**Vinyl Clothing**
Ivory	**Vinyl Tile**
Jade	**Vinyl Wallcovering**
Linoleum	

Wipe up the spill with a cloth dipped in warm, sudsy water to which a few drops of white vinegar have been added. Rinse well and wipe dry.

Alabaster **Marble**

Wipe the stained surface with a cloth dipped in warm, sudsy water to which a few drops of ammonia have been added. Rinse well and wipe dry. If the stain persists, mix a thick paste of water, bleach, and powdered detergent. Apply to the stain and let it remain until the oil has been drawn out and the stain is bleached out. Rinse thoroughly with clear water and wipe dry with a soft cloth.

Leather **Suede**

Note: This may be an impossible stain to remove. First apply leather cleaner to stains on leather. For suede, apply suede cleaner. Rub in the cleaner with a clean, soft cloth. Let it dry. If the stain remains, test cleaning fluid in an inconspicuous place. If the surface isn't damaged, apply the solvent to the stain. Allow the leather or suede to air-dry. On leather only, condition with saddle soap.

Wallpaper

Note: This stain might permanently dye the paper. Rub the area very gently with a damp cloth sprinkled with baking soda. Wipe off the stain with a cloth dampened with cool water, but don't let water streaks run down the wall. Overlap strokes. Use a clean cloth to pat dry.

Wood

Gently wipe up excess shoe polish with a cloth moistened with the suds of mild detergent and water to which a few drops of white vinegar have been added. Rinse with a clean cloth moistened with clear water. Polish or wax the wood as soon as possible.

SMOKE

Acetate	Rayon
Carpet/Synthetic	Silk
Carpet/Wool	Triacetate
Fiberglass	Wool

Note: Fabrics or carpets that are heavily stained with smoke should be laundered or professionally cleaned. For light stains, flush the area with dry-cleaning solvent, taking care not to spread the stain. Apply dry spotter and cover with an absorbent pad dampened with dry spotter. Check the stain every 5 minutes. Before changing pads, press firmly against the stain. Continue the alternate soaking and pressing until no more stain is being lifted. Flush again with dry-cleaning solvent and allow to dry. If any stain remains, try applying wet spotter with a few drops of ammonia added. (Do not use ammonia on silk or wool.) Cover with an absorbent pad dampened with wet spotter. Let stand as long as any stain is being lifted. Flush with clear water. Repeat if necessary; allow to dry.

Acrylic Fabric	Nylon
Cotton	Olefin
Linen	Polyester
Modacrylic	Spandex

Note: Fabrics that have a smoke residue from a fire are best laundered or professionally cleaned. If the stain is small or laundering immediately is not possible, flush it with dry-cleaning solvent. Apply dry spotter to the stain and cover with an absorbent pad dampened with dry spotter. Check the stain often, tamping before changing pads. Continue to alternate soaking and tamping until the stain is removed. Flush with dry-cleaning solvent and allow to dry. If the stain remains, try the same procedure with wet spotter and a few drops of ammonia. Be sure to flush the area with clear water when the stain is lifted. Allow to dry and launder as soon as possible.

Acrylic Plastic	Paint/Flat
Alabaster	Paint/Gloss
Asphalt	Plexiglas
Cork	Polyurethane
Glass	Vinyl Clothing
Linoleum	Vinyl Wallcovering
Marble	

Wipe the stained area with a cloth dipped in warm, sudsy water. Rinse well with clear water and wipe dry with a clean cloth.

Smoke *(continued)*

Bluestone	**Sandstone**
Brick	**Slate**
Masonry Tile	**Terrazzo**

If stain is small, erase as much smoke as possible with an art gum eraser. Mix ½ cup powdered all-purpose cleaner in 1 gallon water and rub the stain with a sponge dipped in the solution. Rinse with clear water to remove all chemicals and allow to dry.

Leather	**Suede**

For light stains, mix a solution of mild soap and lukewarm water. Swish to create a great volume of suds. Apply only the foam with a sponge to the smoke residue. Wipe the area dry with a soft cloth. On leather only, condition with saddle soap.

Wood

Wipe the stained surface with a cloth dampened with sudsy water. Rinse with clear water and wipe it dry immediately because water will damage most finishes. Polish or wax as soon as possible.

SOAP

Acetate	**Olefin**
Acrylic Fabric	**Polyester**
Burlap	**Rayon**
Carpet/Synthetic	**Silk**
Carpet/Wool	**Spandex**
Modacrylic	**Triacetate**
Nylon	**Wool**

Sponge with cool water. If the stain persists, thoroughly flush it with cool water. If the color has been altered or to prevent fading or bleeding, neutralize the spot with a few drops of lemon juice, white vinegar, or 10-percent acetic acid solution. Sponge thoroughly with cool water. If the soap stain has a high lye content, the fabric may be damaged permanently. Silk and wool are weakened and sometimes destroyed by strong soap, so be especially prompt in treatment.

Acrylic Plastic	**Jade**
Alabaster	**Linoleum**

(continued)

Soap *(continued)*

Aluminum	**Marble**
Asphalt	**Opal**
Bamboo	**Paint/Flat**
Brass	**Paint/Gloss**
Bronze	**Pearls**
Cane	**Pewter**
Ceramic Glass/Tile	**Platinum**
Chromium	**Plexiglas**
Copper	**Polyurethane**
Coral	**Porcelain**
Cork	**Rope**
Fiberglass	**Stainless Steel**
Glass	**Tin**
Gold	**Vinyl Clothing**
Grout	**Vinyl Tile**
Iron	**Vinyl Wallcovering**
Ivory	**Zinc**

Rinse well with a sponge dipped in cool water. Wipe dry with a clean, soft cloth. Baking soda applied with a damp cloth should cut soap film. Treat pearls stained with strong soap immediately; they are permanently damaged by strong alkalies.

Bluestone	**Limestone**
Brick	**Masonry Tile**
Concrete	**Sandstone**
Flagstone	**Slate**
Granite	**Terrazzo**

Soap scum is almost impossible to remove. Scrub with a solution of washing soda or nonalkali cleaner and water. Rinse well and dry.

Cotton	**Linen**

Flush the area with cool water until all trace of soap is gone. Launder as soon as possible. The acid treatment recommended for other fabrics cannot be used on cotton or linen because they may be permanently damaged by acids.

Felt

Brush in the direction of the nap with a sponge moistened with cool water. If any stain remains, neutralize it with a few drops of lemon juice,

Soap *(continued)*

white vinegar, or 10-percent acetic acid solution. Sponge thoroughly with cool water. Since felt is composed mainly of wool fibers, strong soap may damage it permanently.

Fur/Natural	Fur/Synthetic

Dip a cloth or sponge in cool water and remove as much of the water as possible. Gently rub with the nap; do not overwet the pelt or backing. Dry away from heat.

Leather	Suede

Dip a cloth into the suds of mild detergent and water. Gently wipe away soap film. Blot with a clean, dry cloth. Dry away from heat. Leather may be conditioned with saddle soap. Treat suede with suede cleaner.

Silver

Wash silver in hot, sudsy water with a soft cloth. Rinse in hot water and dry immediately with a soft cloth.

Wallpaper

Take special care to clean this stain quickly because an alkali like strong soap may dissolve the adhesive behind the paper. Dip a sponge in clear, warm water, wring until the sponge is damp, then gently stroke the stain, overlapping your strokes. Pat dry with a clean cloth.

Wood

Strong soap may dissolve wood polishes. With a sponge dipped in cool water and wrung out until damp, wipe the area without spreading the stain. Wipe dry with a soft cloth. Polish or wax immediately.

SOFT DRINKS/COLA

Acetate	Silk
Fiberglass	Triacetate
Rayon	Wool

Blot up as much of the spill as you can with a clean cloth. Sponge the remaining stain with water. It is imperative to remove all the sugar. Usually

Soft Drinks/Cola *(continued)*

water will completely remove the stain, but if any remains, spray on fabric spot cleaner or apply wet spotter and a few drops of white vinegar. Cover with an absorbent pad and let it stand as long as any stain is being lifted. Change the pad as it picks up the stain. Keep the stain and pad moist with wet spotter and vinegar. Flush well with water. Repeat until the stain is lifted. If any sugar remains and turns yellow, it cannot be removed.

Acrylic Fabric	**Nylon**
Cotton	**Olefin**
Linen	**Polyester**
Modacrylic	**Spandex**

Blot up spilled cola with a clean cloth and flush the area thoroughly with clear water. This is usually enough to remove the stain, but to be certain the sugar is removed, launder immediately. If that is not possible, soak the stain in a solution of 1 quart warm water, ½ teaspoon liquid detergent, and 1 tablespoon white vinegar for 15 minutes. Rinse with water. If it is an old stain and the sugar has not been caramelized by heat, soak the stain in a solution of 1 quart warm water and 1 tablespoon enzyme presoak for 30 minutes. Rinse well with water to remove enzyme and sugar residues. Allow to dry, but launder as soon as possible.

Acrylic Plastic	**Marble**
Alabaster	**Paint/Flat**
Aluminum	**Paint/Gloss**
Asphalt	**Plexiglas**
Bamboo	**Polyurethane**
Cane	**Porcelain**
Ceramic Glass/Tile	**Silver**
Chromium	**Stainless Steel**
Copper	**Vinyl Clothing**
Cork	**Vinyl Tile**
Glass	**Vinyl Wallcovering**
Linoleum	

Blot up the spill. Wipe the surface with a cloth or sponge dipped in warm, sudsy water. Rinse well and wipe dry.

Bluestone	**Limestone**
Brick	**Masonry Tile**
Concrete	**Sandstone**
Flagstone	**Slate**
Granite	**Terrazzo**

Soft Drinks/Cola *(continued)*

Mix a solution of washing soda or detergent (not soap) and water. Gently brush away the stain. Wash with clear water and allow to dry.

Carpet/Synthetic   **Carpet/Wool**

Blot up the spilled cola immediately. It is important to remove as much of the sugar as possible. Sponge the stain with clear water or flush area rugs with water. Blot up as much liquid as possible and apply carpet stain remover, following the directions on the label. If any stain remains, flush with a solution of 1 quart warm water, ½ teaspoon liquid detergent, and 1 tablespoon white vinegar. Rinse well with water and blot with a clean pad. Place an absorbent pad over the area and weight it down. When no more liquid is being absorbed, allow the carpet to air-dry thoroughly.

Leather   **Suede**

Blot up the spill. Mix a solution of mild soap and lukewarm water. Swish to create a great volume of suds. Apply only the foam with a sponge. Rinse well with a clean, damp cloth and wipe dry. If suede needs a conditioner, apply suede cleaner. For leather, condition with saddle soap.

Wood

Mix dishwashing detergent in hot water and swish to make a great volume of suds. Dip a cloth in only the foam and apply to the cola spill. Rinse well with a clean damp cloth and wipe dry. Do not allow water to remain on the surface. Polish or wax as usual.

SOFT DRINKS/NONCOLA

Acetate	Rayon
Carpet/Synthetic	Silk
Carpet/Wool	Triacetate
Fiberglass	Wool

Blot up as much excess as possible and sponge the area with cool water. Spray on fabric spot cleaner or apply wet spotter and a few drops of white vinegar. Cover with an absorbent pad dampened with wet spotter. Let stand as long as any stain is being removed. Keep both the stain and the pad damp with wet spotter. Flush with water. Repeat if necessary. If the stain persists, moisten the area with a solution of 1 teaspoon enzyme presoak and 1 cup warm water—do not use on silk or wool. Cover with a damp cloth

Soft Drinks/Noncola *(continued)*

that has been dipped in this solution and wrung almost dry. Let it stand 30 minutes. Add more solution as needed to keep the stain warm and moist, but be careful not to let the wet area spread. When the stain is gone, flush thoroughly with clear water to remove all sugar residue.

Acrylic Fabric	**Nylon**
Cotton	**Olefin**
Linen	**Polyester**
Modacrylic	**Spandex**

Blot up as much of the spill as you can. Launder as soon as possible, as that usually removes all trace of soft drink. If laundering isn't possible, soak the stain in a solution of 1 quart warm water, ½ teaspoon liquid detergent, and 1 tablespoon white vinegar for 15 minutes. Rinse with clear water, allow to dry, then launder.

Acrylic Plastic	**Marble**
Alabaster	**Paint/Flat**
Aluminum	**Plaint/Gloss**
Asphalt	**Plexiglas**
Bamboo	**Polyurethane**
Ceramic Glass/Tile	**Porcelain**
Chromium	**Stainless Steel**
Copper	**Vinyl Clothing**
Cork	**Vinyl Tile**
Glass	**Vinyl Wallcovering**
Linoleum	

Wipe up the spill. Then wipe the surface with a cloth or sponge dipped in warm, sudsy water. Rinse well and wipe dry.

Bluestone	**Limestone**
Brick	**Masonry Tile**
Concrete	**Sandstone**
Flagstone	**Slate**
Granite	**Terrazzo**

Wipe up the spilled drink. Wash with a solution of washing soda or detergent (never soap) and water. Use a sponge or soft-bristled brush. Rinse thoroughly with clear water and allow to dry.

Leather	**Suede**

Soft Drinks/Noncola *(continued)*

Remove excess soft drink. Mix a solution of mild soap and lukewarm water. Swish to create a great volume of suds. Apply only the foam with a sponge. Wipe dry with a clean, dry cloth. On leather only, follow with saddle soap to condition.

Wood

Wipe the excess spill immediately with a cloth or sponge dipped in warm, sudsy water because soft drinks can damage wood finishes. Rinse with a clean, damp cloth and wipe dry. Polish or wax the wood as soon as possible.

SOUP/CREAMED

(Follow procedures for Cream.)

SOUP/MEAT BASE

Acetate	Rayon
Carpet/Synthetic	Silk
Carpet/Wool	Triacetate
Fiberglass	Wool

Treat the stain as soon as possible. Meat stains that have set can be extremely difficult to remove. Sponge the stain with cold water. If fresh, this should remove it. If any stain remains, spray on fabric spot cleaner or apply wet spotter and a few drops of ammonia. (Omit ammonia on silk and wool.) Cover with an absorbent pad dampened with wet spotter. Continue this treatment as long as any stain is being lifted, changing the pad as it picks up the stain. Keep the stain and pad moist. Flush with cool water, making sure to remove all trace of ammonia. If stain persists, moisten it with a solution of ½ teaspoon enzyme presoak and ½ cup warm water—do not use on silk or wool. Cover it with a pad dampened slightly with this enzyme solution. Let it stand for 30 minutes. Add more solution to keep the stain moist and warm, but do not let the wet area spread. Flush with water and dry thoroughly.

Acrylic Fabric	Nylon
Cotton	Olefin
Linen	Polyester
Modacrylic	Spandex

(continued)

Soup/Meat Base *(continued)*

Fresh meat-soup stains usually can be removed by a thorough washing in cold water. If any stain remains, soak in a solution of 1 quart warm water, ½ teaspoon liquid detergent, and 1 tablespoon ammonia for 15 minutes. Tamp or scrape, blotting occasionally with an absorbent pad. Continue as long as any stain remains. Rinse well with clear water, making sure to remove all trace of ammonia. If the stain remains, soak in a solution of 1 quart warm water and 1 tablespoon enzyme presoak for 30 minutes. Rinse with clear water and dry. Launder as soon as possible.

Acrylic Plastic	**Paint/Gloss**
Alabaster	**Plexiglas**
Aluminum	**Polyurethane**
Asphalt	**Porcelain**
Copper	**Stainless Steel**
Cork	**Vinyl Clothing**
Linoleum	**Vinyl Tile**
Marble	**Vinyl Wallcovering**
Paint/Flat	

Wipe the stain with a sponge dipped in warm, sudsy water. Rinse thoroughly and wipe dry.

Bluestone	**Limestone**
Brick	**Masonry Tile**
Concrete	**Sandstone**
Flagstone	**Slate**
Granite	**Terrazzo**

Wipe up the stain with a sponge dipped in cool water. If any stain remains, wash or brush the stain with a solution of washing soda or detergent (not soap) in warm water. Rinse with clear water and allow to dry.

Carpet/Synthetic	**Carpet/Wool**

Blot up as much soup as you can and sponge the area immediately with cool water. This should remove the stain, but if any remains, apply a carpet stain remover, according to the package directions. If the stain persists, mix 1 teaspoon mild detergent in ½ pint warm water. Apply a small amount of this solution to the carpet and blot the liquid. Take care not to force the stain further into the fibers. Continue until no more stain is removed. Flush thoroughly with water. Place an absorbent pad over the area and weight it down. When no more liquid is drawn out, remove the pad and allow it to air-dry thoroughly.

Soup/Meat Base *(continued)*

Leather **Suede**

Blot up as much soup as you can and follow with leather cleaner, applied according to package directions. Or mix dishwashing detergent in hot water and swish to make a great volume of suds. Dip a cloth in only the foam and wipe the area. Wipe dry with a clean, dry cloth. On leather only, follow with saddle soap.

Wood

Wipe the stain with a clean cloth dipped in warm, sudsy water. Rinse with a damp cloth and wipe dry. Polish or wax as soon as possible.

SOUP/VEGETABLE BASE

Acetate **Silk**
Carpet/Synthetic **Triacetate**
Carpet/Wool **Wool**

Remove excess soup immediately. Sponge the stain with dry-cleaning solvent. Apply dry spotter to the stain and cover with an absorbent pad dampened with dry spotter. Continue this treatment as long as any stain is being removed. Change the pad as it picks up the stain. Keep the stain and pad moist with dry spotter. Flush with dry-cleaning solvent. If any stain remains, moisten the area with a solution of 1 teaspoon enzyme presoak and 1 cup warm water—do not use enzyme presoak on silk or wool. Cover the stain with a pad that has been dipped in this solution and wrung almost dry. Let it stand for 30 minutes. Add more solution to keep the area warm and moist, but do not let the wet area spread. When no more stain is being lifted, flush with clear water and allow to dry.

Acrylic Fabric **Nylon**
Cotton **Olefin**
Linen **Polyester**
Modacrylic **Spandex**

Wipe up spilled soup immediately. Sponge the stain with dry-cleaning solvent. Apply dry spotter and cover with an absorbent pad dampened with dry spotter. Continue this treatment as long as any stain is being removed. Flush with dry-cleaning solvent. If any stain remains, apply a few drops dishwashing detergent and a few drops ammonia to the area, then tamp or scrape to loosen stain. Keep the stain moist with detergent and ammonia

Soup/Vegetable Base *(continued)*

and blot occasionally with an absorbent pad. Flush well with clear water to remove ammonia and launder or allow to dry.

Acrylic Plastic	Marble
Aluminum	Paint/Flat
Asphalt	Paint/Gloss
Bamboo	Plexiglas
Cane	Polyurethane
Ceramic Glass/Tile	Porcelain
Copper	Stainless Steel
Cork	Vinyl Clothing
Glass	Vinyl Tile
Linoleum	Vinyl Wallcovering

Wipe up the spill immediately. Wipe the surface with a cloth or sponge dipped in warm, sudsy water. Rinse well and wipe dry.

Bluestone	Masonry Tile
Brick	Sandstone
Concrete	Slate
Flagstone	Terrazzo
Granite	

Remove excess soup. Wash the area with a solution of washing soda or detergent (never soap) and water. Scrub with a sponge or soft-bristled brush. Rinse the area thoroughly with clear water and allow to dry.

Leather	**Suede**

Carefully blot excess soup from the surface. Mix a solution of mild soap and lukewarm water. Swish to create a great volume of suds. Apply only the foam with a sponge. Wipe dry with a clean cloth. If a greasy stain remains, apply an absorbent, such as cornmeal. Give it plenty of time to work. Gently brush or shake off the cornmeal. Repeat if necessary. On leather only, condition with saddle soap.

Wood

Remove excess soup immediately. Wipe with a cloth dipped in warm, sudsy water. Rinse with a clean cloth dampened with clear water. Polish or wax as soon as possible.

SOUR CREAM

(Follow procedures for Cream.)

SYRUP/CHOCOLATE

(Follow procedures for Chocolate/Cocoa.)

SYRUP/CORN, MAPLE, SUGAR

Acetate	Silk
Fiberglass	Triacetate
Rayon	Wool

Sponge the area with clear water to help remove the sugar, then apply fabric spot cleaner. Or after sponging, apply wet spotter and a few drops of white vinegar. Cover with an absorbent pad moistened with wet spotter. Continue this process as long as any stain is being removed. Change the pad as it picks up the stain. Keep the pad and stain moist with wet spotter and vinegar. Flush with water and repeat until no more stain is being removed. If the stain persists, soak in a solution of 1 quart warm water, ½ teaspoon liquid detergent, and 1 tablespoon vinegar for 15 minutes. Rinse well with water and allow to dry.

Acrylic Fabric	Spandex
Modacrylic	

Sponge the area with water and apply wet spotter and a few drops of white vinegar. Cover with an absorbent pad dampened with wet spotter. Let it stand as long as any stain is being removed. Tamp occasionally and change the pad as it picks up the stain. Flush with water. If a stain persists, soak in a solution of 1 quart warm water, ½ teaspoon liquid detergent, and 1 tablespoon vinegar for 15 minutes. Rinse well with water and launder if possible. If not, soak in a solution of 1 quart warm water and 1 tablespoon enzyme presoak for 30 minutes. Rinse well with clear water and launder.

Acrylic Plastic	Marble
Alabaster	Paint/Flat
Aluminum	Paint/Gloss
Asphalt	Plexiglas

(continued)

Syrup/Corn, Maple, Sugar *(continued)*

Bamboo	**Polyurethane**
Cane	**Stainless Steel**
Ceramic Glass/Tile	**Tin**
Cork	**Vinyl Tile**
Glass	**Vinyl Wallcovering**
Linoleum	**Zinc**

Blot up the spill. Wipe the area with a cloth or sponge dipped in warm, sudsy water. Rinse well and wipe dry.

Bluestone	**Slate**
Flagstone	

Wipe up the spill, then wash with a solution of washing soda or detergent (not soap) and water. Scrub with a cloth or soft-bristled brush. Rinse thoroughly with clear water and allow to dry.

Carpet/Synthetic	**Nylon**
Carpet/Wool	**Olefin**
Cotton	**Polyester**
Linen	

Scrape to remove the spill and sponge the stain with water. Apply wet spotter and a few drops of white vinegar. (Do not use vinegar on cotton or linen.) Cover with an absorbent pad moistened with wet spotter. Continue this process as long as any stain is being removed. Keep both the pad and stain moist with wet spotter and vinegar, changing the pad as it picks up the stain. Flush with clear water and repeat until no more stain is being lifted. If a stain persists, apply rubbing alcohol to the area and cover with an absorbent pad dampened with alcohol. Continue this treatment as long as any stain is being removed. Change the pad as it picks up the stain, and keep the stain and pad moist with alcohol. Allow to dry. If a stain still remains, soak in a solution of 1 quart warm water, ½ teaspoon liquid detergent, and 1 tablespoon white vinegar for 15 minutes. Rinse with water and sponge the stain with alcohol. Launder if possible. If not, soak in a solution of 1 quart warm water and 1 tablespoon enzyme presoak for 30 minutes. Rinse well with clear water and launder as soon as possible. When treating carpets, apply stain remover. Or thoroughly dampen the spot with an enzyme solution and cover with an absorbent pad moistened with the solution. Keep area covered for 30 minutes. Using an absorbent pad, blot up as much excess moisture as possible, then allow area to air-dry thoroughly.

Grout

Syrup/Corn, Maple, Sugar *(continued)*

Wipe up spilled syrup immediately with a cloth dipped in warm, sudsy water. If any stain remains, apply tile-and-grout cleaner or dip a wet toothbrush in baking soda or powdered cleanser and gently scrub the spot. Rinse well and wipe dry.

Leather	Suede

Gently scrape to remove excess syrup. Mix a solution of mild soap in lukewarm water. Swish to create a great volume of suds. Apply only the foam with a sponge. Wipe with a dry cloth. On leather only, condition with saddle soap.

Wood

Wipe up excess syrup. Wipe the stain with a cloth dipped in warm, sudsy water. Rinse with a cloth dampened with clear water and wipe dry. Polish or wax the wood as soon as possible.

TEA

(Follow procedures for Coffee.)

TOBACCO

(Follow procedures for Nicotine/Cigar, Cigarette, Pipe Smoke.)

TOMATO/TOMATO JUICE/TOMATO SAUCE

Acetate	Rope
Carpet/Synthetic	Silk
Carpet/Wool	Triacetate
Fiberglass	Wool
Rayon	

Sponge the stain with cool water, then sponge the area with lemon juice or rub a slice of lemon over the stain (use with caution on wool). Flush with clear water and blot up as much liquid as possible. Let dry. If stain persists, apply wet spotter and cover with an absorbent pad moistened with wet spotter. Continue this treatment as long as any stain is being removed. Change the pad as it picks up the stain. Keep the stain and pad moist with

Tomato/Tomato Juice/Tomato Sauce *(continued)*

wet spotter. Flush with water. If any trace of the stain remains, moisten the area with a solution of 1 cup warm water and 1 teaspoon enzyme presoak—do not use on silk or wool. Cover with a clean pad dampened with the solution and wrung almost dry. Let it stand for 30 minutes. Add enough solution to keep the stain and pad moist and warm, but do not allow the wet area to spread. When no more stain is visible, flush thoroughly with water and allow to dry.

Acrylic Fabric	**Olefin**
Modacrylic	**Polyester**
Nylon	**Spandex**

Sponge the stain with cool water immediately. Then sponge lemon juice on the stain or rub with a lemon slice. Flush with clear water, blotting as much liquid as possible. Allow to dry. If any trace of the stain persists, soak in a solution of 1 quart warm water, ½ teaspoon dishwashing detergent, and 1 tablespoon white vinegar for 15 minutes. Rinse with water and launder if possible. If not, presoak in a solution of 1 quart warm water and 1 tablespoon enzyme presoak product. Rinse well with water and launder.

Acrylic Plastic	**Grout**
Aluminum	**Iron**
Asphalt	**Paint/Flat**
Bamboo	**Paint/Gloss**
Brass	**Plexiglas**
Bronze	**Polyurethane**
Cane	**Porcelain Dishes**
Ceramic Glass/Tile	**Porcelain Fixtures**
Copper	**Stainless Steel**
Enamel	**Vinyl Clothing**
Glass	**Vinyl Wallcovering**

Wipe the stain with a cloth or sponge dipped in warm, sudsy water. Rinse well and wipe dry.

Bluestone	**Granite**
Brick	**Masonry Tile**
Concrete	**Slate**
Flagstone	**Terrazzo**

Wipe up the spill and wash the stain with a solution of washing soda or detergent (not soap) and water. Use a cloth or soft-bristled brush to scrub the stain. Rinse thoroughly with clear water and allow to dry.

Tomato/Tomato Juice/Tomato Sauce *(continued)*

Cork   Vinyl Tile
Linoleum

Wipe up the spill and wash the area with a solution of washing soda or detergent (not soap) and water. Scrub with a cloth or soft-bristled brush. Rinse thoroughly with clear water and allow to dry. If the stain persists, wipe the area with a cloth dampened in a solution of 1 tablespoon oxalic acid and 1 pint water. Rinse well and wipe dry. Polish the surface if needed. **Caution:** Oxalic acid is poisonous; use with care and wear rubber gloves.

Cotton   Linen

Test fabric for colorfastness. If colorfast, stretch the stained fabric over a bowl and fasten in place with a rubber band. Pour boiling water through the fabric from a height of 2 or 3 feet. Avoid splatters. This procedure must be done immediately. If the stain persists, soak in a solution of 1 quart warm water and ½ teaspoon detergent for 15 minutes. Rinse with water. Sponge area with rubbing alcohol and launder if possible. If not, soak for 30 minutes in a solution of 1 quart warm water and 1 tablespoon enzyme presoak product. Rinse well with water and launder.

Leather   Suede

Wipe up excess tomato juice, then mix a solution of mild soap and lukewarm water. Swish to create a great volume of suds. Apply only the foam with a sponge. Wipe with a clean, dry cloth. On leather only, condition with saddle soap.

Marble

After removing excess liquid, wipe the surface with a cloth dipped in warm, sudsy water. Rinse well and wipe dry. If any stain or discoloration remains, mix a thick paste of water, powdered detergent, and bleach. Apply the paste to the stain and cover with a damp cloth to retard evaporation. Leave in place. When stain has been removed, rinse thoroughly with clear water and dry.

Silver

Wash silver in hot, sudsy water as soon as possible. Rinse in hot, clear water and dry immediately with a soft cloth to prevent tarnish.

Wood   *(continued)*

Tomato/Tomato Juice/Tomato Sauce *(continued)*

Mix dishwashing detergent in hot water and swish to make a great volume of suds. Dip a cloth in only the foam and apply to the tomato stain. Rinse with a clean cloth moistened with clear water. If any stain remains, rub the area with a cloth dampened with a solution of 1 tablespoon oxalic acid and 1 pint water. Rinse well and wipe dry. Wax or polish as soon as possible. **Caution:** Oxalic acid is poisonous; use with care and wear rubber gloves.

TURMERIC

(Follow procedures for Mustard.)

UNKNOWN STAINING AGENT

Acetate	Rayon
Carpet/Synthetic	Silk
Carpet/Wool	Triacetate
Fiberglass	Wool

Sponge the area with dry-cleaning solvent. Tamp or scrape to help loosen the stain. Flush with dry-cleaning solvent. If stain persists, apply amyl acetate and tamp again. Flush with solvent and allow to dry. If stain still remains, sponge stain with clear water and apply a few drops of white vinegar. Tamp again. Apply wet spotter and a few drops of ammonia. (Do not use ammonia on silk or wool.) Tamp again. Allow to dry. Sponge with rubbing alcohol and pat with an absorbent pad dampened with alcohol. (Do not use full-strength alcohol on acetate, rayon, or triacetate.) Allow to dry.

Acrylic Fabric	Nylon
Cotton	Olefin
Linen	Polyester
Modacrylic	Spandex

Cover the stain with a pad dampened with rubbing alcohol. Let the pad remain on the stain for a few minutes, then wipe with a cloth moistened with ammonia. If the stain persists, sponge the area with dry-cleaning solvent. Apply dry spotter. Tamp or scrape to help loosen the stain. Flush with liquid dry-cleaning solvent. If stain remains, apply amyl acetate and tamp again. Flush with dry-cleaning solvent. If stain still persists, sponge with clear water, then apply wet spotter and a few drops of white vinegar. (Do not use vinegar on cotton or linen.) Tamp again and apply wet spotter and a few drops of ammonia. Flush with dry-cleaning solvent and allow to dry.

Unknown Staining Agent *(continued)*

Acrylic Plastic	**Gold**
Aluminum	**Paint/Flat**
Bamboo	**Paint/Gloss**
Cane	**Plexiglas**
Ceramic Glass/Tile	**Polyurethane**
Chromium	**Vinyl Clothing**
Copper	**Vinyl Wallcovering**
Glass	

Wipe the stain with a cloth or sponge dipped in warm, sudsy water to which a few drops of ammonia have been added. Rinse well and wipe dry with a soft cloth.

Alabaster	**Marble**

Wipe the stain with a cloth or sponge dipped in warm, sudsy water. Rinse well and wipe dry. If the stain persists, soak an absorbent pad in rubbing alcohol and place it over the stain. Wait 5 minutes, then apply a pad that has been soaked in ammonia and wrung nearly dry. Alternate alcohol and ammonia pads until the stain has been removed. Wipe surface with a damp cloth and then wipe with a dry cloth.

Asphalt	**Linoleum**
Cork	**Vinyl Tile**

Wipe the stain with a cloth dipped in a solution of washing soda or detergent and water. Rinse well with clear water and wipe dry. If any stain remains, cover with an absorbent pad moistened with rubbing alcohol. Let it remain on the stain for several minutes, then wipe the area with a cloth dampened with ammonia. Wash with a cloth dipped in warm, sudsy water. Rinse with clear water and allow to dry.

Bluestone	**Limestone**
Brick	**Masonry Tile**
Concrete	**Sandstone**
Flagstone	**Slate**
Granite	**Terrazzo**

Wash the stained area with a solution of washing soda or detergent (never soap) and water. Scrub with a cloth or soft-bristled brush. Rinse thoroughly with clear water and allow to dry.

Grout

(continued)

Unknown Staining Agent *(continued)*

Wipe the stain with a cloth dipped in warm, sudsy water. If any stain remains, apply tile-and-grout cleaner. If stain persists, dip a wet toothbrush in baking soda or powdered cleanser and gently scrub the spot. Rinse thoroughly with clear water and wipe dry.

Leather	Suede

Mix a solution of mild soap and lukewarm water. Swish to create a great volume of suds. Apply only the foam with a sponge. Rinse with a cloth dampened with clear water. If a greasy or oily residue remains, powder the area with an absorbent, such as cornmeal. Allow plenty of time for the absorbent to work. Gently brush the powder off the hide. Repeat the application of absorbent if necessary. If suede has been subjected to intensive stain-removal treatment, condition it with suede cleaner. On leather, condition with saddle soap.

Wallpaper

Gently rub the stain with an art gum eraser. If stain remains, wipe gently with cloth dampened with lukewarm water. If any trace persists, mix a paste of water and cornmeal (for light colors) or fuller's earth (for dark colors) and press the paste onto stain with the palm of your hand. Let dry, then gently wipe off powder with a soft cloth.

Wood

Mix dishwashing detergent in hot water and swish to make a great volume of suds. Dip a cloth in only the foam and apply to the stain. Rinse with a clean cloth dampened with clear water. Polish or wax the wood as soon as possible.

URINE

Acetate	Rayon
Carpet/Synthetic	Silk
Carpet/Wool	Triacetate
Fiberglass	Wool

Sponge the area with water or club soda immediately to dilute the stain. Apply wet spotter and a few drops of ammonia. (Do not use ammonia on silk or wool.) Cover with an absorbent pad moistened with wet spotter.

Urine *(continued)*

Continue this treatment as long as any stain is being removed. Change the pad as it picks up the stain. Keep both the pad and stain moist with wet spotter and ammonia. Flush with clear water, then apply wet spotter with a few drops of white vinegar. Flush well with water and repeat if necessary. Allow to dry. On carpets, apply rug shampoo.

Acrylic Fabric	**Nylon**
Cotton	**Olefin**
Linen	**Polyester**
Modacrylic	**Spandex**

Flush immediately with water or club soda. Soak the stain in a solution of 1 quart warm water, ½ teaspoon liquid detergent, and 1 tablespoon ammonia for 30 minutes. Rinse well with clear water. If stain persists, soak in a solution of 1 quart warm water and 1 tablespoon white vinegar for 1 hour. (Use white vinegar with care on cotton and linen.) Rinse well and allow to dry. If the stain is set, try applying rubbing alcohol to the area and tamping. (Do not apply full-strength rubbing alcohol to acrylic or modacrylic—dilute with 2 parts water.) As the stain loosens, blot liquid and stain with an absorbent pad. Keep both the stain and pad moist with alcohol and change the pad as it picks up the stain. Allow to dry.

Acrylic Plastic	**Paint/Flat**
Aluminum	**Paint/Gloss**
Bamboo	**Plexiglas**
Cane	**Polyurethane**
Ceramic Glass/Tile	**Vinyl Clothing**
Glass	**Vinyl Wallcovering**

Wipe up liquid with a cloth or sponge dipped in warm, sudsy water. Rinse well and wipe dry with a soft cloth.

Alabaster	**Marble**

Wipe the stain with a cloth or sponge dipped in warm, sudsy water. Rinse well and wipe dry. If a stain persists, soak an absorbent pad in rubbing alcohol and apply it to the stain after wringing nearly dry. Wait 5 minutes, then apply an absorbent pad that has been soaked in ammonia and wrung nearly dry. Alternate alcohol and ammonia pads until stain has been removed. Wipe the surface with a cloth dampened with clear water and dry with a soft cloth.

Urine *(continued)*

Asphalt	Linoleum
Cork	Vinyl Tile

Wipe the stain with a cloth or sponge dipped in warm, sudsy water. Rinse well and wipe dry. If stain remains, cover with an absorbent pad soaked in rubbing alcohol. Let it remain in place for 5 minutes, then wipe the area with a cloth dampened with ammonia. Rinse well with water and wipe dry with a soft cloth.

Bluestone	Granite
Brick	Limestone
Concrete	Masonry Tile
Flagstone	Sandstone

Wash the stain with a solution of washing soda or detergent (never soap) and water. Scrub with a cloth or soft-bristled brush. Rinse thoroughly with clear water and allow to dry.

Grout

Wash the stain with a cloth dipped in warm, sudsy water. If any stain remains, apply tile-and-grout cleaner or dip a wet toothbrush in baking soda or powdered cleanser and gently scrub the stain. Rinse well with clear water and wipe dry.

Leather	Suede

Blot up the stain. Mix a solution of mild soap in lukewarm water. Swish to create a great volume of suds. Apply only the foam with a sponge. Rinse well with a clean, damp cloth and wipe dry. If suede needs a conditioner, apply suede cleaner. For leather, condition with saddle soap.

Wood

Gently wipe the stain with a cloth or sponge dipped in warm, sudsy water. Rinse with a clean cloth moistened with clear water and wipe dry. Polish or wax as soon as possible.

VARNISH

(Follow procedures for Lacquer.)

VEGETABLES/GREEN, YELLOW

Acetate	Rayon
Carpet/Synthetic	Silk
Carpet/Wool	Triacetate
Fiberglass	Wool

Scrape to remove spill. Sponge the area with dry-cleaning solvent. Apply dry spotter and cover with an absorbent pad moistened with dry spotter. Continue this treatment as long as any stain is being removed. Change the pad as it picks up the stain. Keep the stain and pad moist with dry spotter. Flush with liquid dry-cleaning solvent. If any stain remains, moisten the area with a solution of 1 teaspoon enzyme presoak and 1 cup warm water—do not use enzyme presoaks on silk or wool. Cover the stain with a pad that has been dipped in this solution and wrung nearly dry. Let it stand for 30 minutes. Add enough solution to keep the area warm and moist. When no more stain is being lifted, flush with water and allow to dry.

Acrylic Fabric	Nylon
Cotton	Olefin
Linen	Polyester
Modacrylic	Spandex

Scrape to remove the spill. Sponge the area with dry-cleaning solvent. Apply dry spotter and cover with an absorbent pad dampened with dry spotter. Continue this treatment as long as any stain is being removed. Flush with liquid dry-cleaning solvent. If any stain remains, apply a few drops of dishwashing detergent and a few drops of ammonia to the area. Tamp or scrape to help loosen the stain. Keep the stain moist with detergent and ammonia and blot occasionally with an absorbent pad. Flush well with clear water and allow to dry. Launder as soon as possible.

Acrylic Plastic	Marble
Aluminum	Paint/Flat
Asphalt	Paint/Gloss
Bamboo	Plexiglas
Cane	Polyurethane
Ceramic Glass/Tile	Porcelain
Chromium	Stainless Steel
Copper	Vinyl Clothing
Cork	Vinyl Tile
Glass	Vinyl Wallcovering
Linoleum	

(continued)

Vegetables/Green, Yellow *(continued)*

Note: If not removed immediately, the interaction between vegetables and uncoated copper causes "green rust." Wipe up the spill immediately. Wipe the surface with a cloth or sponge dipped in warm, sudsy water. Rinse well with clear water and wipe dry with a soft cloth.

Bluestone	**Limestone**
Brick	**Masonry Tile**
Concrete	**Sandstone**
Flagstone	**Slate**
Granite	**Terrazzo**

Wipe up spilled vegetables. Wash the surface with a solution of washing soda or detergent (never soap) and water. Use a sponge or soft-bristled brush to scrub the stain. Rinse thoroughly with clear water and allow to dry.

Leather	**Suede**

Carefully wipe or scrape to remove the spill. Mix a solution of mild soap and lukewarm water. Swish to create a great volume of suds. Apply only the foam with a sponge. Wipe dry with a clean cloth. If a greasy stain remains, apply an absorbent, such as cornmeal. Give it plenty of time to work. Gently brush off the absorbent. Repeat if necessary. On leather only, condition with saddle soap.

Wood

Wipe up spilled vegetable. Wipe the stain with a cloth dipped in warm, sudsy water. Rinse with a clean cloth dampened with clear water. Polish or wax as soon as possible after drying.

VINEGAR/CIDER, WINE

Acetate	**Linen**
Burlap	**Rayon**
Cotton	**Silk**
Fiberglass	**Triacetate**

Note: Acetate will resist mild acids such as vinegar, but cotton and linen can be destroyed or weakened. Immediate treatment is imperative. Thoroughly flush with water or club soda, taking care not to spread the stain. To stop fabric damage and possibly restore any color change, neutralize the acid by holding the stain over an open bottle of ammonia. Allow the

Vinegar/Cider, Wine *(continued)*

fumes to penetrate the fabric. (Do not use on silk.) Sponging with a solution of baking soda and water also neutralizes the acid. Flush ammonia or baking soda from the fabric with clear water and allow to dry. Launder washable fabrics as soon as possible.

Acrylic Fabric	**Olefin**
Modacrylic	**Polyester**
Nylon	**Spandex**

Sponge the stain with water to which a few drops of ammonia have been added. Flush with cool, clear water or club soda. If stain remains, repeat treatment with water and ammonia solution. Thoroughly flush ammonia from the fabric with cool water and launder as soon as possible.

Acrylic Plastic	**Iron**
Alabaster	**Linoleum**
Aluminum	**Marble**
Asphalt	**Masonry Tile**
Bamboo	**Paint/Flat**
Brass	**Paint/Gloss**
Bronze	**Pewter**
Cane	**Platinum**
Ceramic Glass/Tile	**Plexiglas**
Chromium	**Polyurethane**
Copper	**Stainless Steel**
Cork	**Tin**
Enamel	**Vinyl Clothing**
Glass	**Vinyl Tile**
Gold	**Vinyl Wallcovering**
Grout	**Zinc**

Wipe the spill immediately with a cloth dipped in warm, sudsy water to prevent the acid in the vinegar from damaging the surface. Rinse well with clear water and wipe dry.

Bluestone	**Limestone**
Brick	**Sandstone**
Concrete	**Slate**
Flagstone	**Terrazzo**
Granite	

Mix a solution of washing soda or detergent and warm water. Scrub with a cloth or soft-bristled brush. Rinse thoroughly with clear water and dry.

Vinegar/Cider, Wine *(continued)*

| Carpet/Synthetic | Felt |
| Carpet/Wool | Wool |

Blot up spilled vinegar immediately with an absorbent pad. Sponge the stain with club soda or warm, sudsy water. If possible, prevent soaking the carpet. If a stain remains, add a few drops of ammonia to clear water. Sponge into the stain and blot, using great care with wool because it is sensitive to ammonia. Rinse with clear water. Place an absorbent pad over the stain and blot up as much liquid as possible. Allow to air-dry thoroughly.

| Leather | Suede |

Mix a solution of mild soap and lukewarm water. Swish to create a great volume of suds. Apply only the foam with a sponge. Wipe dry with a clean cloth. On leather only, condition with saddle soap.

| Porcelain Dishes | Silver |
| Porcelain Fixtures | |

Wash in hot, soapy water. Rinse in hot water and dry with a soft cloth. Never let acids like vinegar remain on silver because the acid can pit and corrode the metal.

| Wood |

Mix dishwashing detergent in hot water and swish to make a great volume of suds. Dip a cloth in only the foam and wipe the stain with it. Rinse with a cloth dampened with clear water. Wipe dry and apply polish or wax.

VOMIT

Acetate	Rope
Burlap	Silk
Fiberglass	Triacetate
Rayon	Wool

Gently scrape up solids. Sponge the area with clear water and apply wet spotter and a few drops of ammonia. (Do not use ammonia on silk and wool.) Cover with an absorbent pad moistened with wet spotter and ammonia. Continue this treatment as long as any stain is being picked up. Change the pad as it picks up the stain. Keep the stain and pad moist with wet spotter and ammonia. Flush thoroughly with cool water, making sure

Vomit *(continued)*

to remove all trace of ammonia. If a stain persists, moisten it with a solution of ½ teaspoon enzyme presoak and ½ cup warm water—do not use on silk or wool. Cover stain with an absorbent pad dampened with the solution and let it stand for 30 minutes. Add enough solution to keep the area warm and barely moist. Flush with clear water and dry thoroughly.

Acrylic Fabric	Nylon
Cotton	Olefin
Linen	Polyester
Modacrylic	Spandex

Quickly scrape to remove solids. Soak the stain in a solution of 1 quart warm water, ½ teaspoon liquid detergent, and 1 tablespoon ammonia. Tamp or scrape to help loosen the stain. Blot occasionally with an absorbent pad. Rinse well with water, making sure to remove all trace of ammonia. If stain persists, soak in a solution of 1 quart warm water and 1 tablespoon enzyme presoak for 30 minutes. Rinse well and launder as soon as possible.

Acrylic Plastic	Jade
Aluminum	Linoleum
Asphalt	Paint/Flat
Brass	Paint/Gloss
Bronze	Pewter
Ceramic Glass/Tile	Plexiglas
Chromium	Polyurethane
Copper	Porcelain
Cork	Stainless Steel
Enamel	Tin
Glass	Vinyl Clothing
Gold	Vinyl Tile
Iron	Vinyl Wallcovering
Ivory	

Scrape or wipe up solids, then wash the area with a cloth dipped in warm, sudsy water. Rinse thoroughly and wipe dry with a soft cloth.

Alabaster	Marble

Wipe up the solids, then wipe the stain with a cloth or sponge dipped in cool water. If stain remains, mix a thick paste of water, powdered detergent, and bleach. Apply it to the stain and cover with a damp cloth to retard evaporation. When the stain is bleached out, rinse thoroughly with clear water and wipe dry.

Vomit *(continued)*

Bamboo	Cane

Scrape or wipe up solids, then wash stain with a cloth or soft-bristled brush dipped in warm, soapy water to which a few drops of ammonia have been added. Rinse with clear water and wipe dry.

Bluestone	Limestone
Brick	Masonry Tile
Concrete	Sandstone
Flagstone	Slate
Granite	Terrazzo

Scrape or wipe up solids. Then wash the stained area with a cloth dipped in a solution of washing soda or detergent (not soap) and water. Rinse well with clear water and allow to dry.

Carpet/Synthetic	Carpet/Wool

Scrape up solids, being careful not to force the stain deeper into the pile. Then apply carpet stain remover. Or sponge the area with a solution of 1 teaspoon mild, nonalkali detergent and ½ pint lukewarm water. Blot the liquid with an absorbent pad. Continue sponging and blotting until no more stain is removed. Sponge the area with a solution of 1 tablespoon ammonia and 1 cup warm water. (Do not use ammonia on wool carpets.) Blot excess liquid. Continue until no more stain is being removed. Place an absorbent pad over the damp area and weight it down with a heavy object. When no more liquid is absorbed, remove the pad and allow carpet to air-dry thoroughly.

Fur/Natural	Fur/Synthetic

Carefully wipe up solids. Wipe the stain with a cloth dipped in the suds of mild detergent and water to which a few drops of ammonia have been added. Rinse with a cloth dampened with clear water. Rub with the nap of the fur; take care not to soak or overwet the pelt or backing. Dry away from heat.

Grout

After removing solids, wipe the stain with a cloth dipped in cool water. If any stain remains, apply tile-and-grout cleaner or dip a wet toothbrush in baking soda or powdered cleanser and gently scrub the spot. Rinse thoroughly with water and wipe dry.

Vomit *(continued)*

Leather   Suede

Gently scrape to remove solids. Mix a solution of mild soap and lukewarm water. Swish to create a great volume of suds. Apply only the foam with a sponge. Rinse well with a clean, damp cloth and wipe dry. If suede needs a conditioner, apply suede cleaner. For leather, condition with saddle soap.

Wallpaper

Gently scrape up solids. Wipe the stain with a cloth moistened with cool, clear water. Overlap strokes to prevent streaking. Use a clean cloth to pat dry.

Wood

Wipe up solids. Wipe the stain with a cloth dipped in cool, clear water. Wipe dry with a soft cloth and polish or wax the wood as usual.

WATER SPOTS

Acetate	Nylon
Acrylic Fabric	Olefin
Carpet/Synthetic	Polyester
Carpet/Wool	Rayon
Cotton	Silk
Fiberglass	Spandex
Linen	Triacetate
Modacrylic	Wool

Water spots on fabrics are the result of water dislodging sizing or other finishing agents and causing them to form rings on the material. To remove water spots, dampen the entire area with water and allow to dry. Spots may also be removed by holding the area in the steam from a boiling kettle. If the garment can be ironed, press while still damp.

Acrylic Plastic	Paint/Gloss
Aluminum	Plexiglas
Asphalt	Polyurethane
Ceramic Glass/Tile	Porcelain Dishes
Chromium	Porcelain Fixtures
Copper	Stainless Steel
Cork	Tin
Glass	Vinyl Clothing

(continued)

Water Spots *(continued)*

Linoleum	**Vinyl Tile**
Paint/Flat	**Vinyl Wallcovering**

Wipe the stain with a cloth or sponge dipped in warm, sudsy water to which a few drops of white vinegar have been added. Rinse well and wipe dry.

Alabaster	**Limestone**
Bluestone	**Marble**
Brick	**Masonry Tile**
Concrete	**Sandstone**
Flagstone	**Slate**
Granite	**Terrazzo**

Wash the stain with a solution of washing soda or detergent (not soap) and water. Use a cloth or soft-bristled brush to scrub the stain. Rinse thoroughly with water and allow to dry.

Leather	**Suede**

Test denatured alcohol in an inconspicuous area. If it does not harm the material, rub the stain with a cloth dampened with a few drops of alcohol. On leather, condition with saddle soap. To condition suede, apply suede cleaner.

Silver

Note: Water spots can tarnish silver. Wash as soon as possible in hot, soapy water. Rinse in hot, clear water and dry immediately with a soft cloth.

Wood

Rub the stain with petroleum jelly or boiled linseed oil. Repeat application until stain vanishes. Use a chamois to finish polishing the surface.

WINE/RED, ROSÉ

Acetate	**Rayon**
Fiberglass	**Triacetate**

Blot up the spill with a clean cloth. Spray on fabric spot cleaner. Sponge any remaining stain with water and apply wet spotter and a few drops of

Wine/Red, Rosé *(continued)*

white vinegar. Cover with an absorbent pad moistened with wet spotter. Continue this treatment as long as any stain is being removed. Change the pad as it picks up the stain. Keep the stain and pad moist with wet spotter and vinegar. Flush with clear water. Repeat until no more stain is removed. If the stain remains, moisten it with a solution of 1 teaspoon enzyme presoak and 1 cup warm water. Cover with a clean pad that has been dipped in this solution and wrung nearly dry. Let it stand for 30 minutes. Add enough solution to keep the stain warm and barely moist. When no more stain is removed, flush with water and dry.

Acrylic Fabric	**Olefin**
Modacrylic	**Polyester**
Nylon	**Spandex**

Note: Be sure to remove the sugar residue or it will cause a permanent stain. Blot up the spilled wine and soak the stain in a solution of 1 quart warm water, ½ teaspoon liquid detergent, and 1 tablespoon vinegar for 15 minutes. Rinse with clear water and sponge with rubbing alcohol. Launder as soon as possible. If the stain remains, soak it in a solution of 1 quart warm water and 1 tablespoon enzyme presoak for 30 minutes. Rinse well with water and allow to dry. Launder as soon as possible.

Acrylic Plastic	**Ivory**
Aluminum	**Jade**
Asphalt	**Linoleum**
Bamboo	**Paint/Flat**
Brass	**Paint/Gloss**
Bronze	**Pewter**
Cane	**Plexiglas**
Ceramic Glass/Tile	**Polyurethane**
Copper	**Stainless Steel**
Cork	**Tin**
Enamel	**Vinyl Clothing**
Glass	**Vinyl Tile**
Gold	**Vinyl Wallcovering**
Grout	**Zinc**
Iron	

Blot up the spill. Wipe the surface with a cloth or sponge dipped in warm, sudsy water. Rinse well and wipe dry.

Alabaster	**Marble**	*(continued)*

Wine/Red, Rosé *(continued)*

Blot up spilled wine. Wipe the surface with a cloth dipped in a solution of washing soda or detergent (not soap) and water. Rinse well and wipe dry. If any stain remains, mix a few drops of ammonia with 1 cup 3-percent hydrogen peroxide. Soak a white blotter with this solution and place it over the stain. Weight it down with a heavy object. Continue applying the solution until the stain is bleached out. Rinse well and wipe dry.

Bluestone	**Limestone**
Brick	**Masonry Tile**
Concrete	**Slate**
Flagstone	**Terrazzo**
Granite	

Mix a solution of washing soda or detergent and warm water. Gently brush away stain with cloth or soft-bristled brush dipped in the solution. Rinse with clear water and allow to dry.

Burlap	**Wool**
Silk	

Note: Be sure to remove the sugar residue or it will cause a permanent stain. Blot up excess wine. Spray on fabric spot cleaner or sponge the stain with clear water and apply wet spotter and a few drops of white vinegar. Cover with an absorbent pad dampened with wet spotter. Continue this treatment as long as any stain is being removed. Change the pad as it picks up the stain. Keep the pad and stain moist with wet spotter and vinegar. Flush with water and repeat until no more stain is being lifted. If any stain remains, sponge with rubbing alcohol and cover with an absorbent pad dampened with alcohol. Continue this process as long as any stain is being lifted. Change the pad as it picks up the stain and keep both the stain and pad moist with alcohol. Flush thoroughly with clear water. For stubborn or old stains, try moistening the area with a solution of 1 teaspoon gentle liquid detergent and 1 cup warm water. Cover with an absorbent pad dipped in this solution and wrung nearly dry. Let it stand for 30 minutes, adding enough solution to keep the area warm and moist. When the stain is removed, flush thoroughly with water and allow to dry.

Carpet/Synthetic	**Foam Rubber**
Carpet/Wool	

Note: Be sure to remove the sugar residue or it will cause a permanent stain. Blot up as much spilled wine as you can with an absorbent pad, then apply carpet stain remover. Or flush the stain on an area rug or sponge

Wine/Red, Rosé *(continued)*

carpeting with a solution of 1 quart warm water, ½ teaspoon liquid detergent, and 1 tablespoon white vinegar. Blot with a clean pad and rinse well with clear water. If any stain remains, sponge it with a solution of 1 quart warm water and 1 tablespoon enzyme presoak. Blot and flush alternately until no more stain is removed. Rinse with clear water and blot up the excess liquid with an absorbent pad. Weight down another pad with a heavy object. When no more liquid is absorbed, allow to air-dry thoroughly.

Cotton   **Linen**

Blot up the spill, then pretreat and launder. If that is not possible, soak the stain in a solution of 1 quart warm water and ½ teaspoon liquid detergent and let stand for 15 minutes. Rinse well with clear water and sponge area with rubbing alcohol. Rinse again with water and allow to dry. If the stain persists, soak in a solution of warm water and enzyme presoak according to package directions. Rinse with water and launder as soon as possible.

Felt   **Fur/Synthetic**
Fur/Natural

Blot up the spill. Mix dishwashing detergent in hot water and swish to make a great volume of suds. Dip a cloth in only the foam and apply. Rinse with a cloth dampened with clear water. Allow to dry thoroughly.

Leather   **Suede**

Blot up excess wine. Mix a solution of mild soap and lukewarm water. Swish to create a great volume of suds. Apply only the foam with a sponge. Rinse well with a clean, damp cloth and wipe dry. If suede needs a conditioner, apply a suede cleaner. For leather, condition with saddle soap.

Porcelain Dishes   **Porcelain Fixtures**

Wash the stain with a cloth dipped in warm, sudsy water. Rinse well and wipe dry with a soft cloth. To remove old or set stains in the bottom of a dish, dip a soft, damp cloth in baking soda and wipe away the residue. Rinse well and dry.

Silver

Wash silver in hot, soapy water. Rinse in hot, clear water and dry with a soft cloth.

Wine/Red, Rosé *(continued)*

Wood

Mix dishwashing detergent in hot water and swish to make a great volume of suds. Dip a cloth in only the foam and apply to the stain. Rinse well with a clean cloth dampened with cool water. Polish or wax as soon as possible.

WINE/WHITE

(Follow procedures for Alcoholic Beverages.)

YELLOWING

Acetate	**Silk**
Fiberglass	**Triacetate**
Rayon	**Wool**

Flush the spot with water. Test a mild solution of 3-percent hydrogen peroxide and water in an inconspicuous area—if it does not harm the fabric, apply to the stain. Do not allow the solution to remain on the fabric; flush with water immediately. If any stain remains, it is best not to attempt further cleaning at home.

Acrylic Fabric	**Olefin**
Modacrylic	**Polyester**
Nylon	

Apply lemon juice to the stain, but do not let it dry. Rinse thoroughly with clear water. If possible, launder. If you can't launder, test rust-stain remover on the fabric. If it does not harm the fabric, apply according to package directions. Then flush the area with cool water and launder as soon as possible. Be careful not to spill any rust remover on porcelain or enamel because it will ruin the finish.

Cotton	**Linen**

Rub detergent into the stain and rinse well with water. Launder as soon as possible. If the stain remains, test rust remover in an inconspicuous place. If it does not damage the fabric, apply according to package directions. Flush thoroughly with clear water and launder.

HINTS FOR YOUR HOME

M ost of us want to get through our cleaning as quickly as possible, so we can get back to doing all the other things we need and want to do. But there are some things that have to be done around our homes that we like to slow down and enjoy doing. We want to do these little extras because they'll improve the quality of our lives. Caring for a home may not be much fun, but it does not have to be total drudgery.

In this chapter of *How to Beat Housework*, you'll find a collection of helpful hints from people who have figured out better ways to do things around their homes. When you read some of these terrific tips, you'll probably say to yourself that that's the way you've always done it. When you read others, you may find yourself asking why you never thought of that.

We've told you about the fastest and best ways to clean everything in your home. In "Hints for Your Home," we'll give you some good ideas about decorating, from finding a bargain on furniture to wallpapering your bathroom. There are hints about hanging pictures, getting your kids to hang up their coats, and not getting hung up when you panel a room. You'll find out how to make better use of your home workshop and discover hundreds of ways to make your home a better place to come home to.

Home Furnishing and Decorating

GENERAL PAINTING TIPS

According to manufacturers' calculations, a gallon of paint will cover about 450 square feet. For estimating purposes, figure 400 square feet of coverage per gallon of paint. Never try to stretch paint.

To determine the amount of paint required to cover a wall, multiply the height of the wall by its length and divide by 400. By this reckoning, a gallon of paint will cover a 10-by-15-foot room with one coat. Two coats will take two gallons.

When painting a ceiling with a roller, it's not necessary to try to keep the roller strokes all the same length. The lines won't show when the paint dries.

If you use masking tape around windows while painting the woodwork, remove the masking tape immediately after painting. Otherwise, it may pull off some of the paint.

If you want to paint a window frame and have no masking tape, use strips of dampened newspaper. They will stick to the glass. Peel off the paper when you finish each frame.

To get paint drips off hard-surface flooring, wrap a cloth around a putty knife and gently scrape up the paint. Then wash the areas with warm, soapy water. Don't use solvent; it can damage the finish on the floor.

You can easily make your own stencils by cutting designs out of thin cardboard.

Decorative stencils can be expensive to buy. Make your own out of thin cardboard. Sketch a design, transfer it to tracing paper, and cut it out. Then lay this pattern on a piece of cardboard, trace around it, and cut out the design.

If you're interrupted in the middle of a painting job, wrap aluminum foil or plastic wrap around your brushes and rollers. The wrapping should be loose enough to avoid mashing the bristles on brushes or the pile on rollers but tight enough to keep the air out. Leave the wrapped brushes on a flat surface or hang them up. Put the packet in the freezer to save the brush for a longer period of time.

Prevent drips when painting a drawer front by removing the drawer and painting it face up.

To avoid smearing while painting cabinets, paint the insides of the cabinets first. Then paint the tops, bottoms, and sides of doors before painting the door fronts. If you proceed in this sequence, you won't have to reach over already-painted areas.

Protect doorknobs when painting a door by wrapping the knobs with aluminum foil or by slipping plastic sandwich bags over them.

When painting stairs, paint alternate steps so that you'll have a way out. When those steps dry, paint the others. Or paint one side of each step at a time. Use the other side for foot traffic until the painted side dries, then reverse the process.

If your light-switch plate was painted over along with the wall and you now need to remove it, avoid flaking or chipping any paint by cutting carefully around the switch plate with a single-edge razor blade. Remove the screws and lift off the plate.

Don't wipe your paintbrush against the lip of the paint can. The lip will soon fill up with paint that will run down the side and drip off. Use a coffee can to hold the paint instead.

A paper plate glued to the bottom of a paint can keeps drips off the floor.

Glue paper plates to the bottoms of paint cans to serve as drip catchers. The plates move along with the cans and are more convenient than newspapers.

If you don't want to—or can't—remove hardware when painting adjacent areas, coat the hardware with petroleum jelly before painting. You'll be able to wipe off any paint that accidentally gets on the metal.

If the smell of fresh paint bothers you, you can eliminate it from a room in one day with a dish of ammonia, vinegar, or onion slices in water left out in the room.

To cut the smell when you're decorating with oil-based paint, stir a spoonful of vanilla extract into each can of paint.

If you want to be able to use a previous coat of exterior paint as a base for a new coat, the old paint should be no more than five years old. If you wait longer than that you'll have a major job of scraping, sanding, and spackling.

Wrinkling occurs when too much paint is applied or when the paint is too thick. You can correct wrinkling easily by sanding the surface and brushing on paint of a thinner consistency.

Artificial light darkens color, so paint will look lighter in the daylight. If you're in doubt about a color at the paint store, take the container outside to examine the color.

Color can saturate your eyes. When mixing paint, look away at a white surface for several minutes to allow your eyes to adjust so that you can judge the color accurately.

To get the correct feel for spray painting and to determine the correct spray distance from the object to be painted, first experiment with a sheet of cardboard as the target area.

Record how much paint is required to cover each room by writing the amount on the back of the light-switch plate. When you remove the switch plate before repainting, you'll be reminded of how much paint you need.

To avoid painting a window shut, gently slide the sash up and down as the paint hardens but before it forms a seal.

If you are working on a ladder in front of a closed door, lock the door so that no one can inadvertently swing the door open and send you sprawling.

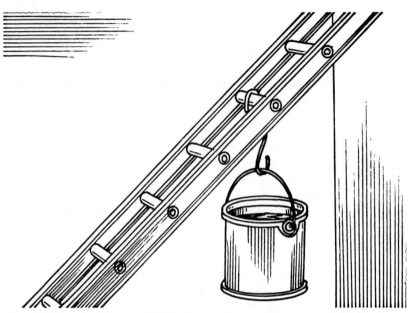

A coat hanger bent into an "S" hook attaches a paint can to a ladder and frees your hands while you paint.

Make a paint holder from a coat hanger to keep your hands free when painting. Open the hanger and bend it in half; then bend it into an "S" to hook over the ladder and hold your paint can.

When tiny spots need a paint touch-up, use a cotton swab instead of a brush. You won't waste paint, and you won't have to clean a brush.

Before using a new paintbrush to apply oil-based paint, soak it for a day in a can of linseed oil. The brush will last longer and be easier to clean.

CLEANUP AND STORAGE
To avoid having to clean a paint tray, press a sheet of aluminum foil into it before use. When you're finished painting, simply wrap up the foil and dispose of it.

Why buy new paint thinner when you can reuse the old? Here's how: Pour paint thinner into an empty coffee can. After you've cleaned your brushes, cover the can tightly and let it stand for several days. When paint from the brushes has settled to the bottom as sediment, drain off the clean thinner into another can and store for reuse.

To clean a paintbrush without making a mess of your hands, pour solvent into a strong, clear plastic bag, and insert the brush. Your hands will stay clean as you work the solvent into the bristles through the plastic.

To clean a paint roller after use, roll it as dry as possible, first on the newly painted surface and then on several sheets of newspaper. Then slide the roller from its support and clean it with water or a solvent, depending on the type of paint used.

Before capping leftover paint for storage, mark the label at the level of the remaining paint so you'll know without opening the can how much is left inside. Label the can with the room the paint was used for, so there's no question which paint to reorder or use for touch-ups.

For easy cleanup of your paint tray, line the tray with a plastic bag before pouring in your paint. After the job's done, you can discard the bag without having to clean the tray.

If you store a partially used can of paint upside down, skin won't form on the surface of the paint. (Be sure lid is tight.)

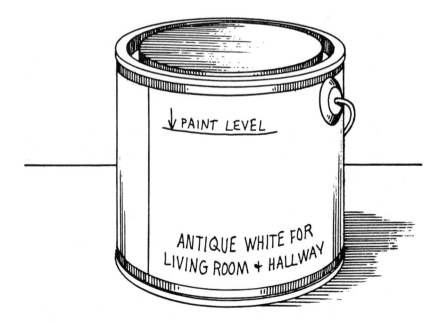

Label paint cans before you store them so you'll know how much paint is left in the can and what room the paint matches.

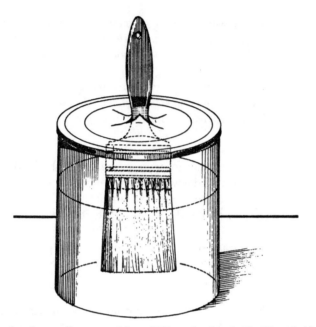

Soak brushes in a coffee can with an "X" cut in the plastic lid to hold the brush handle.

Leftover paint that is lumpy or contains shreds of paint skin can be strained through window screening.

To keep a brush as soft as new, clean it and then rinse it in a solution of fabric softener and water.

An empty coffee can with a plastic lid makes a perfect container for soaking brushes. Just make two slits in the center of the plastic lid to form an "X," push the brush handle up through the "X," and replace the lid. The lid seals the can so the solvent can't evaporate, and the brush is suspended without the bristles resting on the bottom.

White paint won't yellow if you stir in a drop of black paint.

You can remove paint spatters from your hair by rubbing the spots with baby oil.

The best brush that money can buy may not last beyond the first job if it is neglected. A brush will give years of service if it is treated properly.

If you are cleaning brushes or rollers that have been used in oil-based paint, varnish, shellac, or lacquer, work in a well-ventilated area away from open flames.

Before cleaning a brush, rid it of excess paint by tapping it against the inside rim of the can and then vigorously stroking the brush back and forth on a thick pad of folded newspapers until very little paint comes off.

Clean brushes and rollers used for shellac in denatured alcohol, then wash in a detergent solution.

Clean brushes or rollers used for lacquer in lacquer thinner or acetone and then wash in a detergent solution.

Clean brushes or rollers used for oil-based paints and varnishes in turpentine or paint thinner and then wash in a detergent solution.

Clean brushes and rollers used for latex paints in water and then wash in a detergent solution. Do not allow brushes to soak in water; this can loosen the bristles.

Rinse all brushes well after washing and shake vigorously to remove excess water. Comb the bristles with a wire brush to straighten them. Then allow the brush to dry completely before storing it flat or hanging from a rack.

WALLS AND WALL COVERINGS

You get about 30 square feet of coverage from a roll of wallpaper (whatever its width). To calculate how many rolls you need for a room, find the perimeter of the room by measuring the length of each wall and adding the measurements together. Then measure the height. Multiply the first figure by the second and then divide by 30. The result will be the number of rolls you need.

Foil wall coverings, because of their reflective surface, tend to emphasize the smallest bumps or imperfections in the wall surface. To minimize irregularities, use a lining paper under these wall coverings.

Foil wall coverings are easily damaged, so instead of using a regular smoothing brush on them, smooth them in place with a sponge or folded towel. Bond the seams in the same way—a seam roller may dent the foil.

If you're planning to paper all the walls in a room, choose the least conspicuous area as your starting and finishing point. It's almost inevitable that the pattern won't match perfectly.

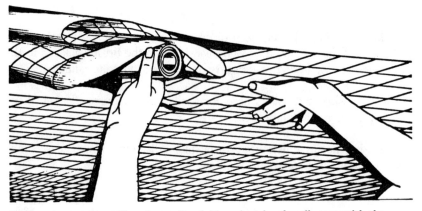

When you paper a ceiling, accordion-fold each strip of wallpaper with the pasted sides together.

Save time when applying wallpaper paste by using a short-napped paint roller.

To make wallpaper hanging easier, a right-handed person should work from left to right and a left-handed person from right to left.

Slightly tint wallpaper paste with food coloring so that you can see exactly where you've applied it.

If there are stubborn grease spots on walls that you're going to paper, seal them with clear nail polish or shellac so that the grease won't soak through the new wallpaper.

However carefully you put up wallpaper, you may still find blisters. Fortunately, they are easy to fix. All you need do is slit the blister twice with a razor blade to form an "X," then peel back the tips of the slit, brush paste into the blister, and smooth the paper down.

Wallpaper a ceiling with the strips positioned crosswise—they're shorter and more manageable. Accordion-fold each strip, pasted area against pasted area, and unfold it as you go along, supporting the paper with one hand and smoothing it onto the ceiling with the other.

When folding wallpaper accordion-style before hanging, the pasted side should not touch the patterned side at any point, and the paper should never be allowed to crease.

After wallpapering a room where there will be a lot of moisture—such as a kitchen or bathroom—cover all seams with clear varnish to help guard against peeling.

When papering over wall anchors or places where you plan to reposition shelves or pictures, insert toothpicks in holes left by screws or picture hooks. As you cover these sections, force the toothpick points through the paper to mark reinstallation points for screws or hooks.

Save time when hanging wallpaper by smoothing it with a clean, dry paint roller. If you attach the roller to a long handle, you can reach the ceiling or the tops of walls without climbing a ladder.

If you don't have a seam roller, rub the wallpaper seam with the back of a spoon.

White glue can substitute for wallpaper paste if you run out of paste before the job is finished.

Use a squeegee to eliminate bubbles and wrinkles in vinyl wall coverings.

To eliminate a bubble in freshly hung wallpaper—while the paste is still wet—puncture it with a sharp needle or pin. Press the blister inward from its edges toward the puncture, squeezing out excess paste. Wipe off this excess with a damp sponge, and then press the area flat with a seam roller or the back of a spoon.

When preparing to remove old wallpaper, soak it first with very hot water applied with a paint roller; add a touch of detergent to the water to hasten the process. If you are removing a foil- or vinyl-coated wall covering, score its surface so water can penetrate.

When removing old wallpaper with a steamer, save the ceiling for last. As you work on the walls, steam rising from the applicator will loosen the ceiling paper. Much of it will start sagging from its own weight, and peeling it off will be easy.

Repairing Wallpaper
Save a large piece of wallpaper for patching. Let it weather and fade at the same rate as the paper on the wall by taping the piece on a closet wall. If you do this, it will correspond in color density as well as pattern to the paper already on the wall.

If you don't have wallpaper scraps for patching, try touching up the design in worn areas. Carefully use felt-tip pens to restore colors.

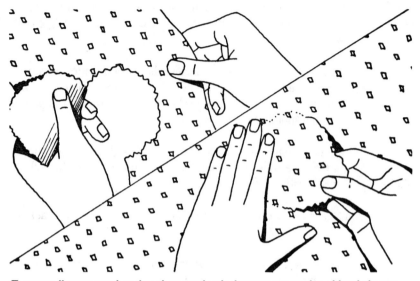

Tear a wallpaper patch rather than cutting it, because torn edges blend almost invisibly.

To repair a damaged section of wallpaper, tear—don't cut—a patch from a piece that's been weathered. Because less-defined torn edges blend imperceptibly with paper already on the wall, the patch will be virtually invisible. **Note:** Don't remove damaged wallpaper before placing a patch on it. Paste the patch directly over the damaged surface.

Other Wall Coverings
If you're stapling fabric to a wall and you want to mask the staples at the top and bottom, glue a band of fabric or a wide, contrasting ribbon over the staples. You also can cover the staples with molding strips.

When paneling a room, let the panels acclimate to the room's humidity for 48 hours before positioning them. This helps prevent them from being installed too tightly or too loosely.

When applying wood paneling to a wall, you can attach panels directly to the studs. However, panels attached this way tend to give a little and are not as soundproof as those installed over either plywood or drywall.

When you're installing wood panels, first lean them against the walls where you want to hang them. This gives you a chance to arrange the panels' wood graining in the manner that pleases you most. When they're positioned the way you want them, number the panels for reference and proceed with the project.

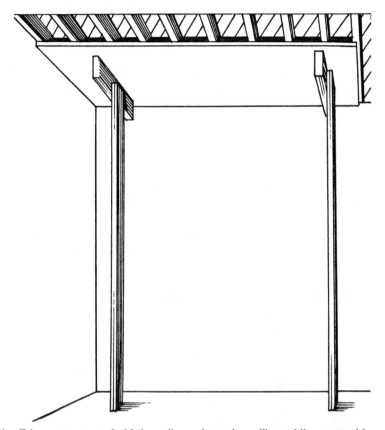

Use T-bar supports to hold drywall panels to the ceiling while you position and secure them.

To save your arm muscles while installing drywall on a ceiling, construct two "deadman" supports. Cut two-by-fours of the proper floor-to-ceiling length and nail T-bars at their tops. The supports effortlessly hold up the panels while you do the final positioning and securing.

Instead of carrying large wallboard sheets into the house and possibly damaging them when navigating awkward corners, measure and cut them to fit before bringing them inside.

When using a handsaw or a table saw to cut a wood panel, cut the panel with the face up. When using a hand-held power saw with a reciprocating blade, cut the panel with the face down.

To discourage nails from popping out of drywall, drive them in pairs, spaced two inches apart. Each nail strengthens the holding power of the other. If you're driving nails into a stud where the edges of two drywall panels butt up against each other, stagger the double nailing on each side of the seam.

To help absorb noise, install acoustical tiles on the doors to playrooms. You could also reduce noise in your home by using acoustical tile to line the room or closet that houses the central-heating and air-conditioning unit.

Wall Repairs

A saucepan lid makes a good container for joint compound, since the knob of the lid lets you hold the bowl easily during application. (When you've finished, rinse out the lid before any residue hardens.)

To prevent a toggle bolt from slipping into the wall cavity, insert a washer under the head of the bolt. (The hole needed for the toggle bolt is larger than the head of the bolt.)

To hold a heavy screw in a masonry wall, taper a dowel and drive it into a hole in the wall. Then drive the screw into the dowel.

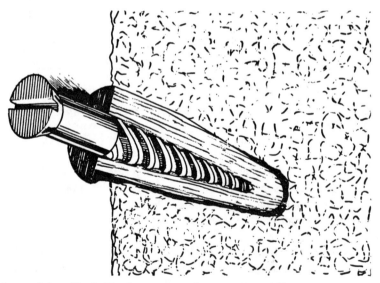

Use a tapered dowel to hold a heavy screw in a masonry wall.

If a screw hole in a wall has become too large to hold the screw, stuff the hole with a cotton ball soaked in white glue. Let it dry for 24 hours. You'll then be able to insert the screw securely using a screwdriver.

A beer-can opener makes a good tool for cutting loose plaster out of a wall before patching a large crack. Use the pointed end of the opener to undercut and widen the opening.

It will be easier to fill a large hole in the wall if you first jam a piece of drywall into the hole, and then mar the surface of the drywall so that it is rough. The spackle will adhere tightly to the wallboard piece and won't sink in and require further applications.

To patch a small hole in drywall you can use a tin-can lid covered by a plaster patch. Thread a wire in and back out through two holes in the lid of the can and then slide the lid behind the wall through horizontal slits cut out from each side of the hole. Pull the lid flat on the inside, and hold it in place while you apply plaster.

A can lid can be used to support a plaster patch in drywall.

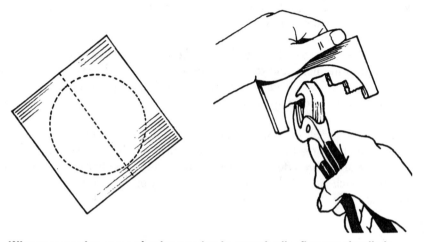

When you need to cut a circular opening in ceramic tile, first cut the tile in half and then cut out semicircles with nippers.

Adding a tablespoon of white vinegar to the water when you mix patching plaster will keep the compound from settling too quickly, allowing you more time to work.

You'll be able to remove a damaged ceramic tile easily if you first drill a hole through its center and score an "X" across it with a glass cutter. Then chisel out the pieces.

To fit a ceramic tile around the stem of a shower pipe, cut the tile in half and then cut semicircles out of each half with tile nippers.

When replacing an individual ceramic wall tile, it helps to tape it securely to surrounding tiles until the adhesive sets.

PICTURES AND MIRRORS

If a picture won't hang straight, wrap masking tape around the wire on both sides of the hook so that the wire can't slip. Or install parallel nails or hooks a short distance apart; two hooks are better than one for keeping pictures in their places.

Squares of double-faced tape affixed to the two lower-back corners of the frame will keep a picture from moving. If you don't have double-faced tape, make two loops with masking tape, sticky side out. Apply to each of the lower-back corners and press the picture against the wall.

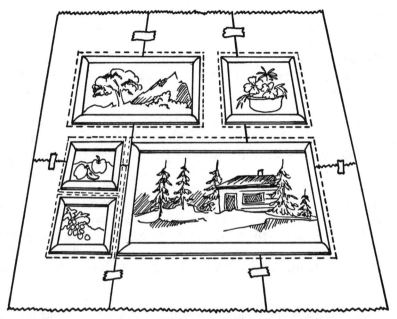

When you want to hang several pictures together, arrange them on paper, mark the locations of the hooks, and use the paper as a guide when you drive the hooks in the wall.

Take the guesswork out of arranging several pictures on a wall. Spread a large sheet of wrapping paper or several taped-together sheets of newspaper on the floor and experiment with frame positions. When you decide on a pleasing grouping, outline the frames on the paper, tape the paper to the wall, and drive hooks through the paper into the wall. Then remove the paper and hang the pictures.

Picture hanging can be frustrating if you simply try to eyeball the right spot to put the hook. Instead, place a picture exactly where you want it the first time with the following method. Cut a sheet of paper to the exact size of the frame. Position the pattern on the back of the picture, pull up taut the wire the picture will hang from, and mark the inverted "V" point on the pattern. Adjust the pattern on the wall, and then poke through it to mark the "V" point on the wall. If you nail the hook there, the picture will hang precisely where you wanted it.

If the picture isn't too heavy, another timesaving method is to hold the picture itself by its wire and decide where you want it positioned. Wet a fingertip and press it on the wall to mark the wire's inverted "V" point. The fingerprint mark will stay wet long enough for you to drive a nail or hook on target.

Don't lose a perfect picture grouping when you repaint a room—insert toothpicks in the hook holes and paint right over them; when the paint dries, remove the toothpicks and rehang your pictures.

To prevent a plaster wall from crumbling when driving in a nail or hook, first form an "X" over the nail spot with two strips of masking tape or transparent tape.

If you're hanging a picture from a molding but don't like the look of exposed picture wire, substitute nylon fishing line. The transparent nylon does a disappearing act that allows your picture to star on its own.

Hang heavy objects by driving nails directly into the wood studs behind walls. There are several ways to locate studs. You can tap a wall gently with your knuckles or a hammer. A wall sounds hollow between studs, solid on top of them. Or move an electric razor (turned on) along a wall; a razor registers a different tone over studs. If nails were used to attach drywall to studs, a magnet will indicate the location of the nails and, therefore, the studs.

When hanging a mirror with screws that go through mounting holes in the glass, don't tighten the screws all the way. Leave enough play to prevent the mirror from cracking if the wall shifts.

Hang mirrors to reflect you but not the sun; some mirror backings are adversely affected by direct sunlight.

Sometimes a picture that has been hanging for a while will leave a dark outline on the wall because dust and dirt have collected against the frame. To prevent this buildup, allow better air circulation by holding pictures slightly away from the wall with thumbtacks pressed firmly into the backs of their frames. You can get the same result by fixing small tabs of self-sticking foam weather stripping to the picture backing.

REFINISHING FURNITURE

If you'd like to know how unfinished furniture would look if it were varnished, try the "wet test." Dampen a cloth with turpentine and wipe it over the surface; the moisture will bring out the grain, showing the contrasts and giving the wood the appearance it would have if varnished.

When refinishing, a flat rubber kitchen spatula can be a useful scraper for removing paint from curved or rounded surfaces, especially since it can be used even on delicate carvings. For greater versatility, buy both wide and narrow sizes.

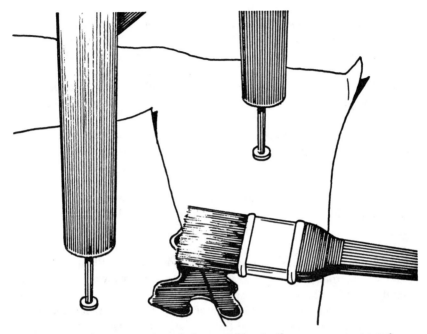

When you finish furniture, keep it from sticking to the newspaper you put down to protect your floor by driving nails into the legs.

Use newspaper to protect your floor or workbench when you're refinishing a piece of furniture, but keep the legs of the piece from sticking to the paper by driving a nail no deeper than ¼ inch into the bottom of each leg.

To sand a furniture spindle or rung without flattening it, hold a sandpaper strip behind the part, one end in each hand, and saw the ends back and forth to smooth the wood.

To smooth wood evenly and thoroughly in the refinishing process, work with successively finer sandpaper grades. Between sandings, brush off or vacuum the sanding debris; then wipe the wood clean with a tack cloth.

Many small items are useful for cleaning furniture crevices and cracks when you're refinishing. Enlist the aid of a nut pick, a plastic playing card, a plastic credit card, the broken end of an ice-cream stick, the tine of an old fork, an orange stick, wooden toothpicks, or an old spoon.

If you need an unusually shaped smoothing tool for use on wet spackling compound or wood fillers, try whittling an ice-cream stick to the required contour.

Sanding concave curves will be easier if you hold the sandpaper around a dowel the same diameter as the curve. Or slit a length of rubber garden hose and wrap the paper around it, with the ends held in the slit.

Use a heavy string to strip the narrow turnings of a spindle furniture leg. Gently move the string back and forth to remove the softened finish.

To avoid gouging wood when using a putty knife to strip furniture, round the putty knife's sharp corners with a metal file or sandpaper. If you're working on large flat surfaces, dull a paint scraper the same way.

To obtain a smooth and evenly finished surface on open-grained wood, treat it with filler after staining. First apply filler in the direction of the grain; then work across the grain to fill all pores completely.

If large knots in unfinished furniture are loose, remove them, apply carpenter's glue around their edges, and replace them flush with the surface. If small knots (pin knots) are loose, remove and discard them and plug the resulting holes with plastic wood or water putty. Since both glue and putty seal the wood, you'll have to sand the patches before staining the piece of furniture.

For a professional patching job on a finished piece of furniture, use shellac sticks to fill cracks and gouges, since they leave the least conspicuous patch.

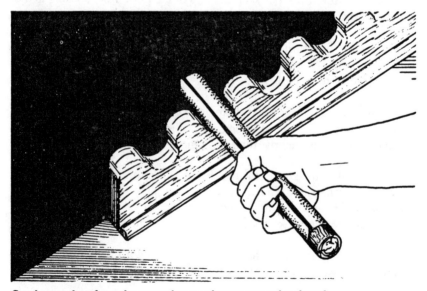

Sand curved surfaces by wrapping sandpaper around a dowel.

It will be easier to apply paint or varnish remover to a piece of furniture if all hardware has been removed. If you label the hardware, it will also be easier to reassemble it correctly.

To slow evaporation after applying a coat of paint remover and to give it more time to work, cover the surface with aluminum foil. Keep in mind that in any case paint remover stops working after about 40 minutes.

You can make a template to patch damaged veneer this way: Lay a sheet of bond paper over the damaged area and rub a soft lead pencil gently over the paper. The edges of the damaged area will be precisely indicated on the paper so you can cut a pattern.

If hardware is spotted with paint or finish, drop it into a pan filled with paint remover. Let it soak while you work on the wood, then wipe it clean.

Small blisters on a veneered surface can sometimes be flattened with heat. Here's how: Lay a sheet of smooth cardboard over the blistered area and press firmly with a medium-hot iron, moving the iron slowly and evenly until the blisters soften and flatten. Leave the cardboard in place and weight down the area for 24 hours.

For more durability, top an antiqued finish with a coat of semigloss or high-gloss varnish.

If you apply a protective shellac coating to cane chair seats, they'll last longer and be easier to clean.

Water-soluble paint and varnish removers should not be used on veneered or inlaid furniture pieces. Water is the enemy of wood and certain glues. The water used to remove the chemicals must be removed from any wood furniture as soon as possible to avoid raising the wood grain or dissolving the glue.

UPHOLSTERING FURNITURE

When you reupholster furniture, put fabric scraps in an envelope and staple the envelope to the underside of the newly covered piece. That way you'll have scraps for patching.

When using ornamental tacks for upholstery, push extras into the frame in an inconspicuous spot so you have replacements if needed.

Before covering kitchen chair seats with plastic, warm the plastic with a heating pad so it will be more pliable and easier to handle.

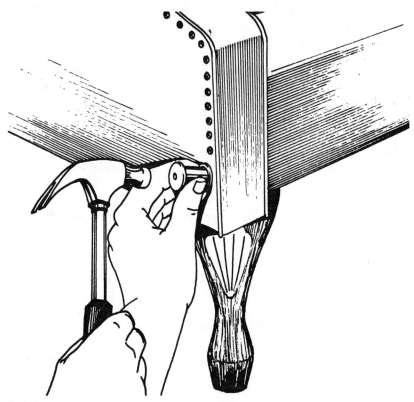

When you upholster furniture, protect the heads of decorative tacks with a wooden spool.

To hammer decorative furniture tacks without damaging their heads, place a wooden spool over each tack and pound on the spool.

When you're refinishing a piece of upholstered furniture and want to keep the upholstery, it's best to remove the fabric before you work on the finish—but only if you are sure you can put it back on again. If the piece is large, have a professional upholsterer remove and replace the fabric.

When examining a sample of upholstery fabric, fold the sample and rub the backs together to make sure that the backing is firmly bonded to the fabric.

You can test whether a fabric is likely to pill easily by rubbing it with a pencil eraser.

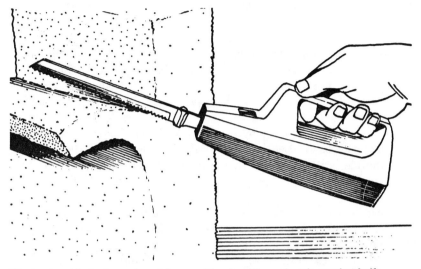

The best and fastest way to cut foam rubber is with an electric carving knife.

For speed and convenience, you can cut foam-rubber upholstery padding with an electric carving knife.

FLOORS AND FLOOR COVERINGS

If you have a squeaky wood floor under tile or carpet, you may be able to eliminate the squeak without removing the floor covering. Try to reset loose boards by pounding a hammer on a block of scrap wood in the area over the squeaky boards. The pressure may force loose nails back into place.

You may be able to silence a squeaky wood floor by using talcum powder as a dry lubricant. Sprinkle powder over the offending areas, and sweep it back and forth until it filters down between the cracks.

Try filling dents in a wood floor with clear nail polish or shellac. Because the floor's color will show through, the dents will not be apparent.

Sometimes you can flatten bulges or curled seams in a linoleum floor by placing aluminum foil over them and ironing them with your iron. (The heat will soften and reactivate the adhesive.) Position weights, such as stacks of books, over treated areas to keep them flat until the adhesive cools and hardens.

To remove a floor tile for replacement, lay a piece of aluminum foil on it and then press down with your iron set at medium. The heat of the iron will soften the tile's adhesive, and you can easily pry up the tile with a putty knife or scraper.

To remove a damaged floor tile, soften it with a propane torch fitted with a flame-spreader nozzle. (Be careful not to damage surrounding tiles.) When the tile is soft, pry it up with a putty knife and scrape the old adhesive off the subfloor so that the replacement tile will bond cleanly.

You can remove a floor tile by covering it with dry ice. Wear work gloves to protect your hands. Let the dry ice stand for ten minutes. The cold will make the tile brittle, so it will shatter easily. Chisel out the tile from the edges to the center.

Laying floor tile will be easier if the room temperature is at least 70 degrees Fahrenheit before you start, because tile is more pliable at higher temperatures. Put all boxes of tile in the room for at least 24 hours prior to positioning tiles on the floor. Try to keep the room temperature at the same level for about a week after laying the tiles, and then wait at least a week before washing the floor.

To prevent scratching the floor when moving heavy furniture across uncarpeted areas, slip scraps of carpeting, pile down, under the furniture legs.

After laying floor tiles, you can help them lie flat by going over them with a rolling pin.

If you want to replace a damaged area of sheet flooring, here's a way to make a perfect patch from scrap flooring: Place the scrap piece over the damaged area so that it overlaps sufficiently, and tape it in place. Then cut through both layers at the same time to make a patch that exactly fits the hole. Replace the damaged area with the tightly fitting patch.

DESIGN AND DECORATION

A room will appear larger if you paint an oversized piece of furniture the same color as the walls.

A small room can be made to look larger if you install mirrors on one wall to reflect the rest of the room.

If you want to make a large room seem cozier, choose a wallpaper with a large, bold pattern. However, don't choose a large pattern for a small room because it will make the available space seem crowded.

When selecting wallpaper for a particular room, keep in mind the dominant colors already present in that room. One or more of those colors should be present in the wallpaper to tie the color scheme together.

To make a high ceiling seem lower, paper it with a bold pattern. To make a low ceiling seem higher, paper it with a small print or a texture.

A wallpaper mural makes a small room appear larger.

There's no need to invest in wallpaper to give your walls new life. A super graphic painted on the wall can make a room exciting.

The texture of your furnishings can brighten or darken a room. Glossy surfaces like satin, glass, and tile reflect light and add brightness to a room; surfaces like brick, carpet, and burlap absorb light and make a room seem less bright.

In a room with a low ceiling, use vertical lines—high-backed chairs, straight draperies—to carry the eye upward and give an illusion of height. Horizontal lines—a long sofa or low bookcases—give a feeling of space and make high ceilings appear lower.

Small rooms will seem even smaller if filled with elaborate patterns or designs. Keep the furniture for a small room simple and the colors fairly restrained.

A darker color on the ceiling will make a room with a high ceiling seem more in proportion. So will low-placed, eye-catching objects such as a low coffee table, low-slung chairs, and plants on the floor.

In a long, narrow room, paint the end walls contrasting colors for a striking effect. Room dividers or furniture positioned in the middle of the room will give the effect of two rooms in one and lessen the feeling of length.

A favorite painting can be the inspiration for the color scheme of a room. Select one dominant color and several contrasting shades to create a pleasing combination.

You've fallen in love with an unusual wallpaper pattern but aren't sure whether you can actually live with it? Tape a sample to the wall of the room where you're thinking of using it and leave it there for a while. You may feel quite differently about it in a week or so.

If you can't afford professional help with your home decoration, consider swapping talents with a friend. Perhaps you know someone who's artistic and would love to redesign or redecorate your room in return for your services as a babysitter, typist, or housecleaner.

If you use the same fabric on two different chairs, it will tie the decor of the room together.

To add color to matchstick blinds, weave rows of colored ribbon through them.

Matchstick blinds can disguise a wall of hobby or utility shelves for a clean, unified look. They also can be used to partition off a closet or dressing area.

There is no need to invest in drapes if your budget is tight. Instead, brighten up inexpensive shades by decorating them with tape to complement the wall color or wallpaper, or by gluing fabric over them.

To give a room a soft glow, spotlight objects in a room instead of lighting the whole room. For example, light a piece of art or a bookcase.

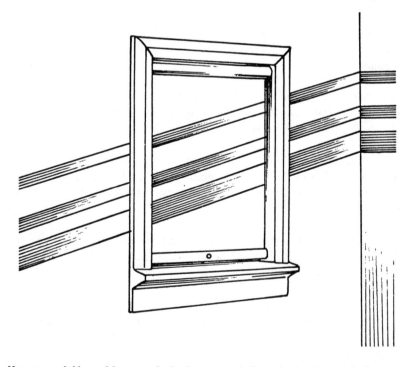

You can quickly and inexpensively decorate window shades to match the decor of your room.

Using plants to curtain a window is especially effective in the bathroom or kitchen.

Hang shiny, metallic blinds vertically or horizontally to help reflect summer sun. This works especially well in south and west windows.

You can make a curtain panel from a bed sheet by knotting the top corners around a bamboo pole.

Your old removable-slat wood blinds can be renovated. Spread the slats outdoors on plastic drop cloths and finish with high-gloss spray paint or brush-on enamel.

A screen of hanging plants can be a great substitute for curtains.

For an insulating window covering, attach wood rings to a patchwork quilt and hang it from a wood rod. Don't do this, however, if the quilt is an antique that could fade or otherwise be damaged by exposure to sunlight.

Hang an Indian print bedspread full-width across a window. Open it diagonally across half the window and secure it with a tieback.

Turn your bathroom into a miniature gallery with pictures that can't be damaged by humidity.

If you don't want to buy furniture, you can rent it at surprisingly reasonable rates. Furniture for rent includes everything from sofas and carpets to lamps and works of art.

To make a quick floor covering for a beach house, stretch natural-colored painter's canvas from wall to wall and staple it to the baseboards.

Mexican serapes and Indian bedspreads make colorful, inexpensive tablecloths—great for picnics, too.

Fasten colorful paper shopping bags to the wall for storage of art supplies and other lightweight items.

Keep your decorative baskets looking healthy by placing them away from dry heat and rinsing them periodically with clear water to remove dust and restore moisture.

Display flowers in unusual vases—a crystal ice bucket, a fluted champagne glass, a bright coffee mug, or a jug. Flowers, in fact, look good in almost any container.

For a quick, easy, and inexpensive way to re-cover a chair, drape a twin-size sheet over the chair, and tie or pin the corners to fit. You can use the same trick to add interest to a small table.

You'll never have trouble tightening screws and bolts if you remember that, for most, right is tight and left is loose.

An easy way to give a room a new look is to update hardware, such as doorknobs, drawer pulls, and curtain rods.

Add a miniature hammock to a corner of a child's room to make a place for all his or her stuffed animals.

Storing a bicycle on wall hooks not only solves your storage problem but adds visual interest to a room.

Solve a bicycle storage problem: A bicycle hanging on a wall becomes a piece of art as well as a means of transportation.

Replace the drab cord or chain on a light fixture with a piece of satin piping or silver cord. Thread a bright ceramic bead at the end of the cord for a finishing touch.

Look for levelers, mechanical devices built into the furniture's base that compensate for uneven floors, when you buy tall pieces of furniture such as china cabinets and wall units.

Furniture upholstered in sturdy fabrics with a high content of durable fibers, such as nylon and olefin, is a good choice for a household with adventurous kids, playful pets, or adults who forget to take off their shoes before putting their feet up on the sofa.

Upholstered furniture should not be placed in constant, direct sunlight or near heating outlets; this can cause fading or discoloration.

If someone in your family has allergies, check the materials used to fill upholstered furniture before you buy. Most states require furniture manufacturers to attach a label stating the materials used to pad the frame and fill the cushions, such as down, feathers, kapok, horsehair, or polyurethane. If you know one of the materials used is likely to be a problem for an allergy-prone family member, you can avoid that piece of furniture.

To keep drying flowers dust-free, cover them with plastic bags punched with air holes. When the flowers have dried, spray them with hair spray. This will serve several purposes: The hair spray will give the flowers a clear mat finish, keep them from shedding, keep insects away, and protect them from moisture.

When drying flowers or herbs, most have to be hung upside down in small bundles in a dark, dry place for a few weeks. Try hanging branches from coat hangers with strings of different lengths. This allows for good air circulation.

Hot peppers threaded on a string make a beautiful kitchen decoration while drying. Garlic and onions also look attractive braided and hung on display.

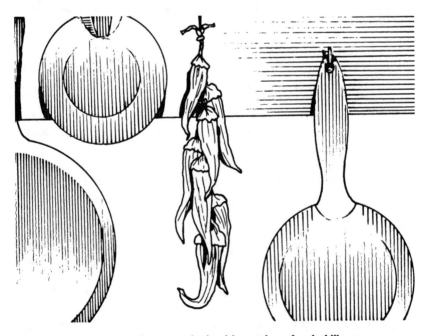

Give your kitchen a southwestern look with a string of red chili peppers.

Some flowers and foliage can be placed in a vase without water and dried upright. Among these are pussy willows, wild grasses, and grains and flowers with large composite heads and sturdy stalks, such as Queen Anne's lace and cockscomb.

A branch cut from any blossoming tree or bush makes an unusual centerpiece.

Glue pieces of felt to the rough bottoms of vases and art objects to keep them from scratching tables.

Use leftover dining room wallpaper to make matching place mats. Paste the paper onto sturdy cardboard, trim the edges neatly, and coat each mat with a plastic spray.

Perk up slightly wilted fabric flowers by holding them over steam from a teakettle or steam iron.

A handy deodorizer for wastebaskets: Place a sheet of fabric softener in the bottom of each.

An old dining table found at a flea market can become a sofa-height coffee table. Just cut the legs to the height you need.

You can make unusual centerpieces in no time by floating flowers in clear glass dishes. Fill the dishes halfway with water, cut the stems from the flowers, and place them in the dishes.

Dime-store bandannas make pretty, inexpensive pillow covers. Buy assorted colors for a striking effect. These bandannas also make wonderful table napkins—especially for a picnic or a barbecue.

Old, carved doorknobs, attached to each end of a dowel, make an attractive curtain rod. Paint or stain the knobs to match your furniture.

An old kimono can be hung on a padded dowel to add an elegant splash of texture and color to a room.

You can make cheap floor rugs by stenciling canvas with nontoxic acrylic paints.

Make an extra closet into a book nook for quiet reading. Remove the door, and install a wall lamp, shelves, and a comfortable chair.

A variation on portable board-and-brick bookcases uses tile pipes to hold the shelves. Glass brick is another option.

Place an unwrapped bar of soap in a drawer or linen closet to give lingerie and linens a pleasant scent.

You can make inexpensive bookcases out of flue tiles or conduit pipes. The cubbyholes are perfect for storing wine.

BEDS AND BEDDING

When outfitting a guest room that's used infrequently, economize by choosing a cheaper mattress. It won't have to withstand daily use.

When shopping for a mattress, be sure that the clerk offering you advice is employed by the store and not by any particular bed manufacturer. A manufacturer's representative will have a vested interest in selling you his or her company's brand, which might be less suited to your needs than a product by another manufacturer.

Sometimes you can silence squeaky bed springs with a coat of spray wax. If bed squeaks are caused by springs touching the frame, pad the frame with pieces of sponge.

If bed slats sometimes slide out of place on the frame, keep them from moving so easily by slipping wide rubber bands over the slat ends.

When you purchase a new bedspread, consider buying a larger size than you need and then cutting the excess to make a matching headboard.

When buying an innerspring mattress, make sure it has thick, strong wire along its borders and a machine-stitched tape covering its outside edges.

Before purchasing a double mattress, lie down on it with your partner to be sure it gives both of you the desired support side by side and at your heads, shoulders, and hips. If one person rolls over, the mattress definitely shouldn't sway. If it does, try another mattress.

Make sure any mattress you buy is warranted against defects in workmanship for 10 to 15 years. Some guarantees aren't valid if the mattress isn't positioned on a frame that conforms to the manufacturer's specifications.

An adjustable ironing board placed beside a bed makes a perfect bed table for someone who's ill and confined to bed.

Bed manufacturers don't share a common system for rating mattress firmness. You'll have to judge each mattress by testing it, not by relying on a "soft," "medium," or "firm" tag.

An ironing board adjusted to bed height keeps the things a convalescing person needs within easy reach.

Save a place on the closet shelf in each bedroom for the sheets and pillowcases you use in that room. That way you don't have to shuffle through the linen closet to find the right bed linens.

Creams and lotions that are kind to your skin aren't kind to your pillowcases. Spread a hand towel over your pillow when you moisturize your face at bedtime.

If you're good with an embroidery needle, monogram your children's bed linens. They may be more willing to make their own beds if their linens have the personal touch.

Stitch a flat mattress pad in the center of an old fitted sheet to make an inexpensive fitted mattress pad.

STORAGE AND SAVING SPACE

If your home is built with studs and drywall, you can add cabinets between the studs, anywhere you need them—they won't take up any space at all. For example, put a liquor cabinet over your bar, or fashion a canned-goods pantry in your kitchen.

Pegboard is most often used on walls, but it can also be used as a room divider or to make the inside of a closet or cabinet door more functional. When installing pegboard, remember to provide space behind the panels for the hooks.

Use flat, roll-out bins for under-the-bed storage. They can hold bed linens, sewing supplies, and infrequently used items.

Nail coffee cans to the wall to make bins for clips, pins, or other small items.

To increase the capacity and efficiency of a drawer, outfit it with a lift-out tray. Fill the tray with items you frequently use, and use the space beneath the tray for articles you seldom need.

Add more storage space in your bedroom by building a headboard storage unit. You can place books, lamps, or a radio on the lid of the unit and inside you can store extra linens and blankets.

For extra closet storage, see if your closets can accommodate a second shelf above the existing one. If you install the main clothes-hanging rod high enough, you may be able to install another rod beneath it on which to hang shorter items such as slacks and shirts.

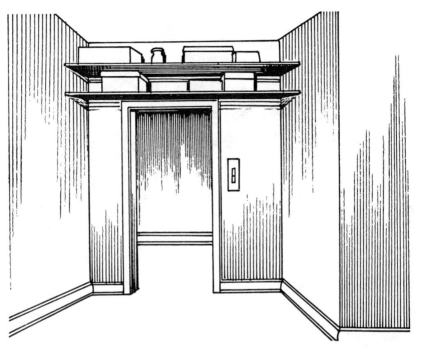

Shelves across a narrow hallway provide needed storage.

A hallway can double as a storage area. Line it with shelves or shallow cabinets, or put shelving across the width of the hallway.

Glass baby-food jars are ideal for storing nails and screws. Better yet, nail the caps to a wood base or wall plaque, and just screw the jars into place. And remember that partly used tubes of glue and artist's paints won't dry out if they're kept in tightly closed jars.

If you're in need of an extra closet for storing items like golf clubs, skis, and camping equipment, angle a decorative folding screen across a little-used corner.

Hooks, shelves, or hanging bins can transform the insides of closet doors into useful storage areas.

Keep a stool and a hooked pole handy for use in a tall closet.

Convert an ordinary closet or chest into a cedar closet or chest by installing thin cedar slats over inside surfaces. Then weather-strip to contain the scent.

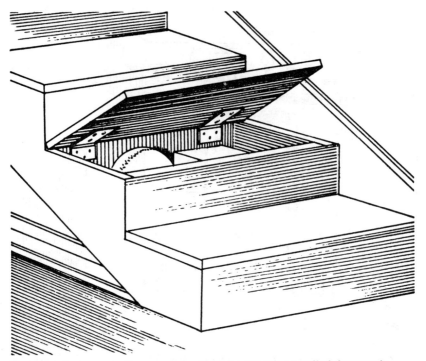

You can gain access to the area under stairs by removing a nailed-down stair tread and replacing it with a hinged step.

If your cedar chest or closet no longer smells of cedar, lightly sand its surfaces. Sanding opens the wood's pores and releases a fresh cedar scent. Remember that the scent doesn't kill moths; it merely repels them. So it's best to clean clothes before storing to remove any moth eggs.

Use a stairway as a storage area by replacing ordinary nailed-in-place steps with hinged steps. The space under the hinged steps can hold boots or sports equipment.

Hang a wicker basket on the bathroom wall for storing towels, tissues, soap, or bath toys.

Put the space under a stairway to work as a storage area. Construct a wheeled, wedge-shaped container that fits into the area beneath the steps.

So that you won't misplace frequently used items, glue small magnets on the walls of the medicine cabinet to hold nail files, cuticle scissors, clippers, and other small metal objects.

Your medicine cabinet will stay neat and clean with shelf paper made of blotters that can absorb medicine or cosmetic spills.

Hang a basket near the front door and keep your keys in it. You'll always know where they are. Also use this basket for bills and letters that need to be mailed. When you grab your keys, you'll remember to pick up the mail as well.

Install two rows of coat hooks on your closet doors—one down low for a child to use, another higher up for you to use.

If you want your kids to hang up their coats, put coat hooks where they can reach them easily.

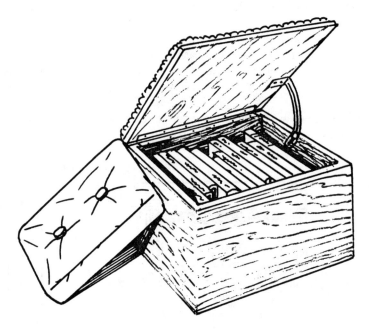

If you build furniture for your home, look for ways to incorporate extra storage. This ottoman opens to store magazines.

For a double-duty ottoman, build a plywood box with a hinged cover. Paint the outside or cover it with fabric, and then cover the top with scrap carpeting. Add a cushion for comfortable sitting, and store your magazines in style.

Extension cords won't get tangled when stored in a drawer if you wind them and secure them with rubber bands—or slip them into toilet-paper or paper-towel tubes.

Keep flashlight batteries fresh by storing them in a sealed plastic bag in the refrigerator.

When storing suitcases, put an unwrapped cake of soap inside each one to prevent musty odors from developing.

A metal garbage can is perfect for storing long-handled yard tools. Hooks can also be attached to the outside of the can for hanging up smaller tools. You can lift up the whole can and move it to whichever part of the yard you're working in.

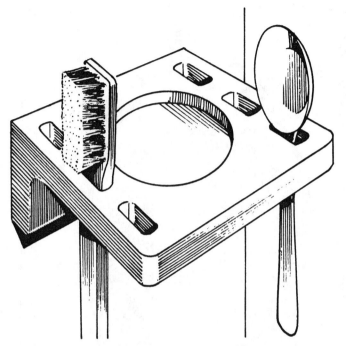

Keep a medicine spoon handy in your toothbrush holder.

Use an extra slot in the toothbrush holder to keep a medicine spoon handy.

Keep toothbrushes handy but neatly out of the way on cup hooks attached to a wall or under a cabinet.

Keep your wet umbrella in the shower where it can drip without making a mess. This is an especially useful strategy when you have company on a rainy day, and everyone has an umbrella.

You'll always know where your photo negatives are if you store them behind corresponding prints in your photo album.

Photographic film will stay fresh longer if stored in your refrigerator.

A good place to store small clothing items is in large, metal potato-chip cans—after the cans are washed.

Put a wine rack next to the door and use it to store your sandy beach shoes and muddy running or gardening shoes.

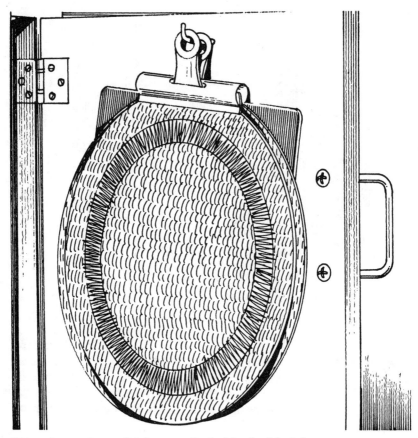

Store place mats on clips hung on the inside of cabinet doors.

Keep place mats flat and out of the way by hanging them on a clipboard hung from a hook inside a cabinet or pantry door.

To give yourself more storage space in a small bathroom, put up shelves on the dead wall space beside the vanity, over the toilet, or behind the door. Such shelves offer convenient storage without intruding on floor space.

To minimize breakages, store loose light bulbs in tumblers. A paper towel wrapped around the bulb before you put it in the tumbler provides added protection.

Make your shower curtain rod do double duty—attach extra curtain hooks to hold a back brush, a net bag for bath toys, each family member's washcloth, and a shower cap.

Smooth out shelf paper with a blackboard eraser.

To make shelves without hammering a nail, upend two narrow wastebaskets on your closet shelf and position another shelf across them. Or use sturdy boxes stacked on their sides to make compartmented shelf space—you can see at a glance what's stored in the boxes, and you can use the tops for little-used items.

If you have trouble with bubbles and creases when applying adhesive-backed paper to shelves or drawers, try smoothing the paper with a blackboard eraser.

CHOOSING FURNITURE

It's risky to buy furniture off the back of a truck. The price—and the sample on view—may be attractive, and the cartons may even bear a good brand name, but by the time you find out that the boxed furniture is of inferior quality the truck and driver will be long gone.

Furniture items advertised for sale "as is" sometimes provide wonderful bargains, but you should be sure to identify the damage before the purchase. A minor scratch may be something you can live with (or fix yourself), but avoid structural damage unless you're willing to pay for repairs.

Good furniture bargains are available at close-out sales, but be sure you won't want to match the piece later. A "close out" is a style the manufacturer is discontinuing, and you will not be able to find replacements or additions once the consignment is gone.

The fabric on the arms of upholstered chairs and sofas will wear twice as long if the piece comes with matching arm caps.

Zippered sofa cushions should not be removed for cleaning or washing. Clean them according to the manufacturer's directions while they are on the cushion.

Vinyl-covered furniture may be a good choice for a family room or high-traffic area, but it's not invulnerable. Body oils and perspiration can harden vinyl, and tears are difficult to repair. Keep this in mind when making your choice.

Lightweight fabrics wear better when they are quilted; the quilting allows the fabric to stretch under stress.

The fabric used to upholster a piece of furniture can boost the price to a surprising degree. If you suspect that a piece you like owes its price to a lush fabric, ask if the piece is available with a less expensive covering.

A fabric that has the design woven in is likely to be more serviceable than one that is printed only on one side.

If your household is particularly hard on furniture—or if you have cats— keep in mind that nubby fabrics are more likely to snag and pill than smooth ones.

There's more to upholstered furniture than meets the eye, so check the frame that supports it. Lift one end of the piece; it shouldn't wobble or creak. If it does, the construction may be inferior.

Push hard on the arms and back of an upholstered chair. You shouldn't be able to feel hard frame edges through the fabric. If you can, the chair is poorly padded and will wear out quickly.

Protect your wood table or desk by keeping a pad under your writing paper when using a ballpoint pen. It's easier than you think to lean on the pen hard enough for the point to mar the wood surface.

Moisten your dust cloth with a spray polish before dusting furniture. A dry cloth can drive the dust into the finish and cause tiny scratches.

Before you go shopping for furniture, make a floor plan of your room. Use grid paper and a scale of one square on the grid to one square foot of floor space. Mark in doors, windows, heating outlets, electrical outlets, and other features that will influence where you can and cannot position a piece of furniture. That way you'll avoid buying a bookcase that blocks your most conveniently placed electrical outlets, or a sofa that has to sit on top of your floor heating duct. Take your floor plan and tape measure when you shop—a chair that looks quite small on the showroom floor may look a lot bigger when you get it into your living room.

If you move frequently, be wary of buying furniture with a specific location in mind. Look instead for items that are adaptable to many spaces and uses.

When buying furniture, comfort should be near the top of your list of criteria. You'll grow tired of even the most elegant chair if it's not comfortable to relax in.

It's a good idea to visit department and furniture stores that display furniture in room-style groupings. It's sometimes much easier to imagine how furniture will look in your own home if you see it in a homelike setting.

When selecting furniture, consider the traffic patterns of your home. That handsome coffee table that looks so good on the showroom floor will be a lot less attractive if it's going to block everyone's route to the kitchen or the stairs.

Fold a printed fabric and rub the printed sides together. If any of the print comes off, don't buy the fabric. It's an inferior product.

Tightly woven fabrics wear better than loosely woven ones. To check the weave, hold the fabric up to the light. Spots of light will show through a loose weave.

Turn the cushions on your chairs and sofas regularly to ensure even wear on the furniture.

Your Home Shop

SHOP TIPS
To protect tools, store them where they aren't subjected to moisture. Keep a thin coating of oil on metal parts, wrap them in plastic wrap, or keep carpenter's chalk, which absorbs moisture, in the toolbox.

To sharpen scissors, snip pieces of sandpaper.

A piece of garden hose, slit open, is a handy protective cover for the teeth of a handsaw between projects.

To guard the teeth of circular saw blades, store the blades in record-album covers. You could even store the covered blades in an ordinary record rack in your workshop.

Clean tools without expensive cleaners: Pour a small amount of kerosene onto the metal parts of a tool and rub vigorously with a soap-filled steel-wool pad. Then wad a piece of aluminum foil into a ball and rub on the surface. Wipe away the residue with newspaper, and coat the tool lightly with olive oil before storing. **Caution:** Kerosene is flammable; do not use it near an open flame.

If you hang tools on pegboard walls, outline the tools with paint so you'll know at a glance where each tool goes. You'll also know when a tool hasn't been replaced.

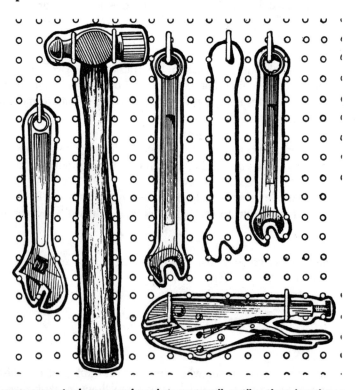

After you arrange tools on a pegboard storage wall, outline them in paint so you'll know where to hang them.

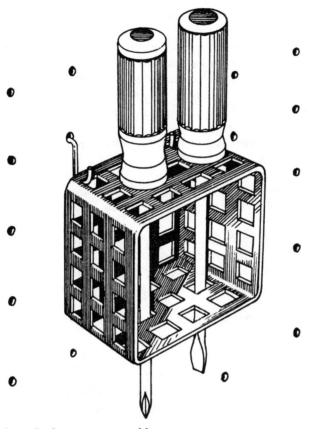

A plastic berry basket stores screwdrivers.

If you want to remind yourself to unplug an electric drill when changing accessories, fasten the chuck key near the plug end of the cord.

Snow won't stick to your shovel if you give it a coating of floor wax.

Keep screwdrivers handy: Slide the blades through the mesh of a plastic berry basket.

Paint all tool handles with an unusual bright color, or wrap reflective tape around them; they'll be easy to identify if borrowed or left in the wrong place.

Don't take a chance of hitting a thumb or finger when hammering a small brad, tack, or nail. Slip the fastener between the teeth of a pocket comb; the comb holds the nail while you hold the comb. A bobby pin or a paper clip can be used the same way as a comb.

Here's a homemade rust-preventive coating for tools, outdoor furniture, and other metal objects: Combine ¼ cup lanolin and 1 cup petroleum jelly in a double boiler over low heat. Stir until the mixture melts and blends completely, then remove from heat and pour into a clean jar, letting the mixture cool partially. Use the mixture while it's still warm. Don't wipe it off—just let it dry on the object. If you have leftover coating, cover it tightly, and rewarm it before you use it again.

An empty soft-drink carton makes a convenient kit for holding and carrying lubricants.

To keep the pores of your hands dirt- or grease-free, wipe on a thin coat of petroleum jelly before starting a messy task.

You won't waste time when picking up spilled nails, screws, or tacks if you collect them with a magnet covered with a paper towel. When the spilled items snap toward the magnet, gather the towel corners over the pieces and then pull the towel bag away from the magnet.

As an aid in measuring lumber or pipe, paint lines a foot apart on your shop or garage floor.

You can pick up spilled tacks quickly with a magnet covered with a paper towel.

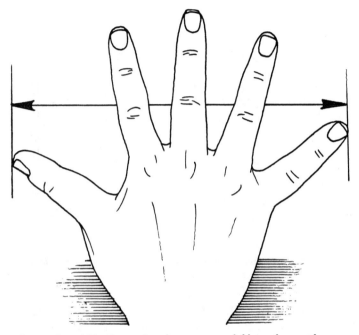

If you know the width of your hand, you can quickly make rough measurements.

You can prevent a knot in nylon rope from working loose by holding it briefly over a small flame. The heat will melt and bond the fibers.

Know the exact width of your hand so you can make rough measurements without using a ruler or tape measure.

Loosen a stubborn screw, bolt, or nut with a shot of penetrating oil. If you don't have oil, use hydrogen peroxide, white vinegar, kerosene, or household ammonia. Should these prove ineffective, heat the metal with an iron, rap it sharply with a hammer while it's still hot, and try again to loosen it. **Caution:** Kerosene is flammable; do not use it near an open flame.

You can often loosen rusted bolts by pouring a carbonated beverage on them.

If a bolt repeatedly loosens due to vibrations, coat the threads with fingernail polish and reinsert it. When you need to remove it, you can break the seal with a little effort.

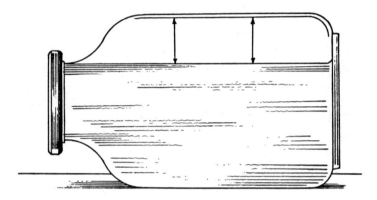

A jar filled three-quarters full of water substitutes for a carpenter's level.

If you don't have a carpenter's level, you can substitute a straight-sided jar with a lid. Fill the jar three-quarters full of water. Lay it on its side on the surface you're testing—when the water is level, the surface is, too.

For easy workshop measuring, fasten a yardstick to the edge of your workbench. Cut keyhole slots in the yardstick so you can remove it when you need it elsewhere.

If you're out of penetrating oil, you can substitute hydrogen peroxide or lemon juice.

An old nylon stocking makes an effective strainer if you're out of cheesecloth.

You can use a coping saw blade to remove a broken-off key from a lock. Slide the blade in beside the key, turn it toward the key so its teeth sink into the key's soft brass, and then pull the blade out along with the key fragment.

To prevent metal tubing from denting when sawing it, insert a dowel that fits the tube's interior tightly.

Dipping the ends of a rope in shellac, varnish, or paint will keep them from unraveling.

To hide a screw head, drill a counter-bored hole, seat the screw, glue a dowel into the counter-bore and sand it flush.

Avoid burning your fingers when lighting a pilot light. Simply clamp the match in an alligator clip at the end of a straightened coat hanger.

HINTS FOR WOODWORKERS

Plywood frequently splinters when you saw it. You can prevent this by applying a strip of masking tape along the line you plan to saw.

To prevent plywood from splintering or splitting when sawing it, use a sharp chisel or pocket knife to score the top layer on both sides of the sheet along the cutoff line.

Use expensive waterproof plywood only for outside projects. Use less-expensive water-resistant plywood when the panels will be exposed to weather infrequently. And use relatively inexpensive dry-bonded plywood when panels will be used indoors.

You can saw a board into almost perfectly equal lengths without measuring it. Simply balance it on a sawhorse. When the board stops wobbling, the center will be the point where the board touches the crossbar of the sawhorse.

To make any sawing task smoother and easier, lubricate the saw blade frequently by running a bar of soap or a candle stub over it.

To prevent dimpling a wood surface when removing a nail with a claw hammer, protect the surface with a small block of wood or a shim; this will also increase your leverage.

When you drill through any kind of wood, a certain amount of splintering will occur at the breakout point. You can prevent splintering by backing the stock you are drilling with a piece of scrap.

Check that wood is perfectly smooth after sanding by covering your hand with a nylon stocking and rubbing it over the surface. You'll be able to detect any rough spots that remain.

Sandpaper clogs fast, and usually before it's worn out. You can clean clogged sandpaper and give it new life by vacuuming it or rubbing a soft-bristled brush across its grit.

Although a hacksaw is designed to cut metal, the thin blade is well suited for cutting small pieces of wood accurately.

When you rip (cut lengthwise) a board, hold the kerf open with a wedge to keep the saw blade from binding.

To prevent a saw from binding when ripping a long board, hold the initial cut open with a nail or wedge. Move the nail or wedge down the cut as you continue to saw.

Whenever you plan to drive a screw into wood, drill a pilot hole to prevent splintering when you insert the screw.

Tack cloths will last longer if they're stored in an airtight container to keep them from drying out. Airtight storage also prevents spontaneous combustion.

A plastic playing card or credit card can serve as a scraper for removing excess wood filler from a surface that you are repairing.

A salt shaker makes a good applicator for distributing pumice evenly on a wood surface.